Glynn Christian's
DELICATESSEN
FOOD HANDBOOK

Glynn Christian's
DELICATESSEN
FOOD HANDBOOK

MACDONALD & CO
LONDON & SYDNEY

First Published in Great Britain in 1982 by
Macdonald and Co (Publishers) Ltd
London and Sydney

Maxwell House
74 Worship Street
London EC2 2EN

ISBN 0 356 09746 3

Printed in Great Britain by A. Wheaton & Co. Ltd., Exeter

CONTENTS

Acknowledgements	6
Introduction	7
Bread and Baked Goods	9
Butter	28
Cheese	33
Chocolate	98
Coffee	102
Cream	114
Dairy Product Substitutes	119
Dried Fruits	120
Eggs	124
Fish and Shellfish	127
Foie Gras	157
Fruit	159
Glacé Fruits	163
Grain	164
Herbs, Spices and Flavourings	196
Ice Cream	245
Margarine	247
Milk	249
Mushrooms, Dried	258
Nuts	259
Oils and Fats	277
Pasta and Noodles	282
Pâtés, Terrines and Galantines	292
Peas, Beans and Lentils	294
Pickles, Preserves and Olives	302
Pork and Beef	312
Salads	332
Snails/Soups	334
Sugars, Syrups and Honey	335
Tea	348
Truffles	356
Vegetables	359
Vinegar	365
Waters, bottled	367
Yoghurt	367
Reference Tables/Index	371

ACKNOWLEDGEMENTS

Nobody could write on this subject, at length, without extraordinary assistance.

I am grateful to those importers, manufacturers and distributors who exposed themselves, giving time and information, both when I was behind my shop's counter and when writing this book. There are hundreds of such benefactors; but those most generous were Petty Wood Limited, Eden Vale, Caby, Harmony Foods, The Swiss Centre, Mr Szyptma, Duncan Rayner, and Peter Leggatt of Duncan Macneill & Company. Schwarz Spices, the Swedish National Tourist Office, Food and Wine from France, the Dutch Dairy Bureau, the Italian Trade Centre and the German Food Centre gave invaluable assistance too – often by just being there.

I was carefully checked, disagreed with and educated by two researchers – Michael Brook and Tristan Whalley. Any errors are mine not theirs, be assured.

None of this would have been possible without the encouragement and support of my partners in the delicatessen business, Gerald and David Leigh, and of Greg Scott, who runs the shop. Richard Broome drove me about France, Judy Popkins walked me around New York, Katie Stapleton showed me the food emporia of Denver, Fred Baumeister knowledgeably introduced me to the West Coast's delights, Kurt Weyrauch revealed the surprises behind the doors of Washington DC, David Williams and the Reverend Jesse Parker did the same in Baltimore.

A big thanks to Sue Fleming for sterling foundation work on the idea and manuscript, to Emma Hogan for sorting out the final structure, and to the patient Panos and Darryll for eating fish and chips or hamburgers for months whilst I typed noisily of better fare, unable even to dictate a more interesting shopping list.

INTRODUCTION

Not long ago, a Sunday columnist defined a delicatessen as 'a newspaper shop that sells milk'. An exaggeration, certainly, but not by much. For the word delicatessen is so ill-defined it is painted up over all kinds of surprising places.

In America, where the word was popularized, a *deli* is where you go to have sandwiches made, or where you go to put together a meal that needs little further preparation. There will be hot salt beef and pastrami, smoked salmon, barrels of salt cucumbers and herrings, cheeses, and a choice of breads. Often – and New York is famed for this – the food will be largely Jewish, for originally a delicatessen was a small German-Jewish shop, a kosher food shop. The name and style were taken to the United States in the great migrations and, like the people who accompanied them, were blended into something quite new. Yet, if you want a very special cheese, spices, something unusual in a tin, or freshly ground coffee, you don't choose a delicatessen in the United States – you find a 'specialty food store'. The two might be combined in supermarkets, or in New York's new 'deli-specialty' star Dean and Delucca, but generally the European tradition of separation prevails.

The word delicatessen is not easily recognized in Europe. Sausage, cheese, pickles and farm produce are the daily fare, and not available in one store. Salami and ham come from one shop, bread from another, cheese somewhere else. The French *charcuterie* sells just pork products; for other meats and prepared dishes you must go to a *traiteur*, a *fromagerie* sells cheese. And even the small villages have a market with farm produce and home-cured sausages, free-range poultry and fresh fish, traditional butter and cheese, milk, eggs and cream.

A delicatessen in the United Kingdom should combine the best of all features, selling a range of fresh, unpackaged foods plus a variety of higher-class and hard-to-find specialities. It should not be confused with a health-food shop, with its limited diet and vitamin supplements. A delicatessen should offer you authentic, mature farmhouse cheeses, unadulterated yoghurts, honest bread, pure ice-cream, salads to go with your sliced meats, unsalted butter, quality coffees and teas, rare nuts, herbs and spices, continental sausages, dried peas and beans—and a host of little treats, simple *and* exotic. In fact if you scratch beneath the surface of most long-established delicatessens you will find they are an echo of the old, general grocer. My own shop, just off Portobello Road, is one of these Within the memory of some of today's customers, the original proprietor used to boil ham, roast coffee, pack butter and age cheeses on the premises. The people behind the counter knew what they were selling, the customers knew what they were buying.

In the end, I believe you get what you deserve, and the worst of the processed foods, meats and cheeses, especially, are there simply because you bought them, perhaps knowing no better.

A great deal of modern, manufactured food is excellent, for not all progress is bad. The combination of modern refrigeration and transport systems have vastly broadened our culinary palettes in just a few years. Once combined with a sense of respect for tradition and authenticity on the part of the manufacturers, and with greater general knowledge, food will be richer for us all. You see, delicatessen food is not about smoked salmon for lunch or sausages made out of pigs' guts. It is also about knowing how to combine smoked pork with pickled cucumbers, how to improve cream cheese with a sprinkle of rose-water, how to choose the proper pasta shape, or to make your own flavour of coffee. Like most of the world's greatest pleasures, the enjoyment of delicatessen food need cost you no more than you would normally spend. Plus a copy of this book.

I hope you find my *Delicatessen Food Handbook* useful. But more than that, I hope it makes food more fascinating and more fun for you. Bon Appetit.

BREAD AND BAKED GOODS

Bread need only be made from flour, water and salt. Bread made without a raising agent (unleavened bread) is one of our oldest foods; even bread raised to lightness by the action of yeast was possibly discovered in ancient Egypt. It is a simple, honest satisfying food, yet it is a reflection on living standards in much of the western hemisphere that we should have go to a specialty store to buy bread that *is* honest, well-made and unadulterated. But bread represents such an emotive part of our heritage that it is always at the mercy of social fashion. At present 'real bread' is the spearhead of the burgeoning movement back to things natural. Stone-grinding of flour is increasingly demanded, wholemeal breads are more widely acceptable socially, and interest in baking with wholemeal or unbleached flours has become widespread. Fashion, rather than a Paulian conversion to the good life, is the major reason. In other parts of the world, sense has long prevailed and bread-making is just as it was ten, one hundred or one thousand years ago.

In the villages, towns and cities of India, Pakistan and Bangladesh, for instance, the unleavened *chapati* and its relatives are still regularly hand-shaped and baked over open fires. The slapping sound of the dough being shaped between the palms of squatting women is an integral part of daily life. Some families may actually buy the coarse wholemeal chapati flour, but most will grind their own as they need it. Similar breads, sometimes made with flours other than wheat but also baked on griddles, are made further north. In Afghanistan the dough is rolled out to be a metre or more in diameter. Armenians make smaller, even thinner chapati-type breads and the Sardinians still make 'paper bread' in their mountain villages.

In the lands of Islam, yeast has long played a part in bread and pastry making. The most common types of bread there are flattish discs, often spiced, and the oval envelopes known widely in Europe as *pitta*. This is also common in Greece, Cyprus and has also become the national bread of Israel. Eaten fresh and warm, *pitta* – whether Israeli, Greek or Arabic – is perfectly delicious.

Countries of the eastern and southern Mediterranean still offer the interested tourist a chance to see a sight once familiar throughout Europe. In the tight alleyways and up the steep-stepped lanes of bazaars and medinas you will see single loaves of leavened dough being carried to a central baker. Each family identifies its loaves with its own mark, a custom which prevailed in some areas of England right up to the turn of the century.

Countries with a traditional high regard for their food forbid their flour to be tampered with, by omission or commission. This is certainly true of France and largely why the French enjoy such good breads; there is also a relative absence of large baking combines in France so the independent village baker reigns supreme. Elsewhere the story is rather different. 'Scientific' advances during the last century have changed bread-making in some parts of the world more than during the previous 3,000 to 4,000 years. Reliable yeasts, better and cheaper wheat flour and ovens with controllable temperatures all coincided and caused a revolution from whose upheaval recovery is still some way off.

THE SLICED-LOAF PHENOMENON

In pursuit of more output for less manpower, man created a continuous bread-making process and introduced bread aerated by chemical interaction, neither of which can give any approximation of true bread flavour, whatever the flour used.

The financially-based delight with which these bread-making innovations were greeted has now died and during the 1960s several countries quietly dropped the new methods and went back to the older, slower, batch-baking methods; chemically-aerated bread, other than soda bread, is no longer made commercially. But the chemically *assisted*, fast-rising, sliced white loaf is. It is marketed mainly in the United States, the United Kingdom, the Netherlands and parts of the British Commonwealth and stimulates a continuing controversy. The essential complaint is that the dough for this product is mixed, risen and being baked within the hour. The gradual stretching of gluten and maturing of the dough's flavour doesn't happen; the first is achieved by extremely fast, brutally rough beating, the second is forgotten or approximated with additives. The end product, to the scientist who created it, smells right, slices like a dream, does not crumble when spread with butter and keeps well. And that, claim the manufacturers, is all bread is expected to do. The flavour seems not to matter and if it does then it must, by definition, be an acceptable flavour because everybody buys it. Not true. But, to be scrupulously fair, I will concede that this type of 'bread' is probably quite good for you, even though the long-term effects of some of the additives are unknown.

BREAD IN YOUR DIET

White bread is regarded as an excellent source of energy, protein and the B vitamin, plus minerals and trace elements. The bran, wheatgerm and wheatgerm oil content of wholemeal bread provides, in addition, Vitamin E. As calcium is added to all flours in the UK, bread is also, for the British, a significant source of calcium.

So-called brown bread is usually made with white flour coloured with caramel. However, it usually contains some bran or malted grains as well, and thiamin and nicotinic acid have been replaced in the flour to give it the same vitamin content as an 80% extraction flour. This puts its dietary value somewhere between that of white and wholemeal breads.

Bread contains no Vitamins A, D, B_{12} or C and the expected bonus of extra vitamins and minerals in wholemeal bread can be a forlorn hope.

Life supporter

No evidence exists to support the common assumption that wholemeal bread is good for you while white bread is damaging to your health. Wholemeal bread does contain bran, however, and should offer both Vitamin E and a higher proportion of minerals and trace elements than white. In practice, according to some dieticians, wholemeal bread could actually be detrimental to health. It seems we are likely to spread it more thickly with butter, jam and other good-tasting comestibles than we might mundane white bread; arguments exist to show that such excesses are far worse for us than the suspected chemical shortcomings of white bread! Research in the USA shows that as long as the rest of the diet has a minimal proportion of high-quality protein, a white bread diet successfully suports life and encourages excellent growth in 5- to 15-year-olds.

During the Second World War, it was thought high-extraction flour (the only type then milled) caused rickets in children. This theory is not far-fetched. Wholemeal flour contains a substance called phytic acid, which is present in the whole grain. In the bowels, this phytic acid locks itself on to valuable calcium, iron and magnesium, preventing the body from absorbing and using them. The British government decreed that chalk, in the form of highly refined calcium carbonate, should be added to all flours other than wholemeal at a rate three times higher than daily requirements. It is still added today, for although the war-time rickets scare has passed, chalk is thought to help prevent some heart diseases.

Additives to flour

The many additives to white flour used throughout the world fall into two categories. Some substances are added for dietary reasons, to redress an imbalance produced in the processing of the flour, some to improve the performance and commercial appeal of the flour.

Dietary additives are usually thiamin (Vitamin B_1), nicotinic acid, riboflavin and iron in certain proportions. There is no international agreement about levels of additives; the level of vitamins added to flour in the UK is far lower than that used in the USA, and Scandinavia insists on twice the amount of riboflavin used in the latter.

LEAVENING

To 'leaven' means to aerate dough or batter. Gas, created as a by-product of a biological or chemical action, is trapped as bubbles in dough or batter. In the heat of the oven, the gas expands even more; continued heat kills the gas-forming action and hardens the balloons formed by the gas, allowing the baked end-product to retain its risen shape.

Yeast

The origins of yeast-leavening are unknown. Like so many basic techniques, it may have been discovered by accident – probably in ancient Egypt. Most early leavening, other than sour-dough leavening, was done with ale barm – the froth from the top of fermenting ale or beer. As beer and bread were usually made in the same room, their eventual combination was highly likely. The Gauls and Spaniards used ale barm to leaven dough in the 1st century AD.

Today, bread doughs are normally leavened with yeast, or with chemicals such as baking soda or baking powder. Sour-dough leavens and salt-raised breads are far less common than they once were.

Without yeasts we would have neither beer, wine

nor bread. Yeasts are an enormous family of minute, single-celled fungi. Each is only about 1/120th of a millimetre (1/3000th of an inch) in diameter, and there are millions of them in the air, almost everywhere. Some are useful, some not. The most important are those that have a special aptitude to convert, by the action of their enzymes, sugar into alcohol and carbon dioxide.

The yeasts on the skins of fruits and vegetables are directly responsible for the fermentation of wines. Yeast for beer-making was grown in a sweet liquid mixed with flour and potatoes, hops or both. A clever brewer's wife would try to use mainly hops with plenty of pollen dust upon them; she may not have known it, but these supported the strongest colonies of the yeasts she wanted.

The barm, which she kept and sold to bakers and housewives, was made and used only within the broadest of guidelines. There was no way of knowing what combination of yeasts had been cultivated or how they would perform in dough. It was this ever-changing broth of many yeasts that necessitated the long risings and provings in former times. Then, in 1850, came German or compressed yeast, made of one yeast only – *Saccharomycescerevisiae*. At last bakers had their own yeast. It worked quickly and consistently on the maltose (sugar) in flour and permanently changed the face of yeast cookery, commercial and domestic.

The new yeast went on the market under three different names: German, compressed and dried. (This has confused many people who have tried baking from old recipes: the chances are that 'dried' yeast means 'compressed' yeast.) Modern compressed yeast is often called fresh yeast. It performs consistently if it is in good condition and can be kept in the refrigerator for weeks or deep-frozen for months.

Dried yeast is much more expensive than the compressed yeast but very much more easily obtainable. Dried yeast granules are twice as strong, weight for weight, as fresh yeast, e.g., 15 g (½ oz) dried yeast equals 25 g (1 oz) fresh yeast. Always use less rather than more dried yeast even if it looks ludicrously little. American recipes usually state the number of packets of yeast required; their packets hold only 7 g (¼ oz) dried yeast, which is the same as 15 g (½ oz) fresh yeast.

Yeast needs only to come into contact with warm liquid to start reproducing and creating gas and alcohol; dried yeast is helped by the presence of a little sugar but sugar should not be added to fresh yeast. Even under refrigeration, yeast is prone to self-digestion which, naturally, makes it rather less potent than it might be. A clean smell, light colour and a tendency to crumble rather than collapse are clear indicators that the yeast is in good condition.

Magical as yeast seems, it can exceed its usefulness in bread. The action that creates gas is accompanied by other enzymic actions that ripen the flour and enhance the dough's flavour. But after a certain point the bread is said to be over-yeasted and the loaf will look and taste decidedly wrong. Bread yeast dies at a temperature of around 55°C, 130°F. This is a gradual process during baking as the heat penetrates from the crust to the centre. Over-proving bread, proving in a hot place or using too much yeast will make a loaf heavy and cause it to stale quickly.

Readers who wish to try out recipes from cookbooks printed before the advent of compressed (fresh) yeast are advised to work backwards from the amount of flour required. For bread doughs, 25 g (1 oz) fresh yeast is more than enough for 1·5 kg (3·31 lb). You can double the amount for sweet brioche-type doughs and sweet buns and cakes. The old yeasts and barms, measured by the pint or cup, contained liquid, so you may have to add extra water, milk or egg if you are adapting an old recipe and using compressed yeast instead of the old types.

Refrigerating yeast   If it is easy for you to buy yeast, then buy exactly the quantity you want, when you want it. If you have to store it, use the coldest part of the refrigerator. Provided the yeast was in good condition and you have bought a good-sized piece, it should last a full two weeks.

Some air circulation helps storage of yeast, so either wrap it loosely in greaseproof paper or store it in a fairly close-fitting container with a little ventilation. Keep it away from strong odours. Melon, slices of which are very often put into refrigerators unwrapped, is a particularly bad offender. There are few things that invade other foods quite so vigorously.

Deep-frozen yeast Those who find it difficult to obtain compressed yeast but own a freezer may safely splash out on yeast when they have the opportunity. Yeast freezes very well, and should produce excellent results for up to three months, possibly longer. Pack the yeast in suitable sizes – say 25 g (1 oz) batches – and seal and label it carefully. Allow frozen yeast to thaw slowly, then dissolve it in lukewarm liquid as usual.

GUIDE TO BAKED AND YEASTED GOODS

Babke: a Polish or Russian sponge-type cake with a dense texture baked in a deep decorative ring mould. The mixture usually incorporates some beaten egg white, so it is often described as a soufflé cake. It might be leavened with yeast or a chemical agent. Serve plain with coffee when fresh. Babke makes an excellent quick pudding or special tea-time treat served with a flavoured cream, doused with syrup or liqueurs, or covered with such cream/fruit mixtures as raspberry fool. Sometimes they are available covered in chocolate.

Bagel: this yeasted, white-dough bread roll is like a doughnut with a hole and varies from 3-5in (8-12cm) in diameter. The ring of dough is poached in water before baking, giving the requisite rather tough crust. Associated with kosher food, particularly with that of New York, it is better eaten warm and is at its most famous when filled with a combination of cream cheese and smoked salmon – the lox and bagel ubiquitous for Sunday breakfast in the Big Apple. Bagels can also be bought sprinkled with caraway seed, salt, poppy seeds or sesame seeds. Seasoned or garlic salt might be added to the dough. Even raw onion can be sprinkled on top, which bakes to a caramelized brown—not, I think, a very social breakfast choice.

Bath Buns: a white-bread bun, the dough of which should contain egg and milk; must have crushed lump sugar on top. Can contain lemon, chopped peel or sultanas but never currants.

Bloomers: these are the oblong, fat and rounded loaves of white bread which are always slashed diagonally and never baked in tins.

Brioches: made of a light, yeasted dough with a high proportion of egg and butter to give a cake-like texture. Sweetness is variable, but are usually baked in tapering, fluted moulds, large or small, and most often eaten warm for breakfast; sometimes plaited.

Unsweetened brioches also make an elegant accompaniment to soups and other light first courses. If the centre is scooped out and replaced with a vegetable or meat purée they make a stunning savoury snack, hot or cold. A big brioche, cut into slices and toasted lightly is nice for tea; these slices also can replace toast to serve with light supper dishes such as chicken or fish with a cream sauce – but again only if the brioche is not too sweet.

Brioche dough baked around a whole coarse, pork sausage is a great treat, hot or cold—Fauchon in Paris do this to salmon and serve it in slices with saffron-flavoured butter. I was eating some outside Notre Dame when a congregation spilled out. Once the Fauchon wrappings were espied literally dozens of Parisians wished me an envious 'bon appetit'. So *that's* how to gain the attention of a Parisian!

Greek Easter Bread (Tsoure Kia) is a brioche mixture flavoured with a little cardamom.

Brown Bread: in the United Kingdom brown bread is simply a white loaf that has been dyed, usually with caramel. If you want wholewheat bread ask for it specifically; many of the large chains and 'hot-bread' shops sell only coloured brown bread and do not have a genuine wholemeal loaf.

Chapati: an unleavened, Indian flat bread which should be made of wholemeal flour – see unleavened breads.

Cheesecakes: Together with the quiche, one of the great successes of the sixties and seventies; without these most small and some big catering businesses would not be businesses at all. But the very popularity of cheesecakes has meant a more discerning customer and, in contrast to quiches, the standard of most commercial cheesecakes is quite high.

I find three basic types, all made with curd cheese or cream cheese, but the division may be purely mine; they are the true cakes, the baked 'wet ones' and the unbaked. Within these categories there are truly thousands of variations, for cheesecakes in one form or another have been with us for as long as we have had cheese.

True cheesecakes are probably the most traditional and have a recognisably cake-like texture, in which cream or curd cheese is simply a flavouring. In the traditional small English chesecakes, baked in a pastry shell, there is usually no cheese at all now; but curd cakes, cheesecakes or curd tarts were always popular, and once flavoured with rose-water, nutmeg, orange, lemon, sherry, lemon or dried fruits.

It is unlikely you will be able to buy this style of cheesecake unless you can find a predominantly Polish, Russian or Jewish area or a shop run for these people. Austrians and Germans also make these, perhaps the richest versions of all.

What I call the 'wet ones' are baked cheesecakes in which cheese is the major ingredient and flour and eggs are there simply to bind it; (home-made ones would include cream or sour cream or, often, yoghurt, too). These are the most common commercial cheesecakes, and usually have a biscuit base and a topping of fruit in a thick syrup or sauce. Provided they are slightly chilled they make a satisfying and attractive snack or pudding. But don't hesitate to add ice cream, cream or a splash of suitable alcohol. Rum or cream or both on blackberry cheesecake, gin or cream or both on pineapple cheesecake, Mandarine Napoléon on strawberry cheesecake – and so on.

The third type of cheesecake is often found in small delicatessens where food is made on the premises. These are the unbaked types, often set with gelatine, which is no bad thing as long as they also contain a measure of whipped cream or yoghurt to give a fluffy, light texture. Those without gelatine often use only flavoured Philadelphia cream cheese and, because this will give no body, are thin and miserable, scarcely thicker than the biscuit base, and that is a swizz and a disappointment.

Whatever your delicatessen does, you should always store cheesecake in a refrigerator, for even if made with the finest ingredients it will go sour in warmth, or it will dry out, or both.

If you can buy some quite plain cheesecake it can be made rather special as the accompaniment to a purée of sharp fruit – black currants, gooseberries, red currants with orange, or rhubarb with orange and a touch of green root ginger would all be good.

Thin slices of chilled cheesecake on beautiful plates are the best way to extend small amounts of exquisite fruits. A slice of lemony cheesecake with just half an exquisite peach, or some passion fruit pulp, with perhaps a slice of mango or with some lime – splashed kiwi fruit slices would leave guests wishing for nothing more – unless of course they knew you had some chilled, well – matured elderflower wine, which goes with all cheesecakes. Some good delicatessens even sell elderflower wine, too. Others at least sell dried elderflowers, which once softened in a little cream make exquisite flavouring for cheesecakes you bake yourself . . . or a topping for those you do not.

Chelsea Buns: to be authentic these buns should be made from a slightly sweetened, white, yeasted dough and must incorporate both lemon zest and some mixed spice. The flavoured dough is rolled flat, covered with a mixture of butter, currants and brown sugar, rolled up and then sliced – to make spirals of dough. They must be laid flat and arranged so that when they prove and swell they just touch one another, giving the authentic slightly square shape. When cooked Chelsea buns must be glazed with a boiled milk and sugar syrup, then sprinkled with castor sugar.

Chollah: essentially a large loaf of yeasted white flour with milk and a little egg, often slightly sweetened, too. The usual shape is a plait, sprinkled with poppyseed. Particularly associated with Jewish food and festivals but not that much different from the small English milk loaves.

Cob/coburg loaf: the name for any round loaf of leavened white, brown or wholemeal bread. They are sometimes slashed or pricked or topped with whole grains but are never baked in a tin.

Cottage loaf: bread loaf of any type made of two rounds of unequal size, the smaller sitting on top of the bigger. Not often made commercially now.

Crisp bread: an unleavened, thin bread from Scandinavia. Made domestically only with rye flour but commercial manufacturing dictates the addition of wheat and other ingredients.

Croissants: one of the heights of yeast baking, croissants are made by rolling up a rich yeasted dough with layers of a great deal of butter – in fact they are really a yeasted puff pastry. Although now far more easily available, even in supermarkets, many of the mass-produced croissants have a metallic taste induced by the use of fats other than butter and are not worth the money. Croissants are found throughout Europe, varying mainly in their sweetness – Polish and Austrian are the sweetest. Several places claim the invention of these crescents of cholesterol – I plump for the Viennese baker who is said first to have fashioned them on the morning the crescents of the invading Turkish army were finally repelled from his city gates.

If not too sweet themselves, croissants go surprisingly well with some of the sweeter meats, especially ham; such combinations make a change in a picnic basket. If you make your own croissants, roll the dough around slices of ham and make the croissants bigger than usual for a more substantial breakfast; these are good hot or cold with herby, chive or garlic butter or with flavoured cream cheese. My shop in London sells some made by the Swiss Centre, and these are filled with rich chocolate; we can't get enough of them. . . .

Crown loaf: a speciality loaf made by baking a circle of rolls of white dough in a tin – they should only just touch. To make it more crown-like, some bakers use two circles, the top one smaller and joined to the bottom in the same way cottage loaves would be.

Danish loaf: a long oval, crusty loaf of white bread with a central slash, lightly floured. Not baked in a tin.

Danish pastries: these are made with a rich, yeasted dough similar to that of croissants but the butter is usually incorporated all in one layer and the dough turned and rolled without further additions. The pastry is then cut into decorative shapes, filled, iced or flavoured in dozens of ways and the finished products are served hot or cold at almost any time of the day. The secret of the fascinating but fugitive flavour of the better ones is ground cardamom. Probably invented in Vienna but specially associated with Scandinavia (the Danes call Danish pastries *Wienerbrod!*).

Diet breads: other than so-called slimming breads diet breads are usually either salt free or gluten free. The former helps in some heart conditions but is fairly unappetizing; the latter is almost impossible to buy but gluten-free flour, something of a contradiction, is available on prescription for sufferers from coeliac disease which is caused by an inability to digest the gliadin in gluten.

Some health food shops sell a gluten-free, bran-bread mixture.

Doughnuts: chunks of leavened white flour dough, sometimes filled with jam or fruit, then fried in fat or oil and smothered in sugar or a thin icing. Extremely widespread. It is mainly Arabs and Americans who make the ones with holes in the middle and these are often chemically leavened. Poles and Russians are addicted to their jam-filled *ponshki*. The Greeks make them smaller then soak them in warm honey and call them *loukoumades*. The Dutch, who normally make boring food, make wonderful doughnuts, stuffed with grated apple and fruit and spices and then give them the delightful name *olliebollen*.

Enriched breads: the additives which enrich the flavour, vitamin or mineral content of breads often improve keeping qualities, too. Milk, eggs, butter and cooking fats or oils are the most common enricheners; but soya flour, bran, wheatgerm, molasses, honey, and sugar are all found in commercial loaves. Most such additives are unnecessary if you regularly eat proper wholemeal bread. In any case the milk or egg was probably added to commercial loaves in powder form.

Farmhouse loaf: a white bread loaf baked in a tin both wider and more shallow than the usual tin loaf. The word farmhouse is imprinted on the side of the loaf, which is sometimes slashed lengthwise and floured.

French bread: the name generally given to any yeasted bread baked in long rolls, even though French flour or techniques may not have been incorporated. Usually called 'stick' or French sticks, but there are correct names for most types. *Baguettes* are the crisp, golden, medium-sized sticks that bulge in the middle. The very long thin ones are properly called *ficelles*. Large, hand-shaped cylindrical or round loaves are usually *pain de campagne* or *pain de ménage*. If French breads are baked in roll pans, which gives them straight, even sides, they are called *longuets*.

Granary loaf: a commercial brown loaf to which is added a measure of malted wheat grains for flavour and texture.

Grissini: these are the thin, well-baked breadsticks so beloved of Italian restaurants. There is no secret to making them yourself other than rolling your dough evenly and thinly.

Gugelhopf: this egg-rich, yeasted cake, also called *kugelhopf*, related to babke and brioche, contains chopped peel and other dried fruit. Dozens of recipes. It may be eaten plain but the very high yeast content means it stales too quickly for the taste of those not from Central Europe. But butter, jam or syrup will put that right. Like babke, gugelhopf may also be covered with chocolate and nuts.

Lardy cake: sometimes available in small independent baker's shops, this is bread dough rolled and folded like a simple puff pastry, except that instead of butter, pure lard, brown sugar and sultanas or mixed fruit are used. The dough should be scored with a sharp knife and the baked lardy cake broken on these marks rather than sliced. It is better warm than cold but either way is wonderful—and extraordinarily bad for you.

Milk loaf: a generic term for white bread mixed with milk or milk and water which gives a sweeter flavour, softer texture and longer life. Often made in small sizes and usually glazed.

Petits pains au chocolat: the ultimate sin in breakfast fare – or at any other times. These are usually made of brioche or croissant dough in which is embedded a chunk of rich dark chocolate, rather like a sweet sausage roll. Such is the sweetness and richness of these delights that those made with a simpler white bread are actually more enjoyable than those made with richer doughs.

Pannetone: a rather dry, yeasted cake from Italy which includes lots of dried fruit and is traditionally found at Christmas time.

Pitta: a flat oval of white or wholemeal bread recently popularized by the growth of interest in Greek and Arabic food. Usually served heated and torn into small squares and used as a scoop. Otherwise it is cut in half and the space inside encouraged to become a pocket which is then filled with salad and sliced hot meats or kebabs.

Pizza: originally a Neapolitan way to fill hungry stomachs cheaply – now an easy way for restaurateurs to fill bank accounts. True Neapolitan pizza (and the better American ones) is a thick slab of yeasted white or wholemeal flour dough mixed with milk to give lightness and more sustenance. It should be very crisp underneath and around the edges thanks to the generous application of olive oil to the baking tray. Originally toppings were simple and yet rich and chosen to blend into the dough rather than curl and crisp on top in the way modern pizza ingredients do. Cheese has become a common ingredient, especially the chewy Mozzarella or grated Cheddar – but neither is authentic. Although now essential, tomato as a topping would originally have been unknown. For a long time after they were introduced to

Europe, tomatoes cooked to a pulp were merely one of the optional sauces you poured over your chunks of hot white dough in Naples. Elizabeth David says the absolutely original pizza-type dish is from Armenia and the topping was of minced lamb. The French pissaladière covers dough (or thick slices of bread fried on one side only) with a mush of onion cooked in olive oil and decorated with black olives and anchovy fillets – a tomato-less pizza, in effect.

Pumpernickel: the many packaged varieties of unleavened German, whole-grain breads are essentially the same, with slightly different emphasis given to one or the other whole grain. Thus pumpernickel and *vollkornbrot* are much the same and versions from Westphalia and Osnabruck differ on purpose, as both these German areas claim to have created the original as far back as 1400. There is just as much controversy over the origin of the word pumpernickel. Some say it is onomatopoeic for the flatulent effect on the eater. (Try saying it with a German accent, and you'll hear what I mean).

It is not easy to make at home; the commercial pumpernickels are often baked for 24 hours at a very low temperature in a closed container. This makes a moist, dense, dark flat loaf which is now usually bought ready sliced. It should be refrigerated when opened. Pumpernickel and similar unleavened loaves, which might include grains other than rye, are excellent bases for open sandwiches; but as they dry and split easily I find it is better to cut each slice into squares or fingers before they are covered. A thin layer of butter keeps pumpernickel slices and pieces supple and prevents them either drying out or becoming soggy when on a buffet.

Rum babas: although a relatively new staple of delicatessens rum babas are part of the classic french repertoire. They are made of a savarin dough, that is a sweet, very highly-yeasted dough, and are baked in small ring moulds. They should be saturated with rum-flavoured syrup, which dissuades the growth of mould but which does not always disguise the taste of staleness which is precipitated by the high yeast content. If they are nice and fresh they can be deorated with chilled fresh fruit and whipped cream to make a super pudding.

Rye bread: a generic term for any bread which contains a proportion of rye flour. The actual content varies from as low as 15 per cent, which gives a light-coloured, light-textured loaf, to 100 per cent, which gives a dark dense loaf. Most often baked in a bloomer shape in this country, with or without carraway seeds; some delicatessens sell sour-dough rye breads, which, surprisingly, are rather sweet. These should be cut in very thin slices.

Sally Lunn: this light sweet bread was either originally sold in the streets of Bath by a woman of the same name or the name is a corruption of the French 'sol et lune' for these delicacies are supposed to look like the sun and the moon – a rich shining golden top over a pale delicate base. Put more simply, a Sally Lun loaf is a white flour, yeast-dough bread mixed with full milk or milk and cream, slightly sweetened, perhaps slightly spiced. It should be glazed with beaten egg yolk and scattered with crushed cube sugar whilst still hot. In Australia and New Zealand they replace the crushed sugar with white icing and dessicated coconut. They would.

Sandwich loaf: white, brown or wholemeal bread baked in an enclosed tin to give a rectangular shape. Usually made only with modern fast-rising 'bread' and then sliced and wrapped.

Soda breads: any breads leavened with baking soda and an acidic milk or with baking powder and a sweet milk. Normally a cob shape, sometimes deeply slashed with a cross.

Slimming breads: also called starch-reduced or high-protein breads as they are generally made with flour to which extra gluten has been added. This creates a bulkier more aerated loaf. Slice for slice these breads have more air and less starch – but ounce for ounce they are exactly the same as other breads. They only assist dieting if you eat the same number of (or fewer) slices than you would normally eat of 'heavier' bread. Some would say bread wasn't the problem anyway, but what we put upon it.

Sour-dough breads: breads leavened by the addition to the dough of some old, soured dough (the souring creates a gas which gives the rise). Usually the action of wild yeasts which feed on the flour assist, and this creates unique flavours. Because there is relatively little yeast content, sour-dough breads tend to last well.

Split-tin loaf: a tin loaf with a long slash down the middle. It can also be made by placing two long rolls of dough side by side in the tin. Almost always made with white dough.

Sweet/savoury breads: not often sold commercially

now, although lardy cake is an example. But once small amounts of dough were always kept back from the batch and used to make fruit breads, cheese breads, herb breads and so on.

Tin loaf: generic term for all loaves baked in metal tins, but specially applied to loaves which are long, rectangular and have a markedly high rise.

Unleavened breads: the unleavened breads of India, Asia and America are used as plates, forks and spoons. Only the *pitta* is slowly gaining popularity in the west but there are others fairly easily available. *Chapatis*, the Indian staple, are well-known to devotees of red-flock wallpaper throughout Europe and although made just of wholemeal flour and water are quite tricky to get right. Indian cookbooks will give instructions and introduce you to more adventurous chapatis, including the vegetable-stuffed *parathas* and the deep-fried *pooris*.

Other easily available unleavened breads are the Jewish *matzoh*, which is crisp and the mexican *tortilla* which is not, unless it is a taco which is a fried *tortilla*.

The Swedish crispbreads and the dense German pumpernickel and vollkornbrot (which simply means whole grain bread) are further examples—strange to think these relative exotica are related to the damper, that flour and water paste wrapped around green sticks, baked over fires and called bread by followers of Baden-Powell.

Vienna loaf: this is a style of bread rather than a shape of loaf and the difference is in the technique used. It is not often made commercially but is essentially a milk dough baked in a bloomer shape. The shape has become so associated with the vienna loaf that ordinary bloomers are sold as 'viennas'.

Wholemeal bread: the extraordinary difference found between domestic and commercial wholemeal loaves available is due to ignorance as much as anything else. Dough made with only 100 per cent wholemeal flour should be handled as little as possible or it will not rise – yes, kneading the dough of wholemeal flour gives worse not better results. If you like to knead, mix a high proportion of strong white flour with wholemeal flour. Commercial or domestic bread makers who turn out a bad loaf that is flat and heavy either have kneaded it too long or have not let it rise long enough.

Zwieback: this means 'twice-baked' and these are

rusks or slices of bread that have been baked dry, but which are usually thicker than commercial French or melba toast, which are made the same way.

QUICHE AND
SAVOURY FLANS

Quiche has gone into the English language and onto the table faster than spaghetti or kebabs ever did. But how woeful most of them are, and how few are quiche at all!

True quiche, the quiche lorraine, is a light, slightly savoury egg custard in short pastry with perhaps some little amount of green bacon and only a scattering of finely sliced leek or onion. The pastry is always pre-baked and the quiche should be eaten warm and quivering – not hot, not cold but warm.

There are some French and German cousins of quiche, absolutely stuffed with bacon or packed with onion. Some do include cheese, it is true. I've had some flavoured with smoked salmon, which were good and, like most people, have suffered countless spinach 'quiches' which swam about in a pool of their own juices because no-one had taught anyone how to drain spinach. But, no matter how good, they are not quiches and each diminishes the reputation of the real thing. Better to call them savoury flans or some similar name, the way we used to do.

With absolute respect for these earnest urban armies of quiche-makers, I know it is virtually impossible to make quiches or savoury flans of high quality or authenticity for commercial sale. The pastry has either to be like cardboard, which is unpleasant, or blind-baked, which is uneconomical. The fillings have to be full of cheese and onion or they would be too expensive for most of us to buy. And the whole arrangement must be able to withstand storage, transport, display-cutting, carrying and re-heating. I've yet to see it done economically *and* authentically for any length of time.

So, when you buy quiche or savoury flan, you really cannot expect what you would make at home. You may be lucky to find someone prepared to make less profit, or you might get to a shop as the delivery is made. If the pastry is crisp and the filling moist and generous with egg custard you will probably be better off not tempting fate – eat it cold. Reheating quiche or savoury flans can compound most ills, for by heating further you can cause the fillings to separate, wetting the pastry even more. If you want your quiche warm, better to stand pieces on a wire cake rack and reheat on that, so the air can crispen the bottom of the pastry whilst it reheats the rest.

Because most wine bars and bistros have microwave ovens now, it is always worth asking how they reheat their quiche if they offer it hot. A microwave is bound to soften the pastry unless the operator is highly skilled, which is as rare as a quiche lorraine. Order something else.

STORING BREAD

There are two great fallacies about bread storage: one concerns refrigeration and the other concerns air. Although refrigeration will certainly slow down the appearance and growth of mould, it also hastens the drying process *particularly* when the bread is in a plastic bag. It also affects granulation of the starch, giving a hard crumb.

The reason why refrigerated bread feels moist is simply that it *is* refrigerated, and therefore attracts condensation from the warmer atmosphere into which it is introduced. By heating refrigerated bread in a hot oven for 10 minutes you can return the starch to a softer state and so render the bread more palatable.

Surprisingly enough, bread keeps better if there is circulation of air. The reason is simple. In a space without an air-flow there will be a build-up of the moisture given off by the bread. A moist atmosphere is a basic requirement for the growth of mould: the more tightly the bread is sealed, the better the chances of it going mouldy.

Any container that can easily be washed and cleaned and that is not porous is suitable for bread storage. If you have a bread bin that does not allow circulation of air, prop the lid open with a few pieces of cork.

Simply wrapping bread in a clean tea-towel and storing it on a cool, airy shelf is just as effective.

Deep freezing is the perfect way to maintain the moisture content of bread, provided each item is absolutely fresh. Each must be well sealed, and any type can be used, although crusty French loaves tend to crack and *must* be refreshed in the oven before use. the oven before use.

The dimensions of most domestic freezers dictate that square-sided loaves are most suitable for storing. They stack more easily, with almost no wasted space. Bread can be thawed either slowly at room temperature, or finished in the oven, or thawed entirely in the oven.

At room temperature a fairly large loaf will take anything up to four hours to thaw completely. Condensation will form inside the freezer bag and settle on the bread, which will affect the crust. The softened crust will shorten the life of the bread. To obtain a better crust, open the bag and take the bread out as soon as you can. Ten minutes in a moderate oven will finish the job and ensure that you avoid serving a loaf with an icy core.

When you need bread immediately and have no time to start unfreezing it at room temperature, transfer the bread directly from the freezer to the oven, unwrapped. Half an hour at a moderate temperature is usually enough, but use a metal skewer to check for a heart of icy crumb.

If you wish, take this opportunity to glaze or re-glaze your loaf by brushing it over quickly with some milk or cream.

See also: flour, milling.

BUTTER

Without mountains of glorious, glistening butter, there would have been no *haute cuisine* – and there would probably be fewer heart disease problems, too. But for me to attempt to live without butter because of possible future health problems would be the same as cutting off a leg in case I might stub a toe. I was brought up eating masses of butter with everything, and that's that. I comfort myself with the knowledge that Australasians don't have a heart disease incidence anywhere near as high as their butter intake might suggest. We're built differently.

Butter-making is a specialized art, involving far more than churning cream for longer than required to make whipped cream. Even today there is no such thing as totally automated butter making. The great stainless steel churns which hold from 1000-1500 gallons of cream all have windows through which watch expert buttermakers, who must stop the churning at a precise moment or risk losing the whole batch.

Basically what happens is this: the rotation of a churn half-full of cream cracks the envelope of non-fat solids that encase each of the fat globules of the cream. When this happens – it is called 'breaking' – the butterfat globules begin to coalesce into pieces about the size of a wheat grain and the other solids are dispersed into the liquid content of the cream, becoming buttermilk. This buttermilk is drawn off and the butter grains are washed with cold water to rinse out any remains of buttermilk which would reduce the butter's quality and keeping ability. Once the water has drained enough to reduce the liquid content to within legally enforced limits, salt may be added. This is a very delicate operation, requiring a balance between market tastes and marketing requirements; the former is purely nationalistic, the latter depends on how long the butter is to be stored or how far it is to travel. As might be expected, the greater the expectations the higher will be the proportion of salt as a preservative. The more salt, the longer the butter will last.

The salted or unsalted grains are then churned a further 10-15 minutes, which is called 'working' and blends the grains into a solid mass. It is now packed into small packets or in large cartons for commercial use; in the latter process it is usually slightly compressed which helps avoid problems of shortened life which can be caused by trapped pockets of air.

The wide variety of flavours offered by butters comes as a surprise to most people. These variations are achieved in three basic ways, starting with the characteristics of the cream used. This relies on the type of cow and the feed it is given. As these vary during the year, so will the resultant butter, but usually the changes are more likely to be in the balance of minerals contained, and flavour differences would be beyond the detection of most of us. Perhaps the most widely used method of flavour manipulation is treatment of the cream.

Provided there has been a preliminary 'holding' of the cream to ensure uniform hardness of the fat globules, you can make butter from sweet cream to which you have done nothing else. But if you then leave it longer to ripen, the naturally-occurring bacteria will multiply and their enzymic actions and side-effects will increase the flavour, by raising the acid content in particular. Such a flavour enhancement or a flavour change can be aided by the addition of a cultured 'starter' as with the making of cheese. All the cream used to make Danish and Dutch butter is culture-treated, thus giving the distinctive and consistent flavour of these countries products. Sweet butter, which tastes like rich clotted cream, and unsalted butter, are *not* the same thing.

Salt is the last and final way of affecting butter's flavour. The combination of basic dairying technique, treatment of the cream and salting gives an enormously wide potential of flavours. Colouring is sometimes added also, but you shouldn't take it for granted that all brilliant butter has such additives. If the cream used is from Jersey or Guernsey cows it will naturally have a brighter glow.

USING BUTTER

Although the Mediterranean and Asian countries tend to prefer oil, the rest of the world relies on butter to add delicious bulk, texture or flavour to a high proportion of its foods. Sauces of melted butter were basic to the simple English way of cooking until jet travel and television had their persuasive way with our palates. But Germans, Russians and lots of Arabs still drench meats, grains and dumplings with the golden liquid. In Morocco, masses of butter is the secret of their unctuous sauces, cooked for hours to reduce and concentrate both flavour and texture.

Without butter we wouldn't have Danish pastries,

or croissants or real shortbread or much else of French and Continental *haute* cuisine. The cry of most men and women trained in this school is 'butter, butter and more butter'. Then they probably add cream as well.

There is a school of French cooking which eschews flour-based sauces. Instead reduced cooking liquids are beaten over heat with butter, which gives bulk and richness.

In Tibet butter is essential to living, for rancidified yak butter is what they scoop into their continual mugs of strong tea; the only man I know who has been to Tibet said you quite soon get used to that for the two robust flavours cancel one another out. But he could never get used to the smell engendered by carrying your own hunk of rancid butter about with you. Indians use butter in much the same way as we would for frying and so on. But they nearly always clarify it first to make *ghee*, which removes non-fat solids, giving even longer life and also means there are not particles to brown and burn which is one of the hazards of cooking with butter.

If bread were tastier in the United States they might eat more butter. As it is they are more likely to spread it with oleo-margarines that have what I can only describe as a 'distinct' flavour difference. This combination of chemical bread and fat is horrifying. They even use their horrid butter substitutes on their wonderful buckwheat pancakes and waffles in the morning. I really wonder about their children's future as enjoyers of real food.

Other English-speaking colonial countries stick to butter with a loyalty little short of addiction. Even the ever-present steak is usually cooked in butter. Indeed, I remember zipping out to buy a whole fillet steak, slitting it and stuffing with a bottleful of fresh rock oysters (about 3 dozen) and then cooking this slowly in the oven with regular bastings of a melted ½ lb (225 g) of butter. In NZ in the early 60s this was a perfectly ordinary meal.

If for financial or health reasons you prefer to use butter substitutes, there is still a case for using butter on special occasions. Perhaps the most important of these to a serious cook is in the finishing of sauces. Just before serving one, sweet or savoury, whisk in a few knobs of butter. This actually polishes the sauce, giving it a shine and a velvety texture that indicates a sincere care about good food – and it tastes good, too. If you prefer simple food, then there is no better accompaniment than a flavoured butter, whether you are serving meat, fish, fowl, vegetables or eggs.

Unsalted butter is not very popular in most English-speaking countries, mainly because of the added 'culture-flavour'; but it is worth the extra expense to experiment with a favourite cake or pastry recipe to see the difference it makes. Most people prefer it in baking once they know about it, even if they can't take it spread on their bread or melted over vegetables. Incidentally, if you are faced with unsalted butter when travelling and don't like it, the solution is dead simple. You simply follow the local custom and sprinkle on a little salt before you spread the jam or marmalade.

TYPES OF BUTTER AVAILABLE IN THE UNITED KINGDOM

There are three main types of butter: salted, slightly salted and unsalted. You can generally judge how much salt there is by ascertaining how far the butter has had to travel; hence butter from New Zealand is likely to have a higher salt content than butter from, say, Wiltshire. There is a certain uniformity to the degree of saltiness in UK-produced butter, the flavour differences being those associated with cream treatment.

So-called farmhouse butter, usually from the western counties, is usually slightly less salty than most, which is one of the contributing factors to its notoriously short life. In my experience it has a special predilection for rancidity, which may be due to inefficient churning and washing or because it is often made close to cheese dairies and picks up foreign flavours. Either way, farmhouse butter should always be given a discreet sniff to ensure it is sweet and wholesome. You should also check for streakiness; this indicates the combination of different batches and possible problems with randicity.

Slightly salted butter gives a blander flavour which suits much continental cooking and many palates.

Unsalted butter is usually the most expensive and potentially the most troublesome kind, for without the preservative advantage that salt gives it is prone to all manner of afflictions. If it has been made with unripened cream, as is the case with some of the French varieties, it will taste rather like a slightly sharp, fresh whipped cream. Again, a trained and perspicacious nose is a definite aid when buying.

COOKING WITH
BUTTER

If you have problems with butter burning when you are frying or melting vegetables, the simplest technique is to lower the heat. Or you can add up to an equal quantity of oil, which allows you to use a much higher heat without the butter burning. Otherwise you have to buy or make clarified butter, which is quite a good thing to keep in your refrigerator. Melt a good quantity of butter over gentle heat then increase the temperature a little until it foams. Now either let this settle and set undisturbed and remove the top layer or pour the hot butter through several layers of butter muslin. Either way you end up with a clear yellow butter, free of solid matter that might burn. This is what the Indians call *ghee*.

STORING
BUTTER

All butter is affected not only by heat but also by light, so it should be kept both cool and dark.

CHEESE

In Dutch the word for it is *kaas*, in Irish *cais*, Welsh *caws*, Spanish *queso*, Portuguese *quiejo*. In English it was *case* or *cyse* before 1100 AD and then went on to become *cease, coese, schese, chease, cheise, chies* and *ches*; but it was probably the same thing all along, as the English are renowned for being unable consistently to spell their own language. Even Shakespeare, who might be thought to have known a thing or two about it, spells his name a different way almost every time he signs himself. But whatever the language or spelling, it is solid milk or, rather, solidified casein plus several other of the components of the milk, depending on how the change in texture was effected.

Put like that it sounds mundane. But of all our foods, cheese is the one that is perhaps the least mundane of all. Cheese and the gift of cheese-making skills have been the comfort, succour and support of king and subject since time immemorial. The pharaohs fancied it and Zoroaster lived desert-bound on it for 20 years. Madame de Pompadour was known to be partial to a bit, David and Jonathan both enjoyed it, together with biblical fellow-travellers; Casanova swore by it, Roman emperors commanded it to be imported – and we, poor unsung mortals, have always turned to it both for simple pleasure and as a mainstay of our very existence.

Cheese is as variable as the faces of man and the places in which he lives. It can start a meal, be a main course, a pudding, a savoury, a snack. It can be given, shared, remembered – even lusted after.

There are undoubtedly over one thousand varieties of cheese made in the world. But this great array breaks down into just a few basic groups; variation within each of these groups is what makes up the numbers and the differences are often so minute as to be distinguishable only because a label tells you it is distinct from others.

The best way to begin to understand the marvel of transforming milk into cheese is simply to know what is happening. To put it in a nutshell, you heat milk, coagulate it, separate the liquid whey and solid curd, salt the curd, mould or press the curd, then eat it fresh or let it lie about for some time to ripen or ferment. Of course, it's absurdly more complicated than that but these basic principles are common to all cheeses.

To be more expansive, milk straight from a cow or any other dairying animal will curdle unfailingly because of the action of enzymes produced by bacteria naturally present in milk. These enzymes work on the lactose – milk sugar – converting it into lactic acid. This is what happens as milk first ripens and then sours. At a certain level of acidity the milk will coagulate, forming solid white curd and liquid whey.

This process of natural coagulation can take some time and is affected by weather and other unpredictable factors. So it is often helped by the addition of rennet. This is made from the fourth stomach of a young ruminant – usually a calf – and its enzymes quickly curdle milk without requiring it first to be sour. The choice of starting with an acidic natural curd or a sweet, renneted curd is an important way to influence the final flavour of any cheese.

Cheese-making was simple but unreliable until the advent of pasteurization. Pasteurized milk will not curdle naturally. It may solidify if left somewhere warm, but this has nothing to do with the formation of lactic acid. Rather, it happens as a result of the action of potentially dangerous spoilage bacteria – so sour pasteurized milk should never be used for cheese or anything else. As well as killing off harmful bacteria, pasteurization also kills off the useful bacteria necessary for curdling milk and for giving cheese its aroma, flavour and texture. Nowadays a 'starter' – a laboratory-grown culture of these cheese-making bacteria – must be put back into pasteurized milk if it is used. Then the milk is allowed to ripen, to develop a pleasing fullness of flavour and slight acidity before it is renneted.

CURDS AND WHEY

Once rennet-assisted or natural separation begins, the soft junket-like curds may be gently sliced and laid in a mould, while the whey slowly drains out over a period of days. Alternatively, the curd may be cut to release the whey more quickly, and then further cut or crumbled by hand. It may even be put through a small mill to break it down into very small particles, the process known as cheddaring. The amount of separation, the time it takes and the temperature at which it is done all help determine the final texture and flavour of the cheese.

Separation is usually accompanied by salting. Soft,

naturally-draining curds will probably be sprinkled with salt as they lie shrinking in their moulds. Drier curd will have to have salt mixed into it. These salted curds will then be transferred to a mould of some type and subjected to a greater or lesser degree of pressure. The amount of pressure and the length of time for which it is applied actively influence the type of cheese which results. Generally, soft, crumbly cheeses and blue cheeses do not have heavily pressed curds. The longer the curd is pressed, the longer the cheese will take to mature and the longer will be its life.

RIPENING

After pressing, the cheese is put in a cool cellar or cave to ripen. Here, the catalogue of influences continues. The temperature, the amount of draught and the humidity of the ripening cellar all count, as does the treatment of the rind, if there is one, and how often the cheese is turned. This last process ensures even aging through the entire cheese and, in particular, even distribution of remaining moisture.

A HISTORY OF
CHEESE

Somewhere on the great, wind-ravaged steppes of Central Asia there should stand a monument as high as a mountain. For here, according to legend, once lived the simple nomad responsible for discovering the action of rennet and cheese as we know it.

The earliest cattle to be domesticated were the Aurochs, a wild breed found throughout Europe and the Middle East. In Mesopotamia they often removed one of the animal's horns, probably for greater safety in the early days of milking. Cheese making quickly followed cattle domestication, but only as a result of natural acid-curding, which took time and made an inherently sour-tasting product. One day, our unknown hero put his fresh milk into an improperly-cured pouch he had made from the stomach of a young goat or sheep. Presto! the action of the stomach's residual rennet curdled the milk in record time, and it was still sweet.

Sweet, solid milk was a phenomenon the tribesmen had noted often in the stomachs of slaughtered, unweaned animals. Being necessarily thrifty they may have eaten it, enjoying the contrast to their usual acidic cheese. Now they had the secret of making it themselves, and a wider world of cheese was created – a world that continues to grow today.

The spread of knowledge

That is only one version of the story. Some have it that the nomad rode with the stomach-bag jiggling on his saddle, others say that it simply sat in the warmth of his tent. Still more reckon it wasn't a nomad at all; the Greeks swear that, like fire, it was a gift of their Olympian gods. However it was discovered, no better substitute has ever been found for rennet, and rennet is still made from the stomachs of young suckling animals. Be it Brie, Chèvre, Roquefort, Gouda or even modern processed cheese, all sweet-curd cheese starts in the same way.

Drifting nomads, conquering hordes, Roman legionaries, Christian monks and the written word slowly spread the knowledge until most of the world made cheese. There were some exceptions; it must be one of the few discoveries not credited to Chinese ingenuity and they've never taken to it. On the Indian continent, some religions taught that milk and cheese consumption robbed animals of their rights. In the Americas the Indians were hunters, not husbandmen; and on the Pacific Islands there were no suitable animals available.

Archaeologists continually astonish our pasteurized society with more and more discoveries of ancient cheese-making knowledge. They cannot tell us how the cheeses were made or what they tasted like, but vessels depicted in sculpture and paint have been identified as ancient cheese moulds and drainers.

Domestication of mammals for their milk probably started in Macedonia in about 6000 BC. Evidence of milk-processing a half-millennium later has been found in recently discovered cave paintings in the Libyan Sahara. This predates by two thousand years our knowledge of similar progress in both Mesopotamia and pharaonic Egypt. The tomb of the Pharaoh Horus-asha yielded vessels containing a substance that scientists have identified as cheese.

By the time the Roman empire stretched across Europe, cheese-making had progressed enormously and a wide variety of types was known. There were even alternatives to rennet, for the juice of plants, flowers and bark can also curdle and flavour milk. In most places goats were the primary source of milk; cows were not to replace them for some centuries, when the influence of Viking husbandry made itself felt.

The conquered and colonized had their own cheeses. Goths, Teutons, and Celts made many varieties which the Romans thought good enough to import and sell in their markets. To the Romans, cheese was a staple. It was carried in every soldier's pack, sold in every market, mixed with honey, herbs, wine and spices for banquets; gratinéed dishes were an imperial speciality. The occupying forces passed on their own sophisticated cheese-making knowledge, too, and had a direct influence on much of the cheese we know today.

Vikings in Istanbul

After the Roman Empire went the way of the world, it was the unworldly brotherhood of Christian monasteries that cherished and preserved the cheese-making heritage of Europe for almost one thousand years. Simple, fresh cheese was an important part of a peasant diet, but large-scale manufacturing was attempted only by dairying monasteries. The Celtic monks of Ireland, unaffected by the waves of vandalism and ignorance that swept Europe after the Fall, were especially responsible for re-establishing the industry.

Most old-established cheeses in France, Italy and Switzerland trace their ancestry back to monastic beginnings, and to this day Port (du) Salut is made only by the monks of the Abbaye d'Entrammes.

Before explorer Tim Severin intrepidly sailed his open leather boat 'Brendan' across the Atlantic in 1977 he came to me for advice on suitable foods: 20th century pre-packs had proven unreliable and unpalatable. I quickly discovered that Appenzell cheese from Switzerland could trace its origins directly back to Irish monks who had arrived about the time of St Brendan's voyage in the 6th century, when he is thought first to have discovered America. So *Brendan* eventually sailed with grains, cheeses, smoked meats and sausages just like its predecessor so long ago. It was good to have one's suspicions about 'old-fashioned' things being better proven so dramatically.

The greatest single contribution to the renaissance of cheese-making came from a most unexpected source – the Vikings. It is not generally appreciated how wide was the sphere of their travelling, trading and influence. Some went as far as Istanbul, where blond bodyguards soon decorated the courts of the lecherous Byzantine emperors. The Vikings used their trading routes to exchange expertise with the herdsmen of the Volga, the Black Sea, the Baltic countries, England and Normandy. They also shipped their cattle to new ports and evolved high-yielding cross-bred species that may still be seen today.

The clash of East and West during the Crusades from the eleventh to thirteenth centuries lifted Europe even further from her caseous Dark Age. The elegant and sophisticated dishes of the Arab and Byzantine world took Europeans by storm when the crusaders brought them home. Even today it is easy to see, in Morocco specially, a series of dishes exactly the same as those claimed to be traditional Olde English, but which in fact had been brought back from the East, together with exotic fruits and flavourings. The new spices – cumin, caraway, pepper – found their way into both fresh and pressed cheeses. But it was the seductive combination of soft cheese with rose-water or orange-blossom water that really awoke the European palate and the romance with these flavours only died when we stopped eating the gargantuan meals of Queen Victoria and her son.

Pressed for trade   Big business and the international marketing of cheese began with the establishment of commercial centres such as Venice and the cities of the Hanseatic League. Cheese was an internationally known and enjoyed food staple and thus an important part of trade. The boom in exporting led to a greater demand for cheeses which travelled and kept well – and hence to the creation of many of the long-lasting hard or pressed cheeses. Even though buying these foreign cheeses was often dangerous to your health, they sold furiously; the very fact that they were foreign was enough to recommend them . . . *plus ça change* etc.

Some cheeses were meant only for immediate consumption and could never travel; they required years of experiment and the advent of refrigeration before they passed into the common domain. It was only late in the nineteenth century that, for example, wooden boxes were invented for transporting Camembert.

You had to have your wits about you in the market place. Hygiene was known to have some bearing on results but there was not very much the maker or buyer could do about that. And there was no way of judging whether the memorable experience offered by unusual mould or bacterial growth would be a taste thrill or an upset stomach. Temperature, acidity, curing and even pressing were arbitrary. Some say that until the advent of pasteurization only one cheese in three was safe to eat; but two out of three cheeses were *not* thrown away.

The beginning of the end

And so it remained right up to the early 19th century, when the new sciences first began to make nature a servant of man.

The work of von Liebig in Germany, Pasteur in France and Metchnikov in Russia explained the curing of cheese and established that by treating milk with heat you could render it pure and safe. It was a technique that spread as fast as the fevers and disease it prevented. Soon advances in sterilization made it possible to offer the world pure 'starter' cultures of selected live bacteria to replace the dead ones in pasteurized milk. Rennet, too, could be standardized.

Burgeoning knowlege soon led to the harnessing of steam and the beginning of the end of manpower. By 1856 Norway was able to set up a cheese-making factory that was successful and profitable. Others followed all over Europe. In less than fifty years the cheese lore of thousands of years had been transformed, never to be the same.

Who else makes cheese?

Apart from the Chinese, who have never regarded milk as quite suitable for human consumption and are nauseated at the idea of eating 'rotten' milk, nearly every country now makes cheese of some kind, even if it is not a long-standing tradition.

The Mongolians make cheese from the milk from their prized mares, and the isolated region of Tibet is highly dependent on its supply of yak milk; I've been told that odd aberrants in China make a cheese from milk curdled by tomato.

In India, greater religious freedom and dietary knowledge have now made the production and eating of cheese possible. Much of India's cheese is actually imported from Nepal, where a relatively new cheese industry has proved both successful and profitable.

Considering the fame of Canadian Cheddar and Wisconsin's huge output of cheese, it is astonishing to think that throughout the entire American continent milk was probably unknown as a human food until European settlement. But, since 1600, North American cheese has pulled together the best of taste and technique from all over the world. Excellent pressed and soft cheeses trace their ancestry directly back to the ancient traditions of several European countries.

The exciting mix of people and cultures, and the constant search for new techniques, have led to the creation of some remarkable American cheeses, such as Pineapple, whose hard shellacked rind can be used as a salad bowl when the softer centre has been scooped out. Processed cheese is also an American invention – one that has become an abused convenience world-wide.

In South America, fresh white cheeses are the most popular for domestic consumption. Argentina exports a large amount of cheese and her Parmesan type has gained for itself a sound reputation abroad.

Australasia, particularly New Zealand's North Island, has perfect dairying climates. The most popular dairying cow there is the gentle Jersey whose carotene-rich, yellow milk gives the cheese excellent flavour, and high nutrition. Indeed, it has been reported that the Stilton made in New Zealand is at least as good as, sometimes better than, the real thing: quite a compliment, for there is barely a dairying country in the world that has not attempted the Stilton coup.

Perhaps the most interesting examples of modern dairying technology are Denmark and Ireland. Although both have been dairying countries for countless centuries, their current place in the world cheese market as manufacturers and exporters has almost nothing to do with their native cheeses. They provide excellent, if not quite authentic, imitations of other country's best-selling cheeses. Some experts maintain that the Irish cheese industry faces the brightest future of any European producer, and that given economic and technical backing it could be turning out the best-quality cheese available in ten or fifteen years.

Danish Mozzarella, Irish Brie, French Cheddar and New Zealand Stilton have all been mastered. And what, you may wonder, do the clever Japanese do? Almost everything is the answer. A wide variety of the world's cheeses is made and marketed in Japan where, earlier this century, cheese was hardly eaten at all. Who knows, but soon we may see Japanese Cheddar in our delicatessens.

BUYING CHEESE	Buying cheese really is putting your money where your mouth is. Although much cheaper than meat as far as nutritional value goes, it is no longer a cheap food. The demise of the corner shop and the blossoming of the supermarket have also robbed the customer of the chance to taste and discuss. But here are a few observations that will help you on your way to better buying.
You and your shop	In an ideal world, cheese would reach the customer in perfect condition, thoughtful retailers refusing to sell anything underripe, overripe or otherwise imperfect. But if you see a cheese that does not look quite right, it does not necessarily mean the retailer has been careless.

A small shopkeeper may be trying to provide a specialist service, building up a trade in traditional and interesting cheeses. Invariably some will sell faster than others, so some may not be in tip-top condition. They are probably perfectly acceptable to many people, sometimes through preference, sometimes through ignorance. They are still worthwhile as a way to learn a little more about cheese – putrefaction and desiccation always excepted. Complain, but don't give up.

The only sure way to help avoid this problem and dissuade your shopkeeper from taking the easy way out – selling pre-packaged basics – is to buy more cheese. When you try something new that you like, tell your friends where you bought it. Try tasting before you buy, so that you can avoid anything that is not quite your style.

In supermarkets the problems are very different and difficult. Supermarket staff need know very little about pre-packed cheese to display it neatly and price it properly. If you buy something really bad from such a source, the wrapping having prevented accurate assessment, complain. Otherwise the cheese-buyer may never know what has gone wrong. It may not even be his fault; his supplier may be sending inferior goods.

Buying blind

Buying an unusual or new cheese is full of pitfalls, even for the initiated. There are no real short-cuts; only experience can help you. You can take out some insurance by going to a reputable shop that still cuts from whole cheeses. If these are good, the rarer, smaller delicacies should be too. If the treat you are looking for is soft and French, remember that these are far more difficult to keep than pressed, domestic cheese.

Once ripe, such cheeses usually have a very short life. Thus, although some of the grander shops flout modern practice and keep these on their counter-tops rather than under refrigeration, this is a matter of display rather than good husbandry. You might be lucky to find something in just the right condition. But often cheese from such a display will be inedible, and because it is new to you, you will not *know* that it is inedible.

Genuine interest in cheese requires planning and application. As with wine, attention to correct storage, temperature, maturity and accompaniments will repay you handsomely.

The subjectiveness of each one's taste buds means no-one can give simple rules for your guidance through the forest of trade names and pre-packaged cheeses. Some are certainly better than others. If you really believe the brand your retailer stocks is inferior to another you know, show him the label, hoping it also reveals the supplier's name. Your shopkeeper will love you for it if you are right; still be interested if he thinks you are wrong. As most small shopkeepers cannot find time to try cheeses which they do not carry as part of their own stock, any specialist help you can give is bound to be appreciated.

Generally, the rules applying to the purchase of most cheeses are very much a matter of good sense and similar to those for other fresh foods; there should be no dryness, cracks, sweating, oiliness, mould in the wrong place or of the wrong type, no sourness, decomposition or excessive crumbling.

A buyer should never reject a piece of cheese simply because it has rind (like Farmhouse Cheddar) or because some foil is included in your weighed portion (as in Dolcelatte). It is fair enough to object, however, if inexpert cutting means there is a disproportionate amount of rind or foil.

Pre-packed cheese should always be checked for date. The packing should never be smeared or cloudy; avoid like the plague any that are puffed up like cushions, even if they are in date.

Instructions for opening, storing and serving packaged cheese should be strictly observed.

SERVING
CHEESE

Full enjoyment of even the most unassuming and inexpensive cheese can be ensured with just a little care; expensive, rare and delicate cheeses demand it by right. As with wine, temperature, atmospheric conditions and the method of serving can have dire or divine effects. Much of the following is simply good sense.

**Serving
temperature**

This is the most important factor in ensuring you enjoy the full flavour of your chosen cheese.

A moderate room temperture is best for most cheeses. When removing cheese from the refrigerator, take into account the effect of central heating in winter or cool kitchen breezes in summer. An average of half to one hour to reach the right temperature is usual.

On balance, it is probably better to serve cheese slightly too cool rather than too warm – warmth leads to sweating and unpleasant taste changes. To avoid the effect of air deterioration and prevent exchange of flavours, **never unwrap cheese until just before serving.**

Cream cheeses are usually served lightly chilled. But as this convention was largely to safeguard freshness, you may enjoy the fuller flavour of a warmer cream cheese, provided you are confident of its wholesomeness.

**The art of
presentation**

The appearance of the cheese you serve is a matter both of good sense and a sense of respect for your choice.

Trim any dry, cracked or mouldy parts if necessary.

Never camouflage the cheese with gardens of salad, forests of pine or crêches of straw. Let the cheese speak for itself on a plain base. A wooden cheese board is traditional; but if you have a large one and want to serve only one or two cheeses, improvise with a small contrasting plate, a bread board or table mat.

The common practice of covering boards or plates for cheese with split-cane table mats is not recommended. Crumbs of cheese and other food can make them very unhygenic; in any case they are difficult to cut on and serve from.

A few choice accompaniments may be served with cheese for those who require them. This is more correct when cheese features as a large part of the meal – say, a light lunch or picnic. Then fruits, nuts, cress, fresh herbs, chutney or pickles may be offered, with regard to complementing rather than masking the flavours of the cheese.

Pickles – especially pickled onions, traditionally served with a ploughman's lunch in pubs – dramatize the astonishing tastelessness of much modern Cheddar. They overwhelm what little *goût* there is – which, perhaps, is no bad thing. With some well-matured, summer-milk, farmhouse cheese a pickle or two can be ideal, but beware you do not swamp the cheese.

Wraps, rinds and tags

Depending on the formality of the meal, any wrappings, such as boxes, should probably be removed; so too should inedible rinds.

Some experts maintain that no rind is edible, including those of Brie and Camembert. Others allow the possibility of eating the rind only of the soft-paste cheeses with washed or bloomy natural rinds. Use your own taste as guide – making sure that if you do serve the rind, it is not dry, ammoniacal or otherwise contaminated.

The idea of putting name-tags on cheese at the dinner table is appalling. If you are unable to remember the names of the cheeses you are presenting, you are probably serving too many. Unfussy presentation of an interesting or rare cheese will create far more of a sensation.

Tags are unhesitatingly recommended in catering establishments with inexperienced staff and at parties specially held to experiment with, or introduce, new cheeses but these should really be the domain of catering schools. Cheese and wine parties are really rather *passé*.

To cut or scoop?

Unless you are serving children or the infirm, never pre-cut cheese into portions; it hastens the deterioration of both flavour and friendship!

But as there are guests who seem to possess an unerring talent for mutilating cheese, there is nothing wrong in actually serving the cheese to your guests yourself. A pile of plates, a sharp knife (two if blue cheese is included) and a nice line in chat will ensure no one feels you are being mean.

Butter should always be available, though its use is a personal matter. A choice of biscuits – some salty, some not – is best at dinner; bread is better at lunch and for snacks. As all cheese is salted to some degree, never offer just salted biscuits. If you are able to serve only one sort of biscuit, choose water crackers, or Bath Olivers, with salted butter. Thumbscrews and the rack are an inadequate response to those who serve cheese-flavoured biscuits.

What about scooping? In a word, never. Although the centre of a properly aged Stilton is certainly the *bluest* part, it is no *riper* than any other section. The flavour simply changes as you move from the rind to the centre, as the amount of blue increases. But no part is in any way a lesser Stilton; it all shares in the fascinating spectrum of tastes presented by a mature cheese.

Defenders of the practice of scooping are incorrect to say they are logically following the process of ripening from the centre to the rind. Cheese ripens anaerobically – without direct air contact. Once air gets at cheese it begins to activate spoilage bacteria. Stilton scooped from the centre slowly changes in texture – certainly. But this change is the result of deterioration and desiccation.

Equally frowned upon is the alcoholic dosing of cheese – again inflicted most often on the noble Stilton. This was originally done, not for a recherché taste thrill, but to keep whole cheeses moist or to disguise bad ones. The practice is unnecessary today. Clearly, the finest port could not improve a bad cheese, a fine cheese would not help an inferior port and excellent examples of both need neither assistance nor disguise. The combination of the two is an insult to the painstaking manufacturers of both; but a chunk of Stilton and a glass of port, both at room temperature and savoured individually, are a sublime experience.

The party's over

As soon as is decent, get the cheese off the table and back into its protective wrapping. Cigarette smoke and a warm atmosphere are hardly a cheese's best friend. As well as protecting flavour, such quick action will mean fewer dried edges to trim and thus will save you money, too.

CHEESE AND WINE

Cheese is incomparably gregarious. It goes well with great and modest vintages and with beer, ale, cider, fruit, herbs and nuts.

There is probably more snobbish rubbish written about the companionship of wine and cheese than about any other food; this cheese must be eaten only with that wine, that with this – the list of arranged marriages is endless. Preferences are subjective in the extreme; one sometimes suspects the unsubtle marketing scheme of an ambitious wine merchant.

A guide without limits

The truth is that very few of us, even the most devoted sybarite, will have the cash or the inclination to go out and buy a highly individual bottle of wine just to complement a cheese. The wine is usually there first – bought to go with the main course or, more likely, left behind after the last party. It is the cheese that is expected to slot in, the cheese that should be bought to match the wine.

The joy of both wine and cheese is that neither has tiny, cramped, limited spheres of conviviality. Whether great or simple, they can adapt to their surroundings.

Broadly speaking, the cheeses and wines of an area do have a natural affinity, particularly if you are drinking the simpler wines. Finer vintages spread their welcoming arms wider. Experience teaches you that this is but a basis for pleasure. A light claret easily replaces a Beaujolais, and a really crisp white wine can more than equal the light reds, and so on. But overripe Brie will never be saved by a superb Bordeaux or Burgundy. Neither will an absolutely perfect cheese salvage or camouflage a sour or vinegary wine. The general rule is to ally full-bodied wines with richer cheeses; the lighter white and rosé wines deserve the fresher and creamier cheeses and the subtlety of light, newly made Chèvres.

Cheese and wine at the dinner table

Your choice of cheese will depend on when it is to be served. If this is to be between the main course and the pudding – as the French do – it is usual to match it to the main-course wine. If you had served a white Meursault, it would be better not to offer a Brie or a tangy Blue Cheshire to eat with the last of that wine. A soft goat's cheese, some flowery Gruyère or a Tomme would be much more balanced choices.

If you have offered a particularly good main-course wine, you should *always* finish it by serving cheese before your pudding.

This is even more important if you are to serve a luscious, sweet, chilled pudding wine. You will thereby ensure full appreciation of both wines and cheese.

On the other hand, any dinner smart enough to change wines is likely to finish with port or madeira, in which case cheese is also a highly suitable accompaniment; but on balance it would still be better to serve it before the pudding.

Those who insist on finishing with cheese, and who have served red wine, might consider avoiding pudding altogether. If they wish both to finish with a sweet pudding wine and cheese, such strongly flavoured cheeses as Roquefort and, say, a Barsac make a sensational combination – if you can afford it.

COOKING WITH CHEESE

Any good cookbook will have numerous recipes incorporating cheese. The following suggestions show how cheese and an enterprising cook can make an inventive contribution to many types of dish.

For a start, hard cheese ends can make super biscuits. Grate them, mix them with plain flour and water to a stiff paste, add a dash of salt and cayenne or pepper if you like. Roll thin, cut into strips or circles and bake in a moderate oven.

A handful of grated cheese makes scones into cheese scones. Sprinkle more on top a few minutes before they are ready to come out of the oven.

Sauerkraut toast is a heartier variation of the bread-and-cheese combination. Top toasted bread with heated sauerkraut, some salt beef, pepper and, finally, thick slices of Emmental cheese. Sprinkle with paprika or caraway seeds before serving. It makes a filling late-night supper or, with soup, a warming lunch on a winter's day.

For lunch or light supper, split open a baked potato and stuff it with grated cheese (Cheddar, Gruyère and Emmental are best), butter and a dab of sour cream or milk. Spice with celery salt, sweet paprika or nutmeg.

Lancashire is the proper cheese for rarebits; add almost anything to the basic mix, from anchovies to chopped ham and pineapple.

Cheese cubes are delicious in salads. The Greeks use Fetta; you could use white Cheshire or white Stilton.

If Parmesan is too expensive, look for the ribbed, round, yellow Pecorinos originally from Sardinia or the Italian mainland but now well made in Belgium. These are wonderful for nibbling, as well as for grating.

Cream cheese is the basis of a luxurious dessert.

Flavour with marrons glacés, crystallized fruit and orange or coffee liqueur, then freeze. That's all there is to it. It will not freeze solid.

Cheese and apple do not have to be served separately or cold. Finish cooking a baked apple with grated cheese, or alternate layers of cheese and apple in your next pie. 'Apple pie without some cheese is like a kiss without a squeeze' is what they are supposed to say up north.

Most vegetables have an affinity with cheese. Add interest by grating cheese over hot vegetables when you serve them; stuff vegetables such as marrows, courgettes, aubergines and large tomatoes with cheese, breadcrumb and herb mixtures.

Cheese grated into a bowl of soup is a fragrant addition – Gruyère on onion is the great classic. The Dutch also grate Gouda on their pea-and-ham soups.

The next time you are making a fish pie, mix cheese into the potato topping. For something more substantial, bake the pie with a cheese scone topping but make sure it is well cooked before serving.

A cheese soufflé is always popular and is easier to produce than one imagines. For a nineteenth-century touch, line your soufflé dish with pastry, blind-bake it, then add the soufflé mixture – Queen Victoria approved. If you are making the pastry yourself, chop fresh herbs into the mixture for an even more appetizing touch.

A simple party or pre-prandial snack is Stilton-stuffed celery. Break off individual stalks and crisp them in iced water. Serve with the leaves on if they are fresh-looking. Cream Stilton and softened butter together, and push into the hollow of the stalks. Cream cheese and chive stuffing is also very popular.

Plain cream cheese can be home-decorated to look and taste every bit as good as the imported varieties. If you are making your own cheese, either drain the renneted full-cream milk over the sink in cheesecloth in the usual way and then pack in a mould to shape – or, if you can find one, use a shaped mould with drainage holes in it. If you use commercial full-cream cheese, just pack it straight into an ordinary pretty mould. Whatever method you choose, you can decorate the result with pistachios, walnuts or pine nuts at a fraction of the commercial price.

Pork and chicken both like cheese. Finish off grilling with a layer of grated cheese, just melted and browned. You can even do this to chicken or pork casseroles.

When vegetables are cheap, bake vegetable and cheese flans. Aubergines, tomatoes and courgettes on a base of Cheddar and sprinkled with Parmesan or Pecorino, for instance. A touch of sharp cheese is also good on hot corn on the cob or fresh asparagus. There is also a traditional heart-shaped cheese dessert, coeur à la crème. The special mould is quite easily available; simply pack it with rich cream cheese and serve with fresh strawberries or raspberries in their juice. If you chop up some preserved ginger and mix that into the cheese it is even more delicious; but let it sit for 24 hours first.

Cheese and beer cannot only be mixed and toasted as a rarebit – they also make an easy dip or fondue. About ⅛-¼ pint (75-150 ml) beer per 1 lb (½ kg) grated Cheddar with a drop of Worcestershire sauce makes a delicious dip or an easy summer lunch.

Grated Cheddar, Parmesan or Pecorino add a terrific lift to plain or flavoured rice; brown rice cooked in chicken stock with sippets of bacon and then tossed in Parmesan is extraordinarily good and quite enough for lunch with some good fruit to follow.

The fragrant flowers of summer – especially the violet, rose and elder – all go very well with cheese and particularly in cheesecake. In any of your favourite cheesecake mixtures add two or three heaping spoonsful of the flowers of elder or violet or the petals of a fragrant rose, trimmed of the white portion at the base. A spoon or two of wine made from the same source helps even more.

Nuts and cheese can combine in more places than on a snack tray. A couple of dozen good walnut halves crushed lightly and mixed with an equal weight of butter and some Parmesan-type cheese should be moistened with some squirts of tomato purée, cooked gently until all nice and unctuous and then poured over tagliatelle or spaghetti. With extra grated cheese, of course. Personally I'd add a little garlic for piquancy and chopped parsley for colour, too.

The *rosti* you so often come across in Switzerland is basically only potatoes and cheese and worth the little attention it takes. For 4 people you would lightly cook about 2 lb (1 kg) of big potatoes in their skins. Let them cool, skin them and then grate them in nice long threads, which you can only do if you have not overcooked them. In a large frying pan, fry the grated potato in at least 4 oz (125 g) of good butter, turning frequently and keeping the heat moderate so that nothing burns. In 15 minutes or so you should have a nice golden brown, slightly crisp panful and so you add 4 oz (125 g) of grated Emmental. Mix quickly, form into a nice shape, cover with another 2 oz (50 g) of Emmental in slices, cover the pan and gently continue heating until the cheese has melted and been absorbed. It can be eaten by itself or as a most self-indulgent additive to almost any meal. Salt and pepper may be added just before the cheese and although not authentic, I'm afraid I like to get a little sophisticated and add a little grated nutmeg, too. And, yes, you guessed, garlic is a wonderful additive. Onion too can be included but it isn't really *rosti* in either of these cases.

If you must cook with blue cheese, then please use Danish Blue instead of Stilton or Roquefort. It's not that I think it is only a 'cooking' cheese – I don't. But I do think Roquefort has had too much time and effort put into it to then be abused or destroyed. After all, you wouldn't cook with a Mouton Rothschild either. One of the things you might do with Danish Blue is use it in a cauliflower cheese sauce, in toasted sandwiches with ham or with a sweeter cheese. It can be mixed with soured cream and nuts and used as a crudité dip, made into a delicious salad sliced thinly with an excellent pear, or crumbled into a salad dressing to make a blue cheese dressing which I think is a filthy combination whatever the cheese but which millions of Americans adore. It can be used instead of Parmesan or Cheddar when you bake cheese straws or used in rarebit mixtures. Of all the things you can do with blue cheese I prefer simply mixing it with equal amounts of butter to make a spread, thus taming its flavour but respecting it at the same time.

STORING CHEESE

The basic rule about storing pieces of cheese is – don't! Buy in small amounts that you can eat quickly. If this is impossible for you, simply remember that successful storage depends on avoiding the effects of heat, air and desiccation.

Although widely heard, it is quite wrong to say that cheese should never be refrigerated, even though a cellar or larder at 50°–60°F/10°–15°C is better. The vegetable container at the bottom of a refrigerator is perfect. But remember both to bring your cheese back to room temperature before eating it and to leave it wrapped until the last moment. The best ways of storing cheese are:

Soft cheeses. Always keep wrapped in cling film or aluminium foil. The same applies to goat cheese.

Pressed cheeses. It is well worth the trouble to wrap these in a cloth moistened with water, light brine or a mild vinegar solution (plain water is easiest and perfectly efficient). Otherwise cling film is fine.

Gruyère and Parmesan. Damp wrapping is good for these and all other cooking and grating cheeses; again cling film is perfectly satisfactory.

Blue cheese. This may be closely wrapped in film or foil, or in a damp cloth; the former method is better.

It is worth noting that a crumbly surface dries faster than a smooth one – draw the flat of a knife over the surface of crumbly cheese (like Cheshire) before storing it.

Fortunately, it is fairly difficult to ruin cheeses totally. Sweated fat can be wiped off, mould can be scraped off – neither is a health risk. Dried cheese can be grated and used as a condiment or cooking ingredient; the simplest ploy with dried blue cheese, which I don't think should be cooked, is to mix it up with butter into a savoury spread. Find a better storage place or method next time and no one will ever know.

For those blessed with neither refrigerator nor cellar, a breezy window ledge or stairwell are good summer substitutes for storing cheese.

What must be avoided at all costs is the cheese dish or cheese bell – a murderer of cheese and incubator of all sorts of undesirable elements and diseases, both of the cheese and of you.

FREEZING
CHEESE

For those who find shopping for a good variety of excellent cheese is difficult freezing can offer a solution. Generally, the higher the fat content of a cheese the better it freezes and a minimum of 45 per cent is usually recommended.

Freezing cheese stops its development and it will not continue to mature during or after freezing. So ensure you freeze it when it is in tip-top condition and just the way you like it.

Recommended storage time is 3-4 months but less is preferable. Otherwise you simply take the usual precautions associated with freezing and ensure you eat them fairly fast after thawing; this is why it's sensible to cut each cheese into smaller portions before freezing.

Thawing time for firm cheese is 3-4 hours for an 8 oz (250 g) piece at an average room temperature; but you could leave it in the refrigerator overnight and then remove it a few hours before you went to use it. The prime requirements of serving cheese in good condition become even more important when it has been frozen – protect it from air, heat and light, particularly the first.

TYPES OF CHEESE

There seems to be no universally accepted method of classifying cheese into types. To do so by texture or taste is impossible; some cheeses change their textures as they mature and would belong to several classes. Taste can only be subjective. Appearance is equally deceptive – human whim, cunning and complication can produce cheeses which look like one thing but are quite another. In this book, classification is by process of manufacture. Within each class, variation is infinite but often a cheese's appearance gives some clue to how it was made. With guidance on this point, you should be able to guess at its condition and taste before you buy.

Fresh cheeses

These include cream cheese, curd cheese and cottage cheese. They may sometimes be lightly pressed after being salted and flavoured; Boursin is one such example. Although fresh cheeses are meant to be eaten fresh, this does not mean to say they may not have been matured for a short period. In England you would once have wrapped your fresh cheese in dock or nettle leaves and placed it in between pewter plates and left it in a cool place for 2-3 weeks; the maturing effect of the plates works without the leaves and you could try either method with very fresh commercial cream or curd cheese that had first been drained and squeezed in muslin.

This sort of maturation is for development of flavour, not change in texture or growth of mould.

1a Cream cheese

True double-cream cheeses need no help from rennet – the rich, unpasteurized cream is simply allowed to solidify, then hung in very fine muslin and allowed to drain. More cream may be worked into the curd, to make double- and triple-cream. Erroneously, many cheeses made only of full-cream milk are defined as cream cheese simply because of their creamy consistency. Most cream cheese sold today is likely to have been renneted for speed and consistent quality.

1b Acid-curd cheese

Acid-curd indicates that the milk has been set by natural bacteriological action and the formation of lactic acid, rather than by rennet. Both untreated raw milk, and pasteurized milk dosed with a soluble starter, will sour and coagulate without further treatment. This natural, time-consuming process is usually reserved nowadays for making soft, fresh cheeses lactic cheeses).

1c Rennet-curd cheeses

Commercial companies make most fresh cheeses – cream cheese, curd cheese, cottage cheese and so on – by renneting. Renneting ensures that the milk is ripe and flavourful, but not sour, when coagulated. Cottage cheese is made from skimmed-milk curds which have been washed and rinsed thoroughly, leaving no trace of fat in the curd or lactose (milk sugar) in they whey.

Ripened cheeses

Ripening is often referred to as fermenting or curing. This is the largest and most diversified group; it is here that some cheeses escape definition by seeming to belong to several groups.

2. Soft paste cheese – bloomy, unwashed rind

The rennet-curd for these cheeses is obtained at a relatively low temperature and never cut and drained, other than when it is sliced and ladled directly into moulds. There is no pressing: the whey drains naturally. Maturity usually takes about a month, and is accompanied by the growth of the *penicillium candidum* mould – a white fur. Brie and Camembert are the best-known varieties and the mould spore is now usually introduced artificially by spraying if the cheeses are being made commercially. These are generally creamy, mild, buttery cheeses. Once ammonia becomes even faintly evident they are overripe – the eccentric who eats Brie or Camembert when it is liquid or highly ammoniacal is foolishly endangering his health and perpetuating the myth that this is how these cheeses should be eaten. Brie and Camembert made with unpasteurized milk are increasingly common; but even their extra 'farmy' taste must never be confused with overripeness.

3. Soft paste cheese – washed rind

The process is similar to that for Brie and Camembert, with the exception that the curd is broken up and stirred before being put into the mould. It is hardly ever pressed. Ripening takes from one to two months. During this time the rinds are frequently washed or rubbed and salted. This prevents the growth of mould but facilitates the growth of bacteria. The bacteria give these cheeses their easily recognizable rinds, which vary from a straw colour to brown-orange. Pont l'Evêque, Munster, Maroilles and Livarot are well-known examples of this group. They invariably have rather a high ammoniacal nose, but, as often as not, are surprisingly sweet if you can get past the protests of your olfactory senses.

4. Scalded cheeses

These are the popular semi-hard cheeses. Scalded cheeses are also called pressed, uncooked cheeses – a classification used as a contrast to the Emmental/Gruyère process. There are two main types of scalded cheese.

4a Lightly pressed

The curd for all scalded cheeses is obtained at a much higher temperature than for soft cheeses. Separation of the curd and whey is achieved by several processes, including pressure and cheddaring. The separation process is always done in a constantly maintained temperature, which might be higher than that for the curding – this is why the cheese is called scalded. When pressed relatively lightly, much whey is still contained, shortening the maturation period and limiting the life of these cheeses. Caerphilly and white Cheshire are prime examples of lightly pressed, scalded cheeses and their moisture content is what leads to their quick souring when not stored properly.

4b Hard pressed

Exactly the same process as **4a,** but the scalded curds are subjected to greater pressure for extended periods, resulting in a firmer-textured cheese that takes longer to mature and lasts longer.

The variations of process in making scalded cheese are innumerable, particularly with regard to the difference in temperature between that for curding and scalding. But this difference is never more than 10°C/15°F – if it were to be so the cheese would be cooked rather than scalded.

Scalded cheeses are given rinds in various ways, including brining (Gouda), spraying with hot water (commercial Cheddar) or wrapping with cheesecloth.

5. Cooked cheeses

After the curd has been obtained at still higher temperatures, the resultant mixture has its temperature raised even more – an increase of up to 20°C/40°F. This cooks the curd and produces a tougher, drier curd altogether. This is then pressed very heavily indeed. This process is used for Emmental and Gruyère-type cheeses. The dry curd and heavy pressing encourage longevity.

6. Plastic-curd cheeses

The best-known cheeses of this type come from Italy – the smooth yellow Provolones, Caciocavallos and Caciottas. Their strange shapes hang like a schoolboy's store of toys and skittles in front of most Italian delicatessens.

The curd is soaked several times in hot whey which makes it very tough and putty-like. It is then k.eaded by hand, making it even more malleable, until it can be moulded and teased into the required shape. This type of cheese is also made in Turkey.

7. Whey cheeses

A prime example of no waste, no want, these are not really cheeses at all, according to strict definition. Instead of being comprised mainly of solidified casein, whey cheeses are a solidification of the albumen of the whey. The solidification happens when the whey is heated, causing the albumen to flocculate – collect in flakes or cloudy masses. In so doing, it picks up some of the remaining fat, vitamins and lactose of the whey. Ricotta and Greek Mitzithra are made like this. Nowadays milk is sometimes added to the hot whey to make a much richer end-product.

8. Albumen cheeses

This is made by heating whole milk, which coagulates both the casein and the albumen. It is not very common but the Swiss Schabzeiger and Greek Galotiri are made this way. Both require some maturation.

9. Blue cheeses

These are usually scalded cheeses that may have been lightly pressed. Light pressing, or no pressing, leaves minute spaces between the curd particles in which the moulds can grow. At one time the invasion of such moulds was by chance, relying on the effect of lack of hygiene, and the hope that most of the dairy and cheese-making equipment was infected with *penicillium roqueforti* or something similar. To hasten and ensure the process suitable cheeses are now inoculated with the bacteria by steel needles. Blueing should not be confused with ripening. A properly mature cheese might well be only slightly blue because the mould did not grow properly. Conversely, an immature cheese may be very blue because it has been (purposely) injected with too much culture or because bad storage conditions encouraged its growth whilst inhibiting the cheese itself.

10. Goat and sheep cheeses

The complete range of cheese can be made with these goat and sheep milks, and many famous cheeses would once have been made with cow, goat and ewe milk as the season changed; both are specially suitable for home-cheese-making.

Today goat cheeses are usually made like the fresh cheeses above, and have either the *penicillium candidum* white mould or ash covering. A few have washed rinds and are sold highly ripened, often also macerated.

Although there is a farmhouse goat's-milk Cheddar-type cheese occasionally on sale in England, this curd is not generally heavily pressed. Sheep's-milk cheese is usually kept soft for home consumption and now a variety of herb-flavoured cheese of this type is being marketed here. In the production of genuine Greek Fetta, sheep's milk curd is lightly pressed for ease of storage and selling. It is blued for Roquefort, and pressed and matured for the wonderful Italian Pecorinos; but these are being artifically produced – and very well – by treating cows' milk with a highly specific starter. These fake Pecorinos are excellent and come from Belgium, one of the trade's best kept secrets.

11. Processed cheeses

Once described as 'a triumph of laboratory technique over conscience', processed cheese is essentially an emulsion of second-rate cheeses, flavoured, stabilized, extended, sterilized and wrapped so as to impede any natural, enzymic or bacteriological action that might conceivably give some identity or flavour. Nonetheless, it is enormously popular with children and unsophisticated palates – probably *because* of its blandness – and is thus an important source of protein for millions of people. Some Australasian and American varieties are specially suited to cooking and, in this guise, very welcome. Fondu cheeses, which look like the French Tommes, and are supposed to, are sometimes rather good. The ubiquitous walnut cheese and the one coated with black grape pips are the most common.

VEGETARIAN CHEESE

No – it's not a joke – nor is it made with dandelion milk! Killing or mistreatment of animals strikes many people as unnecessary, and strict vegetarians usually abstain from cheese because of the use of animal rennet. Observance of Jewish dietary laws presents a similar problem for they forbid the mixing of milk and meat products.

So what is the solution? The juice of plants is used to curdle the milk. It is a technique known for thousands of years and may even pre-date the use of rennet. A number of wild flowers can serve as curdling agents. Ladies' bedstraw, also known by the country name of 'cheese rennet', has been used in England for hundred of years. The ancient Romans used thistle, safflower and fig sap, which is used today by the Bedouins of North Africa. In Portugal's southern mountains the leaves and flowers of a wild thistle are used: Spain's Cordoba also makes a vegetable rennet cheese.

Perhaps the most amazing coagulent ever used was by the monks of the vegetarian Cistercian order in medieval Denmark – they used the digestive juices of the Venus flytrap and sundew.

GUIDE TO EUROPE'S CHEESES

That great cataloguer of mistresses, Casanova, attempted to compile a guide to cheeses during his busy life. It is said to be the only failure to which he readily admitted. Nor have subsequent books succeeded. I know for a fact that one of this country's cheese 'experts' has his purchases from a famous shop individually wrapped and labelled, including Cheddar, Cheshire and other common types. There can be little point in tracking down and describing local specialities which are unavailable outside the mountain village in which they are produced. This guide introduces a range of cheeses that, thanks to modern means of distribution and refrigeration, is generally available for purchase. Opinions will of course differ concerning which varieties of cheese should be included in such a guide, but I think a sound basic list has been provided and is based on what is generally available (i.e. exported) rather than that which is actually made.

Each geographical area is introduced by a general discussion of its cheese, followed by a concise, informative list covering the country's best-known or most widely exported varieties. The list describes the type of milk, process by which the cheese is made, fat content, ripening time if known and seasonal availability. Practical information includes how it should look and smell. Where relevant there is advice on cooking and on any other special points which contribute to enjoyment. The following is an explanation of the symbols used:

Milk type

R – raw, P – pasteurized
R/P – either can be used

F – full milk, S – skim
F/S – mixed

An asterisk (*) after an animal's name, e.g. Cow*, means that the more usual animal already noted may sometimes be replaced by another, either as a matter of tradition or availability. In this case, the other animal is identified in the accompanying text.

Cheese type

Explanations of these categories are given on pages 50–54.
1a – cream
1b – acid-curd
1c – rennet-curd fresh cheese
2 – soft paste, unwashed rind
3 – soft paste, washed rind
4a – scalded, lightly pressed
4b – scalded, heavily pressed
5 – cooked
6 – plastic-curd
7 – whey
8 – albumen
9 – blue
10 – goat and sheep (brackets indicate process)
11 – processed

Fat content

This is shown as a percentage, e.g. 45 per cent.
Great care must be taken when considering the fat content of cheese. The percentage given is that of the

solid matter in a cheese: 45 per cent fat content does not mean 45 per cent of the cheese you eat is fat; it means that of the solid matter of that cheese, 45 per cent will be fat. Therefore a very wet cheese with 45 per cent fat content can have much less fat per mouthful than a drier harder cheese with a lower stated fat content. Remember, fat content figures alone are no instant guide to a cheese's fattening power. To know that you need much more information. Also, protein is an important element of food value.

Ripening time

This provides an indication of the time it takes the cheese to ripen or ferment to the correct condition. By working backwards you can assess the quality of the milk used; but, sadly, this is of diminishing use today, since it can only be used to assess cheeses made with raw milk. For instance, we know it takes abot 4–5 weeks for a Camembert made with pasteurized milk to ripen, although refrigeration may well extend this period. If offered an unpasteurized Camembert Fermier in February, we could be fairly certain it was made with winter milk and that the cows were unlikely to have fed on lush green pastures. The same cheese offered in June would certainly have been made with rich spring milk. Do not forget when counting back in this way that hot mid-summer can mean very little grass, but that the showers of autumn bring the 'second growth' grasses that many believe are even finer for cheese-making than those of spring.

Cheeses made with pasteurized milk are fairly similar all year through, though a trained palate might detect slight differences in flavour.

The superiority of early summer milk is the reason why we still regard Stilton as being at its height at Christmas-time. Once this was correct. Stilton takes a good six months to mature. Therefore Stilton made from the first rich, raw milk of summer would come into season at Christmas.

Now, pasteurized milk means that Stilton can be of prime quality all year round, and any lapse is usually the fault of insufficient ripening rather than the type of milk used.

In the following lists, the ripening period is indicated in months, e.g. 1m, 6m. Those cheeses which continue to mature beyond their minimum ripening time are indicated by a plus sign (+). Thus '6m+' after 'Cheddar' means that though six months is the minimum time needed to produce a fine product, the cheese will continue to ripen after this period, increasing in flavour.

Where a cheese's ripe condition is fugitive and requires refrigeration to keep it wholesome – such as Brie and Camembert – an exclamation mark is added, e.g. Brie 1–2m!

Where the mature version of a cheese is recognized as a different cheese type – as in mature Gouda – a note to this effect will be made.

Season

As a natural extention of the preceding paragraphs, where applicable a cheese's best eating season will be given by indicating the months, e.g. May to July.

P12 indicates pasteurization, and means that the cheese varies little throughout the year.

Characteristics

Now we enter the realms of subjectivity, for the characteristics of a cheese include not only appearance and smell, but also taste. And even if we all privately concur on how a ripe Brie should, it is almost impossible to express it in words.

What you may call sharp, another may call sour; what has an unacceptable smell to others may be bliss to you. Never take anyone else's word, but fiercely stick to your own opinions – provided you have actually tried the cheese in question.

Variations

Quite apart from the confusion caused by calling the same cheeses different names, different cheeses can have the same names. All are subterfuges used by manufacturers of more or less honesty.

Most of the world's best-known cheeses would once have been made almost exclusively of sheep and goat milk. The explosion of population and easy transportation systems of this century have led to such a great demand for cheese that no herd of the low-yielding sheep and goats could ever cope. So the cheeses were made with cow's milk and a subsequent lack of authenticity. This does not make the new versions inferior; they are simply different, although called by the same name. On the other hand, many cheeses were always made with whatever milk was best or easiest at the time. If you are out of the country and are offered a goat's-milk Cheddar, cow's-milk Banon or sheep's-milk Petit Suisse, don't question the validity of the cheese or of this book or imagine ignorance on the maker's part: it's a healthy sign that somewhere the good old days are still with us.

BRITISH
CHEESES

France may have given the world its king of cheeses in Brie; England gave it the most popular and most copied: Cheddar. 'Cheddar' has even become a verb, describing how curds are treated in the manufacture of a certain type of cheese. It is made in most western cheese-producing countries. At one time it used only raw summer milk, often coloured with saffron or marigolds, and sometimes enriched with butter. English Farmhouse Cheddar could – and still can – offer unbeatable taste delights. Today's conglomeration of pre-packed, pasteurized unripened Cheddar from France, Ireland, New Zealand or the United Kingdom offers all manner of shapes, flavours and textures. Many think this is a good thing; the imitations, competent though they be, cannot fail to highlight the original.

Other English cheeses are older, and Cheshire was always better known and more highly regarded on the Continent. Even relatively modern French guides to cheese mention only Cheshire (le Chester), Cheddar and Stilton. These are grudgingly admitted to the hallowed, chauvinistic halls of French epicurean opinion; but the effect is spoiled by reference to Blue Cheshire as Blue Cheddar and an insistence that Stilton be moistened with port. If God had meant Stilton to contain port . . .

Quite as interesting as what Europeans think of British cheese, is why the cheese itself differs from that across the Channel, and why eating habits vary, too.

Invaders and conquerors

England is perfect cheese country. The climate is just right; the superb summer milk from its rich pasturelands makes fine cheese, an important source of winter protein. As British shores were conquered and invaded, new cheese-making techniques and types of cattle were constantly introduced, giving the country an enormous variety of widely contrasting cheeses.

There were all manner of shapes and sizes. Hard, soft, blued, greened, herb-flavoured and coloured, herb-curded, goat and, in particular, sheep. There were big ones, small ones, round, square and oblong ones. Some travelled farther than others; a few were so common that they picked up several names – York and Cambridge cheeses were identical.

It is not too difficult to buy close approximations of what our ancestors knew – but only in the pressed and blue types. The soft and cream cheeses that were once a basic part of dairy management and domestic life have all but disappeared from the cook's repertoire. Even at the turn of the century there were not many recipes for curd puddings or cheesecakes which did not begin with the instruction to 'earn' a quart, chopin or mutchkin of new milk – meaning to turn it with rennet. No popping round to the supermarket then.

The same books even gave recipes for making your own rennet. *A New System of Domestic Cookery* (the first 19th-century cookbook, incidentally, to allow the possibility of foreign recipes) presents a wonderful rennet flavoured with the evocative ingredients suggested only in such books: hawthorn tops, rose leaves, knotted marjoram, sweetbriar . . . what cheeses that might make!

English soft cheeses were flavoured with essences and spices; sweet herbs were layered between slices of velvety curd. Cheese was drained on split rushes, pressed in bricks, matured in leaves of dock, nettle and chestnut, or between plates of pewter.

The continuing Industrial Revolution, the railways and this century's international holocausts put paid to all that.

Farmyard to factory

Before the railways there was no alternative to home – or at least locally – produced milk. The poor state of the roads made transportation of raw milk impossible. Although cities and towns were geographically close to the country, cow- and goat-keepers were common sights around market places and town squares. Hygiene in the country was hardly of the highest; that in the towns was, literally, breathtaking. The rapid and not entirely unexpected spread of cattle plague through the town herds in 1865–67 luckily coincided with the development of railways. Trains were used to speed fresh country milk to the towns for the very first time. Concurrently, the revolutionary fever for big business led to the establishment of the first dairy factory in Derby in 1870. Others followed. No longer was the production of milk based solely on local demand and the productivity of hired help. Indeed, who better to make this new factory cheese than the milk-maids and dairy-hands? The country lads and lasses followed their milk to the better conditions and pay of the creameries.

Down on the farm

Conditions down on the farm steadily deteriorated. They had neither spare milk nor hands to make cheese, not even the fast, soft cheeses for their own consumption. The creameries were not interested in these cheeses either, for how would they keep them edible? So they were forgottten, presumed to have no place in the modern world.

Then came the two world wars. During the first, more 'dairy-maid' traditions and wisdom were forgotten. Resident bacteria evacuated themselves from old dairying-rooms and equipment, never to be reidentified or to return. During the second, rationing actually forbade making some of the few traditional cheeses left. In any case, the establishment between the wars of the new National Milk and Dairy Boards meant that farmers could earn as much for good plain milk as for going to the trouble of making it into cheese. Thus Blue Vinny, Cottenham (considered better than Stilton), and countless others, great and small, became extinct.

Even ten years after the end of the last war people were wondering whether they would ever see Blue Wensleydale or Sage Derby or Double Gloucester or Blue Cheshire again.

Throughout the long decades which witnessed the erosion of their traditional cheeses, the English – ever more willing to complain about the price of food rather than its quality – let them slip further and further away. Perversely, they served garlic- and herb-flavoured cheese from across the Channel, wide-eyed at the cleverness of the French, forgetting that a few years before they would have made it themselves – albeit not with *that* much garlic.

New pleasures

Things have improved tremendously. The glorious revival of interest in the home-made, the farm-made, the natural, whole and traditional has led to a resurgence of interest in, and consumption of, farmhouse-made, single-herd cheeses. Financial strictures have also turned the thoughts of many firmly towards cheese and it is regaining its old importance as 'white meat'.

The whole farmhouse cheese-making industry is growing rapidly and in the last two years we have seen the reintroduction of two farmhouse cheeses not sold commercially since before the last war: Caerphilly and Sage Lancashire. Both perfectly illustrate the difference between chalk and cheese;

the latter is fearsomely difficult to find, but oh! the pleasure when you do. Blue Cheshire and Blue Wensleydale are well re-established and Blue Vinny has been sold. Blue Vinny, however, it almost certainly was not.

Over the last fifty years, memories of the savour of this cheese have increased in inverse proportion to the amount seen and actually tasted. If you have been offered a Blue Vinny you would certainly have noticed a peculiar flavour, for it was the only major English cheese made with skim milk to have survived into this century. It was not veined in a Stilton or Cheshire manner, but clouded or streaked by a bacterium still not properly identified. It was said to have been made only from milk from around Sherbourne; to set the seal on the unlikelihood of your having enjoyed the real thing, bear in mind that it was a very hard cheese indeed. You have probably been given an adolescent Stilton or an infantile Blue Wensleydale.

There is a growing interest in the re-creation of some of the vanished soft cheeses, and with modern refrigeration and transport at our service, there seems no reason for the venture's failure. Already some of the rare goat and sheep milk cheese is to be found more readily. Between the wars there was a company flavouring its cream cheeses with chutney, caviare, lobster, and an astonishing range of other flavours, some of them 'compost-grown'. Cost, if nothing else, one hopes, will prevent the resurgence of such excess. But the pleasure of sitting down to a genuine English country cheese, ripened to perfection and flavoured with naturally grown herbs, is certainly worth a little of someone's exertion.

English eating habits

Wine and the way he drank it is largely responsible for the Englishman's habit of eating cheese at the end of a meal rather than between the main course and the sweet course. Some erroneous views of the stomach's functionings contributed too.

The English owned Bordeaux for 300 years, from the mid-12th century, and they drank huge amounts of its bounty – but after, not with, the gargantuan mid-afternoon main meals of the day. Only soft or cream cheeses were included in the menu, and then often as an ingredient much fussed about with saffron, elderflower, spinach, tansy, rose-water and the like. Only the peasants ate hard cheese as a basic food, and most of this was made from the skim milk thought too rugged for the palates of gentlemen.

These same gentlemen might, however, consume a little hard cheese just before repairing to bed – to seal the stomach: they may also have nibbled some during their mammoth drinking sessions.

Gradually, eating and social habits changed. The main meal of the day was taken later and later, wine was served with it and eventually the small, light supper of cheese followed straight on from it. So there cheese stayed, still as a final stopping up. And is this not exactly the way the English still regard cheese? As a filler and topper-up? It is a 500-year-old echo of the belief that cheese's fat sealed the stomach, keeping the food and wine – be there ever so much of it – in place, while you slept and it did whatever it had to do.

The French always had more regard for cheese as a basic part of their diet. They served it in the Middle Ages as they still do, to finish the red wine that accompanied the roasts, and to signal a change of wine for the sweet courses. Fashionable Victorian society adopted a distaste for ordinary cheese. If we remember that only one in every three was supposed to be edible before pasteurization, this may have been good sense rather than bad fashion.

Now cheese of all kinds finds itself on all kinds of tables, at snacks, banquets, and picnics. Yet old habits die hard. The English persist in serving cheese at the end of a meal, relegating it to an anti-climatical position after the cherries jubilee or spotted dick, rather than presenting it as a minor sensation before a triumphant dessert. Port is still thrown into Stilton and this cheese is still served with a scoop. And not so very long ago when faced with the sight of a Frenchman enjoying food and wine together, a native wit observed that an Englishman should never be expected to do two things at the same time. Such feigned fragility belongs firmly in the extinct world of Oscar Wilde's drawing-room comedies.

Scotland and the Islands

In spite of Scotland's long alliance with France, it has neither a palate for, nor a strong tradition of, cheese. Dunlop is the best known, but, like Derby, it is fated usually to play second fiddle to the ubiquitous Cheddar, which it closely resembles; enthusiasts would deny this.

The Orkney and other islands have started more

aggressively to market their interesting, small, coloured cheeses, but they are not sufficiently distinctive to make much mark. Also, their size, from about 1lb (½kg) and up, makes them too small to be cut at delicatessen counters and too big for casual purchase.

Northern Ireland and Eire

The policy of the governments since the beginning of this century has been to stimulate the dairy industry as a whole and cheese-making in particular. So Ireland makes other people's cheeses, and generally makes them very well. Together with most of the traditional English pressed cheeses, she makes Emmental, Gruyère, and Gouda as well as Brie and Camembert. Some old books, such as *Cheddar Gorge*, give recipes for cheeses based on the old traditions; these are worth making, especially if you live on the Emerald Isle, for those innumerable ballads about green hills are an accurate indication of the richness of the pastures.

BUYING BRITISH CHEESES
Caerphilly

PF Cow: 4a. 45–48 per cent. 2–4 weeks. P12.
White, granular texture, slightly crumbly; clean, sharp smell; sourish, buttermilk flavour. White/grey mould acceptable on farmhouse cheeses. Suitable ingredient, but an acquired taste, in cooking. Creamery Caerphilly is more sour and turns quickly; excess moisture or yellowing is bad.

Cambridge

R/PF Cow. 1c. 24–36 hours.
Still occasionally made and available commercially. Small oblong with creamy top, orange central stripe, sitting on a straw mat. Fresh, slightly sharp but full flavour. Must be eaten very fresh. Also called York cheese.

Cheddar, Farmhouse

FP Cow. 5b. 45–48 per cent. 6m+. P12.
Smooth, yellowish, waxy texture: full, sweet nose, rich nutty flavour. Slight after-taste bite which increases with greater maturity – as does crumbliness of texture. Useful in all cooking. Creamery or foreign Cheddars often have bite but no flavour owing to use of unripened milk or careless ageing. NB true farmhouse Cheddar is never made in oblong blocks.

Cheshire	**Red** FP Cow. 5a. 45–48 per cent. 6–8 weeks +. P12. Crumbly, moister and less compact than Cheddar. Salmony pink. Mellow/sweet flavour with salty overtones; light clean smell. **White** Faster ripening variation, uncoloured. Acidifies easily. Not much to recommend it; but sometimes used as substitute for Fetta. **Blue** One of the world's greatest cheeses. Look for opulent marigold colour and buttery texture. Brown discolouring acceptable when close to rind. Quite unique flavour, very rich, full, nutty and tangy. You may like to temper it with butter. Surprisingly, many women prefer its robust flavour to that of Stilton.
Cotswold	Double Gloucester cheese flavoured with chives; a fantastic modern commercial success. Rather artificial, moist, plastic texture. Good keeper. Like garlic, it is better if everyone at the table eats it.
Derby	FP Cow. 5b. 45–48 per cent. 4 weeks +. P12. Flakier and moister than Cheddar, paler and more delicate in flavour, too. 'Lesser Cheddar' is an apt but sadly damning description of this subtle and overlooked cheese. The first English cheese to be made in a creamery, in 1870. **Sage** Marbled artifically, coloured and flavoured with sage oil. Highly individual, rather perfumed flavour; best appreciated in rather small amounts. Interesting when lightly grated over tomato salad.
Double Gloucester	PF Cow. 5b. 45–48 per cent. P12. Yellow rather than pink, smooth mellow flavour even when mature. Must never bite. Particular affinity with fruit and salad. Single Gloucester – also called Berkeley – was a faster maturing cheese of the same diameter but half the depth. Sadly, extinct.
Ilchester	Another modern conglomerate. Tremendously popular in the 'sixties and now finding favour again. A mixture of Cheddar, beer, chives and garlic.
Lancashire	PF Cow. 5b. 45–48 per cent. 2m+. P12. White, crumbly but butter-soft texture. A unique blend of curds from several days. Mild but rich flavour and the cheese for cooking and melting; the proper cheese for rarebits. Mature Lancashire has a wonderfully full flavour.

Leicester PF Cow. 5b. 45–48 per cent. 6m+. P12.
Rich russet-red colour, granular looking but actually
moist, elastic texture. Clean buttery flavour. Often
marketed too young, as the flavour develops before
the texture. So avoid dry, crumbly-looking cheeses.

Shropshire Blue PF Cow. 10. 45 per cent. 6m! P12.
Invented only a few years ago in association with
Paxton and Whitfield of Jermyn Street, London, one
of the world's oldest cheese shops. It fits neatly in
between Stilton and Blue Cheshire in texture and
flavour, with a touch more bite than Stilton but not
the aggression of Cheshire. Its colour is somewhat
more golden than the Cheshire, too. Very good
indeed and perhaps the first new *proper* cheese to
come onto the market for over 100 years. I'm not
sure why they called it Blue Shropshire, as there
never was a Shropshire of any other hue.

Stilton **Blue** PF Cow. 10. 45–48 per cent. 6m!. P12.
Soft buttery texture, blue-green veins radiating from
centre to crust. Wrinkled brown/grey skin. Some
brown discolouration close to the skin is acceptable,
but anywhere else it is a sign of inferior milk or bad
manufacturing. Neither flavour nor smell should be
sharp or strong. Do not accept white and chalky
(unfortunately not a rare commodity) or yellow and
oily Stilton. One is too young, the other too old. Can,
but should not, be used in cooking. Port is an
accompaniment, not an ingredient.
White Crumbly, very white cheese with strong
nose but deceptively milder, slightly sour, flavour.
Ideal substitute for Fetta in Greek salads – but that's
about all.

Walton Astonishingly popular mash of Cheddar, Stilton and
walnuts. The murky look and musty flavour are
intentional. Refined manufacturing should improve
the appearance; but so far it hasn't.

Wensleydale **Blue** PF Cow. 10. 45–48 per cent. 6m+!. P12.
Though smoother, whiter, smaller and less veined, it
is undeniably similar to Stilton. Grey corrugated
crust. Wensleydale curd is never soured, giving it
potential for a richer, rounder flavour. A perfect
example could well rival Stilton.
White A lightly-pressed, rapid-maturing cheese that
has a definite character of its own. But appreciation

of its subtle, mellow, honey-like flavour requires the possession of a fairly well-tuned palate. Sourness and yellowness indicate excess age. It has no rival as an accompaniment to apple pie – a classic English combination of flavours well worth discovering.

Windsor, Red
A Cheddar-based cheese with hysterical marbling of electric-red liquid, reputed to be wine. A fit mate for Walton.

SCOTLAND
Caboc
PF Cow. 1c + oatmeal. ?. P12.
Newish, small full-cream cheese coated in oatmeal. Slightly sharp nutty taste; check carefully for mould or deterioration on the oatmeal.

Dunlop
PF Cow. 5b. 45–48 per cent. 2–3 months +. P12.
Like Derby, this popular Scottish cheese is similar to Cheddar and to Double Gloucester. It is paler, blander and moister. Naturally enough it is best with Scottish accompaniments, oatcakes in particular.

Orkney and Islay
Small soft cheeses with an authentic provenance but such a similarity to better-known English cheeses that their purchase is on impulse rather than cultivated demand. They are delicious, nonetheless, so do buy if you see them.

FRENCH
CHEESES
A different cheese every day, and a choice on high days and holidays: that's the range of cheeses made in France. If you are determined enough to nose out the specialities known and eaten only in remote areas, the choice becomes even wider.

Few people interested in food manage to go long without encountering Brie and Camembert, and probably also know of something called Roquefort which is blue, and certain others which are smelly. This is barely the tip of the French cheese mountain. Their cheeses run the gamut of taste, from gentle to harsh. They exhaust geometric possibilities in their shapes, can be purest white or coloured and speckled, and vary from rock hard to as soft as lightly whipped cream. Some, as they grow slowly from meek infancy to robust maturity, offer such a variety of tastes they are rarely without friends; others bloom for just a day or two – uninteresting before, inedible afterwards. Many of these cheeses are as strictly protected, nationally and internationally, as the famous wines. France is rightly jealous of her heritage.

But just as she allows Brie and Camembert to be made elsewhere (with the proviso that the manufacturing country's name must appear before the words Brie or Camembert) she in return makes the cheeses of other countries. Fetta, Gouda, Cheddar and dozens of other imitations are actually exported back to the countries from which the types originated.

Cultural conservation

How have so many French cheeses managed to survive in an era when cottage industry is an exception? Mainly because France never suffered anything comparable to the Industrial Revolution of 19th-century Britain, which lured hundreds of thousands of land workers from their rural life. And because the traditional peasant-based rhythm of the French countryside was difficult to upset by war. On the contrary, rations and deprivations made farmers and peasants even more determined to stay on the land, which guaranteed them something on the table in return for honest work, a reward with which the towns could never compete.

Each of France's contrasting provinces is a patchwork of self-sufficient micro-cultures. In these the character of its wine and cheese is determined inescapably by the nature of its soil. Viniculture is the touchstone, for the *vin ordinaire* of an area is largely unalterable, and to change it would be to add unnecessary expense to a very cheap essential. Cheese, on the other hand, is easily adapted to be milder or stronger. The affinity of wine and cheese, both single-ingredient foods based on the flavouring properties of the local soil, is the solid foundation for most provincial cuisines. Where wine is light, the cheese will be too; but when sun and soil produce robust reds and flinty whites, the cheese will be equally strong.

Vigilance and a demand for quality have also played a part in the preservation of gastronomic tradition. While other European nations have seen their farmhouse production decline – and in Britain's case, entire cheese types disappear – the French housewife or *ménagère* has ever been insistent that convenience does not destroy traditional pleasures.

It would be fatuous to pretend that no changes have been made. Pasteurization and commercial techniques have caused a difference. But most of France's millions of small landowners still treasure a milk-producing animal (usually a goat) of some kind, and make their own cheeses.

At the other end of the scale, commercial production of cheese is staggering, considering a vast proportion is directed toward the speciality or gourmet market. Well over 500,000 Camemberts are made every day in creameries alone; this discounts those made traditionally on farms. It is a sobering experience not to be able to buy genuine farmhouse Cheddar in an English market town, but to be offered a choice of Camemberts.

Types of French cheese

There are three types of cheese at which the French excel, and which are made to a much lesser extent by other countries: washed rind, goat and macerated cheeses. The washed rind cheeses are the ones with the bad reputations – the smelly cheeses. The process is explained on pages 51–2 and certainly does produce cheeses with a most definite presence. But do not let this fool you. Most are sweet-tasting and are more mellow than the nose would suggest. The taste may need to be acquired, but is often an accurate taste picture of the pasture and flowers from which the cheese was made.

Goat cheeses are legion, from the tiny Chabichous to big, snowy logs. Their popularity is based not just on flavour, but on the fact that goat's milk is easier to digest than that of cows. These cheeses can be eaten fresh or aged almost to liquefaction. Many are covered in ashes to prevent growth of mould. They are always fairly expensive, partly because the yield of goats is not high, and partly because the goat dairy farmer refuses to be organized into factory production.

Sometimes combination cheeses are made by adding cow's cream to goat's milk. These are the creamier 'mi-chèvres', often found flavoured with such herbs as summer savoury *(sariette)* and thyme.

Macerated cheeses are not often sent abroad. In these the divine combination of wine and cheese is taken to its limits. Fresh – or sometimes mature – cheeses are aged or given their rind in alcohol – more often than not in *marc*, the fiery *eau-de-vie* distilled from the leftovers of wine-making.

Always individual, France has her own Gruyère and Emmental, rarely exported, and a Cheddar type called Cantal. There are bland cheeses produced by monks – the Port Salut of the Trappists – and of course Roquefort, made solely from the milk of the Larzac sheep. Now that sheep are mechanically milked, the basic white cheese is also made on Corsica and shipped to the caves of Combalou to be blued. It remains one of the world's greatest cheeses. It has been around for over 1200 years – known by the Romans, enjoyed by Charlemagne and mentioned by the ubiquitous Casanova in his memoirs.

BUYING FRENCH CHEESES

There are perhaps about one hundred French cheeses exported in sufficient quantity to make it worth your while searching for them, and many are included in the following list. The majority are traditional, though up-dated. Every year sees the emergence of new cheeses, few of which offer something startlingly new or original. Therefore, a cheese you know and love may not appear here; this is not necessarily an oversight. It is more likely to be a rose by some other name. The comparative sweetness is for you to taste and then judge.

Banon Laitier
Provence

Cow*. 45 per cent. 2 weeks. 12m.
Small disc, traditionally wrapped in chestnut leaves but now often in plastic. Lactic smell and refreshing sharpish taste when fresh; sometimes eaten when matured further. Banon bought in the United Kingdom should not smell high or ammoniacal.
*Also made (less frequently) with goat and sheep milk, and/or sometimes marinated in *eau de vie*.

Beaufort
mountains of Savoy

PF Cow. 5. 50 per cent. 6m+.
Best in winter, spring and summer. French Gruyère/Emmental type. Few or no holes. Fruity flavour and smell. Not often seen in the United Kingdom.

Bleu d'Auvergne
Auvergne

P/RF Cow. 10. 40–50 per cent. 4–6 weeks+. P12.
A cow's-milk Roquefort, sharp, salty and rich. Foil-wrapped cylinder; thin, pinkish skin. Avoid stickiness or over-bluing, which looks grey-green. Light and melting on the tongue.

Bleu de Bresse
Jura region

PF Cow. 10. 50 per cent. Depends on size. P12.
Three sizes of small cylinder. Slightly mouldy smell; thin, bluish rind. Is often creamy-blue with a less-sharp Gorgonzola-like piquancy. Avoid sharp

smell, greyish body colour. Not one of the best blues.

Bleu des Causses
Aquitaine

Very like Bleu d'Auvergne, but matured in caves. Another economical Roquefort substitute. Rather variable, though.

Bonbel

A brand name for small, commercially made Saint-Paulin-style cheeses. The zip pack or wax covering means that it lasts well. Bland, mild, popular with children.

Bondon
Normandy

PF Cow. 1c. 50 per cent. 24 hours. P12.
An unripened Neufchatel (or Neufchatel-type) cheese. Shaped like a small barrel bung. Fresh, slightly salty flavour, almost no smell. Avoid if smelly or soft. Its ancestry can be traced back 1,000 years or more in Normandy.

Boursault
Ile-de-France,
Normandy

PF Cow + cream. 3. 75 per cent. 3–4 weeks. P12.
Also called Lucullus. Small cylinder, downy-pink rind, romantic smell, mild, nutty, rich flavour. Avoid red surface, runniness or shrunkenness.

Boursin
Ile-de-France,
Normandy

PF Cow + cream. 1c. 70 per cent. Fresh. P12.
Available plain, with garlic and parsley, or surrounded with black pepper. Rich, creamy and tangy. It is cheaper to make your own. Otherwise check the sell-by date on the pack and smell for rancidity. Avoid stained packs.

Brie Latier
Ile-de-France,
Burgundy,
Champagne,
Lorraine

PF Cow. 3. 45 per cent. F-SP Cow. 2. 50 per cent. 3 weeks. P12.
The most common Brie, creamery-made. Comes in three sizes and two degrees of fat content. The white, floury rind may have some brown marking around the edge; smell should be that of mushrooms and mould, not ammonia. Texture smooth and homogeneous, with no chalkiness or excessive runniness. The flavour is full, mellow and almost buttery. It is incorrect (and dangerous) to eat ammoniacal or liquid Brie. Many of the packaged portions are excellent, but difficult to check on in supermarkets.

Brie Fermier
Ile-de-France

RF Cow (occasionaly pasteurized). 3. 50 per cent. 4 weeks +. Summer, autumn, early winter.
The most commonly available farmhouse Brie is Brie

de Meaux. It is bigger than a Laitier with a much browner surface, even when immature. The smell and flavour are tangier, but still clean, lactic, with no trace of ammonia. Enjoyable even when slightly young and with a chalky centre. This was voted King of Cheeses in 1814 by the Congress of Vienna. Expect to pay quite a lot (up to 50 per cent more) if and when you can find it.

Camembert Laitier
Normandy

FP Cow. 3. 45–55 per cent. 2 months +. P12.
The basic, creamery-made Camembert. Fat content varies with richness of milk. Small flat disc, white rind, some edge-browning. Full mould aroma, not ammoniacal. Creamier colour than Brie. If perfect, should have no chalkiness or excessive colouration of rind, or liquidity. Flavours vary from milky mellowness to a richer lactic. Not as strong as most people expect. Demi-Camembert and portions easier to check by feeling. Can be ripened at home in moderate temperature, but keep wrapped. Avoid high nose, shrunkenness in packaging or liquidity. Go for genuine Normandy product at first, though imitations are quite good.

Camembert Fermier
Normandy

RF Cow. 3. 45–50 per cent. 4 weeks. Late spring, summer, autumn.
The real thing! Bears the description 'non-pasteurisé' on chipboard container. Increasingly available, often made with milk from unsprayed grass. Like Brie Fermier it is browner and tangier, delicious when slightly young. Expensive, but worth every penny.

Cantal
Auvergne

FP Cow. 5b. 45 per cent. 3–6 months +. Late summer, autumn.
This fragrant grey-rinded, yellow cheese is often likened to Cheddar. Snap it up if you ever see it. If it is labelled Haute Montagne it will be particularly special and taste even more of Alpine herbs and flowers.

Caprice des Dieux
Champagne

PF Cow + cream. 3. 60 per cent. P12.
Really an enriched Brie-style cheese, small oval-loaf shaped. Choose for individuality rather than exciting flavour, observing the same caveats as for Brie.

Carré de l'Est
Champagne,
Lorraine

PF Cow. 3. About 50 per cent. 3 weeks. P12.
A flattish, square Camembert-type, but slightly softer and milder. Must have snow-white rind, so no

discolouration, no dryness or runniness. This is relatively expensive when compared to its finer cousins.

Chabichou
Cabichou, Poitou

RF Goat. 11. 45 per cent. 2 weeks +. Scarce in winter.
These small, truncated goat's-cheese cones are made in several ways. They have a strong animal smell and a very full flavour. Some farm-made examples can still be found. They should be firm and white-rinded but never hard, grey or blackened.

Chèvre

This is a generic name for a host of goat cheeses which are as varied as the range of cows'-milk cheeses. The soft *blancs* should have a sharp sweetness, the logs should be firm, a little crumbly, and downy. Very few goat cheeses should be bought when actually hard, or with rinds that are markedly discoloured. Those with very blackened outsides are the *cendrés* and have been cured in cinders to inhibit surface-mould growth.
Some of the more well-known cheeses include Chèvrotin, Chèvreton d'Ambert, and Sainte-Maure. All have fat contents of 45 per cent. Chèvres are easily digestible and form a good introduction to more exciting cheeses.

Compté
Franche-Compté

RF/S Cow. 5b. 45 per cent. 3–6 months. End summer, autumn, winter.
Although a Gruyère-style cheese, this is not cooked, and has large holes. It tastes like a stronger, fruitier Emmental and is rarely seen outside France, where it is enormously popular.

Coulommiers Petit Brie
Il-de-France

PF Cow. 3. 45–50 per cent. 4 weeks +. P12.
Basically a smaller Brie, sometimes enriched slightly, but with a taste closer to Camembert. Usually sold on straw mats and, in France, eaten relatively unripe, at the first appearance of the surface mould. Insecure packaging often encourages unacceptable dryness. Perfect dinner-party fare. Fair amount of browning acceptable. Sometimes available made with unpasteurized milk.

Fondu au Raisin

see **Tomme**

Fontainebleau
Isle-de-France

PF Cow + whipped cream. 1c. 60 per cent. P12.
A cream-enriched white cheese, fairly firm. Flavour

not pronounced, therefore some prefer it older, when it is sourish. Avoid a brown or slimy-looking outside. Many cheeses of this kind are marketed. St. André is particularly rich – 75 per cent fat – and has a fuller, flavour. Explorateur is another such cheese.

Fougéru
Ile-de-France

This is a Coulommiers-type cheese, usually made with unpasteurized milk, cured in a fern leaf. Some types of Fougéru cheese (fern cheese) are now so rare as to be almost extinct. Excellent farmy, lactic flavour, even when very young. A memorable experience.

Fourme d'Ambert
Auvergne

PW Cow. Lightly pressed. 45 per cent. 3 months +.
Summer, autumn.
Tall, slim, cylindrical. Sometimes called a French Stilton. Pinkish-grey rind, salty, full flavour with intriguing after-taste. Some bitterness, light musty smell. Popular at Giscard d'Estaing's banquets. Avoid sticky, cracking rind, overbluing or grey/brown appearance. Bitterness and smell should not be pronounced.

Fromage Blanc

PS Cow. 1c. 0 per cent.
Sold under many names, Jockey and Bon Blanc being best known. Refreshing and popular as a sort of yoghurt substitute because of its very low or non-existent fat content. Fromage Blanc is also used, in France, as a family name for all fresh cheeses, even when full-fat. The basis of sauces in the over-rated Cuisine Minceur, which is *not* the same as Nouvelle Cuisine.

Gaperon
d'Auvergne

PS Cow. Low. Pressed, surface ripened. Available year round according to degree of curing preferred. This rather expensive mound of garlic-flavoured low-fat cheese is often made with buttermilk. It should have a greyish-white skin and is even acceptable with a technicolour beard several inches long; but this is the old-fashioned way of enjoying it. Mildish garlic-and-pepper flavour. It should be a little moist outside or you will lose a lot of the interior. A conversation piece for a difficult dinner-party, it was once a basic part of an Auvergne girl's dowry and rows would be hung in front windows for the local swain's to count!

Livarot Normandy

PF/S Cow. 4 40–45 per cent. 3 months +! P12.

About the size of a Camembert but thicker; traditionally banded with sedge but now appearing with useless, coloured raffia. It has a strong, briny smell, slightly ammoniacal (like town drains running into the sea). The flavour is spicy and pungent, more than most other similar cheeses. Flavour and smell are caused by unventilated curing rooms. Difficult to tell when the smell and flavour begin to indicate a real putrescence – and a very expensive mistake to make.

Maroilles
Hainault, Flanders

PF Cow. 4. 45 per cent. 3 months +. P12.
Small, square and with much presence. The reddish rind has an assertive smell, the pale shiny homogenous body is vigorous and strong without being sharp. Ammonia should not be detectable, nor should dryness or runniness.
Variations include Le Dauphin, flavoured with herbs and pepper.

Mi-Chèvre

This is another generic name for goat's-milk cheese that is either mixed with cow's milk or enriched with cow's cream. It makes a fairly light, rich aromatic white cheese when fresh, but it goes off rapidly. Often flavoured with herbs such as summer savory, then called Sariette.

Monsieur, Fromage de Normandy

PF Cow + cream. 3. 60 per cent. 6 weeks +. P12.
A small, white-furred cylinder of cheese that is yet another variation on the Brie theme, invented at the end of the last century. It is richer in flavour, with a stronger smell. Avoid shrunken or excessively red examples.

Munster Latier
Alsace

PF Cow. 4. 45–50 per cent. 4–6 weeks (small), 2–3 weeks (larger). P12.
A famed cheese with a heritage said to date from the settling of seventh-century Irish monks – (see Swiss Appenzell). Round, flat, orange-red rind and rich yellow body. The typical washed-rind cheese smell is penetrating, the flavour equally strong. Locally eaten quite young. The German version differs mainly by having an umlaut over the 'u', as in Münster. Some farmhouse versions are made.

Neufchâtel
Normandy

PF Cow. 3. 45 per cent. 3–4 weeks! P12.
In the United Kingdom we see more of the heart-shaped Coeur de Neufchâtel than the other

shapes, which include barrels and squares. Its coat should be snowy-white and downy, with perhaps a little red pigmentation. The flavour is slightly more salty but, again, Brie is the best platform for comparison. Should never be sharp, runny or brownish. Excellent eaten young (see Bondon). Neufchâtel is a protected name.

Petit Suisse
throughout France

PF Cow enriched with cream. 1c. 60–75 per cent. Eaten fresh.
These small cylinders of fresh cheese should have a slight saltiness and a touch of sour-sharpness to enhance the light creamy taste. Avoid those showing signs of yellowness. Good with all fruit, great with raspberries – and yes, with extra cream too, if you must.

Poivre d'Auvergne

A delicious modern Tomme, with moderate flavouring of black pepper. Horrible black plastic/wax coating.

Pont l'Evêque
Normandy

P/RF Cow. 4. 30 per cent. 6 weeks. P12.
The real Pont l'Evêque about 4 in (10 cm) square is expensive (usually) and not too common in the United Kingdom for such a famous cheese. It should have a smooth gold-yellow rind, sometimes with straw indentations, a tangy sweet flavour and a moderately strong smell. Many variations include the larger Pavé from which better shops will cut a portion: even bigger – 12 in (30 cm) square or more – is the Tour Grise. This is equally expensive, but you can buy smaller pieces. Same caveats as for all washed-rind cheeses.

Port du Salut

PF Cow. Pressed 4. 2 Months. P12.
The original Trappist cheese, first made by monks in the 13th century. Although a washed-rind cheese it is very mild, almost bland. Excellent keeper. Ignore a slight growth of surface mould: salt water will remove it. Sometimes the growth is caused by exposure to excessive heat, so check for wholesomeness. A commercial version, Port Salut, is more commonly available. A wedge cut from the whole cheese tastes better than a prepacked wedge. Saint Paulin, although made slightly differently, is almost indistinguishable, other than being a little cheaper. Oka is a Canadian version made by the Trappists of Quebec.

Reblochon Savoy
PF Cow. Pressed 4. 45–50 per cent. 4–6 weeks. P12.
A flattened disc weighing just over 1 lb (½ kg). The
skin is pinkish-grey and smooth, with a slightly
mouldy smell. The creamy, sweet but throaty flavour
is not as pronounced as might be expected. A
relatively expensive cheese; unpasteurized farmhouse
versions are very expensive. Worth it to experience
an ancient *goût verité*, for the milk is processed when
still warm from the cow.

Roquefort
Causse plateau
Sheep. 10–11. 50 per cent. 3 months in caves of
Combalou. 12 months by using Corsican-made
cheese.
One of the world's most famous cheeses. A clean,
sharp smell and pronounced, sheepy flavour with
rich, salty aftertaste. The bluing should be even, the
body white. Although many cheeses are made with
Corsican sheep's milk, these are actually ripened in
Combalou. Corsican sheep lactate at different times
of the year, thus ensuring us a year-round supply of
the cheese, although it might be harder to track
down in early winter. The texture should be buttery,
but if you ask for a small portion from a block expect
some crumbling of the edge. The locals eat it with
butter; others think this heresy. Known since Roman
times and eaten with chilled ham by Casanova.

Saint Marcellin
Isère
FP Cow. 3. 50 per cent. 2 weeks. P12.
The modern cow's-milk version, about 3 in (1¼ cm)
in diameter, is made like Brie and Camembert but
will develop a blue-moulded thin rind. Fairly mild
with a little lactic bite. Served at the Louvre as early
as the mid-fifteenth century, when it was made with
goat's milk, or a mix. Sometimes still found made
like this in Savoie.

Saint Nectaire
Auvergne
PF Cow. 4 + pressed. 8 weeks – better when much
older. Available most of the year.
About 8 in (20 cm) in diameter. Has a dry
violet-to-pink thin rind with a slightly mouldy smell.
Firm texture, fruity flavour with slight bite; but not
strong. Farmhouse version still made. Melts well on
toast; sometimes stirred into soup.

Saint-Paulin
See Port du Salut

Tomme
Savoy
PF/S Cow. Pressed 4. 45 per cent. 2 months. P12.
Tomme is another family which in general are

uncooked, pressed cheeses which thus have a velvety-smooth texture and relatively mild flavour – sadly similar to processed cheeses, which they can resemble. The most popular in the United Kingdom is that with a plasticized black mixture of dried grape-skins and pips – Tomme aux Raisins. Cheaper versions can have a low fat content through being made with part or all skim milk. As some develop a sour or bitterish taste it can be difficult to judge the state. Authentic Tommes are often macerated in marc or flavoured, such as the Poivre d'Auvergne now on the market.

This family is also called Fondu.

GREEK CHEESES

Ancient Greeks regarded knowledge of cheese-making as a gift from the gods and honoured the lonely life of the vital shepherds and shepherdesses in song and story. The priapic gods and their amorous consorts seemed to pay them a good deal of personal attention, too, offering a kind of job satisfaction that was nothing if not heavenly. True or not, cheese has certainly been part of the Greek diet since history began. Homer recounts that the one-eyed giant Polyphemus, the captor of Ulysses, had his cave stacked with rack upon rack of cheeses and barrels overflowing with whey. In Athens cheese was a luxurious and rich commodity; in the sweaty gymnasiums and open fields of athletic Sparta it was a simple essential in a libido-controlled diet.

More per head

The poverty of much of Greece's soil is such that there was never much hope of raising animals for both meat and milk; it was one or the other. Thus the Greek diet has always relied on fruit, cultivated grain, olives, wine and cheese. Meat-eating was for important occasions, and still is. Today the Greeks eat more cheese per head than any other race.

Greek cheese is limited in range and simple in manufacture. But its individuality – achieved by only the slightest of margins – has led to a tremendous upsurge of interest and consumption in the past few years. European demands, mainly from nostalgic holidaymakers but also from displaced nationals, have caused a dairying phenomenon – Denmark has begun manufacturing and exporting Fetta. Of course, it is not quite the real thing, but then neither is a great deal of what you may buy in Greece nowadays

Fetta is the most universally known Greek cheese. Originally and authentically made only from sheep's milk, it is the result of quite a fascinating process. The milk is allowed to coagulate naturally (acid-curding). Then the curds and whey are heated, causing flocculation of albumen and any other remaining protein.

Most modern Fetta is an approximation of the real thing, and almost certainly made from cow's milk. To be acceptable to the Greeks, this must be bleached to give the finished cheese an acceptable whiteness. But as long as the lightly-pressed curd is allowed to ripen in its own whey, diluted with brine, it will develop an acceptable flavour.

Mitzithra is becoming quite well known, too, most often in the Greek kebab houses which have sprung up throughout London. It is a whey cheese, similar to Ricotta, but is now often enriched by the addition of milk. Throughout Greece and her myriad islands, goat's milk and sheep's milk are used separately or mixed together. The resultant unexported and sometimes unnamed cheeses are used not only as an essential part of almost every meal but as the starting point for some spectacular but simple recipes.

BUYING GREEK CHEESES

Fetta

RF Sheep*. 1b + pickling. 45–60 per cent. Fresh or ripened. P12.

Genuine sheep's-milk Fetta is made from naturally curdled milk which is then heated to flocculate the remaining casein and albumen protein. It is then cured in a mixture of its own whey and brine.

Commercially-made Fetta is usually made with pasteurized cow's milk, sometimes bleached, sometimes with sheep's or goat's milk added. In any case it should always be very white, moist and slightly crumbly. Taste is salty-sour, but refreshing. It should be stored in its brine/whey mixture; otherwise avoid excess generation of moisture or separating – don't buy the pre-packed cheese if the plastic pack has swollen.

Most Fetta seen in England is from Denmark, a consequence of the difficulty in importing the authentic Greek version in good condition.

Mitzithra

RF Sheep*. 10. low fat content. fresh or cured. This is a Greek version of Ricotta and, like the

Italian whey cheese, is subject to infinite variation, since full or skimmed milk may be added to the hot whey to increase both the yield and the richness of the product. May be dried so that it is suitable for grating. Commercial Mitzithra is usually made from the whey of pasteurized cow's milk.

ITALIAN CHEESE

Can you conjure up Italy and Italian food without thinking of cheese? Can you imagine those fabulous platters of steaming pasta without the tang of Parmesan, those tomato, aubergine and basil sauces without the same celestial sprinkling? Or sizzling wheels of herb-fragrant pizza without Mozzarella? It's impossible, of course.

Barefoot in barbarity

Like so much of her heritage, Italy's tradition of cheesemaking has had effects of enormous proportions throughout the world. Cheese was known and important well before the establishment of the great Roman Empire. Sheep and goat herds were very popular as they required less attention and less food than cattle. Knowledge of hygiene's importance was acknowledged and practised. *De Agricultura*, the oldest known Latin book, makes this point continuously. From such books we learn many ancient cheesemaking customs, relevant today. Thistle, green-fig bark and various herbs were used to obtain and flavour curds. Many cheeses were heavily smoked, not only because the flavour was enjoyed but because cheese was an important part in the pack of each legionary as he marched across Europe. It is thought these same soldiers may well have been responsible for introducing more sophisticated cheesemaking methods to Britain. In any case, Rome's great cheese market imported from all over its empire and English Cheshire cheese was prominently featured and commanded a premium.

When the Empire went it was the unworldly priests who preserved and fostered knowledge of the Empire's cheesemaking as they settled in monasteries far away from the ravages of the Dark Ages. Only they could afford to keep the animals in safety. And only they could re-introduce the knowledge as they tramped barefooted back into Europe replacing the horrors of barbaric centuries with messages of brotherhood and husbandry. Of course there had been tiny pockets of self-sufficiency where cheesemaking in the old way continued in Italy, but generally it was not until as late as the 10th century that there was a revival of more sophisticated or adventurous cheesemaking here.

From Scotland, too

Parmesan (one of the Grana family of hard cheeses) is probably the most authentic pre-Fall cheese made in an unbroken line. They are relatively low in fat through being made with skimmed milk. They take years to mature and the oldest and ripest are claimed to be bullet-proof. The blue cheeses of Italy are all based on Gorgonzola, one of the earliest products of the Renaissance of Italian cheese, and known for over 1000 years. Once the butt of jokes because of its smell (remember Dagwood's sandwiches?) it is now an altogether milder thing, mainly through the use of pasteurized milk and a shorter maturation period. It has two claims to uniqueness – it has always been made only of cow's milk and the mould, although of the penicillin family, is not the roquefort strain.

Pasta Filata is the Italian generic name for a weird and wonderful range of plastic-curd cheeses – the Provolones, Caciottas and Caciocavallos and so on. These strangely shaped, straw- or earth-coloured cheeses often hang in pairs outside and inside shops, like so many implements for esoteric team games. They, too, are ancient, and can be seen in 15th-century frescoes. Those exported or made abroad are generally soft, bland and slightly sweet cheeses; but back home many are matured and/or smoked, becoming piquant and hard enough for grating and use as a condiment.

World consumption of the white Mozzarella is so enormous it is usually made in the country where it is eaten. Stainless steel creameries make it in Denmark and export it. It is made in London's Soho, and – as if purposely to addle the shopper's brain – in Scotland, and distributed throughout the United Kingdom.

Nostalgia for home

Most of the goat cheese tradition has gone but you might find Caprino, a soft cheese. Sheep's milk cheese is easier to trade, mainly as the related Fiore Sardo and the Pecorinos, sold both fresh for table use and hard for grating. Rarely exported are the luscious soft cheeses, often eaten as sweets with the addition of cognac, coffee, Chartreuse or crystallized fruits. Sometimes even the name will have a suitable ring of decadence. Mascarpone for instance, is truly something to savour with and on the tongue.

Italian cheese and food is copied right round the
world, constantly praised and envied. When the
country marketed a new cheese in the 20s they called
it Bel Paese – beautiful country. It was a good choice
for this is exactly what poets, writers – and eaters –
had called their country for centuries.

There are some shops that will offer you dozens of
Italian cheeses, but most of them will be the same
basic pastes as detailed below, with any discernible
differences rooted only in their purchasers' nostalgic
attachment to their home town.

**BUYING
ITALIAN
CHEESES
Bel Paese**

PF Cow. 4. 28–29 per cent. 6–12 weeks. P12. Firm
pearly-white texture with full fruity nose. Clean
creamy taste, sweetish after-taste. A mild, Washed-
rind cheese perfected about 1920 in Lombardy. Great
keeper; but beware of an excess of paraffin under the
foil, a fault easily detected by your nose.

Caciocavallo

see Provolone (the main difference is in shape.)

Crema Bel Paese

Is a very soft, apparently processed, version of Bel
Paese, sold in small round packs.

**Dolcelatte (see also
Gorgonzola)**

This is a milder, creamier version of that robust
favourite. In essence, a providential combination of
modern factory production and marketing
techniques, but no less good for all that.

Fiore Sardo

RF Sheep. 5a. 40 per cent. 6 months +.
A protected cheese type from Sardinia, sharp and
delicious like Pecorino, to which family it belongs.

Fontal

This is Fontina (see below) made with pasteurized
milk.

Fontina

RF Cow*. 6. 45 per cent. 3 months +. July to
December/January.
The great Piedmontese cheese, slightly yellow, sweet
aroma, delicate nutty flavour. A few small round
eyes. Melts well and grates when matured and hard.
Once made with ewe's milk, and sometimes still is.

Gorgonzola

PF Cow. 10. 48 per cent. 90 days +. P12.
Soft texture and blue-green veins in a yellowish
paste. More elastic than other blue cheeses. Sharp
smell and rich but not pungent taste. Beware a
brown appearance, bitterness or sourness. Made for

over a thousand years with a mix of two milkings.
Named after a village near Milan.

Some companies make layered Gorgonzolas,
which when cut reveal stripes of the creamy blue
cheese and one other cheese. The best is made in
conjunction with the smooth white and rich
Mascarpone. Sometimes there is additional
flavouring too, such as nuts or herbs. They are very
expensive but at least are made from real cheeses.

Grana

Basically the same as Parmesan (which is, in fact, a
Grana) in manufacture, but both names are strictly
controlled according to the area of manufacture.
Whereas Parmesan Parmigiano is made north of the
Po where cows are fed clover and lucerne, Grana is a
family of similarly produced cheeses made all over
Lombardy from cows fed on grass and hay. Grana is
generally lighter in colour, faster to mature and
flakier. Excellent in cooking as it does not form
threads. Grana Padano, made with pasteurized milk
all year round, is widely distributed.

Mozzarella

PF Cow*. 7. 45–50 per cent. fresh.
Pale and plastic-looking: unobtrusive smell and
flavour mainly sweet with a little bite. Eaten raw (try
it sliced and marinated in vinaigrette, with orange
slices and a few chillis, dry or fresh) or cooked on
pizza, etc. Should be kept in light brine if
paper-wrapped, refrigerated if plastic-packed.
Originally a buffalo-milk cheese.

**Parmesan
(Parmigiano
Reggiano)**

RS/F Cow. 6. 32 per cent. 2–3 years – 4 years
maximum.
The salt and pepper of Italian cuisine, now
exorbitant in price. Although hard and crumbly,
Parmesan literally melts in the mouth with a rich,
pithy flavour that belies its very low fat content.
Young Parmesan, Giovane, is a truly delicious table
cheese; Tipico, Stravecchio, and Vecchio are
progressively older, harder and more highly
flavoured. More costly too. Ready-grated Parmesan
must be lesser flavoured and, if you work it out,
breathtakingly expensive. You would be better off
using Pecorino or mature Cheddar.

Pecorino

RF Sheep. 5b. 35–40 per cent. 8 months +.
Pecorino is the family name for Italian sheep-milk
cheeses, the most famous of which, Pecorino

Romano or Sicilano, are rarely seen in the UK. (see also Fiore Sardo.) It is often a golden yellow wheel with a convex rim about 8 in (20 cm) in diameter, with rush or straw markings, sometimes artificially added these days. Equally it can be shaped like a simple Cheddar. Similar sharp nutty flavour to Parmesan and a good substitute. Excellent table cheese and keeper. Grates well even if fairly soft. Store wrapped in a moist cloth in the refrigerator. Occasionally you can buy a fresh white Pecorino, with or without crushed black pepper. Fabulous. Note: Much Pecorino sold is actually made in Belgium from cow's milk.

Provolone

PF Cow. 7. 44–47 per cent. 2–3 months soft; 6–9 months sharp.
Seen in several sizes and shapes but usually a small (6 in/15 cm) or large (18 in/45 cm) across. Glossy golden rind, dense creamy paste, delicate and mild when young, piquant when old. Must not have internal holes. Calf's rennet is used for the sweeter types, kid's rennet for the sharper ones.

Ragusano

RF Cow. 7. 44 per cent. 6 months +.
A pasta filata sometimes found smoked but always quite hard. White to yellow body; sweet when young but sharpening with age.

Ricotta

Cow/Sheep/Goat. 8. 20–30 per cent. Fresh.
Once made simply by heating whey, but nowadays full or skimmed milk is usually added for a greater and richer yield. It is fresh, white and crumbly, slightly sweet and similar to cottage cheese. Can be sweetened, but usually is mixed with other ingredients to stuff pasta. It may be dried and grated as a condiment. Sours rather easily.

Taleggio

RF Cow. 4. 48 per cent. 6–8 weeks. P12.
This was created either early this century or a thousand years ago, depending on the reference book you choose to believe. It is a creamy, full cheese with a subtle bite. The rind should be a pinkish-grey, but is often seen in the United Kingdom with rather a lot of blue-grey mould. Provided the body of the cheese is relatively firm and evenly coloured it is still an acceptable purchase, but it should not be misshapen.

GERMAN, DUTCH AND SWISS CHEESES

The cheeses of Germany, the Netherlands and Switzerland have more in common than a first glance and their incredibly contrasting scenery might suggest.

Common borders, common traditions

With Germany and the Netherlands on the route of every would-be conqueror, and Switzerland the traditional neutral refuge of those wanting to avoid such conflict, there has long been an exchange of cheese lore. The early establishment of international trading centres in Holland and Germany also guaranteed constant exposure to advances in techniques.

It is impossible to make the same sort of cheese with the milk of the great, brown Swiss cows as with the pied Friesians of the Lowlands. The grass is different, and life in the Alps – where dairymen and their cows disappear to the high slopes for the entire summer – has nothing in common with that in countries where the herd is usually on your back doorstep and often actually under your roof. Cross-fertilization of ideas and techniques rather than blatant copying led to the very early consolidation of all of these countries' basic cheese styles.

Switzerland has been an exporter of fine, long-lived, hard-pressed, cooked cheeses since the 13th century, when the St Gotthard Pass opened up a trade route with Italy and the rest of Europe.

Cheeses were much smaller then, but advances by the mid-16th century saw great golden cartwheels of cheese floated by barge down the Rhine and to the maritime markets of Holland.

These cheeses were traditionally made high in the mountains by only a few men, the Sennen. Most of the dairymen were fully occupied in watching the cows, so the yield from each milking was pooled and made into cheese at a few central points. The cheeses were stored communally until it was time to lead the cows back to the valley and safety during the winter. Two very important celebrations are associated with this time of the year, both of which are often conducted in the traditional manner. One is the great sharing-out of the cheeses. The other is the formal procession of the milking animals down from the Alps – the Alpabfahrt. These long, meandering lines of belled cows, some decorated with truly fantastic headdresses, are welcomed by the whole village – joy no doubt associated in no small way with the return of cowherd husband to wife.

Holes and herbs

There is much confusion about which Swiss cheese has the holes. If it is Swiss, it's Emmental. If it is French, then Gruyère has the holes and Emmental is blind. There is also an important difference in the cooking attributes of Gruyère and Emmental. Blander Emmental tends to draw threads when heated; fruitier Gruyère does not. A mixture of the two produces a cheese fondu with a well-balanced flavour and texture.

Nowadays such cheeses are no longer an exclusive product of the mountains, for it has been discovered that valley grazing, if beefed-out with modern foodstuffs, produces milk and cheese indistinguishable from the 'real thing'.

Mountain-made Appenzell has a peculiar claim to fame. It was introduced to Switzerland by 8th-century Irish monks.

Holland's famous Goudas and Edams were among the very earliest international bestsellers. Organized dairy-trade centres were set up in mid-13th century Haarlem for the sale and distribution of cheese. At the same time, British merchants were regularly buying cheese in Gouda.

Although there is a town called Edam, today it is Alkmaar upon which Edam cheese trade centres. While it is one of Holland's most important and colourful tourist attractions, it still serves a very necessary and commercial purpose. Each Friday you can see straw-hatted cheese-bearers offering their shining wares for sale from long wooden sledges, just as in medieval days. Most other authentic Dutch cheeses are simply variations on the Gouda and Edam themes.

Germany's most popular cheeses – at least in terms of national consumption – are fresh cheeses of varying fat content, all strictly controlled, and Quark, a low-fat curd cheese. Quark is used in every facet of cooking and finds its way into every type of comestible combination.

Far better known abroad are three smelly cheese styles, one of which is genuinely German, the other two of which are not. The first are the hand cheeses – Handkäses – made from soured Quark, or Quark made with sour milk, or from whey treated in the same manner as Ricotta (*see* Italian cheeses). The equally smelly Limburger and Münster cheeses were originally Belgian and French, respectively, but the Germans have made such a success of their manufacture, particularly of Limburger and its derivatives, that they are now regarded as authentic German cheeses. German Münster has an umlaut; otherwise it is French Munster from Alsace-Lorraine.

Schnittkäse are the slicing, snack cheeses made in every conceivable shape and size. They fall roughly into the flavour categories of Edam, Gouda and Tilsit. German processed cheese (Schmelzkäse) is mainly from Bavaria whence thousands of tons are exported annually. The 'smoked' cheese is best known; others include bacon and nut-flavoured varieties but they have little to recommend them to serious eaters or respecters of cheese. But German Camembert isn't bad at all. Austria is mainly a maker of other peoples' cheeses; as well as Emmental and Gruyère types she makes mountains of processed cheese. Indeed one of her best known manufacturers claims to have been the first to have smoked this substance.

BUYING DUTCH, GERMAN AND SWISS CHEESES

Appenzell
Switzerland

PF Cow. 6 with rind treatment. 45 per cent. 3 months +. P12.

This Swiss cheese has no holes, is rather firm, and can be as mild as an Emmental or fruity as a Gruyère. During curing it is regularly washed in brine flavoured with wine, cider, herbs and pepper. It is good in cooking, usually as an addition. A well-ripened Appenzell has a rich sharpness which may be better appreciated in a hot dish rather than on its own.It should not be cracked, hard or dry. Fairly rare in the United Kingdom; usually found pre-packed rather than whole, when it is about 14 in (35 cm) across and only a few inches thick.

Cambazola
Germany

Often erroneously called a Blue Brie this new cheese is a fantastic and deserved success. It is actually a soft cheese with a white camembert mould on the rind and a blue Gorgonzola (*not* Roquefort) mould internally. The Danish Nycella is similar but smaller. Cambazola is usually cut from a disc and should be creamy in texture and flavour, the bite coming from the blue rather than the rind.

Edam
Netherlands

PF+S Cow. 4a/b. 40 per cent. 4 weeks +. P12.
Whey and brine baths and salting complete the rind
of this internationally famous spherical cheese after it
has been pressed at medium pressure. It is full-
flavoured despite its low-fat content, but is
usually sold well before this flavour has had time to
develop. Has been called the cheese for people who
hate cheese, owing to its sometimes innocuous
flavour. Sourness is a give-away sign of youth. Only
export cheeses are coloured red. Quite useful in
cooking; a good filler, too, as it is still one of the
cheapest cheeses around. Remarkable keeping
properties.

Emmental
Switzerland

RF Cow. 5. 45 per cent. 6–12 months +.
Additional use of pasteurized valley milk means
year-round manufacture and supply. These great
wheels can weigh almost 200 lb (80 kg), in spite of
all those great holes or eyes. The eyes should be
fairly evenly distributed, the body a light yellow, the
rind smooth and free from mould (which may,
nonetheless, easily be wiped off, and causes no ill
effect). The smell and taste should be sweet and
clean, not bitter or assertive in any way. The milk is
usually only from the mottled Emmental cows of the
Emme valley and hills.
  Useful in cooking but will draw threads if heated
too highly. Real Emmental always has 'Switzerland'
stamped on the rind in red. A drop of moisture or
'tear' in the eyes is a very good sign of a perfectly
mature and well-developed cheese.

Gouda
Netherlands

PF Cow. 4a/b. 48 per cent. 2–3 months +. P12.
Richer, larger, yellower than Edam, with a bigger
flavour, too. Salt rubbed on the rind helps develop
the flavour, which continues to improve for over a
year. Mature Gouda, usually coloured gold, is a real
treat and tastes like a completely different cheese. An
excellent cooker whatever the age, and a reasonable
substitute for Gruyère and Cheddar. Melted with
milk it makes a Dutch fondu – the Kaasdoop or
cheesedip.

Gruyère
Switzerland

PF Cow. 5 with washed rind growth. 6–12 months
+. Year-round manufacture and availability.
Only half the size of Emmental but different curing
and the development of rind flora gives a much
fuller, fruitier flavour. The texture is supple with

very few holes, no larger than a cherry.
Check for the 'Switzerland' stamp on the surface.
Some sliminess on the rind can be dealt with and
ignored, as long as the cheese has not become bitter
or sharp. Beware of gritty or grainy texture,
sometimes brought on by cracks in the rind. Great
cooker; hardly draws threads at all. Made in West
Switzerland around Lake Gruyère from a black and
white cow bred exclusively there.

Leiden
Netherlands

PF+S+buttermilk. 4a. 30–40 per cent. 2–3 months
+. P12.
This cheese is kneaded when in the curd stage (in
former times it was trodden). Some farmhouse
cheeses still made. Usually flavoured with cumin.

Limburger
Germany, but
originally Belgium

PF Cow. 3. 30–50 per cent. 13 weeks. P12.
Oblong, loaf-shaped; bigger than most washed-rind
cheeses, therefore there is more of the brick-red rind
to assail your nostrils. Usually foil-wrapped. The
rind should be smooth and only just moist; the
yellow, smooth-textured body has a very full flavour,
less assertive than the farmhouse odour might
suggest. Beware ammonia in the penetrating smell,
shrunkenness and firmness.

Mainzerkäse
German Handkäse
– Sauermilchkäse

PS Cow. 1b pressed. varying. P12.
These opaque yellow cheeses are made from naturally
curdled sour milk, and hand-shaped in various
forms. Those usually found in the United Kingdom
are small, indented logs wrapped in cellophane. They
have a penetrating smell and the close-textured body
is, at the very least, piquant and usually downright
overpowering.

Munster
Germany

PF Cow. 3. 45 per cent. 5 weeks or 13 weeks! P12.
Made in several sizes, hence the difference in curing
times above, but all are flattish discs.
White-to-yellow body, thin skin rather than rind,
strong smell but slightly sharp sweetness of flavour.
Watch for dryness, cracking, etc., or very moist
slimy skin.

Royalp
Switzerland

RF Cow. PF Cow. 3. 20–55 per cent. 4–7 months.
This is a softish, washed rind cheese based on Tilsit
and only introduced to Switzerland about the turn of
the century. But this has now become a distinctive
cheese in its own right. The lower the fat content the

stronger the flavour; but generally a sweetish mild cheese. The pasteurized version is that much less good and assertive. Often used in salads. Generally made in the east of Switzerland and has a distinctive red label.

Sbrinz
Switzerland

RF Cow. 5. 45 per cent. 1½–2 years.
This is Switzerland's Parmesan, cooked to a higher temperature than Emmenthal or Gruyère and made for over 400 years in the Lucerne valley from its distinctive brown cows. Aromatic and full-flavoured, it is very easy to digest. Serve broken or shaved into thin slices or grated finely in sauces, on rice or in soups. Doesn't string.

Tilsit
Germany –
originally Prussia

PF Cow. 3. 45 per cent. 4 months. P12.
This style of mild soft cheese, usually made in big oblongs, was first made by Dutchmen living in Prussia and has been copied by many countries in the vicinity. The flavour can vary from very fruity to bland and it is usually sliced very thin.

SCANDINAVIAN
AND DANISH
CHEESES

Those big, blond Vikings of yesteryear needed similarly butch food to fortify them through freezing winters at home and perilous sackings and pillagings abroad. Most of it was salted and smoked to a uniform degree of horridness – except for their cheese.

A separate tradition

Northerly pastures boast little of the sweet-tasting grasses or savoury herbs of the warmer south and so produce less rich milk. This was a blessing to those old Scandinavians, for, as cheese, they could preserve this blandness with minimal salting and no smoking. Imagine the relief of biting into soft, sweet cheese after a heavy meal of salted raw fish and smoked mutton.

Such bland cheeses have long been the mainstay of native production and diet. Then, of course, there is whey cheese; quite another story altogether.

An important product of any thrifty Scandinavian dairying community, this golden-brown milk by-product is not strictly a cheese and has a pungency and individuality of flavour that allows no indecision – you either love it or hate it. Called Mysost in Norway and Mesost in Sweden, it is made by boiling down whey from cow's milk. But rather than stopping when the solids flocculate, as with Ricotta, the whole mass is kept on the simmer until all extraneous whey liquid has evaporated. The brown colour and peculiar bite of these cheeses results from the caramelization of the lactose. If all or some of the milk is from goat, the cheese becomes Gjetost, a Norwegian speciality and perhaps the best-known of these cheeses. It totals 30 per cent of that country's cheese production.

A diet staple

The Swedes, Norwegians and Danes, as well as their neighbours to the south, the Dutch and the Deutsch, eat a great deal of cheese. Even at breakfast time it is scraped paper thin with a special implement and served with salamis and cold meats. Nowadays their choice of cheese runs the full gamut of flavours, mainly because of wide experimentation in the 19th century and the influence of advisers from Switzerland and Holland.

Danablu, or Danish Blue, is probably the best example of a new Scandinavian cheese. It was invented as a purely commercial venture early this century and proved internationally successful. This story is typical of the forward-looking Danish dairy industry. Danish herds were the first in the world to be tuberculosis-free, and the current standards of hygiene are exemplary. As far as cheese of the future is concerned, Denmark is certainly a country to watch.

Norwegian and Swedish cheeses are not widely exported or known, with the exception of Norway's Jarlsberg. Once it was on the point of extinction, but modern scientific research rescued it; modern marketing has made it popular. It is to Norway we must also give our thanks for the idea of communal creameries and co-opertives. They set up the world's first in 1856.

BUYING SCANDINAVIAN CHEESES

Ambassadeur   **common name for Esrom**

Castello   **see Mycella**

Danablu
Denmark

FP Cow. 9. 50–60 per cent. 8–10 weeks. P12. Invented in this century. Sharp saltiness belies its richness, due to the use of homogenized milk. Should be white rather than creamy, with blue rather than green veins. Crumbliness acceptable if there is plenty of moisture. Often used as a substitute for Roquefort in cheese mousses, blue-cheese dressings and other Americanisms. Mixed with butter it makes an excellent savoury spread.

Danblo see **Samso**

Elbo see **Samso**

Esrom PF Cow. 3. 45–60 per cent. 4 weeks. P12.
Denmark A Danish Port Salut but with a much more aggressive mind and a presence of its own. Firm and buttery with small holes. Rich, sweet flavour which continues to develop. Aficionados swear you must eat the rind.

Gjetost Same details as Mysost but made with goat's-milk
Norway whey or cow's and goat's mixed. When pure goat's milk whey is used, it is called Ekte ('real') Gjetost (even more an acquired taste.). Sliced very thinly, this nutty-flavoured cheese is a great complement to herring and fish dishes.

Havarti FPC. 4a+3. 30–60 per cent. 8 weeks. P12.
Denmark There are two kinds of Havarti – that with a dry rind and that with a washed rind which develops a sharper flavour. The dry-rind version is similar to Tilsit and was once called Danish Tilsit. Aromatic but basically bland flavour. Small holes. Made in flat rounds or loaves.

Jarlsberg FP Cow. 45 per cent. ?. P12.
Norway An old Emmental-type cheese revived this century and widely marketed. Large holes in creamy yellow body. Soft, smooth and mildly aromatic, but less so than Emmental.

Mycella FP Cow. 9. 50 per cent. 8–10 weeks. P12.
Denmark The Danish Gorgonzola: full but unaggressive flavour, yellowish, supple body and green, not blue, veins. Avoid brownness or over-bluing, sharp smell or bitter flavour. Castello is Mycella with a surface, Camembert-type mould as well, which is intentional.

Mysost PF Cow. 7. 10–33 per cent. fresh. P12.
Norway This pungent, brown, whey cheese is not truly a cheese at all. Addition of whole milk or cream adds to the fat content. Usually sliced thin but is used in

Scandinavian cooking, particularly sauces. Can be stored quite well.

Samso
Denmark

FP Cow. 5. 30–45 per cent. 6 months +. 10 weeks. P12.

Originally a Danish Emmental substitute, but now recognized as a distinct family, probably Denmark's most important. All the cheeses with 'o' on the end are related (see below); the first part of the name indicates the cheese's origin. Samso is firm, yellow and nutty with cherry-sized holes and a flavour which varies from mild sweetness to distinctive strength. It is made in a cartwheel shape.

Preference is highly personal and rather arbitrary; varying fat content may have some bearing. Very useful in cooking and probably best defined as between Cheddars and Emmentals.

Danbo This is square and sometimes caraway-flavoured.

Elbo This is rather firm, loaf-shaped, and has few holes.

Tybo This is brick-shaped, very firm and red-rinded.

Tybo (Denmark – see Samso)

TRAVELLERS'
CHEESES

Generally speaking, most countries offer national favourites not exported – or at least not in any great quantity. Like many fresh, simple country wines, these cheeses may not travel well – or perhaps it is just that fresh mountain breezes and a glass of the local vintage gives them a character that no export market can reproduce. Certainly the adage 'If it's good, it's shipped' is not necessarily true. Often these local cheeses are so good that there is none left over for foreigners.

**Regional
specialities**

The French Gruyère, Comtè Beaufort and Emmental, are made in vast quantities but consumed almost exclusively in France. In Germany, besides the ubiquitous Quark and other Frischkäses, there are limitless varieties of Handkäses – discs, cylinders and squares – which change from village to village and farm to farm. The more 'nosey' of these will actually drive grown – but uninitiated – men from the table.

The Scandinavian and North Sea countries have hundreds of cheeses but not many rarities to offer, but you will find it worthwhile looking for

Gammelost in Norway. This is a smallish cheese with
an ancient history. During its manufacture the long
furry surface mould is worked back into the cheese.
Some of Sweden's spiced cheese is excellent.

Holland, Belgium and Germany all offer
Limburger variations, and the cumin-and-clove
Nagelkaas of the first is a delight to be tried on a visit
to Friesland.

A trip to Switzerland gives you the chance to enjoy
Raclette. Raclette is not a specific cheese, but a
generic name for a group of mountain-made cheeses
which melt well. All skiers know the pleasure and
companionship of a Raclette feast around an open
fire after an exhilarating day on the slopes.
Unfortunately there is no real substitute for Raclette
cheeses – a fact sadly related by Swiss all over the
world who have dutifully experimented with local
cheeses. Schabzieger is 'condiment' cheese which
deserves attention. It is a very hard, greenish cone
that is usually grated onto buttered bread. It is quite
pungent and actually smells like meat-extract cubes.
Used responsibly it is different enough to become
addictive it is exported in small quantities, sometimes
already grated.

Italy boasts a number of curiosities amongst the
plastic-curd Caciocavallo or Provolone type.
Interesting, but not by any means sensational, are the
Burrinos – small, pale plastic-curd cheeses which
contain a pat of sweet butter. A far more exciting
discovery is Mascarpone, the rich cream cheese often
flavoured with crystallized fruit; or the rare Caprino;
or genuine Pecorio Romano. And genuine
Stravecchio – very aged Parmesan – is really worth
searching out. The small piquant mountain
Gorgonzolas and Mozzarellas made with buffalo milk
are two great rarities now found only in some of the
less frequented areas.

Something of the same is true in Greece; only in
mountain villages are you likely to find real Fetta.
Perhaps in the islands you may find something
unique, but practically speaking, hygiene and
indeterminate feedstuffs can make such
experimentation too adventurous for any but the
dedicated.

France, of course, offers the best pickings,
especially if you are a goat's-cheese fanatic. Local
cream cheeses too are fascinating. But remember that
this is the twentieth century. What may be presented

as a local speciality might be a recent invention – but may be none the less good for all that.

Belgium now makes a lot of cheese but has none of her own to speak of; her trade is in making that of other countries and they are generally rather good.

As always, the inventive Americans offer much of interest. East Coast sage cheeses are delicious, and some American Cheddar types are exceptionally good. Many 'copies' are actually authentic cheeses made by imigrant families or their descendants. Three indigenous cheeses are 'brick' cheese, a small-holed, mellow variety; Liederkranz, a spreadable mild Limburger; and Monterey 'Jack' cheese, a mild tangy white Californian cheese slightly related to Cheddar – a notable addition to Mexican dishes. Tellemey is very creamy and white with a plasticity about which I am equivocal; but in combination with sharp pickles and rich salami it is most satisfying.

Californian Brie and Camembert shouldn't be so called, even though the tradition is 100 years old. Their relationshp to the French ones is that of shape only and although I *know* that their Brie is sold as Camembert and vice versa, the Marin County trendies discuss their relative and comparative merits for hours. South America offers many fresh white cheeses; those spiced with chilli are an experience. Argentina's large cheese production features quite an acceptable Parmesan-type.

A universal food

As well as watching out for new cheeses abroad, it is particularly interesting to look for different ways of using cheese. Such ideas are easier and safer to transport home. Examples include Turkish and Greek squares of deep-fried pastry filled with cheese; Australian meat dishes with fruit and cheese; and South American fried hard cheeses spread with marmalade.

An interest in food makes any travelling that much more worthwhile. Local shopkeepers – language difficulties notwithstanding – will usually be delighted to tell you about their wares. Cheese is one thing almost everyone has in common. Use it as your passport to more interesting travel and more original travellers' tales.

CHOCOLATE AND COCOA

Until I was 14 I had never tasted coffee, and I was 18 before I could be persuaded to try tea. Cocoa was the hot drink that fortified me through the rigours of Cub camps, bible class socials and school examinations. It would not have if it had been like the first chocolate drinks Europe enjoyed, which were bitter, fatty, thickened and scummy. Clearly, fashion was as much part of its popularity as pleasure, and the entire history of chocolate is equally redolent of the unexpected. It involves Columbus and Montezuma, a disgusted Pope, an Italian entrepreneur, Jewish exiles, a Dutch invention, crusading Quakers – and that's just cocoa and drinking chocolate. Solid chocolate in bars was an English invention that only emerged, with some nicety of timing, in the middle of Victoria's reign. Thence, their backbones further fortified by Mr Fry's novelty, Englishmen more readily went out to conquer; and still no mountaineer or explorer feels right unless there is a bar of chocolate about his or her person. But how many pause in mid-traverse to ponder the vital part cocoa beans played in the fertility and puberty rites of the Mayans? or that Madame du Barry employed hot chocolate as an aphrodisiac? or that Casanova found it more invogorating than champagne? or that only English speakers say cocoa rather than the correct cacao? (apparently it was decided we couldn't pronounce the latter, so we didn't).

The cacao tree probably originated in the Amazon Basin, being taken to the Yucatan by Mayans about 600AD. Columbus carried some beans back to the Catholic Kings, but they showed little interest. Later, when Cortes was greeted by Montezuma, gorgeous in gold and shimmering feathers, he was presented with a placatory drink of frothy, bitter chocolate, for he was thought to be the saviour promised to the Aztecs. Cortes was to take rather than give life; yet throughout the slaughter and greed that followed, he recognised the restorative and energy-giving qualities (it contains caffeine) of the drink, and Spain monopolized the product for the next century. Once Spanish grandees learned to mellow the drink with vanilla and sugar it became quite the thing. It seems to have been nuns who discovered it was infinitely better hot, and by 1569 hot chocolate had been brought to the attention of Pope Pius V. He didn't ban it during Lent, as he could not concieve anyone would ever care willingly to drink something he found disgusting.

Spain's monopoly was broken in 1606 by Antonio Carletti who managed to take the secrets of the fragrant drink back to Italy and by 1700 the famed coffee houses of Venice and Florence were equally acclaimed for their chocolate. The French were introduced to it by Jewish exiles from Spain and Switzerland, now Master Chocolatier to the world, learned of it in 1697 from one Heinrich Fischer on his return from Brussels. 1657 seems to be the first time it was mentioned in England, and by 1662 Henry Stubbs, a doctor returned from Jamaica, wrote a whole book about chocolate, *The Indian Nectar*.

London's coffee houses quickly learned to serve chocolate to those who could afford it, and Pepys used it to settle his stomach after the debauches that marked the coronation of Charles I. Yet it was not until 1828 that Coenraad J. van Houten invented a press that extracted two-thirds of the fat from the chocolate, leaving a dry powder we would recognise as cocoa, thus making possible a simpler and more reliable form of chocolate drink. Only 20 years later Joseph Fry of Bristol discovered how to combine that extracted fat – cocoa butter – with other parts of the cocoa bean plus sugar to make eating chocolate.

The new drink of cocoa was cheap enough to be useful to the poor and was siezed upon vigorously by the Temperance societies of the 19th century. Both the Cadburys and the Rowntrees were Quaker families and dedicated to the movement. They combined the manufacture and marketing of cocoa with a drive for social reform here and abroad and much of the profit they made went to practical, socially-responsible projects – they even organized boycotts in Europe as protest against the conditions of slaves in Portuguese Africa.

Cocoa (and chocolate as a drink) are now far less important. It is to solid chocolate that most of the world loos for the voluptous thrill of the cacao tree's products. Indeed, chocolate is perhaps one of the world's most enduring and universal treats, as much appreciated in sweets on remote Pacific Islands as in the lavish presentation boxes of hand-dipped confections without which many sophisticated urban celebrations would be incomplete. But what is it and how is it made?

Pictures of cocoa trees always make me smile, and

my first view of a real one, on St Lucia, actually made me laugh outright. They *don't* look real. The tree has large glossy leaves and white or pink blossoms which appear all year round and become ridged pods up to 10 in (28 cm) long. These slowly turn from green to yellow through purples and reds to a russet brown – and that is the attraction. At any one time scarcely two of the pods are the same colour, giving the tree a perfectly ridiculous musical-comedy look.

Despite the tree's constant readiness, possibly why it was so worshipped in South America, it is harvested only twice a year. The pods are taken from the tree and split and the beans, or seeds, are left out on the ground for two-to-nine days to ferment, which diminishes some bitterness and develops the fat content. Then the beans are shipped to a factory, at home or abroad. The finest beans, the *criollo*, still come from Central and South America, but the major crop is the *forastero* from West Africa and Brazil and these have a somewhat coarser flavour. Judicious blending of the two is often the secret of specific flavour or price advantage – or otherwise.

Processing continues with a roasting (again secret) which dries the outer skin of the beans. This is removed together with the germ, leaving what are known as cocoa nibs. Once these have been ground into a paste with some application of heat, the cocoa butter can be removed under pressure, leaving a paste called chocolate liqour. This sets on cooling, and is the basic, unsweetened chocolate. The liquor might be further pressed, which results in cocoa powder. Or it can be blended with more cocoa butter sugar and flavouring (including dried milk powder for milk chocolate) before the final process, conching. This is really a slow whipping which ensures even texture and a good gloss. Of course every part of the process, from roasting to flavouring and beating, can be varied to produce different tastes and textures, but I find it fascinating that so many of the names associated with pioneering eating chocolate are still with us and still noted for excellence and quality.

The chocolate factory beneath Harrods, and that of Fortnum and Masons, which was upstairs, no longer exist, for too few can afford to eat confections that are filled by hand, dipped by hand, even polished by hand before packing. Even some of the few chocolate boutiques which survive in London's West End have to admit to a degree of mechanization. But we must do what we can to encourage these small businesses.

COOKING WITH CHOCOLATE

The basic types of chocolate are few, variations being the result of both content and manufacturing technique. Since cocoa products rose so dramatically in price a few years ago it is ever more difficult to buy good, plain, unsweetened chocolate, known also as baker's chocolate. If you need some for a recipe and it is unobtainable, substitute a mixture of 3 tablespoons (¾ oz/20 g) cocoa powder plus ½ oz (15 g) unsalted butter for each ounce (25 g) of dark chocolate.

So-called white chocolate isn't white chocolate at all but cocoa butter, quite possibly with flavouring and substances to make it do what is expected. Neither should cocoa and drinking chocolate be confused; the latter contains milk powder and sugar and thus is always sweet and pallid. No matter how much you use in baking you will get a sweet rather than a chocolate flavour.

In Australasia, chocolate is often combined with orange to make a flavour they call jaffa. It is quite wonderful: try grated orange rind or an orange liqueur on (or in) some chocolate ice cream, or make a butter icing for a plain cake with orange juice and cocoa. Fresh lime too makes an interesting but more demanding combination.

Rose-water mixes with chocolate to great advantage and a chocolate cake is the best way to prove how well it combines with red soft fruits such as raspberries, strawberries, currants and cherries. Mint is really the only herb I can think of that works with chocolate but most of the sweet spices have a natural affinity, especially as additions to hot chocolate drinks or in icings for cakes and biscuits.

Perhaps the most astonishing use of chocolate is as the perfect finisher of any rich spicy game sauce. Try it the next time you make a casserole of hare, pigeon or venison. Just add a square of dark chocolate per person to the sauce, but taste as you go – it should only just be noticeable, and *only* if you know.

A final point: When you are melting chocolate, it is better to do it over low heat and with a small amount of water. Too much heat, or steam, makes it go solid.

Coffee

It is extraordinary to think that the watery instant beverage millions drink is known by the same name as a drink which, for centuries after its discovery, was considered a gift from God, and which properly made smells and tastes quite as though mixed by that very divine hand.

Coffee has been forbidden in Mecca, by a governor who was later put to death, blessed by a pope, accused of making men 'unfruitful', banned by Frederick the Great, and written about by Bach in a temporal cantata. English coffee houses were temporarily closed by Charles II, but nonetheless changed the city of London forever.

Coffee, national drink of the Americas and of the Middle East, had its origins in the latter. Legend or tradition suggests it was first recognized in Ethiopia, by a shepherd who noticed a distinct spriteliness in his sheep after they had eaten a certain red berry. Even he, the shepherd Khaldi, felt invigorated after trying some, and passed the knowledge on to local Sufi mystics. Deciding such pleasure could only be associated with the devil, the monks threw the berries on to the fire; the heavenly aroma that ensued convinced them of an opposite provenance. They raked out the remaining charred seeds, threw them into water . . . and so on.

The stimulus given by this new drink sharpened men's ability to worship god, and so monks kept coffee secret for years. But no-one keeps secrets from followers of Islam, who adopted the drink with fervour, for it helped them through long and repeated religious services. The first public coffee house opened in Mecca about 1511 and thence the habit of combining the stimulus of society and caffeine spread north via Constantinople into Europe. By 1645, anyone who was anyone, or hoped to be, had taken coffee with Signor Floriano in Venice, as noted for his prodigious propensity to gossip as for the excellence of the coffee he served on the Piazza di San Marco. The first coffee houses in Paris were lavish and oriental, captivating bored society by having the drink served on bended knee by Turkish slaves, which would recommend most things to Parisians. In England, coffee houses became centres for democratic discussion, where for a penny a cup all could be assured of commerce and conversation. There was one in Oxford in 1650 and two years later London had its first, in Cornhill.

They were restless, exciting places where you could hear uncensored news but they soon had their day. Although remaining a vital part of much European life, the coffee house in this country disappeared, the few that survived altered out of all recognition into clubs or institutions. The Commercial Union, Baltic Exchange and Lloyds all have their roots in coffee houses.

The Americans began by drinking tea, turning to coffee in protest at taxes on tea that went to England rather than to their benefit. Once they turned the East India Company's tea out of chests and into Boston harbour, coffee became a demonstration of independent thinking. It is interesting to note that the American's modern tea blends are far paler and more fragrant than those of England, a clear memory of the style of China tea their forefathers would have known, before India had been made into a tea-growing phenomenon.

But is it just colonial interests that have made the English so addicted to tea? In coffee's heyday it was often flavoured with mustard, boiled unconscionably, mixed with oatmeal, ale, wine, butter or spices. I think the English prefer simpler food, and tea had to triumph. More coffee is being drunk again, one is told, but witness the rise and fall of the fifties' coffee bars. It was a chance to become a coffee nation again, but was refused. I suspect this is largely because there is so much mystique about coffee making, and it is much easier to ruin coffee than any other beverage. Many who have persevered for years as makers of 'real' coffee have still to taste a good cupful. It is far easier to make tea, much easier to appreciate its differing blends and styles; or you can drink instant coffee, the worst of which at least have the merit of being simple to make and consistent. It is tradition rather than ceremony the English like with familiar food and drink; the care and ceremony concerned with coffee is just too foreign and unrewarding. At least that is how it seems to me, and the more I know about coffee the more I know that getting value and flavour is never easy and cannot be cheap. Yet little else can be so rewarding if you succeed. The path from coffee tree to you is no less fraught with danger, mystery and failure.

The coffee bean is the seed of an evergreen shrub with glossy green, lance-like leaves and a white flower with the heady scent of jasmine. Its fruit is known as cherries, for this is what they resemble as they ripen from green to purple. Harvesting should be done berry by berry as they ripen to the precise degree, for green or over-ripe berries will add inferior flavour to the finished drink.

Each fruit has a skin, a pulp, a tough parchment, a thin sliver skin and the seeds or beans, in that order. Normally there are two seeds, facing each other with their flatter sides together, but sometimes only one bean will develop, and this rounder seed is sometimes separated out and sold as peaberry coffee. Theoretically it should be more flavourful: but in fact such berries usually come from stunted or old trees and the liquor made from them is no different; but they look nice. There are three basic types of coffee shrub, and within those confines there will be hybrids and newly developed strains, popular for heavier cropping or an ability to cope with differing climates rather than for quality or flavour.

The finest coffee is *coffea arabica*, originally from Ethiopia. The other two, *coffea robusta* (originally from Zaire) and *coffea liberica* (from Liberia) grow more easily, produce more prolifically and grow over a broader geographical range than arabica, but the coffee they produce is muddier and less refined; it has the advantage of being cheaper and more suited to the making of instant coffee and so even in Brazil robusta is an important crop. The arabica will grow higher above sea level than other varieties and usually the higher it is grown, the better will be the coffee.

Most modern foods are grown and processed with speed and economy in mind, and coffee is no exception. Only rarely is it now picked by hand or with any real care. Instead whole branches are pulled mechanically away with an admixture of beans in many states, the hope being that processing will extract and separate the good and the bad. What happens next is just as important. The pulp and skins can be removed from the beans in two ways – the wet or the dry. The wet method is far preferable but requires great amounts of water, not necessarily available where coffee is grown.

Wet or washed coffees: an initial rinsing floats off much debris, including the unripe cherries, then a pulper removes most of the outside skin and flesh. Next the beans are fermented, which softens the remaining mucilage which may then be washed off.

This fermentation must be most carefully timed for it affects both appearance and flavour. The beans are now known as parchment beans, and the parchment and silver skin are removed by a machine similar to the roller mill, and washed beans are often given a polish in another machine which makes both colour and quality more durable. The treatment undeniably gives finer coffee, but often the crop will be so big that available machinery cannot cope and the older, dry method will be used.

Dry coffee: the coffee cherries are dried in the sun until crisp. They need constant attention so that they dry evenly. Rain or dew means the cherries must be covered, and as soon as the sun comes out they must be spread again or they will mould. I did not expect to find coffee being grown throughout Polynesia during my expedition to Pitcairn Island in 1980. On Rapa, the most remote of French Polynesian islands, populated mainly by women whom Thor Heyerdahl thought the most rapacious he had ever met, I watched as huge women squatted on plastic sheets turning over and over the precious beans whenever sun fitfully appeared. We drank some of this, my first ever homegrown coffee, and it was rather good – all to do with the French influence I suppose.

Once the drying is thoroughly done, often with mechanical help today, the pulp and parchment can easily be removed. The drawback with the 'dry' method is that there is no guarantee of consistency of colour or quality, and often lesser beans and other debris are included in the final product in spite of careful grading.

The green coffee beans will last well – indeed some, such as the Java, are said to improve for up to twenty years; but the flavour we appreciate so much comes only after the bean is (usually) blended with others and then roasted, which releases the oils and aromas present and adds others.

CHOOSING COFFEE

Most coffee we drink is blended, that is coffees from different countries, or of different types from a country, are mixed to obtain this sort of flavour, that sort of mellowness, another type of strength. The variety at the hand of the blender is extraordinary, as varied as the thousands of styles of wines, and within each country and type of bean from that country, there are grades, based on quality of bean.

Most blenders would agree that, whatever they

wish to achieve, they should blend within the same or similar grades, and with some reference to how the coffee bean is to be roasted. This latter point is an important consideration for those who like to blend their own flavour of ready-roasted bean.

The flavour of coffee is achieved by what I call 'the two Bs' – the bean and the burn. The less roasting given a bean, the more it must rely on its intrinsic quality, rather than the flavour of caramel. It follows that if a bean is to be very highly roasted it need only be a lesser quality, for the drink will savour of the burn rather than of the bean.

So, just as it is wrong to blend fine beans with those from the other end of the scale before roasting, it is wrong to blend highly roasted beans with lightly roasted beans, even if it does look pretty. It is the equivalent of stretching a fine, vintage claret with some Corsican plonk you brought home in the back of the car. Those who blend dark and lightly roasted coffee will find that good Kenyan or Brazilian blends will usually give the mixture of flavour and bite they wish.

There are other points to look for in buying roasted coffee in the bean. Coffee that has been blended before roasting should have a fairly uniform appearance; that is, the beans should be approximately the same size and colour after roasting. Differing colours and sizes mean blending across the spectrum of quality. In higher-priced blends there should be no misshapen or broken beans, although this is what you might expect as you travel down the market. The most expensive coffee in your shop should be very even in appearance and lightly roasted. Never pay as much for a dark roast as a medium or light roast unless you have chosen the beans from green yourself *and* know what you are doing. If you can, smell the container of beans, checking for any smell of rancidity for this is quickly picked up by beans; the higher the roast, the more the problem, as some 'Continental' roasts are finished by polishing the beans with a little butter.

Apart from the sight and smell tests it is terribly difficult to give advice on coffee based on names alone, for the finest Blue Mountain coffee from Jamaica might look well, but actually be suffering from inadequate or too prolonged storage and only a highly trained nose would be able to tell without actually brewing a cupful. And then, the way you make coffee can destroy the finesse of something special; so can the type of water that comes from your tap, the condition of your milk or cream. *But,* there are some general rules of guidance.

STYLES OF COFFEE

Because Brazil is by far the biggest grower of coffee (which makes the name familiar) it is a common misconception that it only grows the finest. Not so. There is an awful lot of coffee in Brazil, but an awful lot of it is almost undrinkable. Brazilian coffee is a recognized class of its own. Within that class there is everything from the elegant Santos or Bourbon Santos down to real rubbish. Most of the enormous crop is used for blending and a large amount goes for higher roasted blends and instant coffees, which will give you some idea.

The second style of coffee is called Mild, and this embodies every type of washed arabica coffee grown outside Brazil.

Then you get the *robustas* and *libericas* which because of their high yield compete heavily with the equally inferior Brazilian coffees. Their flavour stands up to processing better than that of arabica coffees, which is why they are chosen to bulk most of the world's instant coffees.

Otherwise I think simply to divide the world into coffee growing areas and indicating the style of coffee that usually comes from them is the best help I can give through this pit-ridden jungle. Again, Brazil needs to be treated separately, and all the following are arabica coffees.

Africa

Kenya and Tanzania are the most important coffee producers, the latter coffee being slightly thinner. Kenyan coffee is of superb quality and offers a full sweet flavour when lightly roasted; when roasted on to After Dinner (or medium roast) it develops an acidity that is delicious because also accompanied by an increase in basic flavour. The Kenya Peaberry is the only such bean in which better flavour is fairly universal, and so sells at a premium. If you like the flavour of Kenyan coffee but would like less acidity go for a Colombian or Caribbean coffee.

Ethiopian coffee is even sharper but has a syrupy wine-like richness that some think as good as Mocha.

Arabia

The Yemen does (or did, who knows about its state today?) grow the original and only real Mocha. So full-flavoured it tastes as though mixed with chocolate, it has a flavour described as gamey. It is unlikely that much coffee bought as Mocha has come from the Yemen; it is probably blended to taste as though it does, or did. The proper coffee for pulverizing as the basis of Arabic (Turkish/Greek) coffee. Very often blended with Java or Mysore coffee beans.

There is much West African coffee from Angola, Cameroun, Zaire and other countries; it doesn't belong in this list of arabicas for it is virtually all robusta, strong in flavour but lacking character, subtlety or variety.

Brazil

Can mean anything but should mean full-flavoured coffee with little acid and not too deep a colour. It should be smooth and sweet, and a Bourton Santos is best of all.

Lower-priced Brazilian blends of coffee beans have a little more acidity, and those who ill-advisedly mix Kenya and Continental beans will find these Brazilians give the same flavour more honestly and perhaps cheaper.

Caribbean

High-grown Jamaican Blue Mountain coffee is said to be the best in the world. It is rich and sweet and mellow on the tongue – but virtually none has been seen in the United Kingdom for more than five years. The Japanese and the Americans snap up the relatively small crop. With one exception, what we buy here, if you look closely at the label, is a Blue Mountain Blend, which means only that it is blended to approximate the real thing. The blenders might do what they like, for few have tasted authentic Blue Mountain Coffee.

Generally you can expect all the Caribbean coffees to have mellow, sweet and mild characteristics. Cuban coffees are similar to Jamaican, and Haiti produces excellent flavour at the top of the scale. The Dominican Republic and Puerto Rico also produce respectable coffees.

Central America

I find these have the flavour of Brazil or the Caribbean, including their sweetness, but there is always an acidity, too, so they are not dissimilar to Kenyan coffees. The well-perfumed Costa Rican coffees of quality are amongst the best if you like some tang. Coffee also comes from Guatemala, El

Salvador, Nicaragua, Honduras and Mexico.

Hawaii

This is perfectly delicious, with the finest mellow body of the best South American or Caribbean coffees, plus a special flavour of its own described as nutty. Try it if you ever see it. The most expensive instant coffee I ever bought was made from Hawaiian arabica (I don't think they bother with robusta) and it was wonderful. Hawaiian coffee is always sold as Kona, except in Portugal where that is a fearfully rude word.

India

Mysore is the only one you are likely to meet. It is mellow and quite light and usually used in blends, especially with Mocha. I have found it somewhat muddy.

Indonesia

Java coffee is famous for its heavy, rich, almost spicy flavour. Old Java, (properly Old Government Java) a somewhat misused phrase today I believe, was once a guarantee that the beans had been stored in the tropics a minimum of 10 years to develop their unique flavour. Properly aged, such beans would have changed from green to a prized brown. Sumatra and the Celebes, Bali and Timor all produce pretty good coffees but the star of the area nowadays is undoubtedly Papua New Guinea. I know it isn't Indonesia, but from up here that is close enough; and the coffee tastes every bit as good as that from Kenya, whence came the stock.

South America

Having extracted Brazil earlier we are still left with one of the world's most important, biggest and best producers of coffee – Colombia. For my money these are best of all, for only here do I find flavour and strength and acid without any excess of the latter. Colombian beans actually produce more coffee liquor per bean than Brazil's top beans.

Venezuelan coffees are like Colombian but perhaps more delicate and light. Peruvian coffee has more tang and body, and Ecuador's is rather thin and sharp and thus appears anonymously in blends.

Decaffeinated coffee

Caffeine, the substance in coffee that gives you the lift, is also found in tea and chocolate. It upsets many a stomach when too strong (Swedish coffee is a real killer in the mornings) and is universally blamed for many sleepless nights. Caffeine is an odourless, slightly bitter alkaline with the following improbable formula; $C_8H_{10}N_4O_2$. The content in coffee can range from just over .5 per cent to about 2.8 per cent but the average is usually around 1.2 per cent, which means, .1 gram per strong cup of coffee.

In 1905 Dr Ludwig Roselius, a Bremen coffee merchant, discovered that caffeine could be dissolved out of the green coffee bean or out of ground coffee. The process includes chlorine and the de-caffeinated grounds are subsequently heated to remove all traces of the solvent, hence much of the other more delicate aromas and flavours inevitably go, too. Advances in making instant coffee powders, and the increasing variety of coffee from which to choose means that decaffeinated coffee has suddenly improved dramatically in quality.

Doubtless there have been improvements in the decaffeinating process too.

It is always a good sign when a restaurant does have a decaffeinated coffee for customers, but why must they bring the bottle and lukewarm water to the table, to advertise your insomnia? Mightn't they make it in a small pot in the kitchen?

Instant coffee

Suddenly, there are types of instant coffee on the market that are better than the worst sorts of real coffee. It is probably impossible to emulate the flavour of freshly brewed coffee made from freshly roasted arabica beans, but the judicious mixing of the benefits of the many robustas from around the world plus new techniques of making dry solubles from coffee are getting infinitely better. It isn't coffee, but it can be an excellent drink, especially when made very strong and diluted with hot milk for breakfast, or in iced coffee.

The best instant coffees are made by freeze-drying, which seems a contradiction in terms. Freshly brewed coffee liquor is frozen and ground. When the grounds are passed through a vacuum tunnel, the solid water content turns to steam and is exhausted without first having changed into a liquid. The particles are left dry, and containing rather a lot of what they began with.

But most instant coffees are powders made by spray-drying a concentrated coffee brew. The heat required drives off much of the valuable oils and aromas, which is why these powders have a flavour all of their own, even though they are 100 per cent coffee, in the sense that they contain nothing added to compensate for what has been lost.

Coffee additives

The best known additive to coffee is chicory, which is toasted and ground, and added, for the sake of its bitterness and for economy. Understandable in times of war or famine, during which extraordinary foods have been used to eke our coffee, and chicory has always had its adherents and its enemies. Its popularity is slightly on the decline in this country, where it has never had a really large following, but it is still popular in parts of France. What is becoming more popular here is so-called Viennese coffee, which includes ground dried figs. The added flavour is fascinating, but I can't really see the point.

Spices are perhaps the best known additions to coffee – cardamom, clove or cinnamon being the most usual. The first two might be added in a pinch, ground, or as a seed or two put into the coffee pot. A simple way to use cinnamon is to stir the coffee with a cinnamon stick until the desired flavour is reached. Otherwise sprinkle some ground cinnamon on top of whipped cream on each cup.

The mixtures of coffee and liquor are legion and very few alcohols are actually awful with hot coffee. It is certainly the most warming and stimulating drink imaginable when you are very cold or unhappy. But don't do it by half measures in small cups or you will not be able to use a practical amount of alcohol without making the coffee cold. At dinner parties it is no longer fashionable to serve liqueurs in coffee; but if you decide it would complement your meal or your clients, then use cups rather bigger than the demi-tasse or hold back on the alcohol. Far better to enjoy coffee and liqueur from their individual containers. But if you are doing something rugged outdoors, and if you use rougher *eau de vie* like calvados, a mixture is obligatory and practical.

Irish coffee, which originated at Irishman's Wharf, San Francisco, is a good example of an ordinary thing becoming popular when generosity with the liqueurs is possible; is it the only thing Irish about which no-one has made a joke?

STORING
COFFEE

The moment beans are roasted – light, medium or dark – the essential oils released, which give the flavour, begin to evaporate. Once the beans are ground, these evaporate even faster. Those that remain turn rancid. For value for money, coffee should be made from freshly-roasted and freshly-ground beans and the time between roasting and grinding should be short.

Roasted coffee beans can be stored for up to two weeks if they are kept relatively cool; but after that the loss of flavour will be noticeable. Ground coffee kept in an airtight tin will last no more than a week.

There is much discussion about storing coffee in the refrigerator but I don't keep coffee long enough to know if this works to any noticeable degree; it is possibly more important that the coffee grounds are kept closely wrapped in foil. Very finely ground coffee, packed tight, lasts longer than coarsely ground coffee, through which air can pass more easily.

Coffee beans can be frozen but after a month the oils go temperamental. If you really have to store coffee for a long time, buy it in vacuum sealed bags or tins. Many shops now buy their bulk roasted coffee for grinding like this, a great advantage to the customer, especially of the slower moving coffees.

MAKING COFFEE

Buy the books! Discussions about coffee making are unlikely to reach consensus without bloodshed or an insincere capitulation. Although the Arabs boil it, and Americans percolate it, which is almost the same thing, and although both those methods and the superheated Italian esspresso machines all produce drinkable coffee sometimes, it is as well to forget all of this in favour of one cardinal rule: *use boiling water, but never boil coffee.*

When I make coffee I ask for it to be ground just finer than medium, put it into a heated jug, pour on boiling water, stir once, and strain it as I serve it five minutes later. That's right, just like tea. It is sometimes a little cloudy and if you don't like that, then the filter or drip methods are almost as good. That's all I dare say. . . .

When I drank rather more coffee than I do now I compared the use of hot and cold milk and hot or cold cups, for there is a school that says bitterness develops when hot coffee is put into a cold container or mixed with a cold liquid. I think there might be something in it; certainly hot milk appears to give a silkiness to coffee that cold milk seems not to do. And using a cup that has been rinsed with hot water will at least keep your drink hotter for longer.

It is very important that all your coffee making implements are scrupulously clean.

What I most dislike about coffee is (a) the drinking of it from mugs and (b) the precious and inexplicable habit of cupping hands around mugs or cups of coffee. I hasten to add that on expeditions, or deep in farmland, both these habits may have sense in them, but not in kitchens or offices, surely. If pressed I'll grant you the mug, but not the cupped hands.

COOKING

Coffee is not used much in cooking although I'm quite pleased with a spiced coffee marinade I made on BBC TV's Pebble Mill at One for lamb. The Swedes often cook legs of lamb with a coffee marinade and in the United States they finish it with cream. You would need about ½ pint (300 ml) good strong coffee.

Mixed with chocolate, coffee makes a favourite flavour called mocha because it echoes the flavour of real mocha coffee.

Iced coffee can be made with a coffee syrup or leftover coffee, in which case it is probably not strong enough to be put into a glass with masses of ice. Chill, add a little cream, or half-melted ice cream, and put into a tall glass. Even people who normally drink black coffee seem to prefer it with some dairy additive when iced. Finish with a squirt of whipped cream and some grated orange peel or grated chocolate. Of course a suitable coffee, chocolate or orange liqueur would be nice too.

When using coffee in cooking, I cannot see the sense of using real or high quality coffee; and so coffee essence or instant coffee should be used. But if you are making a mousse, or a coffee-flavoured icing, for instance, then by all means use real coffee, simply ensuring you have made it strong enough to survive the dilution tht will follow – or use Tia Maria or the American Kahlua, coffee based liqueurs.

CREAM

Cream is the lighter, fatty portion of full milk and contains all the major components of milk but in a different balance. It is largely water but also contains most of the butterfat; in single cream this is up to 20 per cent of the volume but in double cream it is about 48 per cent and is then the biggest component.

Cream may be separated from milk in two ways. You can let full milk rest for 12–24 hours during which time the cream will float to the top, and is then skimmed off by hand. But you always include some of the milk and the composition of your cream is thus constantly varying. Mechanical separators first heat the full milk and then pipe it to a stainless steel bowl, fitted with conical plates, which revolves at about 6000 rpm. The heavier milk is thrown to the outer edges of the bowl whilst the cream flows towards the centre and each is collected through different outlet pipes. The skim milk is usually then heat-treated to clear it of bacteria and used for making milk products or for feeding to animals.

Different types of cream are obtained not by subsequent dilution, as I had thought, but by different degrees of separation, so that single cream for instance has more of the original milk in it and double cream has less. To make single cream from double cream or to make double cream go further when you are whipping it, dilute with full or skimmed milk.

TYPES OF
CREAM

Most cream for sale is pasteurized to improve its keeping quality without affecting its flavour. You can buy untreated cream from accredited herds quite readily and if it is from Jersey cows (such as that from Loseley Park) it is altogether thicker, richer, yellower and tastier, and has a slight extra acidity which makes it a particularly good accompaniment to soft fruits. And chocolate cake.

Like milk, pasteurized cream is sold with colour-coded tops.

Double cream: this has the blue-and-silver top and has a minimum butterfat content of 48 per cent. It does everything, and can be diluted with milk to extend it. Reduced to half its volume by gentle simmering and then flavoured with herbs or a vegetable puree, double cream gives the simplest rich sauce of all.

Whipping cream: with its green top this is now becoming more readily available since the price of milk and its derivatives began to climb. It has a minimum butterfat content of 35 per cent, which is the ideal for getting maximum whipped cream from your liquid cream. Because you have to whip it longer than double cream you incorporate more air, giving more ultimate bulk. Perhaps this is of interest to caterers, but I prefer the taste and texture of whipped double cream to such mouthsful of air.

Single cream: this must have 18 per cent butterfat and is used as a pouring cream. It can be whipped if you incorporate egg white into it. It has the red foil label and is always homogenized to prevent separation of the cream and milk.

Half cream: not widely available, this has a butterfat content of no less than 12 per cent. It's what is usually called coffee cream in Europe and Half and Half in America. Really a sort of super-rich homogenized milk, it is perhaps too rich for day-to-day drinking but excellent for cooking, for the higher fat content would help cakes and biscuits to keep longer.

Clotted cream: still not available enough in the big cities here (although Marks and Spencer's excellent food shops are now selling it), this is the richest and most heavenly cream of all and still mainly produced in Devon and Cornwall. It has a minimum fat content of 55 per ent and is made by putting full milk in shallow pans which are left until the cream has risen. Then you slowly heat this to a temperature of 82°C and allow it to cool overnight. In the morning the coagulated, lumpy cream can simply be skimmed off. Commercially, the same effect is obtained by scalding separated cream in shallow pans and then transferring that into tins or bottles; I don't think it tastes as good, but this may be because it is subsequently sterilized.

A continuous controversy rages over the proper use of clotted cream in a traditional cream tea. Do you put your cream onto the scone and then add jam or do you do it the other way round? Those who argue for the former say that as the cream is replacing butter it must go on first; but then you can't spread jam over the cream and so you miss out the combination of flavours for most mouthsful. Those who spread the jam first and then dollop on the cream are assured of the best possible tastes with every mouthful and that's the way I prefer it; perhaps because that way you can have butter on the scone as well.

Sterilized cream: made exactly the same way as sterilized milk but packed in smaller containers. It usually has a butterfat content of about 23 per cent (between single and whipping cream) but can also be made from half cream (12 per cent). It is homogenized and the treatment gives it a unique flavour that does not compensate for its ability to keep virtually indefinitely until opened.

Bottled cream/long-keeping cream: this is now tending to disappear from the shops but a lot of old people like it for nostalgic reasons. It fits neatly in all respects between pasteurized cream and sterilized cream, both in keeping ability and flavour, and this applies to single, double or clotted cream, all of which are treated this way.

UHT – Long life cream: treated exactly the same way as UHT milk to give a very long life with no refrigeration. It should mean that the individual portions of liquid used in trains, hotels and planes for your tea or coffee *are* milk or cream, for there is no wastage problem with UHT treated items. But if you look carefully, those litttle pyramids of liquid are nearly all totally artificial.

Soured cream: note the name – it is *soured* not *sour*. This is single cream which has had a culture of bacteria added to it after homogenization and pasteurization. The culture forms acid as a by product, giving the subsequent thickening and acidic flavour. It keeps very well under refrigeration and is perfectly indispensable once you know about it. If you can't buy it you can appreciate the flavour and texture by reducing double cream over heat, cooling, and adding lemon juice; a better bet is to whip or sieve cottage cheese and then add a little milk or cream – cheaper too.

EATING CREAM ABROAD

One of the most frustrating habits of the French is to serve *crème fraiche* with absolutely everything. You might think that this translates as fresh cream; entymologically it might, but not on the tongue. Crème fraiche has been allowed to ferment long enough to develop a lactic bite, not exactly sour but not sweet either. It is not true, as I have seen put about in the United States, that French cream has more lactic acid in it – it has been allowed to *develop* lactic acid, as any cream would do. To get fresh sweet cream you must ask for *crème fleurette* and if you get it you'll be lucky. In America, cream is pretty much the same as here but with different names: our double is called heavy, our single is their light and coffee cream is Half and Half. *But* our whipping cream is not theirs. American whipping cream usually has the lowest possible fat content to comply with its definition – about 30 per cent – and gets its texture from added vegetable fats and oils that behave in the same way as cream. You can also buy it in aerosol packs.

COOKING WITH CREAM

To boil or not to boil is a very vexed question and there is a great deal of disagreement both within each country and between countries. Some of the hysteria is probably because cream is often added in association with egg to thicken and enrich – this will naturally curdle if heated too much. In my experience cream can be boiled and it can be simmered in sauces, and so can soured cream. There will be sauces or cooking liquids that have such high acidity that the cream will curdle when added but often curdling is a matter of bad technique, i.e. you must add potentially troublesome liquids in a certain way – you should always pour the thicker into the thinner (do it the other way and curdling is almost certain). If your sauce has a flour base, curdling is less likely. Reduction of cream or a cream sauce is basic to fine food and when making a cream sauce I always reduce the double cream by a third or a half before adding it. The flavouring liquid is reduced even more drastically, if possible, for curdling seems more a problem when you have large amounts of liquid. Reduction is essential for nothing is worse than a so-called cream sauce that has no coating consistency or body. You do not get globules of butterfat and any other fat that rises in can be beaten in; indeed the beating in of butter is again basic to the proper finishing of sauces. English soured cream does not curdle in sauces in my experience, but perhaps I have been lucky for there are others who swear it always happens to them. I use soured cream more and more to finish wine-based sauces, partly because it is cheaper and partly because it gives extra dimension of flavour.

Nouvelle cuisine cream

In the *nouvelles cuisines* of France, especially *cuisine minceur*, cream is replaced by a number of things. Usually they are based on *fromage blanc*, a totally fat-free soft cheese, sold under such trade names as

Bon Blanc and Jockey. They don't give a very good texture when used just by themselves so I incorporate some curd cheese, which although having some fat content isn't enough to worry about. You could whip lower-fatted cottage cheese and use that, too. Generally the proportions are equal but you might vary them to get certain flavours or textures that suit you better.

STORING CREAM

Pasteurized cream should keep in a refrigerator for an average of six days. Frozen single cream tends to separate, but double cream freezes very well giving best results if it is slightly sweetened. It should always be well stirred or whipped after defrosting.

Dairy Product Substitutes

There is now a huge international industry based on the manufacture of substitutes for dairy products, in the main based on surrogates for butterfat. They were originated in the interests of economy, with flavour and health coming rather miserable seconds. Now evidence and opinion favours the theory that too high an intake of saturated animal fats is detrimental to your health in general and your heart in particular. So all manner of substitutes for milk, butter, cream and ice cream are blithely accepted, which once would have been treated with disdain for their exploitation of our fears; athletes before aesthetes is a dangerous maxim.

Margarines, which at least have the excuse of being popularized through the necessities of the Depression and subsequent global turmoils, are based on a number of different oils, which can be chemically hardened and then whipped into shape. Most of them relate the specific oil they have used. Their relative balance of saturated, unsaturated and poly-unsturated oils, and their attributes, are discussed in the section on oils, starting on page 277.

For items which are frozen, or that are sprinkled on hot drinks (whiteners) or that can be whipped like cream, the basis is usually palm oil, which explains the soapiness of some of these products.

Obviously there are many people to whom these products are a godsend. But I really think they should be thought of as alternatives rather than substitutes, in the same way that instant coffee makes only a passing reference to fresh coffee.

If you want really high quality non-dairy substitutes, I suggest you look for an establishment selling kosher *Pareve* products. *Pareve* means *totally* milk free, with not even skimmed milk powder or lactose included. *Pareve* ice creams, whipping creams and margarine are of very high quality because they have been developed over a longer period, due to the Jewish requirement not to mix milk and meat in the same meal.

The biggest new non-dairy product of recent times is the creamer or whitener, a powder you sprinkle onto hot drinks. This will sometimes include skimmed milk powder, but is more often just made from palm oil plus lots of anonymous chemicals to make it behave like milk. It would seem safer, simpler and cheaper to drink your tea or coffee without their dubious influence.

DRIED FRUITS

An important source of sweetening and of sugar during winter for our ancestors, dried fruits are a most ancient food. Today there is some chemical assistance likely to improve colour or keeping qualities, and often they are dried without the aid of the sun, but the basis of preserving fruit by reducing the moisture content, allowing the natural sugars to act as a preservative, remains unchanged.

Apples

One of the most useful of dried fruits, as they retain their Vitamin C content. 1 lb (½ kg) of dried apple is the equivalent of 6-9 lb (3-4 kg) of fresh fruit. They rehydrate nicely, often becoming rather fluffy and therefore good for purées. They are also a good stretcher of other fruits in pies, crumbles and so on. They are rather rubbery when dried but chopped into smaller pieces make a worthwhile addition to muesli.

Apricots

Always dried without their stones, whether whole or halves. 5½ lb (3 kg) of fresh fruit yield 1 lb (½ kg) of dried. I once found them drying under trees in Ibiza, directed thence by the wondrous scent on the air. They were tended by one of those black-swathed Mediterranean women. Now that site is a hotel or two. Apricots are more often dried in hot air after having been exposed to sulphur dioxide which gives a brighter colour. My favourite dried fruit, it often tastes better like this than when fresh. The greatest of all snacks, pie fillings or breakfast fruit. Thin slices improve muesli more than anything else I can think of.

In Cypriot, Turkish and Arabic shops you can buy something called Armadine. This is sheets of dried apricot purée. You can simply rehydrate it in a little water or wine, cook it smoother, watching it carefully, and serve it chilled with cream and almonds as a smooth apricot cream. I added eggs, black rum, sugar and vanilla, poached the mixture in individual containers, turned them out on a nut pastry and served them very cold with thin cream flavoured with more rum and vanilla. Very beaut.

Bananas

These usually come from South America and are naturally sun-dried. 2 lb (1 kg) of bananas make ½ lb (225 g) of dried ones. Golden brown, very sweet and chewy, they are an addictive snack, but can lead to a fairly determined loosening of the bowels. They may be soaked in water overnight and eaten with lemon and orange juice plus brown sugar – again black rum would find itself most welcome.

They can be chopped and used as any other dried fruit in breads, cakes and puddings.

Chopped or sliced they make a fascinating addition to any cereal, hot or cold.

Recently I have seen a new product which is long thin chips of crisp, dry banana, creamy coloured, and coated with honey. If you don't mind the extra sugar this is terrific at breakfast time.

Dates

Iraq alone grows 400 different types of date, to give you some idea of the complication of writing about dates. They contain so much sugar that even the dried ones are sticky and moist, and they last for years after picking.

The Iraqi dates you most usually eat are the Halawi or the Sayir; from Tunisia or Morocco it is most likely the Deglet Noor, but it is not often you have a choice, so that may be useless information.

To many people dates are cloying and filling and so you should serve them in small amounts. They really are most enjoyed when offered as a sweetmeat after a meal, or as a very high energy booster snack when doing something exhausting like climbing a mountain or sailing. I don't much like dates that are filled with marzipan or cream cheese, but lots of people think they look nice. The only time I have used them in cooking was to recreate a Moroccan recipe that was also current here as a Lenten dish in medieval times.

You take a nice big baking fish and clean it thoroughly. Then cook some rice until it is just done. When it is good and dry, mix in some ground almonds, cinnamon and a touch of sugar. Stuff some dates with this mixture, and close each with a smear of butter. Put the dates and as much extra rice as will fit into the cavity of the fish and sew it up or hold together with toothpicks – sewing really is better this time. Put the fish in a baking dish with a little water, smear it with butter, and sprinkle with more cinnamon and bake under foil. You can sprinkle onion over the fish and lay it on a bed of onion, which will make a more savoury liquid for basting and for pouring over the finished dish. It is very good.

Figs

I don't wish to pry, but if you think you have private problems, spare a thought for the fig. Figs have their flowers *inside* their fruit, and the palaver that they and certain wasps have to go through to get fertilized makes each fig a miracle of perversity and perseverance.

The Smyrna or Turkish fig is one of the most popular varieties for drying, originally named for the town through which most were exported from Turkey, now called Izmir.

They are best known for their assistance to the constipated and useful as a snack but little used in cooking.

Prunes

These are dried plums and now that the Californians have taken to producing them, have changed out of all recognition in the last few years. Rather than those hard, small things of yesteryear we have jumbo prunes and soft prunes and ready-soaked prunes and goodness knows what else.

If you must eat them for breakfast, then add a little orange juice or spice to the water you use for cooking, and serve them very cold.

The very finest prunes of all are the French Pruneaux d'Agen and it seems a pity to muck about with them, but people do. Carlsbad plums are actually prunes, and like the best of dried fruits meant to be eaten at the end of the meal. They are available in wooden boxes but are so expensive they must be eaten instead of a meal. The Portuguese make a cheaper version called Elvas plums and the Poles provide us with something even better and even cheaper. They are called plums in chocolate and are stoned small plums (which is to say prunes), filled with a delicious soft toffee and coated with chocolate and decoratively wrapped. They make stunning gifts for everyone expects them to have cost far more than they do. Always a success.

Purées of cooked prune make excellent sorbets and ice creams; or you can flavour it with, say, orange or a little praline, add egg in the usual custard-making proportion and bake it in a flan case.

Prunes are common in stuffings but I prefer them thus, which is an idea I found in the *Guardian* many years ago, when I read it. Take some prunes and cover them with red wine; add some cinnamon, mace, a clove or two, a slither of orange peel and, most important, quite a few bay leaves. Let this cook for a long while, gently, until the prunes are plump and the flavours have blended. Complete the flavour by adding some brown sugar or redcurrant jelly if you think some sweetness would be an improvement. Remove the prunes and strain the spices from the sauce. Serve hot or cold with game, ham, duck or goose.

Vine fruits

It is thought the Egyptians discovered they could dry grapes in the sun, and what a good idea that turned out to be. Dried vine fruits have eight times more invert sugar than other types of fruit; as invert sugar is really pre-digested sucrose, the body is able to use it very quickly, and hence the usefulness of such fruit as snacks when you are labouring or having an adventure.

Generally, 1 lb (½ kg) of dried vine fruit was once 4 lb (2 kg) of fresh, and the types you will come across are:

Currants: these are not dried black currants but a special type of seedless black grape. Originally they were from Corinth in Greece, hence the name, but now most come from Australia.

Sultanas: are made from seedless white grapes. They were a speciality of Smyrna, now Izmir, and were often called Smyrna raisins. I find these the most delicious of all in cooking, and when you want a rich mellow flavour, in mixed fruit cakes and puddings, add extra sultanas rather than currants or raisins.

Raisins: these are dried red grapes of several types, sometimes seedless. The biggest and sweetest are the muscatels, which can be found without seeds if you look hard enough.

General note

Dried fruits should be thought of as treats in their own right, rather than as substitutes for the real thing. Apricots, especially, are used in all sorts of ways in the Middle East, savoury and sweet, and a dip into such cookbooks is always rewarding. Peaches can be used the same way but I think they are less rewarding, and so are pears.

One of the recipes you will come across when pursuing Middle Eastern food is simply to soak a mixture of dried fruits for 48 hours in just enough water to cover them. Add sugar plus a sprinkle of rose-water and orange-flower water. Serve with a contrasting scatter of chopped pistachios. It is amazingly good for almost no effort.

EGGS

It is only in delicatessen shops that you are likely to have a *choice* of eggs, a possibility that may not have occurred. But there are three distinct types of hen eggs, as well as eggs from other birds that are worth including in your repertoire. There are three kinds of egg-producing hen.

Battery: here the chickens are tightly confined in cases: Their food arrives and the eggs depart by conveyor. There *is* great control over hygiene and disease, but the chickens can scarcely move, are noticeably neurotic (literally hen-pecked) and the food they eat is not their natural diet. The eggs themselves probably differ little from other eggs as far as nutrition goes, even though the flavour may not be as good. But the cruelty to the birds is now arousing international concern and there are moves to improve the lot of the battery hen. Until then, if you have the choice, go for either of the following:

Deep-litter: seemingly the perfect compromise, these birds are kept under cover but scratch around, on a litter of specially treated oak-chips, which enable them to pick up the important enzymes and bacteria of their natural diet.

Free-range: eggs and chickens as our grandmothers would know. *But* even though the more mixed diet might give better flavoured eggs, and the chickens squawk around in fresh air and sunlight, this is no guarantee of health or wholesomeness. Indeed, because the chickens can eat what they like from the soil and lay eggs where they like, the eggs can be tainted, contaminated or horrid, have thin shells, thick shells or very dirty. Yet if you are a creature of principle, these really are the eggs to go for. Shops which say they sell free-range eggs should also display the FREGGS sign, which guarantees certain standards.

Other eggs: I've never eaten *plovers' eggs*, because now they may no longer be gathered, but they are supposed to be the best of the small eggs. Generally you can buy *gulls' eggs* in the summer, which are considered a good substitute. These greeny-blue eggs, dappled with brown and slightly more pointed than hen's eggs and 1-2 in (2½-5 cm) long, taste exactly like hens' eggs, with none of the fishy taste that many expect. If anything they are rather more mellow than the usual breakfast egg. Although they look very pretty in their shells, I deplore the habit of serving gulls' eggs so at buffets and cocktail parties.

How do you peel an egg and balance a glass? Even if
you manage, what do you do with the shell? Serve
them shelled, slightly chilled, with bowls of
mayonnaise, celery salt, sweet paprika and slices of
brown bread. You can always display the shells
around the dish or bowl or basket, to show the eggs
are not from some frightful extruding machine
(which incidentally are responsible for most of the
sliced eggs you find in or on catering food these days
– yes they actually make a sausage of egg and slice
that!)

Quails' eggs, much smaller and now available fresh
most of the year – if you know where to shop – are
served the same way as gulls' eggs, but, being
cheaper, can be eaten more often. If you can buy
them fresh, boil for just one minute. The tinned ones
from China, shelled, are very good, indeed. Either
way, serve them as is, or include them in a special
salad, or in mayonnaise with lobster, prawns or other
shellfish. They look very nice served with cold
asparagus mayonnaise, and are very special with hot
asparagus and a Sauce Maltese (hollandaise flavoured
with blood orange). The Connaught Hotel serves
them soft-boiled on pastry bateaux with a bed of
much reduced mushroom purée, coated with
hollandaise and they or gulls' eggs on a nest of
mayonnaise sauce are the perfect accompaniment to
cold salmon, smoked salmon or pickled salmon
(*gravad lax*) especially if you chop plenty of fresh dill
into the mayonnaise, and/or mix a portion of
whipped cream in, too.

Some enterprising farm shops and speciality shops
in the country will often offer other eggs; I have
bought in London guinea fowl eggs, pheasant eggs
and bantam eggs. All these and others are good,
interesting for their size rather than their flavour,
although pheasant eggs seem to have something
extra. If you are lucky you might also be able to find
duck eggs.

Duck eggs, rich and flavourful, are popular with
children because of their pretty green-blue shell. Let
them be eaten, by all means, but *never* serve
soft-boiled duck eggs. Because the shells are so thin,
and because they are laid in wet and dirty places,
duck eggs contain much higher levels of bacteria than
any others you are likely to eat. They must be
thoroughly cooked. The better use for duck eggs is
for cake-making, especially whisked sponges. They

can be used in combination with hens' eggs or alone to give improved colour and flavour. I remember sitting on a high stool in the kitchen as a child, whisking duck eggs for my mother; then she would make a sponge and win a prize at the local church. I can still smell the rich creaminess of those eggs now, and taste the sponge.

COOKING EGGS

The freshest eggs taste best, but eggs for baking are better for being several days old. Test for freshness by putting into water, the flatter an egg lies the fresher it is. It is alright but a bit old if it stands up, but once it starts to float in the water, crack open to check it has not gone off. If it floats *on* the water, throw it away.

Fresh eggs should display three distinct textures when broken: the yolk, supported by a thick cushion of white, itself surrounded by less viscous liquid. As the eggs get older the white become more watery and eventually the yolk also flattens out. These may still taste alright but don't look too good poached or fried – use them for baking.

When baking, always bring eggs back to room temperature first. You will get more volume and lighter results; it is specially important to have the whites at room temperature when making meringue.

STORING EGGS

Remember that eggs are not designed as human food, but as the nursery and cradle of a bird. The shells are porous and thus can collect flavours, smells and germs. If shells are dirty *and* wet, eat these eggs quickly; always eat right away any eggs you have had to wash.

Keep eggs cool and away from other strong smelling foods. They actually last much longer than is usually thought but buy in small quantity.

ANCHOVY

Once you've been introduced to anchovies you either love them to distraction or hate them with a passion engendered by no other finny thing I know. They belong to the herring family and although inferior to them when fresh are much superior when preserved. Basically, the anchovy should be thought of as a flavouring agent rather than a major ingredient of a dish.

Native to the Mediterranean and the English Channel, the anchovy is nevertheless caught as far away as the Black Sea and Scandinavia. The best are said to come from the area between Nice and the Spanish province of Catalonia, as do many of the best recipes for their use. The simple method of salting and preserving whole anchovies originated with the Greeks and Romans, who also used them as the basis for their fermented fish sauce, *garum*. Like herrings they are often preserved in fillets, flat or curled, which are considered easier for packing and selling these days. They are sold in many forms, whole or filleted, in brine, in oil or in vinegar, although whole anchovies in salt are difficult to buy these days. The Russians preserve them in a spiced vinegar, the Norwegians in a spiced brine.

You can sometimes buy fresh anchovies and they are easily distinguishable. A maximum of 4-5 in (20 cm) long, they have an extraordinarily big mouth which stretches back almost as far as their gills. I have soused them and also served them freshly grilled, but they were not very good.

Anchovy essence, which comes in all manner of mixtures and strengths, is perfectly magical, with the special ability to pull together flavours which aren't melding and to make something new and wonderful. Naturally good in fish dishes, it can be used to advantage if employed with discretion in many meat dishes. It can add intriguing life to rice dishes, to mayonnaise and, perhaps best of all, to vegetables. Broccoli or spinach take very well to a litttle anchovy essence mixed with butter. Used secretly and in small amounts, anchovy essence or pounded anchovy can be used as a marinade for lamb and mutton before roasting, but better not tell your guests, even if they implore you for the secret. I once saw someone vomit on receipt of such information.

Basic use

Anchovies packed in brine or oil are interchangeable, although the former should be rinsed with water or milk and the latter are less highly flavoured. The most common uses for flat fillets or curls of anchovy are on pizza, in salads (such as Salade Niçoise) and for assertive canapés.

Along the edge of the Mediterranean and on some of her islands they make an extraordinary type of sauce-come-dip, usually known as *anchoiade* or by some similar name. Often composed of an anchovy paste (usually made from salted whole ones) parsley, oil and garlic, spread on oil-soaked bread and baked until brown, it is really a peasant version of the anchovy toast served as a savoury in London's men's clubs. The Piedmontese of Italy make something called *bagna cauda*, which is used as a sauce for pasta, or as a hot dip for bread or raw vegetables, and always regarded as being perfectly indigestible unless you've been brought up to it from birth. You simply heat 3 oz (75 g) each of butter and olive oil then add 3 oz (75 g) of anchovies in pieces and 3 oz (75 g) (that's right) of finely sliced garlic. Simmer for 10 minutes then keep hot over a spirit lamp. As Elizabeth David points out in her *Italian Food*, it requires great quantities of coarse red wine and the constitution of an ox. I think I prefer the French olive-and-anchovy paste called *tapénade*, or the civility of Patum Pepperium, the Gentleman's Relish, which is anchovy-based and bliss when spread on hot toast with decent tea in front of a drawing-room fire.

Appetisers and savouries

Anchovies are usually used as a flavouring rather than as a main ingredient, but not so when it comes to appetisers or savouries at the end of a formal meal – then their piquancy is most fully appreciated. Here are some ideas.

1 To make anchovy butter, mix ½-1 oz (15-25 g) butter with each pounded anchovy fillet. Only you will know how strong you like it.

2 Soak about 20 big Pruneaux d'Agen or Californian prunes in cold water overnight, dry them and carefully stone them by opening down one side. Then, pound the hardboiled yolk of 2 eggs with 1 oz (25 g) of butter and some anchovy paste or essence. Pass this through a sieve then pipe it into the prunes, making a nice swirl. Decorate with 1 anchovy fillet cut into thin strips. Spread the remaining stuffing on small pieces of toast and put stuffed prune on each. Decorate overall with a little watercress.

3 Anchovy-stuffed mushrooms are a very simple and very good idea. Mix some pounded anchovy fillets, some anchovy paste or some essence with cream or curd cheese then beat in 1 egg to each 4 oz (100 g) of cheese. Put this into peeled mushroom caps (they don't have to be too big) and bake in a dish until the cheese has started to set and the mushrooms are well heated through.

4 If you can get your hands on some smoked salmon pieces mix these into some cheese (as above) first and then sharpen the flavour with anchovy. Very glamorous as long as you don't use too much anchovy and do have the smoked salmon chopped very small, almost to a paste.

CAVIARE

Those languid heroines of Russian sagas who existed on but a spoonful of caviare and a sip of champagne knew a thing or two. The hard roe of the female sturgeon has twice the nutriment of most meat and is equal to the finest pork flesh. But its powers of sustainment are not why caviare is so esteemed. It is worshipped both because of its scarcity and its superlative flavour. The latter is often hotly debated, usually by those who have never tasted it, with hissed platitudes about 'acquired taste' and 'just because it costs so much'. That's as may be, but I've adored it ever since I breakfasted upon a pot of Beluga aboard a luxurious American cruise liner on January 1 1961, my nineteenth birthday.

Genuine caviare comes only from the sturgeon, a fish once so common in Europe that its roe was used as bait. Caviare was eaten occasionally in England but did not become popular until the 19th century. For all commercial purposes most caviare sturgeon are caught in the Caspian Sea, by the Russians in the North and the Iranians in the south, and all fishing is in government hands. There are other minor sources, and as well as the twelve or so types of caviare sturgeon in those waters there is one in the waters of France's Gironde river. The biggest sturgeon, the Beluga, can weigh anything up to 25 cwt and as much as 350 lb (158 kg) of roe has been taken from a single fish; the usual haul is between 8-35 lbs (4–15 kg), depending on the species.

Caviare can vary in colour from a yellow or brown to light grey and black and varies tremendously in size. The colour and size has little bearing on flavour, for the most important factors are the time of year, age of the fish and method of preservation; the Beluga, for instance must be eighteen to twenty years old before its roe is considered suitable. It is generally considered that the earlier in the season and the lighter the salting, the better the flavour.

The fabled golden caviare is obtained two ways. In the days of the great Russian Empire, patriotic and hardy Cossacks would hack holes through the late winter/early spring ice, through which they would spear sturgeons. Their immature roe was golden-yellow, with a rich flavour that made the senses reel, so it is said. The golden 'Shah's caviare' of Iran could be found throughout the season but comes only from an albino Oscietre; as even normally-coloured fish of this type are rare you can imagine the value placed upon such golden treasure. James Bond loves it.

Sturgeons are usually caught in the deltas of the rivers which flow into the Black and Caspian seas. They are bled before gutting to avoid contamination of the roe, which is sieved several times to remove the connecting tissues of the eggs, and then lightly salted. All caviare so treated will be labelled *malassol*, which actually means little salt, and this is considered the greatest delicacy of all. The Soviets also employ a more sophisticated and productive method of obtaining the eggs. They perform a sort of marine caesarian, after which the female is returned to the water to continue her reproductive cycle all over again.

As the summer gets hotter the caviare needs more salt to preserve it and the 'hot season' caviare is packed in small wooden tubs and labelled 'fresh salted'; this is very rarely seen in Europe. Towards the end of the season the inferior roe of this time is salted and pressed and usually sold in tubes for relatively little – it makes pretty canapés and offers lots of decorative possibilities.

Of all the types of sturgeon from which we get caviare the most productive is the monster *Beluga*, the white sturgeon. It provides the largest and many think the best, but Beluga caviare is also the most fragile and does not keep well. Next most important source is the *Sevruga* which never exceeds 4 feet (1¼ metres) in length and usually never gives more than about 8 lb (4 kg) of very small-grained roe. Many hold that this fineness gives a better flavour than the coarser Beluga, but this is a subjective argument that can never be solved. The third most important source is the common sturgeon which provides masses of eggs that vary from grey to black and are medium in size. It is these three that provide the majority of caviare sold in the United Kingdom and United States. But you might also come across tins labelled Ketovia or *Keta*. This is the hard roe of the dog salmon, common in both Canada and Russia. This 'lesser-caviare' is pink and large and much cheaper. But in candlelight and with overawed friends I have known it presented as the legendary golden caviare with total success.

American caviare is almost certainly from the same or similar species of salmon. But the golden eggs are as big as tapioca and quite salty and fishy – would *you* eat fishy tapioca?

Presentation

You'll note I have not said *basic preparation;* it seemed vulgar in this context.

Caviare has two natural enemies and hundreds of thousands of unnatural ones. The first two are air and metal. Caviare deteriorates rapidly when exposed to the air and the finer the caviare the faster the deterioration. It might last for an hour but if it has not been treated properly before opening it will oxidize and sour sooner – much sooner. You should open caviare to the air for no more than the moments it takes to transport it to the table. Those carved extravaganzas of ice into which you are invited to dip at buffets are a pretentious guarantee that the caviare they contain will be awful. Hours of exposure to hot, probably smoky, air mean it will first oxidize and then freeze. Next, you should avoid touching it with metal; bone, horn, wood or semi-precious stones are best. You might remember that one of the star exhibits at London's Victoria & Albert Museum's Fabergé exhibition was a caviare scoop of amber. Its exquisite simplicity and delicacy was perfectly in harmony with its intended use.

Now for those hundreds of thousands of enemies. These are the people who perpetuate the malpractices of our Victorian and Edwardian forebears who could not conceive of food being served simply. Their presentation of caviare with chopped eggs, pickles and, worst of all, raw onion, is sacrilege of the first degree. Those who so eat caviare only reinforce the opinion of others that they do it not because they like the taste, but because it costs so much. You cannot appreciate the flavour of caviare (or much else) with the harsh, acidic bite of onion in your mouth. Raw onion masks every other flavour even after it has been swallowed and anyone who argues to the contrary is a fool, or has no palate. Either way they should be forbidden caviare.

So, a fine *malassol* Beluga or Sevruga caviare should be lightly chilled in its container then, just before serving, turned into a delicate dish of the finest, whitest porcelain and taken to the table over ice, with a scoop of something non-metallic per person. Some thin buckwheat pancakes *(blinis)* or very good thin toast spread with unsalted butter are the only possible accompaniments. Even lemon juice will destroy the full flavour. If you don't have implements of horn or lapis or malachite, which I conceive is possible, then dip into the caviare with your *blinis* or toast. And make sure you finish every scrap.

I'm all for experiment and new taste thrills. But frankly, when it comes to caviare, if you're not prepared to eat it straight, you shouldn't be allowed it at all . . . oh, all right, perhaps with just the tiniest squeeze of lemon.

Caviare does accompany smoked salmon beautifully, but keep the lemon juice for the salmon and if possible, don't use it at all. For something sensational serve caviare with oysters, a dish calculated to make only bank managers cry.

Mock caviare

The Danes, bless them, have given us a black and red 'caviare-type' product at a most reasonable price and not too bad a flavour. Used to accompany smoked salmon or on canapés of thin, buttered toast, it is pretty and expensive looking. Once, desperate for a new idea for a dip for crudités, I mixed a pot of the black version with a little mayonnaise, lemon juice and cream cheese. It was an absolute sensation. Not for the flavour, but for the colour. It turned a bright blue and both children and adults ate it with mixed gusto and horror. Blue food tends to do that.

These caviare substitutes are made from the roe of something called lumpfish, and have brought a new meaning to the phrase 'like it or lump it'. You can like caviare but serve lumpfish roe instead.

Caviare storing

Optimum storage for *malassol* caviare is 30°F (−2°C) but this does not mean deep freezing. A deep freeze is fatal to caviare, reducing it to a sorry sort of soup. Unopened tins and jars keep well for several weeks in a domestic refrigerator. As this is usually the way the biggest and smallest stores keep them it is always a bit risky to buy from anywhere that does not have a fast turnover – even then I could tell you a story or two!

EEL

No one knows a lot about the private life of the eel, except that it lives in the sea and spawns in the rivers; where it lives precisely has never been discovered but it is thought the Sargasso Sea is one of the liveliest spots.

The Romans liked eel so much they used to farm it, but we seem slowly to have lost our interest in eating it in Great Britain. True there are still places where jellied eel is available, but where are the shops that used to sell nothing else? Now, the English catch their own eels and send them to Dutchmen to smoke, who send them back to us, expensively.

Basic preparation

It is in smoked or tinned form that you will find eel on sale in your delicatessen. You can find smoked eels in two forms. First is the whole thing, head, tail and fins included. Chunks are cut off and you take it home to skin it and serve it quite plainly. Otherwise you will find long, thin, smoked fillets, which are often frozen. These taste not unlike raw kipper; with a sharp knife and equivalent turn of phrase you can make substitution of one for the other at considerable benefit to your pocket. Eel fillets go very well with other smoked fish as a starter – they like hot or cold scrambled eggs, and their shape is terrific for decorating such creations as a seafood mousse. I have been served them with chilled melon and I'm still trying to make my mind up about it seven years later. Probably not a good idea, I suspect.

The Spanish like very baby eel, elvers, which they call *anguillas*. They are white and matchstick-like, and available here in small tins. Being pre-cooked they are soft and delicate, with a nutty rather than fishy taste. Drain them gently and serve with a little oil, lemon juice and garlic. Or put them into a light frying batter to make fritters, which is how I like them best. In New Zealand, these elvers are what we call whitebait, and whitebait fritters are part of the standard diet. The crunch of the bones and stare of the eyes of European whitebait (which is the fry of herrings and sprats) have turned many a colonial's thoughts to home faster than snow and ice ever did. New Zealand's eels are quite the most hideous things you can imagine and thus they are not eaten much there (other than by the Maoris who are delighted to have this delicacy to themselves). Or almost. Now an eel pâté is being tinned and exported. It is very good as far as tinned fish pâtés go, but I prefer it used to make mousses or soufflés; the recipe on the tin is a little ambitious but if you reduce the ingredients by one-third of everything except the eel you will be well pleased.

CLAMS

Baltimore is one of the blackest cities in the United States and, being considerably smaller and much whiter than virtually everybody on the streets, I wasn't really having a good time. But there were things that had to be done, which included visiting the famous Lexington Market. It didn't seem American at all, with its noise and untidiness and hundreds of small garish stalls selling everything edible and a few items that, although once falling into that catgegory, were right over the top. Actually, it was nice to see Americans being unhygienic about food for a change.

Right at the back of the market was an oyster bar and as we were on Chesapeake Bay which is famed for all manner of seafood, we had to make our way there. Far more than an oyster bar, it sold all manner of extraordinary fish, sea urchins, a variety of hard and soft shelled crabs plus some skinned animals that I'm sure were possums and others that I think were squirrels, and others. . . . But I digress. Around a circular bar, men and women were slurping great raw oysters accompanied by special sauces and ice-cold beer. As well, they were eating clams, *raw* clams. Raw clams? I'd never heard of such a thing, and when I saw the size of them I still couldn't believe it. You had to cut each in two, at least I would have, but the experts here managed to slip the lot into their mouth, chew a couple of times and swallow slowly with bliss beaming on their faces.

Enquiries and many clam meals later proved that eating clams raw was indeed very common and uncommonly good. Not at all like the tiny things in Italian spaghetti or Japanese tins.

In the British Isles you are only likely to be able to buy tinned clams or clam juice.

Tinned clams or baby clams	These are an essential in any store cupboard once you know them, and can be either Japanese or Spanish. There are far more in each can than you would imagine and almost any brand is alright as long as they are in brine or a light soup of their own juices. They are cooked, of course, and can be used straight from the tin with the least preparation, just some lemon juice, perhaps some oil and garlic or a special mayonnaise. But they help all other seafood dishes too. Mix them with prawns to make the usual boring cocktail more interesting, or use them instead of prawns in fish sauces, stuffings and so on. Chop them roughly into batter and make fritters for lunch or as an extraordinary accompaniment to roast chicken or turkey, which were once regularly stuffed with oysters. Put them at the bottom of fish soufflés in lots of garlicky butter or stir them into pilaffs of saffron rice. Like all shellfish they toughen if cooked too long, so don't.
Clam juice	Constantly come across in American cookbooks and occasionally on the shelves of better stores here. It is the liquor left after clams have been steamed open nd is certainly the best stock for fish sauces or fishy flavouring. It *makes* a fish pie, and finishes a soup or can be the basis of one, cream or otherwise. It is also a rather interesting mixer with alcoholic drinks and is becoming so popular as an ingredient in Bloody Marys that you can now buy it ready mixed with tomato – it is called Clamato, wouldn't you believe?
CRAB	The problem with buying much of the imported crabmeat on the delicatessen shelf is working out exactly what is inside the pack, frozen or canned.
Dressed crab	This usually means that inferior brown meat (from inside the shell) plus other impertinences have been mixed with a small proportion of white meat, often into a khaki-coloured paste. Full details are usually revealed by perusal of the list of ingredients on the pack, and those who do not do this may regret their inattention to detail. Even where white and brown meat is included but kept apart in products sold as dressed crab, the proportion of white may be distressingly low in the interest of marketability. Buy warily, or do your own dressing.
Crabmeat	Frozen or canned, this is usually better value for

money as there is unlikely to be any adulteration. Indeed, you may be buying just white meat. Russian and Alaskan crabmeat is considered superlatively good and interchangeable as they come from the same geographical area. Any Russian crab from the Kamchatka Peninsula is sold under that name and this generally signifies that the crab was processed within hours of being caught and the can will contain only the leg and claw meat of male crabs, plus natural juices. This is usually what the Americans would sell as Alaskan King Crab.

America is a marvellous place for crab lovers to be. Either their crabs are more numerous or Americans like the meat more, but you can certainly buy and enjoy crab easily. One of the greatest American treats is soft-shelled crabs. If you see them on a menu, and ensure they have been cooked very simply indeed, order them. They are smallish, 4–5 in (15–18 cm) crabs that have just shed one shell and are waiting for the next to grow. You eat all of them. I sat rigid with disbelief for quite some time in the august New York Yacht Club when told this, for the fact had not been vouchsafed until the creatures were placed in front of me. Once I was able physically to put a fork with a couple of claws and half a shell into my mouth (and that took some doing) I found the effort very worthwhile.

Further south, around Chesapeake Bay, you are very much in crab country and can hardly drive more than a few minutes without being exhorted by billboard and neon to try the 'only authentic' Baltimore or Maryland crabcake. I never tasted one worth the fuss. Frankly, I found them all over-peppered and under-crabbed. Perhaps I just didn't get to where the *authentic* ones are.

If you love the idea of crab but can't face the expense, use it as a flavouring rather than an ingredient. In an excellent but subtle cream or tomato sauce with some fine white fish fillets or even in a mayonnaise over a seafood salad, a little goes a long way. For the ultimate cheat, use it in a sauce over pieces of gently poached monkfish, which has the same texture and flavour as lobster. (Make sure you have a dollop of brandy in the sauce, which is one of the most important ingredients of all in any fish sauce, hot or cold. It makes an extraordinary difference). Crab is excellent with avocado, pineapple, mango and other tropical fruit; a small

amount added to a stir-fried mixture of vegetables or
of vegetables and chicken will be a triumph.

HERRINGS

Herrings are one of man's oldest foods from the sea;
remains have been identified in prehistoric
settlements in Denmark, France and Portugal.
Native to the north Atlantic, herrings migrate in
huge numbers from the polar seas to the English
Channel and thereabouts, starting in March.

Considering that each female herring lays some 50
million eggs a year it is little wonder shortages were
rare until recently. They remain one of the cheapest
fresh fish, yet are surprisingly unpopular in the
British Isles, perhaps because of their association
with poverty in the past.

Herring flesh is equal in nutrition to that of
salmon, and a damned sight moister and more
interesting much of the time. There is the problem of
the bones, of course, but a little practice licks that.
Start at the tail end and pull the flesh towards it, the
way the bones point. Anyway, you can eat the bones,
they are very good for you.

Most of the herrings eaten in Scandinavia and
Europe are preserved, usually by salting. Today the
catch is deep-chilled at sea and mixed with coarse salt
in great concrete vats on return. There is a great art
to the salting; to be right the salt should have
combined with the liquid extracted from the fish and
fully dissolved to form a strong brine in 10 days.
This is your basic salted herring. It is distinctly
inedible, but will last for ages.

Smoked herrings must also be salted to some
degree; and depending on the exact cure, or the
habits of an area, the fish will either be smoked close
to the smoke source, which is called hot-smoking and
slightly cooks the flesh, or they will be smoked where
they are not heated at all, and that is cold smoking.

Distinctions between types of salted and smoked
herring are easily blurred, but I think the following
list will explain most of what you are likely to come
across.

**Smoked English
herrings**

Bloaters: in spite of today's excellent cold storage
and transport systems, these have virtually
disappeared because they 'don't keep'. Bloaters are
whole herrings salted for a very short time (in brine
rather than dry salt) then cold-smoked. The very best
are supposed to have come from Yarmouth during

October and November and were eaten almost as soon as they had come from the smokehouse. 'The epicure will eat them before he goes to bed rather than wait for breakfast', said the Wine and Food Society in 1944, when you could still get them. They were grilled or lightly fried and a very few shops in Norfolk are said to make them still. Harrods have them.

Buckling: these are lightly brined after having been beheaded and gutted, but they are unsplit and the roe or milt will be left in place. They are hot-smoked and so keep quite well. Increasingly more difficult to buy, they may be eaten cold or grilled and make an excellent paste. Bucklings are made in other countries (they were originally German), but the Dutch *Bokking* is still the entire fish, cold-smoked, and must be cleaned before consumption.

Kippers: relatively new on the scene, and probably introduced no more than a century ago. Kippering is a way of treating fish, salmon in particular, by splitting, brining, then smoking it. What we call smoked salmon was once called kippered salmon. If either salmon or herring is cooked before smoking it may not be called kippered.

Only the Isle of Man and a few places in Scotland still make proper kippers smoked over oak chips. Most of those you buy have been cooked in some way to prolong their life, and the colour and flavour of smoking has been painted on so they are not really kippers. You only have to see one real kipper to be able to detect fakes; real ones have a glorious pale golden glow rather than a dark, treacle-like coating.

Discussion on how to prepare kippers can lead to blows. I'll play safe and detail all those I know and you can choose your own.

Grilling: this gets rid of some of the excess oil, but must be done gently or you will also dry out the flesh and further toughen the outer layer; open *all* the windows. Serve with a pat of butter.

Slow roasting: if you have an Aga or some other slow-combustion kitchen range with a permanently luke-warm compartment, place your kippers in a covered container with some butter and perhaps a little milk and leave overnight.

Steeping: boil some water, pour it over the kippers until they are just covered and leave for a few minutes, until they are warmed through. *Jugged kippers* are done like this too, except they are plunged vertically into a jug, but you do risk the tail coming off when you remove the fish. Steeping gives very moist results and the water also dissolves some of the salt. I think it is the best way.

Flaming: it is said Irish enthusiasts pour heated whiskey over their kippers, set it alight, then set-to when the flames die. Can you imagine an Irishman (or anyone else, for that matter) burning his whiskey?

The best time for kippers from the Isle of Man is July and August, when the herrings are at their fattest.

Kippers make excellent pâtés but you may as well buy the boned fillets for this. Uncooked kippers, skinned and divided into long strips, are a successful substitute for smoked eel, but good enough to serve without subterfuge. A little cold, creamy scrambled egg, some dill-pickled cucumber, a slice of lemon and some black olives would all make good accompaniments.

Red herrings: you can rarely buy these nowadays, but they used to be the most important of standbys before refrigeration. Red herrings were highly salted and highly smoked and thus almost indestructible. If you find some, soak them for many hours in milk or water before grilling or poaching. A soft-poached egg, cooked without salt, is a perfect foil, as with so many smoked fish.

Continental herrings

Bismarck: these are fresh herring fillets marinated in vinegar with onion, so are fairly rugged.
Fillets: in bulk or in jars, this is the way tons of herring are eaten. The fillets have usually been salted, then soaked and treated in a number of ways. Some go into a red wine sauce, some into a tomato sauce, some are in oil. There are dozens of varieties commercially available and hundreds more are made in the home. The Danish range, bought in jars, keep excellently in the refrigerator; use the fillets as part of an hors d'œuvre, or slice them small for use in potato salads. They can be mashed into a paste with stewed, or chopped, raw apple and with egg yolk as a simple pâté. Most fillets are called *matjesfillet* (but they may not be, so see below).
Matjesherring: used very generally for all herring fillets or salted herrings but properly means a herring gathered in early summer when the roe is still developing. They may be treated two ways – either

lightly brined with some sugar content or heavily brined in the usual way of salt herring. If you are buying them 'straight', i.e. direct from the brine, I think it likely that *matjesfillets* have been lightly salted and whole *matjesherrings* are more heavily treated. In either case, soak them in water or milk to remove the salt you do not want. If preserved other than in brine, of course you will not need to soak them.

They may be eaten just like that, especially the fillets, or perhaps with onion – and in Holland green beans are usual. Or you can then make a marinade, warm or cold, and flavour them according to taste.

Rollmops: These are totally eviscerated fresh herrings, the two fillets joined together only by skin. No bone or fins should remain. The double fillets are rolled around pickled cucumber, sometimes with carrot and onion, and kept in an acidic-brine liquid, usually made with a white vinegar. It is easy to play with this idea at home, using spices and apple with cider vinegar for instance. Sour cream, dill and more pickled cucumbers are by far the best accompaniments. Oh, and ice-cold vodka or aquavit. It is said rollmops are a great cure for hangovers – but I suspect the accompanying liquor is far more useful.

Salt herring: the basic preserved herring, which must be soaked for at least 24 hours before it can be used. Fillet this and serve it with sour cream, pickled beetroot and cucumber, onion rings, potatoes, hard-boiled eggs, gherkins and decent wholemeal or rye bread. Once soaked the whole or filleted herrings can be vinegar-pickled or put into any number of mustard, tomato, onion or sour cream sauces.

Strömming: this is a *sort* of herring, the Baltic herring, which is smaller and leaner than the Atlantic variety. It is less likely to be highly salted and once soaked is usually put into *mild* pickles, with mustard and dill sauces or in sour cream and dill – using small amounts of raw onion rather than vinegar to provide any acidity. The Swedes use an acid they call Attika, which I think is acetic acid and has a pleasant sweetness. All-in-all I think I prefer the serving style of the Baltic herring to the more fierce German and Dutch herring types. If you are ever offered something called *surströmming*, think very carefully before agreeing. These are Baltic herrings which have been packed with only half the normal amount of salt then sealed in barrels which are left in the sun. Alan Davidson's *North Atlantic Seafood* says that birds drop dead from the sky when the barrels are opened. It is acceptable to find tinned *surströmming* bulging, a sign of proper fermentation. Open these tins in the open air, standing up wind, and have on hand some water for rinsing and some ready-chopped red onion which allows you to get the fillets to your mouth before your nose realises what is happening. Thank you – but no thank you . . .

MACKEREL
tinned, smoked, pâtés

Although its cheapness means it is often ignored, the mackerel is quite one of the most fascinating – and delicious – fish there is. Even the reason for its name is bizarre. Mackerel is simply the English version of the French nickname for the fish, *Maquereau*. *Maquereau* means 'pimp' or 'procurer', and the name was given because the female makes a point of escorting inexperienced female shad to ripe males; for this American gourmets, Eartha Kitt and Nöel Coward are grateful. When waiters bring shad roe to discerning diners, they bring what is arguably the most delicious of all roes to table – only caviare excepted. When in the United States, and on the Atlantic coast during winter, it's certainly worth singing for. But, back to mackerel.

The mackerel has a furious temper when in schools, which it usually is, and so brave it attacks fish far larger than itself. Indeed, in Norway there is a story of a sailor being dragged underwater by mackerel while swimming and released ten minutes later bereft of most of his flesh. It is also a stupid fish, and frightfully easy to catch. It has the highest proportion of fatty matter of any fish and this deteriorates very fast; it was once the only fish allowed to be sold on the streets of London on a Sunday.

Like so many fish, they spawn in August and September and fresh or smoked mackerel should be avoided then. In October they start putting on condition, and by December are quite perfect. I tend not to rate tinned mackerel of any kind or provenance, especially the ghastly smoked mackerel pâtés, which are overburdened with farinacea (as, in my opinion, are most English-produced seafood soups – but perhaps you have better luck). Many mackerel products come from abroad and are thus a slightly different and always inferior species, by common consent.

But smoked English mackerel is something else, and when good surpasses any trout I have ever eaten. The boned, smoked mackerel fillets – flat and torpedo shaped – that are staples of many a wine bar, are overcooked and then artifically coloured and smoke-flavoured, a process that often reduces the flesh to a gummy paste. But, when you find mackerel whole, with only the head and gut missing, their skins a pale, iridescent gold rather than lurid copper, well then you've found the real thing – almost certainly from Cornwall and quite superb. When buying them, avoid a slimy skin (which will actually be poisonous) and go for something firm but not rigid.

Interestingly, mackerel may be sexed at sight; those with wavy lines on their bodies are female, those with straight lines are male, and much tastier.

Basic preparation

Smoked mackerel is best served quite simply and it is cheap enough to allow ventures into pâté making or mousses, something I don't normally hold with in something of this quality.

Whether serving a whole or a half smoked mackerel, you should take the spine out. This is simply achieved by first extending the slit in the gut right back to the tail. Then with the point of a sharp knife gently fold the top half of the fish back, having a pair of poultry scissors on hand to cut any intransigent bones. You can now lift out the whole backbone and it remains only to remove the finer ones that remain around the stomach cavity.

For basic serving I like them slightly chilled, served with lemon wedges and a good, creamy horseradish sauce, which is indispensable when presenting mackerel in any form.

Cubed beetroot also goes exceptionally well with smoked mackerel. For a stunning but simple buffet presentation, arrange boned halves of smoked mackerel like the spokes of a wheel, with the pointed tail ends in the middle. Pile cubed beetroot in the centre. Pipe horseradish cream down the centre of each mackerel half and sprinkle this with a little sweet paprika. Fill the space between each fish half with upturned, thin lemon wedges and large sprigs of parsley. This is specially popular with men, who fall upon its hearty flavour with relief.

Marika Hanbury Tenison's *New Fish Cookery*
(Granada) suggests a salad of flaked smoked
mackerel, apple and a horseradish-flavoured
mayonnaise, which would be very good; she also
recommends making kedgeree with smoked
mackerel. Simply substitute mackerel for the more
usual haddock. For extra interest, finish with cream
rather than butter, again flavoured with a little
horseradish.

You can lightly grill smoked mackerel, which then
need something quite sharp to accompany them. I
would suggest spiced red cabbage and a purée of
celeriac, into which you have stirred a lot of finely
chopped parsley and garlic. Great on a cold, boring
winter's day for lunch or supper.

MUSSELS

In New Zealand, mussels are huge, so huge that after
de-bearding and de-tonguing they must be cut in
half, at least. They have a certain rugged appeal, I
remember, but cannot ever equal the sweeter delights
of the smaller European mussels.

Although available packed with flavours ranging
from tomato to onion and pickles, or with vinegar, I
find mussels packed in tins or bottles with brine and
their own juices by far the best. They are usually
from Scandinavia, Norway's Limfjord being perhaps
the best source. They are exceptionally useful, not
least of all because they have enough size and colour
to make a contribution to the eye as well as the
tongue.

Pasta salads seem specially good receptacles for
ready-prepared mussels. Seafood sauces to put into
pastry cases or to complement poached fish fillets are
much more interesting with mussels than with
prawns.

If you follow my instructions for cooking rice, add
some saffron and use the juices from a tin or bottle to
make up the cooking liquid. When the water level
reduces to that of the rice, lay the mussels on top of
the rice, then cover the saucepan and proceed as
usual. They will be steamed to a succulent softness,
any juices they lose being transferred to the rice.
When it is ready, stir gently with a fork and you have
a supper or lunch dish that is attractive, filling and
satisfying.

Deep fried in a decent batter, heated in hot butter,
garlic and parsley, tossed in a dressing with orange
segments and Mozzarella cheese or served in a hot

white wine sauce on rice, mussels are worth your attention if they have so far escaped it.

OYSTERS

It would be possible to write an entire book on oysters, and I suppose someone has. In this country they were once a staple of the grateful poor, as was salmon, and not so very long ago, either. Now like many simple local foods they have become rare and expensive and likely to be served fancifully and badly.

The oysters of most European and American sources have been transplanted, cross-bred and artificially brought-on to a degree that has eroded some of the ancient clear-cut distinctions of flavour. Most fishmongers who still sell oysters on the shell couldn't tell you what type they are. A far cry from France, where in the tiniest inland market the fish stalls will offer a choice of eight or nine varieties for prices that start at under £1 for 10. The one really to go for there is the *Marenne verte*, which is a bright, cuprous green – my hat goes off to the man who was first brave enough to put one in his mouth.

America has a wide variety of interesting oysters, some of them bordering on the monster-sized and needing to be cut up before ingestion. The coastal towns and cities make much of their local seafoods and you can usually get good advice and buy specifically. In Australasia the choice is more limited but those who know vote the Rock Oyster of the eastern Australian coast as amongst the most succulent in the world. When I was last there, twelve of these amazing creatures served over ice in a top-class restaurant cost just £2. They have the added advantage of being equally suited to cooking.

In ancient Greece, where paper was short, you voted to ostracise someone by marking an oyster shell.

Smoked oysters, which usually come in tins from Japan and are eaten by old bachelors with as much relish as spinsters eat soft roes, are delicious. But they're often ruined by being served in the filthy cotton-seed oil in which they are preserved. They should be carefully drained and then sprinkled with the smallest amount of lemon juice. For special occasions I would take the trouble to pat them dry of oil with kitchen tissue and then present them in a nice, gentle lemon juice and oil mixture.

Basic preparation

Smoked oysters may be treated with a little more

abandon that the fresh variety. Minced or chopped, their flavour goes a long way to flavour sauces for garnish or filling puff pastry cases. You can make the most of their flavour to replace bacon on skewers of seafood for your grill or barbecue.

ROE

It will come as something of a shock to many a spinster to learn that her favourite light supper of soft roes is not fish eggs but the milt or sperm of the male. But perhaps it is precisely this that explains their popularity. It's certainly a deliciously wicked thing to reveal as they are being enjoyed, and can quite spoil the most determined appetite, male or female. It is the hard roe which is the egg of the female fish.

Roe of both sorts are popular right round the world. In the Occident, the general agreement on flavour, in ascending order, is: mackerel, herring then shad and carp equal first. Most of the soft roe sold in fish shops or in cans is cod roe, but it can be herring, too.

Greeks are specially partial to the eggs of the grey mullet, and this is the proper basis for *taramasalata*. But try telling that to the shrill-accented debs in striped aprons behind a thousand deli counters. They'll dish out a pink paste by the hundredweight and swear it's better than they had in Corfu or Kos or Katerini. It'll certainly be *different*, for although the smoked cod's roe used is a good substitute for that of mullet, the *taramasalata* is really only an emulsion of low-grade bread and oil with some little amount of roe and a great deal of colouring. When we made it properly (albeit with cod roe) at my delicatessen we sold it as fast as it could be made – until the cod war put up the cost of the roe astronomically. I didn't have the nerve of some Greek entrepreneurs in London who have made it down to a price rather than up to a standard. Pity. I'd never have needed to touch a typewriter again, for now they make virtually all that is sold in Lopndon – yes, even for the big stores and tiny delis that pride themselves on quality.

Basic preparation

Smoked roe, usually hard cod's roe, can be dipped in batter and fried, chilled and served sliced with light vinaigrette dressing, placed on toast and covered with a well-seasoned white sauce – but it really is rather too strong for most people's taste. It's better as an addition to a fish sauce or a garnish to something relatively bland of a fishy nature. There is one exception in my experience and that happened in New Zealand. There you can buy the firm smoked roe of both the schnapper and the blue cod (the latter when smoked was described by André Simon as like Finnan Haddock gone to heaven). When served unpretentiously in thin delicate slices in a most successful small restaurant in Auckland called Clundy's. It was accompanied by a perfect light vinaigrette and a garlic mayonnaise. Quite worth getting off your jet to experience.

PILCHARDS

Often described either as a type of herring or a type of sardine, the pilchard is cleverly both. A timid member of the herring family, it is actually an adult sardine, and thus by any measure good and fatty and delicious when fresh. They are a specialty of the Devon and Cornish coast between July and December but great care is needed when buying them, as they spoil extremely quickly.

The most famous dish made with fresh pilchards is the variety of stargazey pies of the West of England, which can be several shapes and sizes all noted for being baked with whole fish, whose heads protrude from their pastry cases. This is done to incorporate the rich oil from the head in the finished pie, without covering the heads with pastry, which would make eating difficult. You'd be lucky to get stargazey pies of any kinds these days, dead lucky if they included pilchards, whole or beheaded.

I'm not fond of tinned fish, a feeling particularly reinforced in the case of pilchards by seeing how many people buy them to feed to their pets. We are most likely to eat them whole as part of an Italian mixed *antipasto*. Otherwise, the type in tomato sauce, mashed with a little vinegar, lemon juice and cream cheese can make a fish paste of sorts that would go nicely on hot toast. A little chopped onion, capers, olives or anchovies, that enchanted saviour of the banal, might help.

PRAWNS AND
SHRIMPS

Although different from one another, prawns and shrimps look alike enough to be called by one another's name. In the United Kingdom you are usually safe calling little ones shrimps and big ones prawns. In America they are all called shrimp; but the giant Pacific variety, a favourite ingredient of many American menus, are often called prawns for the sake of alliteration.

I am constantly astonished at how good tinned prawns can be, and how cheap. Perhaps those from Malaysia can be a disappointment for they are often shrimps, tiny and floury. Usually, though, tins are packed full of moist plump, pink, crustacea, their shells removed. The initial outlay might seem high for such a small object, but the value for money is comparable with frozen prawns.

There are several pitfalls and pieces of advice to heed when buying frozen prawns. Some types are free-flowing, that is, each prawn has a protective ice-glaze. This means you are paying for water rather than seafood, and in the case of some Indian prawns the water is highly salted. I have ruined a very fine sauce for 100 people by adding these prawns, liquid and all.

I think you should carefully consider the size of prawn you want to use. Generally larger ones look better and they behave better if they are to be served hot. Prawns will inevitably shrink when cooked or when reheated. If cooked or heated for too long they will also toughen. Indeed, unless you are buying cooked prawns and they are to be used for stuffing something elegant, or puréed, or used as a garnish, bigger is always far better.

It is important that you defrost frozen prawns very slowly, or you will lose flavour, texture and moistness. The best way is to leave them in their bag in the refrigerator overnight. They will then be moist and plump and have retained most of their natural juices. If they are then to go into a hot sauce, first bring them to room temperature. Then they can be popped into the sauce just for the few minutes needed to cook them or heat them through. They do not need to be piping hot and the sauce should never be boiled.

Potted shrimps, the ones you buy commercially, are very good and easily copied at home, for they have simply been packed in butter flavoured with a little spice, mainly mace. But they should be served warm, with the seasoned butter in glistening pools. It makes me angry that rather famous fish restaurants, unable to make potted shrimps themselves, cannot read the labels on the ones they buy frozen and serve them ice-cold with limp toast made from plastic bread.

I do not understand the combination of avocado and prawns; both are bland and often even have the same texture. If you want something pink and green, then peel and cut some kiwi fruit into segments (not slices), soak those in Pernod for a while and serve your prawns on them with a mayonnaise flavoured with fresh lime juice and grated lime peel.

You can also extend prawns with cheaper seafood, especially mussels, as long as they have been tinned in brine rather than vinegar. The two are specially good in pasta sauces, or in hot sauces to stuff vol-au-vents.

To make a truly excellent prawn pâté or spread, liquidize cooked prawns with half their weight of warm melted butter. Add white vermouth to taste. Let cool. Then whip some cream in the proportion of ½ pint (300 ml) to ½ lb (250 g) of prawns. Gently fold the two together, keeping as much air in the mixture as possible. Add a little white pepper if you like. Fresh or dried dill is a most refreshing addition, and you might also like a squeeze or two of lemon juice or a touch of brandy. If you want to use less cream, substitute half the amount for curd cheese, cream cheese, or cottage cheese you have seived.

Other flavours which go well with prawns are horseradish, tomato, garlic, basil, ground cumin and coriander, sweet or hot paprika and, of course, cucumber.

SALT COD

Salt cod was the most important staple flesh of the medieval Catholic world, and continued so for much of the time after the introduction of Protestantism. During the long, universally observed Lent and the twice-weekly fish days salt cod kept the wolf from the door. For the sake of Christian observance, millions of tons of cod have been pulled from the waters of the Atlantic and it was in search of bigger harvests that the first English colonies in the New World were established. In fact, so important was the catching and salting of cod to Massachusetts that they incorporated one in the design of their Great Seal of the State.

As Catholicism gradually lost its grip on Europe, and the great explorers introduced new foods, salt fish became less and less important in Britain. Just as well, when you ponder the problems caused by latter-day overfishing and the struggles for territorial rights which led to the recent unpleasant cod wars.

Now, the past importance of salt cod to our ancestors is hard to believe, considering the difficulty of buying it in the United Kingdom. West Indian communities usually have shops displaying the dried, crusty sides hung from the ceiling. And one enterprising company is now prepackaging smaller amounts and these are available at supermarkets where there is an ethnic demand. Good Portuguese, Spanish, Italian and Greek shops should also sell it. Sadly, like herrings, it is considered too cheap to be fashionable. But it is well worth the attention of any true gastronome.

Basic preparation

Preparation of salt cod requires some forethought, as it should be soaked for a full 36 hours in several changes of water to hydrate and de-salt it. A 24-hour treatment will probably suffice, however. When soaked you drain off the last water, then put it in a saucepan with masses of cold water and then bring the lot very slowly to the boil. It should now simmer, with the water barely moving, until the flesh flakes easily. It must never ever boil again, so if you have a large cooker like an Aga, even better results can be obtained if you simply leave the saucepan, once it has boiled, on the back where there will be just enough heat to give the desired results; that is how the Icelanders recommend you do it.

If you haven't planned ahead you can put the dried salt cod in cold water, bring it slowly to the simmer, discard the water and repeat the process several times. But it won't be as nice.

The classic English way of presenting salt cod is predictably boring, for it is simply boiled and served with a sauce of hard-boiled eggs. It is only when you start looking at the kitchens of the Brazilians and Portuguese, the Spanish and Creoles, that it becomes remotely exciting.

There is a Norwegian salted cod called *Stockfish*, which is especially popular in Germany, Belgium and Holland; you may treat it as though it were ordinary salt cod.

Ling is the name given the largest variety of cod, and as this is the type usually salted, salt cod was once known as ling, a point to be aware of when using old cook books.

SALMON

Smoked salmon is rightly regarded as one of the world's greatest delicacies, and the best is probably

Scottish salmon smoked in London. The proper term is kippered salmon, as kippering is what is done to it: the salmon are beheaded and gutted, split, salted and then cold-smoked. The kippering process was only applied to herrings some time last century.

It should not be forgotten that this luxury food was once simply a way for the poor fisherman to preserve food to eat in wintertime.

As with all old-established food processes there are many variations: some smokers will cook the salmon a little before smoking it (which is not true kippering). Some will hot-smoke it. Some will burn this type of woodchip and some will use others. I know of one company that uses Drambuie in its method, giving the salmon a most appealing golden brown colour and a definite extra flavour; but they won't reveal how and when the Drambuie is employed.

As many a person is foxed by being given a side of smoked salmon at Christmas time, without having the slightest knowledge of how to slice it, I'll give you instructions. But first, to whet the appetite, some points about buying it and some ways to serve it.

The best Scotch smoked salmon is pink-red and firm in texture; when it is cut, it should be slightly transparent and waxy. The smaller fish, the grilse, have a more delicate flavour and need to be sliced slightly thickly. Only the larger and more mature adults have enough flavour in them to be sliced finely – at least that is my opinion.

Canadian smoked salmon you will find to be redder in colour, drier in texture, and denser. You might find it saltier, too, for it is expected to last longer, what with having to be transported here, and waiting for people to get over their natural inclination against it. Really, there is nothing wrong with Canadian smoked salmon other than being overcharged for it. And if you are catering for a lot of drunks, or family friends who haven't much knowledge of these things, it is a waste of money to serve the best Scotch smoked salmon.

Although it is the custom to serve smoked salmon with slices of lemon it really is too awful to spray it with such sharp liquid, for this immediately masks the delicate flavour that so many have laboured to create. Neither should it be too cold, for this will also mask the flavour. To get the absolutely best flavour from smoked salmon take it from the refrigerator about half an hour before you wish to serve it, less if you have already put it on the plates. Instead of allowing your guests to squirt lemon juice over it, rub each plate with a cut lemon wedge or a little grated peel, which is better. The perfume of the lemon juice or zest will soon penetrate the flesh with altogether more delicious results.

Of all the things that go well with smoked salmon, scrambled eggs are probably my favourite, hot or cold. HRH Prince Charles is said to be happiest of all when confronted by such a dish, a man of regal taste indeed. For a really marvellous starter for an important meal, roll smoked salmon around cold, creamy scrambled eggs to make a stuffed horn, and sprinkle the overflowing egg with black cariare, real or otherwise. For hot scrambled eggs, you simply slice the salmon into fingers and throw it over the eggs as you are serving them or lay it on the toast on which the eggs are presented. A very small amount of smoked salmon makes a wonderful addition to sauce for quite plain fish and should be put in at the last moment or it will be tough.

A flavour that does help smoked salmon is anchovy. If you mix some smoked salmon leftovers with cream cheese you have an excellent spread made even better by the addition of a little mashed anchovy or some anchovy essence. Better still, add one whole egg per 4 oz (100 g) of mixture and pile this into large mushrooms. Cook in a hot oven until the outside is just browning and the inside is still moist. Serve immediately as a savoury at the end of a meal or as a hot starter.

To slice

Slicing smoked salmon is not difficult; only getting practice is. When I was training people I found there are those who can and those who can't slice salmon, a gift easily discerned by watching those same people cut anything else. A man or woman who cuts a crooked slice of bread, or who always manages to crush bread while cutting it, does not understand knives. People like this think that pressure is what cuts and will not let the knife edge do the work. Try it. Hold a knife lightly and instead of pushing the blade through, let the blade slip through the bread as you go back and forth with only the lightest pressure. You'll get a thin, even slice and, unless you can do this, you'll never be able to cut smoked salmon finely and should either find someone else or be resigned to thick slices, which incidentally I find much more delicious than the very thin ones which you have to curl up and fold to get any suggestion of flavour in your mouth.

If you are presented with an unboned side of smoked salmon, this is what you do. First, cut off the fins and remaining bones at the bigger, gill end of the side. Now put the salmon on the edge of a table or draining board, skin side down, and using your fingertip, ease back the skin along the edges. If you can, peel it back under the flesh a little. Now slice off that peeled-back skin, including the soft foundations of the fins, all the way back to the tail. Next you have to attack the bones. Keeping a long, thin knife horizontal, take a thin slice off the highest part of the salmon, starting at the gill and working towards the tail. As you slice the smoked layer away you will, or should, expose the tops of the tiny white bones, which is what you are going to remove. The best tools are an eyebrow tweezer that has ribbed ends or a pair of pliers that have a long thin nose. So as not to tear the flesh, don't pull each bone out by yanking up vertically. Instead, pull gently in the same direction as the bones lie; you will be pulling towards the gill end. Once these are out you can start slicing and there are two ways to do this.

Short slices: In this method, which is the easier of the two, you start slicing about one third of the way along and slice towards the tail. (I *know* Selfridges slice towards the other end, but they are the only people in the world who do). The knife should be only very slightly angled and aimed so that you are cutting in towards the skin. Each time you take another slice you start a slither further back and keep the angle the same and soon you will have a slice that starts at the top, goes through the flesh and ends up at the skin. This is exactly right for as you continue this method you will have no wastage and the flesh close to the skin will be used at the same rate as the rest and not left, as is the case with –

Long slices: You start at the gill end and slice all the way along, with a flat knife trying to get slices that are as wide and long as possible. It is certainly very satisfactory to be able to slice a large salmon in thin tissues that could simply be laid one upon another to form the entire shape again. But this can only be contemplated privately or in catering when you know you can use all the fish. In a shop you tend to get left with the last ¼ in (½ cm) of flesh, which, because you can see the skin through it, looks dark and unappetising. Indeed, if it has been waiting for a customer for some time, it will be dried and possibly rancid.

Storage

Smoked salmon freezes and defrosts extremely well and provided it is allowed to do the latter slowly can be as good as fresh; but, like all other frozen foods you only get out what you put in, and frozen salmon should be as high a quality as possible.

There are now a number of vacuum packs of smoked salmon on the market and they are an excellent way to transport salmon for they do not need refrigerating; however I'm told that refrigeration will extend the life of such salmon even further. Be assiduous in protecting the plastic from puncturing and only accept those that are tightly bound to the fish by vacuum. If there is the slightest looseness anywhere in the packaging or, worse, ballooning, the vacuum has been broken and the fish may be harbouring and nourishing a great number of organisms that may be dangerous *before* you can smell them.

Otherwise a side of smoked salmon will keep for ages in refrigeration if the air is allowed to circulate; ideally it should be hung. Even a cold larder is cold enough to keep smoked salmon good for many weeks before it is cut.

See also tinned salmon, below.

TINNED SALMON

I vividly remember the first time I saw salmon in tins in shops. It was from Russia and it must have been in the early fifties when the Russians were, to us in New Zealand anyway, something rather terrible. For them to be supplying us with luxuries was thought a bit much. Nonetheless it was with great relief that I found we were one of the first families to eat it; and it was wonderful. Later everyone was eating Russian salmon like mad and it seemed less appealing, even though it was only the finest red salmon being imported. Later still, the taste for tinned salmon rose to its pre-war level and cheaper pink salmon flooded the market. Shocked at its easy availability, I stopped eating both colours on the pretext that I was sick of it and never touched it for almost 20 years when I found a Robert Carrier recipe for an Easy Tinned

Salmon Soufflé. I was prepared to laugh – you may still – but it turned out to be excellent. Of course, one had to add a little of this and a little of that; but it remains one of my most basic stand-bys and bringer of some of my greatest compliments, and has the appeal of being all the better for the use of cheaper pink salmon. If you come across little white crystals in your tinned salmon that look like glass, they aren't. They are a harmless chemical called magnesium ammonium phosphate, which is the sort of thing that can occur naturally in man in the tartar film on teeth. You can check that these crystals are not glass by squashing one between a fingernail and a hard surface. Glass would not crush. The substance is also known as struvite and dissolves in the digestive juices of the stomach with no harm to the ingestee.

STURGEON

Traditionally, the sturgeon is 'royal'. The first one taken each season (August to March) is given to the sovereign, and someone did this in 1978 when one braved our polluted waters for long enough to get caught. It's a shark-like migratory fish, living in the sea but going into fresh water to spawn. Found from the Caspian Sea to North America, it grows to well over 20 feet (6½ m) in the Balkans and Russia. Its female roe is caviare, greatest of all the hard roe dishes; its air bladder makes isinglass, an archaic type of gelatine that the Swiss Family Robinson used for windows.

The royal status of sturgeons is both ancient and universal. Throughout Imperial China commoners forbore to eat it, reserving it for the palate of the Celestial Emperor, who then cunningly used it to tempt other parts of his favourites. The Roman Emperor Severus had it served honoured with coronets and serenaded with musicians; Alexandre Dumas suggests doing this, too. It needs razzmatazz, for the firm flesh is difficult to prepare and present tastefully. Strangely, one is counselled to hang it for some days. Then it tastes like veal and is often cooked in exactly the same manner, and served with the same sauces.

We less-than-royal mortals are more likely to see it smoked, but rarely. The flesh is still very firm but tends to crumble, so it benefits from being served with a little excellent oil. I've only eaten it at a West End hotel where their prices gave the impression that our small party was expected to reimburse the establishment for all the newly-completed redecoration! The smoked sturgeon was insensitively inundated with a too-sharp vinaigrette. Voluble displeasure brought new, untouched slithers. With the merest whisper of oil and zephyr of lemon zest it was quite delicious – but not quite as delicious as smoked salmon.

There is a case for using expensive smoked salmon to make exorbitant smoked sturgeon go further. Arranged in rosettes of alternating colour, the pair make a luxurious start to a meal. Fresh dill weed and a delicate cucumber mousse would be better and prettier than parsley with either or both.

TROUT

The trout belongs to the same group of fish as salmon and the many types of trout divide broadly into two groups – plus one type that devilishly spans both. Basically, either trout migrate to and from the sea, or they don't.

The pretty rainbow trout confuses these categorizations by living in fresh water lakes but migrating up their incoming rivers to spawn. It is a native of California but has now been established with enormous success in New Zealand, Chile and Britain. The American brook trout is actually a char, as is their Dolly Varden trout.

The smoked trout you buy in countries where they are taken in the wild and smoked naturally is superb. But I cannot help thinking the creatures we buy here, which are both farm-bred and then artificially coloured and smoke-flavoured, are a wee bit pricey for the pleasure they give. Still, they are an important basic component of many a menu and probably better than avocado and prawns, a mixture of blandness I've never understood. But you have to be very good at coping with tiny bones, and such difficulty can outweigh any pleasure the hard-won flesh might eventually give the victor.

Basic preparation

Smoked trout should always be peeled before serving and it would be churlish to serve anything less than a whole one per person. A little lemon and freshly ground pepper is adequate accompaniment. If you have the time and skill you might like to take the trout off the bone and arrange it in strips with some of the more esoteric salad vegetables; I think raw fennel lightly dressed with oil and lemon excellent with trout. Flavoured mayonnaises go well too; perhaps present a choice of a tomato, fresh herb and horseradish flavours. Alternatively, serve the trout plain but with thin soldiers of brown bread spread with a variety of flavoured butters, which are simply made and keep for ages.

FOIE GRAS

Foie gras is the grossly bloated liver of large breeds of geese or of certain ducks, which have been forcibly fattened with grain to such a degree that the livers rupture with fat, sometimes growing to weigh as much as 3½ lbs (½ kg). It is very cruel, and an expensive process; only 15 per cent of the geese so treated provide a liver that answers the gourmet's specifications. The other 85 per cent are made into mousses and pâtés, but remain pretty expensive all the same.

I've only eaten absolutely fresh foie gras once, and it was superb – rich, unctuous, explosive with flavour. It is unlikely you will do so in Britain, as its importation is prohibited, but I thought you'd like to know. You might be able to buy whole or sliced ones in tins, and those are actually rather good. I have joined the band that regards fattened duck livers as being as good as geese ones as far as eating is concerned; and they are cheaper.

Fattened geese and duck livers are usually thought of as being the specialty of the area around Perigord, home of the black truffle, as indeed they are. But they are also a specialty of the Landes and of Alsace. Until the Second World War foie gras was produced widely along the Danube, as it was popular with middle European jews. Hungary and Czechoslovakia used to export their livers to France and today their industry is increasing again. Poland has joined them and Israel is a major producer.

Fattened geese livers are nothing new, for the Romans and Greeks adored them and the ancient Egyptians seemed to have force-fed their geese with dried figs. It was probably the Romans who brought the idea to Gaul, as they called France.

If you manage to get a fresh goose or duck foie gras, take exceptional care and suspend all you know about cooking liver. Fresh foie gras must not be served pink, unless it is virtually straight from the bird and is to be eaten in its entirety as soon as it is cooked.

Otherwise it is available in a number of states, not all of which are seen in this country, and there are also very strict rules, in France at least, about labelling. If you've ever wondered what all the fuss was about when you have opened a tin of a pâté de foie gras from which you expected a mouthful of delight, you will shortly discover that the content of foie gras was not very high.

Semi-cooked or semi preserved foie gras	This is considered the finest way of keeping livers. They are cooked gently with little extra seasoning in a tightly closed container. The juices which come out during cooking are soaked back into the liver – nothing is lost, nothing gained. Provided the seal is not broken, and the liver has been cooked right through, and it is kept between 0°C and 5°C, it may last 6 to 8 months, but it is not fully sterilized. Not normally available commercially.
Preserved Foie gras	A fancy way of saying tinned whole foie gras. Fully sterilized in the usual way of canning and probably the way it is most seen. It is important that the preserved liver is allowed to mature after processing – it needs 6–8 months at least.
Labelling	When French products are made only with goose liver, they need only say 'Foie Gras'; if they are made from duck they then need to say 'Foie Gras de Canard'.
Natural	This indicates the content of the tin will be foie gras in one or several pieces. If there is a marinade or seasoning, that will be shown on the label.
Block, Lingot, Tombeau, Massif, Terrine, Roll Pâté	Any of these used as adjectives preceding foie gras means a minimum of 75 per cent foie gras with pork, veal or poultry meat added.
Purée, Mousse or Cream	These adjectives indicate a minimum of 75 per cent foie gras, plus pork, veal, or poultry plus eggs, milk, wheat or cornflour up to a maximum of 3 per cent.
Mousse – Foie d'Oie	The trick is to notice that it is foie d'oie not foie gras. It is ordinary goose liver and the mousse need only contain 50 per cent of it. Most foie gras products include truffles, but I'm still not sure they add anything other than expense.
	The purées and mousses are mainly used as pâtés, spread on toast, but are often used in scoops or slices as garnish and should be cold.
	If you are lucky enough to get whole foie gras, it is traditionally served chilled as a first course with an excellent wine – some say the best accompaniment is a chilled sweet Sauterne and certainly something with a hint of fruit and sweetness is good. A Verdelho Madiera or the rare Paolo Cortado sherry would be my other choices.

FRUIT

A lot of tinned or bottled fruits are useful only for inferior fruit salads or for quick meals for children; the combination of sweetening and long cooking in the can changes flavour and texture too much for me. But some are extremely useful as a short cut to making unusual foods, ice creams or baked puddings.

When you want a quick pie filling, look for tins which say 'solid pack'; apples, peaches and cherries are all very good but need much added flavour – sugar, citrus and so on.

Apricots

Strangely, tinned apricots often have far more flavour than fresh. With a little lemon juice, and perhaps some crushed macaroons or amaretti, which are flavoured with apricot kernels, they can make an excellent pie or crumble filling.

Bilberries

Usually found in bottles from Poland, and that sort of country, bilberries grow wild in Britain but are neglected. They are related to the blueberry, but smaller. Use them wherever you see a blueberry mentioned – with waffles, in batters, on ice cream, in ice cream, in soufflés, or as a sauce for soufflés. They may need dressing up with sweet spices, with a little liqueur or citrus juice, and also like a combination with vanilla. Or simply thicken the syrup with cornflour return the fruit and bake between layers of pastry, with thick slices of apple and lots of cinnamon and nutmeg.

Black cherries

Such a bore to do yourself, and the higher-quality tinned ones, ready stoned, are just what you want for filling chocolate cakes, mixing with chestnut purée and whipped cream, or heating in red wine or brandy with bay and a little spice to serve with pork. Puréed and very slightly thickened with arrowroot or cornflour then flavoured with black rum, they make a sensational chilled sauce for profiteroles.

Cranberries

Although some grow in this country they are largely ignored. We rely on imports from the United States, which are very good and not expensive. Fresh or frozen, they last for ages and are an excellent standby in the freezer or refrigerator. A handful in a stuffing for poultry, lamb or fish lends an attractive sharpness, and I've used them to add interest and colour to apple pies and apple sauce.

Cranberry sauces made commercially are generally not bad but much sweeter than they need to be. To make your own, there are several simple rules. First, eschew water and use red or white wine together with some orange juice and a little very finely grated or sliced rind. Next, cook the cranberries only until they just begin to burst. Include some spice, preferably a connamon stick which can be removed, and add sugar *only* after the berries have begun to open or you will toughen the skin. That will give you a sauce so much nicer than anything you can buy.

It is a mistake only to have cranberries with turkey. The home-made sauce is excellent with ham, with duck, with well-flavoured, garlicky sausages, and it is perfectly marvellous with hot or cold tongue.

Gooseberries

They will have lost their colour and much texture but a purée of tinned gooseberries, strained, is the basis of a quick fool especially when given a lift with cinnamon and grated lemon or orange. I never purée fresh gooseberries for a fool, preferring simply to mash them slightly, which gives a far more fascinating result – every mouthful different. The blander tinned ones, and the strange texture of their skins, makes this version less successful, in my experience.

The tinned ones are too sweet to use as the base for fish sauces.

Greengages

Occasionally seen from France. If they are very small ones (and sometimes they are savoury rather than sweet) they are interesting accompaniments to cold hams and other summer meats. Or they make an excellent purée for frozen or cream desserts.

Kumquats

Fragrant, citrus-related fruits, eaten skin and all. They make unexpected garnishes, or fruit salad contents, when used with great discretion; particularly good scattered over or through soft red fruits.

Lychees

Generally as good tinned as fresh, with almost the same texture. Improved by being slightly chilled. If you liquidize a tinful of fruit and strain that, reduce the accompanying sugar-syrup until just 5–6 dessertspoonsful, mix them together and flavour with a little rose-water, you have a show-stopping sorbet, all the better for being rebeaten during freezing and folded into a whipped egg white, which improves the texture. Drained of syrup and sharpened with lemon or lime juice, or soaked in vodka or dry sherry, lychees may be used as an ingredient of stir-fried Chinese dishes or served with roasted duck. But they are superb by themselves, helped perhaps by rose-water, which flavours are almost similar.

Mango

It is only worth buying mangos in tins if they are from India and are of the Alphonso variety – at least, that is so if you wish to use them as is. But for ice creams, fools, sauces and so on, other varieties, where the texture is less important, may be used. This most beguiling of all fruit makes the most bewitching of all drinks, which I call a Moghul Fizz – liquidize some mango, using lime or orange juice to get a light texture, whisk in a very small amount of clear honey. Put into champagne or sparkling wine. This book was commissioned on the night the drink was invented . . .

Morello cherries

Red, and less sweet than black cherries, morellos are thought better by some for inclusion in chocolate cake fillings. They *are* tastier in their sharp way, it is true, and are certainly much better for making pies. Drained of most syrup, added to white wine, heated with spices and slightly thickened with cornflour or arrowroot, they make an attractive sauce for pork or chicken; sharpen with lemon juice at the last moment.

Paw Paw

I'm trying not to be negative in this or any section, but I don't think this works; yet tinned paw paw can add interest to a tropical sort of fruit salad and work better when chilled and in combination with some fresh passion fruit pulp – bottled or tinned passion fruit pulp is universally beastly.

Pineapple

Although a world away from fresh, some tinned pineapple products are most worthwhile when treated with interest and care. I think the yellower, sweeter pineapples from Hawaii and from Malaysia are well worth paying extra for, if asked.

Crushed pineapple, a standby of cooking and eating in Australasia, should be used more here. Drained (or otherwise) it can be used in cakes, in batters to make pancakes or fritters, or thickened with spices and butter to make sauces sweet or savoury. It can be set with gelatine in flans or on cheesecakes, or used in cheesecakes. Pineapple has a special affinity with gin, and drained crushed pineapple mixed with gin makes a very special hot pancake filling; you could even flame gin over the top, too. Butter-fried pineapple rings or chunks make an unusual but popular addition to bacon and eggs but are more likely to be found with baked pork chops, roasted pork or chicken; spread with a little mustard for more flavour interest.

When decorating cakes with pineapple pieces, it is also an idea to drain and marinate them in gin. It adds much flavour and contrasts better with the sweetness of the cake and icing.

Plums

Puréed plums, of any colour, make good bases for fools, ice creams or sauces. Spiked with a little red wine vinegar and mellowed with a little tomato purée, a slightly spicy plum sauce is tremendously good with any sweet meat, fowl or game. It's a sort of instant plum chutney in a way. Use brown sugar if you want it sweeter and include a little ground clove.

At the other end of the meal, even tinned plums blossom for a dash or two of mirabelle *eau de vie* and a slice of ice cream or custard sauce. Tinned plums are good for pies and sponge puddings and crumbles, but remember they are already cooked so keep cooking times to an absolute minimum.

Soft fruits

Most soft fruits do not react well to processing. I cannot understand why anyone would want to buy tinned strawberries or raspberries, which have artificial colour and little resemblence in texture or flavour to the original fruit. Some of the darker berries like loganberries and boysenberries are better. I once slightly thickened the contents of a tin of loganberries and served them as a hot sauce to a hot chocolate soufflé. There was rose-water in one and black rum in other, and it was superb.

White peaches

These are delicious and as few of us have ever eaten one fresh, can be enjoyed just for what they are. Often used as a garnish by the purveyors of *nouvelle cuisine*. I had some on a slice of fresh foie gras but it wasn't enough really to taste, but I thought I'd better include them. Expensive and seasonal, and apparently an appreciated Christmas present.

GLACE FRUITS

These have always been a luxury, but now are very expensive indeed if made in Europe. Because of the current high price of sugar, glacé, crystallized or candied fruits mainly appear as presents at Christmas time but are excellent standbys in your store cupboard. We now import crystallized fruits from South Africa, which are relatively cheap because of lower labour costs, but I don't think much of the quality.

France is one of the better known manufacturers of luxurious sugar-preserved fruits and Apt in the Vaucluse region is one of the oldest centres. It was not until the mid-19th century that glacé fruits were readily available in Britain, when they began regularly to be imported from France. The most popular lines are apricots and mandarins but pears, greengages, figs, pineapple, melon and cherries are quite common. Chestnuts (marrons glacés), ginger and kumquats are rarer and more expensive. The manufacturing process is still barely mechanized. The fruit must be picked before it is fully ripe or it will be too fragile to withstand the processing. Once it is sorted and graded the fruit is generally stored in waxed underground tanks filled with brine. When required the fruit is rinsed, stalked and pitted and then subjected to a process called osmosis, in which all the natural fruit sugars are replaced by sucrose as a result of being soaked in increasingly stronger sugar solutions. Some fruit is then further coated with a sugar solution and lightly baked.

A light deposit of sulphur on such fruit prevents clouding and acts as a further preservative.

Moist, succulent and sweet, glacé fruits are the ultimate snack although explosively laden with calories. But I like to linger rather longer than the few mouthsful needed to demolish, say, a glacé apricot. So I slice them to use as an exquisite topping for fresh fruits – apricots or mandarins on strawberries, *marrons* on raspberries. Of course they are perfectly wonderful with ice creams or with cream, whipped and frozen together. Indeed you can make yourself wickedly ill simply by mixing some sliced glacé fruits into such excessively rich cream cheese as a Mascarpone and don't even bother to freeze it. A hint of rose-water adds the ultimate touch of degeneracy and thus is urged.

GRAIN

Grain is simply the seeds of various types of grass, yet it is largely responsible for man's long climb from primitive carnivore to his modern peak of dietetic sophistication. The switch from meat to eating grain as a primary food signals the change from semi-independent hunting and foraging on a nomadic basis to a settled community existence. Grain needed continuous care. The newly-formed groups who gave it, received, in return, new comfort and security plus a staple that could be stored for use in winter, when there was suddenly free time to explore emerging skills and interests. Meat remained an important part of the diet, of course, but hunting became less crucial to survival and developed as more of a recreation; in any case the mutually dependent and defended groups were also learning to domesticate the animals on which they liked to feast. While man ate grain, the cattle and other animals ate the straw that remained after harvesting. A balance had been struck that became the basis for civilization.

The new reliance on grains began about 10,000 years ago, and subsequently Babylon, Egypt, Greece and the Roman Empire were founded on the cultivation of wheat, barley, rye and oats; in the Far East it was millet and rice, in the Americas, maize. The villages, towns, cities and empires that everywhere arose through the decision to cultivate grain stimulated the cooperation that eventually shot men from the plains to the planets.

Our most perfect natural food?

The leaders of those ancient civilizations had learned by observation or intuition what we know scientifically – that grains supply most of our nutritional needs, and in precisely the proportions required by our intricate metabolism. Even now, five-eights of our teeth are shaped for grinding and crushing, as opposed to the tearing and shredding teeth required by natural meat-eaters. Our saliva contains the specific enzyme needed to begin the perfect digestion of grains and our relatively long intestines are adapted to derive maximum food-value from such a diet. One of the greatest advantages of eating grains is that their high proportion of starches is only slowly broken down into energy-giving sugars, providing a steady and sustaining flow of stimulation. The bran (outer husk) of whole grains is equally vital, contributing vitamins and minerals to the supply of necessary roughage, which keeps the

digestive system healthy and active.
Thus grain is potentially the chief giver of health
and energy. Whole grains supply significantly more
nutrition than crushed grains or whole-grain flours.
For once a grain has been crushed or ground, the
vitamin-rich oils in the germ (see *wheat*) begin to
oxidize and lose food value, eventually becoming
rancid and sometimes dangerous. If you are
determined always to get full food-value from flours,
you would have to grind them yourself and use them
immediately. Many commercial products made of
grain are de-germinated precisely to avoid
oxidization, giving long, trouble-free shelf life at the
expense of nutrition.

Against the grain

Moderation and time should be observed if you
decide to include substantially more whole grains in
your diet. As with a change to pulses (see pages
00-00) as a protein source, the digestive system needs
time to adjust and I recommend you increase your
intake slowly or the accompanying flatulence may
make your company go very much *against* the grain
with others. But your patience will be well rewarded,
for not only should you look and feel brighter, you
will be saving inordinate amounts of money.

Full assimilation

It is worth soaking many kinds of grains before use,
especially wheat and rye. The prime reason is not to
shorten cooking time but to improve flavour and
usefulness to the body. Soaking in water begins the
germination (malting) process, activating a digestive
enzyme similar to that in our mouths. This process
converts starches into sugars – maltose particularly –
making the grain sweeter and tastier and promoting
fuller and more efficient assimilation. Once cooked,
some grains continue to sweeten and improve in
flavour, the result of a broadly similar process.

There can be a serious digestive problem with the
grains that include gluten, which expands to contain
bubbles of gas in bread doughs. Coeliac disease is the
result of an inability to digest the gliadin in gluten.
This malabsorption problem is of relatively recent
discovery, but now there are many books on the
subject – including those that tell you how to cook
without gluten. Gluten-free wheat flour is available
on prescription and some shops stock excellent
substitutes. Ther is also a Coeliac Society to which
you may write at P.O. Box 181, London NW2.

INSIDE A GRAIN   With minor variations, all grains are constructed in the same way. The outer part, a fibrous container, comprises six layers of skin. This is the bran, only recently recognized as being a mineral-rich food as well as an invaluable source of roughage. The innermost bran skin, the aleurone layer, contains important additional protein and fat.

The germ is the embryo of the wheat plant. As it must sustain the early growth of the grain, it can be likened to the yolk of an egg. In wheat, its protein content, 25-33 per cent, is similar to that of dried milk or meat. The germ also contains significant quantities of essential vitamin E.

The endosperm makes up more than four-fifths of the wheat grain. It is mainly starch, which goes to make white flour (when sifted from the bran and germ). In its natural state the endosperm, ground or milled into flour, is a creamy colour. With ageing it slowly turns white. It is in pursuit of ever-more, ever-whiter endosperm ever-faster, that man has made his most remarkable advances in grain breeding; but it is in the treatment of such endosperm with bleaches and other chemical 'improvers' that some people consider excessive and, even, dangerous measures have been taken.

FLOUR MILLING   As you may already be aware, the endosperm is the starchy, major part of any grain. The purpose of milling is to break open a grain to expose the endosperm. Then, once a liquid has been added the interaction with the starch and other components allows you to make a dough, batter or porridge. Man's first attempts at milling crushed the grain rather than shearing or grinding it, giving a very coarse meal contaminated with grit, stones and other foreign matter. After the laborious task of cracking the grain open by pounding one stone upon another, the meal was mixed with water and cooked in the sun. You had to eat the results hot, for once cold they would be as hard as the boulders on which they had been baked.

As refinements were slowly made to the process of the friction of two stones upon each other, crushing became grinding. The domestic hand mills, or querns, still in common use throughout the world have always been tiresome and slow to use, whether employing a circular or up-and-down motion, and made a centralized grinding service impossible. It took enough time and energy to grind your own grain, let alone somebody else's. In Europe, the advent of the windmill changed that dramatically.

New freedom

Considering that wind had long since been harnessed to propel boats and ships, it is strange that the water wheel preceded the windmill by over one thousand years. Water mills originated with the ancient Greeks and were introduced to Europe by the Romans. But historians cannot agree as to who invented the windmill, or where; they are mentioned in 10th and 11th century manuscripts from Persia and soon afterwards were known in Europe. It is possible they developed independently, but either way wind and water-powered mills gave local people an extraordinary new social freedom; freedom to grow either more grain than they needed and sell it for profit or to grow and grind none at all. The control miller quickly became all-powerful as he bought, sold and, most important, stored grain. Mills freed men from the toil of absolute self-sufficiency and the centre of any thriving community had to be a miller and his mill – without them progress was impossible. Without them there simply wasn't the time to progress.

So it continued right up to the late 19th century. Then men perfected both the heavy-cropping Turkey Red strain of wheat and the first-ever, consistent, compressed baker's yeast. Next, the roller mill was introduced from Hungary, and that allowed milling on a scale undreamed of before. In the United Kingdom, once the first roller mill started operating in Glasgow in 1872, the old water and windmills were soon out of business.

Stone grinding

The time-honoured system of grinding grain in a big central mill was based on two huge, circular stones of a special granite, each weighing well over one tonne. The bottom stone is stationary and the top is revolved. Both are corrugated or grooved in such a way that the grain is sheared and the top stone may be raised or lowered to control the fineness of the grinding. The culmination of the movement and the corrugation of the wheels enable grain fed through a hopper at the eye of the upper stone to work itself gradually out to the edge, where it escapes through the apertures which are the ends of the grooves in the bottom stone.

This process, known as stone-grinding, can only produce a 100 per cent wholemeal flour (if whole wheat grains are fed in to it). The heat and pressure generated during the operation serve to distribute the vital wheatgerm and its vitamin E through the endosperm in such a way that they cannot subsequently be separated and this is the great advantage of this system and of this flour.

To get white flour from a stone-ground wholemeal flour you must sift – or bolt – away the bran. It takes time and time has always cost money – thus the rarity and expense of white flour in the past, when only the rich and the clergy could afford it as a matter of course. It would not be considered as white by most people today, as there were always some tiny pieces of bran left. Even after being sifted of its bran to leave a high proportion of endosperm only, this stone-ground white flour would have been more nutritious than today's roller-milled version, for it was in full possession of its share of the vital wheatgerm and wheatgerm oil.

Roller mills

Roller-milling makes flour by gradually breaking down the grain in a series of processes, rather than the single operation of the stone method. First, fluted steel rollers gently crack open the grain. The endosperm is immediately separated and goes off to closer and closer set rollers which reduce it to flour; meanwhile, the bran and wheatgerm go their separate ways to similar processes. White flour made this way clearly cannot have an iota of the vitamin or mineral content of the germ or bran. In the United Kingdom legislation ensures that some of these are replaced; the replacement vitamins are usually synthetic, but not known to be less good for that.

In many countries, roller-milled flour has further indecencies perpetrated upon it in the interests of commerce and at the expense of nutrition; the worst of these is considered to be bleaching, which is specially common in the United Kingdom and United States. Freshly-milled wheat flour is normally a lovely pale cream colour, but will gradually whiten if left for six to nine months during which other natural changes occur which improve its performance in baking. White, very white, flour is what the public has come to demand but having hundreds of thousands of tons of flour sitting about waiting to whiten is not the kind of idea that appeals to big business. In France, where food is second only to God in importance, they have managed to keep what might be called a healthy respect for the cream-coloured flour and no tampering is allowed.

But elsewhere flour is artificially bleached with a variety of highly technical, complex additives. There is no hard evidence to show there is any cumulative harm in these additives but the reverse has by no means been proven either. Increased consumer interest in commercial manufacturing processes has recently lead to the wider availability of both stone-ground wholemeal flour and of unbleached white flour.

BARLEY

Although it was among the earliest grains eaten and cultivated by man, barley is rarely eaten nowadays – until, perhaps, the first, crisp, golden-leaved days of autumn put us in mind of the pleasures of steaming barley-thick meat-soups and pottages. Yet it is much more important than this. Without barley we would not have our fine Scotch whiskies and there would be no Guinness. There would be no malted drinks, no malt flour and no malt extract, all of which are used to a greater extent than can be imagined. And half the world's barley crop feeds livestock, making us dependent on it second-hand, at least.

Hardy and widely grown, barley has little changed over the centuries. It is essentially the same grain that was a staple in China over 4 000 years ago. It was popular with both the nobles and the workers of pharaonic Egypt some 7 000 years ago, and was used in the training diets of the shapely Greek athletes. In Europe it was extremely important as a major bread grain right up to the end of the 18th century: it grew where the fickle wheat would not, and this was vital when most people were too poor to eat any food that had to be imported or transported.

Today, barley is a staple food in much of Eastern Europe and in parts of Africa. Being almost gluten-free, it makes a heavy, moist bread, not at all to the modern palate. Its lumpiness dictated a round, flat form, perfect for use as the absorbent bread platters, or trenchers, that were so economical and filling in primitive and remote cottages where every drop of gravy counted.

Basic forms of barley

Pearl barley is the most common form, and is invaluable for thickening soups and stews as it has a natural affinity for fatty liquids, both in performance and flavour. It is the barley grain, husked, steamed and then polished to give the characteristic rounded shiny appearance. The dark line down one side is a remnant of the husk.

Pot barley, also called scotch barley, has only the indigestible part of the husk removed, so it is extra nutty and nutritious. It is more commonly available in health or wholefood shops.

Flaked barley is lightly-rolled grains, usually of pot barley. This is my favourite for breakfast porridge, soothing, chewy and satisfying. Make it with milk rather than water and sweeten with a natural brown sugar.

Barley meal and barley flour are difficult but not impossible to find. Terms are confused and transposed but generally the coarser meal is made from pot barley and finer flour from pearl barley. Harmony Foods grind pot barley and then sift it to make something between the two. Country dwellers of determination could apply to their local animal foodstuffs dealer and sift the coarse ground barley meal they will find there. The best use for barley flour or meal in breadmaking is as the basis for a sour-dough starter, otherwise simply substitute some for 15 per cent or so of your normal flour or flours, to add a sweet and wholesome flavour.

Barley sugar, twisted and golden, is increasingly hard to find and probably isn't the real thing anyway. It was so called because barley water was used in its manufacture and you would be hard-pressed to find companies prepared to go to such bother nowadays. Basically it was a superior boiled sweet, and saffron gave it its lovely golden colour, as well as a subtle extra flavour.

Barley water: to make this old fashioned treat, put 2 oz (50 g) pearl barley into 1 pint (600 ml) of cold water. Bring to the boil, simmer 15 minutes, drain, then replace with 2 pints (1 litre) boiling water. Simmer until reduced by half. Strain. Sweeten or dilute according to taste, and add extra flavour with lemon, orange or lime juice.

Cooking barley

Barley is always improved by being soaked overnight. And if you like a roasted flavour, first stir your barley in a hot pan with a little vegetable oil until it colours. Do this also to barley flakes. When cooking barley use three parts liquid to one of grain.

I like to use good chicken stock or, failing that, try to put something fatty like a chunk of bacon into the saucepan. Pot barley will take about 45 minutes to cook, pearl barley considerably less.

The flakes can be added to muesli as well as being used to make porridge.

I think barley's most under-rated use is as a fascinating and unusual alternative to rice in pilaffs, something I first came across in Denver, Colorado. Made with either roasted or unroasted barley, such a pilaff is naturally wonderful with fat-rich lamb, mutton and chicken casseroles.

Barley excels with game birds. I like to pack cooked, roasted barley into individual moulds (ramekins will do) and turn them onto the plates just before serving. Then, dribble over all those mixed bird-and-bacon juices. Rich, I know, but I often think much of the best flavour is lost when you pour away the fat from a pan in which, say, a pheasant has been roasting.

Individual quails, pan-roasted with fresh tarragon sprigs and then flamed in brandy, should be perched in hollowed nests of barley pilaff, both for effect and for scrumptiousness. If you wished to add some fun, you might secrete a few peeled grapes at the bottom of each nest to imitate quails' eggs; but the inclusion of real ones, softly boiled then shelled, would be a *coup de table véritable*.

Storing barley

There are no problems in storing barley provided it is protected from heat, light and damp. Common sense, really.

BUCKWHEAT

Cooked and eaten as a cereal grain, buckwheat is actually the fruit of a herbaceous plant related to dock, sorrel and rhubarb. Its pretty pink flower is a great favourite with those devoted to the natural floral arrangement. Because buckwheat thrives in a harsh climate it has been a staple in northern Europe, Asia and Russia for untold centuries. Buckwheat is often called *kasha* but this is incorrect. Kasha is the collective name commonly used in eastern Europe and western Russia for almost any grain-based dish, whether porridge-like or dry and puffed up in the manner of a pilaff; it just happens that such kashas are usually made with buckwheat. Buckwheat has also been an important food in Japan for a very long time and the recent Western interest in the

Zen-based macrobiotic diet has introduced some to its oriental usages; for instance, there is a Japanese buckwheat spaghetti called soba, which may be found in wholefood shops in the UK.

Buckwheat was also popular in western Europe right up until the end of the last century. Now we eat only 10 per cent of what we did a century ago and it is really only popular in northern France and Belgium, where it is known as black wheat *(blé noir)* or saracen wheat *(sarrasin)* as it is thought to have been brought to this part of Europe by returning Crusaders.

It was the Dutch who introduced it to the American continent, when they founded Nieuw Amsterdam in the 17th century; and there it has remained very much in favour. The popular American habit of eating buckwheat cakes (pancakes) with syrup for breakfast is not one of their own ideas – this is exactly what you would have found in the breakfast rooms of the better-off gentlemen of the court of Elizabeth I.

Buckwheat cakes with hot maple syrup were, as a boy, as magical and romantic to me as Roy Rogers, Lois Lane or Lassie were to other kids. Somehow I just knew they would be terrific. I had to wait until I was 17 before I finally tasted the combination, on an American cruise ship, SS *Mariposa*, in Auckland harbour. Until that moment I had been the ship's agent's office boy. From then on I was their slave.

Although I've had many and varied American breakfasts since, and even enjoyed some of their more extraordinary combinations (would you believe blueberry muffins with ice cream and bacon) I always return to where I began. I like about five smallish buckwheat pancakes, preferably leavened with yeast, *hot* maple syrup and butter, two fried eggs with runny centres sunny-side up, and some strips of really crisp, hickory-smoked bacon. Once, in Washington DC, I ate this for breakfast, lunch and dinner – I could happily have gone to meet my Maker.

Basic forms of buckwheat

The small, whole grains are triangular-shaped and reminiscent of the beech nut: the Germans actually call buckwheat 'beech wheat'. The whole grain is mainly used in Russia and Eastern Europe in as many guises and disguises as their politics. Buckwheat can also be bought coarsely-ground, when it is cooked in exactly the same way but with more speed. Both forms are available roasted or unroasted although the first is undoubtedly tastier; you can roast it yourself by stirring over heat in a pan with a little vegetable oil. Buckwheat is not usually soaked before using but there is no reason why it should not be.

The attractively speckled buckwheat flour gives a remarkable flavour to batters and bread doughs and complements such equally assertive flavours as game. In Brittany, buckwheat is the major ingredient of the famed *galette,* a huge, thin, savoury-filled pancake that is the staple of the peasants there – *and* of the cognoscenti of chic crêperies in Paris, London and . . . Brighton. The Russian *blini,* made to accompany caviare, is perhaps the noblest buckwheat pancake of all. But the English, with typical eccentricity, mainly give buckwheat to gamekeepers who feed it to pheasants, with excellent results.

Cooking buckwheat There is one basic way of cooking roasted or unroasted buckwheat. You seal the outside of whole or of coarsely ground buckwheat in a little hot oil, then cover it with water in the proportion of three-to-one. Replace the lid of the saucepan and cook gently until the liquid is absorbed. Made a little moister by the addition of milk or more water, it can be eaten with milk or cream and sugar, or you can fry some sliced onions, garlic and bacon in the pan first to make a sort of pilaff. Both these dishes can be called kasha.

Coarsely-ground buckwheat (groats) roasted and then soaked, makes an interesting addition to crisp biscuits or cakes; the more-finely ground version (not quite a flour) can be used similarly. You only need a few spoonsful in a basic pancake or bread dough to enjoy its warm haunting flavour.

Buckwheat flour has no gluten content, this must always be mixed with wheat flour in yeast-baking.

Storing buckwheat As with all grains you should buy only in quantities that will last no more than a week or two, unless you have perfect cool and dry storage. Once you introduce warmth you induce the reproduction of creepy-crawlies, especially with organic produce which tends not to be treated with insecticides.

CORN In modern English, corn means maize, but it was

once used as a collective noun for all bread-making grains, including wheat, and such usage may sometimes still be heard in unsophisticated areas. Corn is the only grain native to the Americas and was the basis of the extraordinary civilisations of the Mayas, Incas, Aztecs and other almost unknown peoples of Central and South America. The smaller tribal societies of North America also relied upon it and in all parts of the continent it was worshipped.

Probably cultivated for over 7,000 years, it came to Europe only with the successors of Christopher Columbus, the Spanish conquistadores. It spread round the world like wildfire, and was known in China by as early as 1550. It is from here that one of my favourite kinds of corn comes – the Chinese can finger-sized ears of baby corn which make delicious snacks with drinks and are indispensible when making exotic salads or stir-frying eastern-style meals.

Basic forms of corn

There are three types of corn – sweet corn, maize grain and popcorn.

Sweet corn, known as corn on the cob in its natural state, is soft and succulent and eaten as a vegetable rather than as a grain. After picking, it degenerates in goodness and sweetness with breathtaking rapidity; North American Indians teach that you should walk to a cornfield and run back to the pot. Once you have eaten newly-plucked freshly-cooked sweet corn, you may find difficulty in enjoying cobs you have bought frozen, or tinned, or shrink-wrapped in a supermarket.

Sweet corn, fresh and tinned, is very popular in Australia, New Zealand and America. The kernels stripped from the cob are often used in salads, especially when combined with green or red peppers or made into fritters, which are excellent with poultry and de rigueur with proper fried Chicken Maryland. Creamed sweet corn is also used in batters but more usually served as a hot vegetable, and is very good with pork. In Australasia you might be offered it on toast for breakfast; in Europe, though, sweet corn is largely unknown and confused with maize grain. When I, fresh from New Zealand, asked for some corn in a restaurant in Torremolinos, I was told with mixed horror and pity for my background that, in Spain, corn was for animals. Something similar happened to me at a high-class grocer in

Hampton Court where I asked for pumpkin to roast with my Sunday beef. The reply was 'In this country, sir, pumpkin goes *in* beef, not *with* it'.

Maize grain, which is gluten-free, has a tough fibrous outer layer, making it difficult to cook whole. It is better used in the traditional Indian ways, ground to a meal or flour. The coarsest meals are mainly used for fast, non-yeasted breads but also make a delicious addition to wheat bread. It is generally better to use them sparingly in yeasted breads as they tend to produce a crumbly, cake-like texture. This is why the American breads made only of cornmeal are usually eaten by the spoonful straight from the shallow pan in which they are baked – hence the name spoon bread.

Maize meal is the basis of the Mexican staple bread, the tortilla. The maize is first treated with a solution of lime in water and the special meal obtained after grinding is called *masa harina*. It is now marketed by several of the giant US food companies, mainly for American devotees of so-called Tex-Mex food, a mélange of Texan and Mexican cuisine.

Polenta is not a type of corn meal but a dish made with yellow cornmeal; it is so common in northern Italy that the chief ingredient has been given the name of the cooked dish. Any corn meal will make polenta, which is made by boiling meal until very thick, letting it get cold, cutting it into slices and then frying it. It is usually served with fatty gravies and sometimes has small birds baked in it so that all their juices are retained. Once cooked it can also be layered with cheese, herbs, mushrooms, etc., then baked in the oven; a coating of bechamel sauce is a good idea, too.

Mealie-mealie is finely-cut maize with most of the vital bran and germ removed and is an important staple food in Africa. It is cooked into a rather noisome porridge that has the advantage of being warming but there is little else to say for it, considering its importance.

Cornflour and corn meal are gluten-free, light and sweet and especially good for desserts like custards, blancmanges or baked puddings. Substituting cornflour for some of your soft white flour when baking cakes gives excellent results. Mix one part of corn flour to three of wheat flour and keep it aside as a special baking mix. The most important use of cornflour is in the lump-free thickening of sauces.

Although when first added it makes any liquid cloudy, cooking gives a nice clear sauce; thus it is much used in Chinese cooking. Instructions for use are always given on the packet. The white colour of cornflour is artifically induced. Its disadvantage is that cornflour sauces will eventually begin to thin again if cooked for too long.

Hominy is whole dried maize without its yellow hull and was the chief food of the enslaved American negro.

It was usually cooked in water until the white grains were very soft and swollen. Eaten with gravy and meat or with milk and sugar, or simply with salt and butter, it is still a great favourite throughout the southern United States. Cooked hominy can be incorporated into muffins and cakes or fried in lard.

Grits is the name given to coarsely ground dried maize. Yellow grits are made from the whole grain, including the outer hull; white grits are most often served as a mush or porridge, boiled or baked in the oven and, like hominy, leftovers are often incorporated into the rest of the day's baking and cooking.

Popcorn The kernels of this strain of corn have a skin that is under greater tension than the other varieties, hence its propensity to explode dramatically when heated.

Homemade popcorn can be cooked in hundreds of interesting ways, though this form of corn gives less nutrition than the others. Still, it's fun to run up a batch of garlic-and-herb-butter popcorn to serve with some roasted chicken and then watch your guests' amazed faces. They usually can't decide if it is their first course or their pudding (and if it is either what the hell is it doing on the plate now). Popcorn can appear during any part of the meal and between as well – not that you'd think so when confronted with the electric-blue stuff squirted at you in fairgrounds.

So-called Indian corn and Indian popping corn is close to being the original strain of corn grain and easily recognizable by its high proportion of bright red kernels. Although undoubtedly prettier, it is less good at popping than the newer, all-gold strains.

Most maize-grain products are sold de-germinated to extend their shelf life, and this is specially true of corn meal, hominy and grits. If you can find the whole product it is much better in every way but you will need to follow the storage instructions most carefully.

Cooking popcorn	Just in case your popcorn doesn't have instructions for cooking, you cover the bottom of a saucepan with a thin layer of oil (butter burns too easily for this job) and a layer of popcorn. Cover and shake gently over a high flame until you hear one grain pop. Remove from the flame and continue shaking for another minute. Then put back on to the flame. Shake more vigorously until popping stops then quickly turn into a bowl and add the flavouring you've chosen, (for plain salted popcorn simply add butter and salt).

Here are some other ideas from Harmony Foods:

1. Put 1 tablespoon (15 ml) peanut butter (crunchy is best) in a pan with 2 tablespoons (30 ml) butter. Melt together, add salt and mix with the popcorn.

2. Melt 3 heaped tablespoons (45 ml) butter, then add 3 crushed cloves of garlic, chopped parsley and salt.

3. Melt 2-3 tablespoons (30-45 ml) butter and add several good squeezes of lemon juice and then a good pinch of dried parsley, sage, rosemary and thyme. You could call this Scarborough Fair popcorn and serve it to your folksinging friends.

4. To 2 tablespoons (30 ml) melted butter add 1 teaspoon (5 ml) coriander, 1 of cumin and 1 of turmeric. Toss together and add salt to taste.

You could also add lemon juice and garlic to this – or you could cheat and simply reach for the tin of curry powder.

5. For dessert popcorn, melt 2 oz (50 g) butter in a pan with 4 oz (125 g) sugar and grate in the rind of one orange and half a lemon. Cook until it starts to caramellize. Add the juice of two oranges and a lemon. Stir to make a thick, smooth sauce. Add the popcorn and toss until covered. Serve with cream.

Storing corn	Corn should, like any other grain, be treated with special care, for whole corn meal still contains the fragile germ. In some cases you might be able to buy corn products which have been 'stabilized'. Achieved at the expense of a few of its nutrients, this stabilization prevents the germ oil going rancid and is higher in nutrition than products that have been de-germinated.

MILLET	To much of Europe, millet's *raison d'être* is to feed caged birds. But for almost a third of the world – from northern Manchuria to the Sahara and especially in north China, India, Pakistan and North

Africa – it is their staple grain. It is the third most important grain in the world after rice and wheat and is actually a generic term for a variety of small-seeded grains. Sorghum wheat and Kaffir corn are other generic names, the first being used a lot in America, where sorghum syrup is sold as a substitute for cane sugar syrup. The millet we best know in Europe is yellow millet, which has many tiny, spherical kernels on each head.

African millet is usually Kaffir corn and is ground to a meal and cooked into a sort of porridge. It must always be very freshly ground because it goes rancid very quickly indeed. Japan and China use the grain like rice.

All millet has the unique property amongst grains of being alkaline rather than acid, and its blandness makes it an excellent foil for strong flavours and spices. It is blessed with another distinct advantage to the poorer nations – it hydrates astonishingly, so that 1 lb (½ kg) of kernels will easily feed eight people when cooked.

Basic forms

Millet is nearly always eaten whole as the pilaff base for stews, curries and so on. It mixes well with oats for an interesting porridge and in English cooking you are most likely to find it used for a baked pudding like semolina. References to it can be found in the oldest cookbooks; I found one in a manuscript recipe book owned by my greatgreatgreatgreatgreat-greatgrandmother, a Senhouse of Netherhall in Cumberland and grandmother of Fletcher Christian, leader of the *Bounty* mutiny.

Millet flakes are quite common and make simple additions either to porridges or to muesli where their alkalinity is an advantage.

Millet flour is fairly rare but is gluten-free. It is easily made at home if you have a strong liquidizer. The flour itself makes a flat bread and one such product is the national loaf in Ethiopia.

Cooking millet

Millet should first be browned slightly in a very little vegetable oil in a saucepan. In the meantime, put the kettle on and then pour the boiling water onto the pan-roasted millet in the proportion of four-to-one. If you have it, a stock or vegetable water would be even better. For a wetter, softer result you can add a higher proportion of liquid, but this is entirely a matter of personal taste. It will take about 20 minutes over a medium heat for the grains to absorb the water. Toss lightly with a fork then season with salt and a few herbs – even something as simple as fresh parsley, mint and garlic chopped together.

Perhaps the best way of enjoying millet is to cook it in the same liquid as your vegetables or meat to create a main dish or substantial pilaff. This way you keep all the goodness of all the ingredients. And nothing could be simpler, cheaper or better for you. It's no surprise that most such recipes come from Russian peasant cooking. If you really must have meat with a meal, accompany a millet pilaff with a few slices of bacon, or some garlic-laden boiled Polish sausage – perhaps a couple of *mazurska* or some thick slices of *zywieska*.

Plain cooked millet can also be sweetened with sugar or honey and mixed with fresh fruit and chopped nuts for a light delicious pudding. Yoghurt is a good foil for this, but if you are using sharp-tasting fruit then pile on the cream instead.

You can use millet flour as a thickening agent in soups and stews, but I prefer the whole grains to do this for less trouble and more interest.

Storing millet

Treat millet of any type like other grains: keep it cool, dry and dark and buy in small amounts.

OATS

Oats probably originated somewhere in the east and slowly walked their way westwards as a weed. Their hardiness and very high, sustaining fat content appealed to the hardworking and cold inhabitants of the northern regions, and thus it is to the Scots we must give thanks for nurturing them in this country. Like rye or barley bread, oat bread was made where wheat would not grow; but even when bigger crops and better transport made wheat flour more widely available there were many who preferred the way the heavy oat breads lay longer in your stomach, warming and strengthening you as you toiled in mines, fields and highlands.

Basic forms

Oats are bought as whole grains, rough cut (sometimes called groats) medium or fine meal, or as flakes. Grains are best for porridges, groats are best for thickening stews or broths and for oatcakes. Medium oatmeal is the one for mixing with other flours to make scones, bannocks and such; fine oatmeal is best for pancakes, for flouring grilled herrings or making a thin, gruel-type porridge.

Quick-cook grains and flakes have been partly pre-cooked; in the process of husking, oats are steamed, and an extension of this process followed by kiln-drying gives you this time-saving version with only little loss of dietary value. Jumbo oatflakes are rolled whole flakes; all others have been cut into smaller pieces. Oatmeals which are 'steelcut' are considered superior nutritionally as they have not been subjected to any heat during processing.

Cooking oats

When cooking whole or flaked oats for breakfast there is no doubt they are better if allowed to simmer gently overnight. But with the cost of today's fuel this is sadly impractical other than for very special occasions, or unless you have an economical Aga or similar stove of that nature. Best alternative is to soak your oats overnight and then cook as long as is practical in the morning. For a change, roast your oat grains or flakes first. This can be done over low heat in a pan with some oil or in a tray in the oven. They should only just turn colour.

Another way to make porridge overnight is to bring it to the boil with five times its volume of water and then leave it overnight before cooking again for twenty minutes in the morning. Scots may well blanch at the thought but the inclusion of dried fruits such as apricots or peaches adds a great deal of interest and further nutrition. Some say that sliced fresh bananas are good, too – yes, with *hot* porridge!

Be bold with your porridge and mix the same ingredients as go into your muesli – all sorts of other grain flakes, sunflower seeds, dried apple, coconut, chopped nuts, soaked whole grains. Then top it with molasses or treacle, with a choice of unrefined sugars and, of course, plenty of salt. The only food that goes with muesli that I don't like with porridge is yoghurt. You may think otherwise.

In fancy baking for high teas and special occasions, oat flakes have long been used as a sweet addition to scone and cake doughs. To take regular advantage of the rich food value, you can sprinkle flakes over bread dough before baking, sprinkle meal into the greased baking tins or knead some soaked oats into the dough. Other traditional uses include stuffings and sausages. White pudding should include a measure of oatmeal and Cumbrian oyster sausages rely upon it; indeed, where the Manx and

Scandinavians would use oatmeal to flour the humble herring, the English feed it to the aristocratic oyster.

Incidentally, if you always include citrus juice or vitamin C in any meal in which you eat oats, you will get far more of that important iron content into your blood.

Muesli

Where would the wholefood and healthfood trade be without muesli – even though such shops dislike being mentioned in the same sentence. It is muesli that has encouraged most people into their first faltering steps towards better, healthier eating; indeed, for some it is their only step. Invented about the turn of the century by the visionary Swiss Dr Bircher-Benner, it has become enormously popular in the past twenty years – Marks and Spencer even market a muesli-flavoured yoghurt.

Like so many things that are good for you muesli can be a bit of an effort to make, but make it you should for most manufactured mixes are far too expensive. The ideal balance is:

2 tablespoonsful (30 ml) oats (or oats plus some other grain)
1 chopped hazelnut
1 small apple
honey or unrefined sugar
lemon juice
2 tablespoons (30 ml) yoghurt
milk to taste.

Some people prefer to soak their oats overnight in some of the milk or yoghurt, which makes them less chewy. You can experiment endlessly with combinations, so I recommend buying a few of the more serious (and less advertized) varieties for a start and then copying the one you like best. I like Jordans Country Muesli best and love mixing it with their Crunchy with Honey and Almonds and topping that with yoghurt and honey. Whatever fresh fruit there is gets added, even the exotic peach and melon. This company also makes an excellent five-grain muesli base which saves you time but still allows you to add your individual touch. If I had to give up every muesli ingredient but grains and one other, I would keep chopped dried apricots. Their acidity and colour work beautifully with the contrasted flavours and textures of the grain flakes. But above all the key with muesli is to be bold. Start with flakes of oat, wheat, millet. Then add or substitute rye, rice and barley. Now all manner of seeds – pumpkin, sesame, sunflower and roasted poppyseed. Plus hazelnuts and almonds, peanuts and walnuts, then fresh and dried fruits.

Storing oats

Keep your oats calm by keeping them cool, dark and dry and don't go wild and buy in large quantities.

RICE

As well as being the most important grain, rice has the distinction of being probably the single most important food source in the world. It supports the cultures of China, Japan, India, south-west Asia and much of the Middle East. Its origins are in the Far East, and one ancient Sanskrit word for it means 'sustainer of the human race'.

The beauty of whole-grain (or brown) rice is its ideal balance of essential nutrients – carbohydrate, protein, oil, vitamins and minerals – in a soft, digestible bran which allows it to be cooked and eaten as whole kernels, with only the husk removed.

Mainly grown on submerged land, the romantic paddy field, there are as many varieties of rice as there are climates to which it is adapted. Although expected by travellers in Asia, the shocking, violent green of young rice shoots is a surprise when encountered outside Valencia in Spain, in northern Italy or southern France. Louisiana, the Carolinas, Arkansas and California grow great quantities of rice of extremely high quality, and so does Australia. Once it was grown in England, but as an increasing population caused the draining of marshy areas, the rice-fields became more suited to pasture or other grain crops.

Basic forms

Rice is the one grain where the layman can easily identify and enjoy a variety of whole grains, thereby ringing dietary changes with ease. The basic choice is between brown and white, short or long grain.

Brown rice is whole rice, with only the outer husk removed; once the bran has also been removed by milling, you have **white rice,** which is usually polished with a mixture of glucose and talcum. When such naked rice became fashionable amongst the Eastern rich, as white bread did in the West, the masses clamoured for it. Eventually they got it. And ghastly endemic diseases followed, including beri beri and pellagra, caused by deficiencies of thiamin (vitamin B1) and nicotinic acid respectively. Even in brown rice thiamin is fugitive, being quickly leached out into cooking water; up to 30 per cent can be lost even when using the technique which absorbs all the cooking liquid (see page 185).

Slowly the lesson is being learned and whole rice is replacing white rice as a staple food in those countries where rice is often the *only* food available.

Today, in the West, brown and white rices are available in a wide variety, each with flavour affinities or cooking performances peculiar to themselves. The new interest in brown rice has stimulated a remarkable range of imports, from the elegant, pale, true long-grain of Surinam to a variety of shapes and flavours from California.

In general, white **short grain rice** is sweeter and more absorbent than long grain, and more suited to puddings; indeed it is often sold as **pudding rice**. This rule of flavour is not so with brown rice. Enthusiasts who like a bit of a chew recommend Californian short and medium-grain brown rice for all general purposes, sweet or savoury. It is also from California that the astonishing, **naturally-sweet brown rice** comes; I thoroughly recommend you try this in your favourite rice pudding or bread mixtures.

It was to help reduce the terrible toll of vitamin deficiency disease that **par-boiled** or **converted rice** was introduced. The whole brown rice is soaked and then boiled for a short time before husking and milling. This forces thiamin and nicotinic acid into the grain, so that even though it looks white, it has almost the nutritional value of brown grains, thus satisfying the requirements of both society and sense.

Of all the rare and weird specialty rices you can buy there are only two of real importance, to my mind. First is **arborio**, fat, white, short and Italian. It's the only rice for a true risotto made in the northern Italian style, which should be served rather on the wet side and as an unaccompanied first course; **cristallo** is par-boiled arborio.

Second is **basmatti**, aristocratic, perfumed, long and Asian. It is irreplaceable for curries, and the little extra expense is amply repaid by its fragrance and flavour. Brown basmatti rice has proven difficult to import for some reason; so if you see any, snap it up.

There is, among the many rice oddities, one specially grown to do what we pray every other rice won't – stick together. So-called **sticky rice**, glutinous and fascinatingly scented, is specially popular in the north of Thailand in April and May, where it is eaten with sharp, nutty slices of green mango, until the latter start to ripen. Then sticky rice is used to make fluorescent cakes and sweetmeats, flavoured with coconut or jasmine and baked in folded banana leaves.

And then there is **wild rice**, perhaps better called wild price. It's fantastically expensive – and isn't even a rice, but the seed of a tall aquatic grass native to remote parts of North America. Although something similar has been found in a few places in France and Italy it has proven impossible to cultivate, even in its native haunts. So, it must be laboriously harvested from where it chooses to grow on the edges of rivers, lakes and marshes, usually by one man in a canoe, which explains why there is so little for so much. But you see it so often in exotic rice mixtures and in dehydrated prepackaged stuffings and meals in the glittering supermarkets of the United States that I suspect they must have discovered some way of synthesizing the flavour.

The proper way to prepare wild rice is to 'butterfly' it. You simply pour boiling water over the thin brown-green grains, let it cool and drain it off. This is repeated three or even four times until each grain is opened and fluffy.

Rice flakes, like other grain flakes, are the result of a steaming and rolling process; they can be made either from whole or white rice and used for a faster cooking porridge, for baking and for muesli.

Rice flour may be used in bread and cake making but gives a dry, rather flat product. It is better combined with wheat and cornflour mixtures in this context. Otherwise it can be used to set interesting milk and fruit puddings and delicacies, the like of which fragile Victorian women could just manage to absorb at tea time.

Cooking rice

Personally, I *refuse*, to listen to one more person telling me how they cook rice. Everyone thinks they know best. In case you don't, read on, otherwise, skip the next few paragraphs.

Here's how I cook rice of all kinds. First I gently sauté the rice in butter or oil until it is opaque but not browned. My experience is that this is the best way to neutralize any stray starch, talcum, glucose or whatever else might cause stickiness; I *never* wash rice. Then I add some sort of liquid in the proportion of exactly twice the volume of rice, using the same cup or plastic bag or measuring jug, plus salt and a bay leaf or two. This is brought to the boil and simmered at a steady pace with no lid on the pan until the water is level with the rice and a few bubbling holes can be seen. A folded tea towel, clean and dry, is put over the pan and the lid clamped very firmly on. If cooking with electricity I then turn the heat off and put the pan on the edge of the element; if gas, I put it on an asbestos mat over the lowest possible heat. Either way, the rice is left for seven minutes exactly and is then ready. That's it. You may find your saucepan is thicker or your burners are hotter and have to adjust the final timing. Otherwise it is simple, unfussy and easy to do at the last moment, avoiding the horror of soaking, washing rinsing and reheating, all of which reduces or loses altogether what vitamin content there might be. My way conserves the maximum possible.

If you are making an Italian risotto you may like to add slightly more water or stock, to give the authentic moistness. Or if you can be bothered to go to a little trouble the Iranian method is fun, too. Use about one-quarter less water than normal then, when the rice has absorbed all the water and is still a little hard, transfer it to another saucepan in which there are a few spoonsful of water plus an ounce or so (25–50 g) of butter. Put more butter over the top, cover with a cloth and lid as above and let steam over low heat for 15–20 minutes. The rice will then be cooked and separate but have a crisp golden coating on the bottom. They call this *dig* and it is a great honour to be served it.

To cook brown rice I use exactly the same method as above. But I cook it uncovered, and it can take up to 45 minutes. But, white or brown, *you must never, ever, stir rice when it is cooking* for this more than anything else will make the grains sticky.

Rice is easy to keep hot if covered with foil and kept in an oven with a few dabs of butter. But it's better to do it over steam, which is the way to get those really light and fluffy grains that are so maddeningly delicious in good eastern restaurants, especially if they have used basmatti rice. If in spite of all precautions you end up with sticky rice unintentionally, a 15-minute steam should save the day if you have the time. Simply put the rice in a strainer or colander over a saucepan of boiling water, cover with a cloth and a lid and keep over gentle heat. Once you see the grains start to separate – after, say, 10 minutes – you can fork it over gently.

Leftover rice, brown or white, makes an excellent addition to yeast-leavened baking. If it has also been allowed to sour slightly, by being kept at room temperature, it is remarkably good in the heavier 'health' breads favoured by followers of grain and vegetable-based diets. *The Tassajara Bread Book* is good on this type of recipe.

Even in the United States it can be prohibitively expensive to serve a pilaff or stuffing exclusively of wild rice. But used to flavour a rice-based stuffing it is a memorable experience, especially with poultry or game. As the flavour is so strong and pervasive you can mix it with up to two or three times the amount of white or brown rice and it will still be fully appreciated. A sprinkling in a salad of cold chicken mixed with a flavoured mayonnaise is terrific and I once incorporated some into cream with which I decorated a cucumber mould to be served with poached salmon. Another time I topped wild rice with some quickly-cooked chanterelles and morilles and arranged this salad in a scooped-out pumpkin. This rich earthy-tasting mixture was dressed with olive oil and lime juice and the glistening browns against the bright orange receptacle were a wonderful sight, made even better by a ring of poached cucumber crescents, almost transparent and fluorescent. I really think it is better to serve wild rice in such combinations than on its own, whatever your finances; besides it's tiresome to eat solo as it requires major mastication.

Coconut rice: the cooking of Indonesia, Thailand and all south-east Asia is full of fascinating ideas for using rice. One of the simplest you'll come across is coconut rice, made simply by cooking long-grain rice in coconut milk. Fabulous. It can also be flavoured with the addition of a curry leaf and some lemon grass, both of which are available at oriental food shops. But a good squeeze of lemon or lime juice is equally rewarding. It may also be coloured and further flavoured with some yellow turmeric powder. Either way it is very good with curries and other spiced dishes, or simply with cooked chicken.

Pudding rice cooked in coconut milk and sugar is an idea I found on Pitcairn Island. It became a firm (but sticky) favourite of my expedition, especially

when served with a little hot orange, lime or lemon juice. A sprinkle of black rum is wonderful too.
Fried rice, the left-over-standby of many provincial Chinese take-aways rising to greater heights in Indonesia: it's called Nasi Goreng and should be accompanied by or include strips of beef, chillies, prawns and soya sauce, topped with soft-fried eggs, or sliced omelette. They also do it very well in the Indonesian restaurants of Amsterdam. In Thailand fried rice would include pork and the inevitable chopped green coriander leaf.

But there's no great secret to making fried rice. You simply fry cooked rice in hot oil until nice and brown, then stir in all manner of bits and pieces, especially crunchy and colourful goodies like shrimps, bits of bacon, cubes of ham or flakes of fish, sliced up omelette, green or red pepper, onion, chives, herbs, garlic, green ginger, chillies, apple, pineapple, leftover vegetables etc. When well heated through, dish onto a platter and serve accompanied by soya sauce, and an Asian hot sauce or Worcestershire sauce.

All fried rices are strangely improved by the inclusion of cucumber cubes, sticks or slices. But don't ask my why.
Savoury rice: this is what supermarkets and small-town restaurants would call a *pilaff, pilau* or *plov*. There are so many recipes in so many books I won't bore you with any more. For hot or cold buffets I always colour rice with saffron or turmeric and mix it at the last moment with chopped pistachios and some pine kernels that have been gently turned brown in a little oil. Both these nuts are expensive but a little goes a long way and make a considerable and luxurious difference.
Middle Eastern way simply by preparing your favourite stew of meat or poultry and then adding rice for the last half hour of cooking, which will then absorb the liquid. That's all there is to it really. And this is also the basis for the famous Creole Jambalayas.

RYE

A very important bread-making grain in Scandinavia and the USSR, rye can be cultivated in conditions where other grains fail. Once it used to be sown with wheat as a matter of course, so that if the wheat failed there would still be something to harvest. The mixture of wheat and rye which was thus the usual crop was known as maslin and used as it came with little regard to the proportions of each grain; but as this added interest and variety to an otherwise repetitive diet, the inconsistency was probably welcomed. For some genetic reason, wheat and rye never crossed with one another; but now this has been achieved by science and the new grain is called triticale.

Bread-making is by far the most important use of rye and a loaf made with 100 per cent rye flour is dense, dark, nutty and dry, for there is not enough gluten in rye to allow a high absorption of moisture or a good rise. This dark, so-called black bread is often further coloured and flavoured, especially if made with a mixture of rye and wheat flour. Caraway seeds are the most common additives but others are molasses and caramel. One American recipe I saw advocated the use of instant coffee powder.

In many rural areas a dry loaf is actually preferred for its long keeping qualities and ability to sop up gravies, and far more of Europe makes such loaves than I first thought. I best remember sawing chunks off a huge, low, round rye loaf of this type at Hautfort, near Perigord, though it had been bought at a village some distance away. The surprise of finding such a loaf there was somewhat diminished – overwhelmed perhaps – by eating it in the huge kitchen of a magnificently-restored château, accompanied by homemade *foie gras*, local truffles, omelettes of scorzonera flowers and a wine called 'charming fart'. Not, one imagines, such a bread's usual milieu.

It's commonly accepted in Eastern Europe and Russia that dark or light rye bread is better if made by the sour-dough technique. Pumpernickel breads are usually based on rye and other whole grains but the name is loosely applied to a range of breads.

In the past, rye straw was invaluable for thatching, packing and brickmaking. But for all its positive uses, rye was also a potential killer as it is subject to attack by a fungus called ergot. This extraordinary mould is responsible for a disease of the nervous system called St Anthony's Fire, which was specially prevalent during the Middle Ages in northern Europe, but huge epidemics caused by infected rye bread were common before and after this. The last small epidemic in England was in Manchester in 1927, but in France it was seen as late as 1951 in the

aptly-named village, Pont-Saint-Esprit. The medieval epidemics must truly have been frightening, as the uncontrolled dancing, trances and hallucinations could only have been explained as witchcraft. Ergot-infected rye was actually used as a human abortive, its effect presented and disguised with the mumbo-jumbo of black or white magic.
Interestingly, in learning how to control ergot-infestation, we have learned how to turn it to advantage as well. It helps induce labour in difficult or late childbirth and, not surprisingly, is a source of lysergic acid, LSD.

It was ergot problems that lead to rye bread being dropped like hot cakes whenever wheat became a viable alternative. For some, though, old habits die hard and in most towns with a Jewish or Eastern European community you will easily buy rye bread. In the United Kingdom, London, Manchester, Leeds and Edinburgh are good bets. In the United States rye breads of all kinds are a staple of the delicatessens – well, who hasn't heard of salt beef on rye?

Cooking rye

It is unusual (and unrewarding) to serve cooked whole rye by itself but it makes a worthwhile contribution when added to other grains or as a bulker in casseroles. Treat it like wheat berries, by soaking overnight and then cooking for about 1½ hours. Even so you might have to cook the grains on in a soup or casserole to get them really tender.

Basic forms

Rye flakes are good in mixed grain porridges or in muesli. For general use I think they are best when used in or on bread doughs, after soaking and cooking.
Rye flour is quite easy to obtain and only useful for breadmaking. Most countries like a mixture of rye and wheat (say 15 per cent rye to 85 per cent wheat for a light-coloured and tasty loaf) and other than making such a flour mixture you might use rye flour for your sour-dough starter and then use wheat flour for the rest of the dough. I don't know of any other major use of rye flour, other than for the unleavened Scandinavian crispbreads.

Storing rye

Keep all rye products cool, dry and dark and they will store well. Ideally, buy only as much as you can use in a relatively short time. Buying in bulk has distinct disadvantages, especially in summer when the hotter weather encourages the reproduction of all manner of grain pests.

SPROUTING GRAINS AND SEEDS

Without in any way wishing to convert you to wholefood freakiness, I do recommend you consider the inclusion of sprouts of one type or another in your cooking. They are invaluable nutritionally, and also specially welcome as a reliable crunch when you want some texture contrast.

The two most common sprouts found are alfalfa and aduki beans; the former are smaller and the latter are the ones used to excess in mean chinese take-aways. Both should be eaten before there is a tinge of green apparent, for at this stage they both develop bitterness and lose much of their vitamin vitality.

They are best eaten raw or barely cooked. So add them to soups or stews just before serving. You can add them to nutloafs, omelettes, scrambled eggs, stuffings or vegetable purées. Salads are a common place to find them but I really prefer them served hot. Try them tossed in lots of butter with garlic and lemon juice as a vegetable. *Much* nicer.

It's so easy to sprout your own grains I thought I'd tell you how. As well as the alfalfa and aduki, you might also experiment with chick peas, mung beans, whole lentils, peas, soya beans, beans, whole rices, wheat, fenugreek, barley and sesame seeds. But chick peas and fenugreek usually give the fastest results.

This is what you do:
1. Put 2 oz (50 g) of seeds or grains into a jam jar.
2. Cover the seeds with luke-warm water.
3. Tie a piece of muslin or very coarse cotton over the mouth of the jar.
4. Let the seeds absorb the water overnight, adding more water if required as some seeds will more than double their size. Chick peas swell so fast they get jammed, so free them gently.
5. After 8 hours, drain off the excess water and leave the jar to stand.
6. Twice a day rinse the seeds with cold water. Then invert the jar and gently shake it to prevent sprouting roots tangling. Leave for a few minutes to allow water to drain thoroughly, then invert again.
7. When the shoots are three times the length of the seeds but before tiny leaves appear the sprouts are at their peak. If you don't want to eat them immediately,

put them in the refrigerator to inhibit (but not stop) further growth.

TRITICALE

Until quite recently, although wheat and rye almost always grew together, they never crossbred. This was finally achieved scientifically in Sweden in the 1930s, when the resultant cross was called triticale, a combination of the latin names of both grains. Work on further development continues in Mexico City and Manitoba.

The main advantages of this artifically inseminated grain are nutritional, for it seems that triticale can always be relied upon to give a higher yield of protein, amino acid balance and general food value than any wheat strain under the same conditions.

Triticale does have a gluten content higher than rye but lower than wheat. It is also somewhat fragile, so treat triticale lightly and never knead its bread dough other than with feather-light fingers. Otherwise, you can use triticale like other whole grains to add interest and nutrition to pilaffs, porridges, mueslis, breads and biscuits.

WHEAT

Over 90 per cent of the flour consumed in western Europe, the United States and the countries of the old commonwealth is made from wheat. It is without doubt the western world's most important grain, and always has been.

Archeological evidence shows that wheat has been cultivated since about 7 000 BC, which suggests its use for a much longer period. It is a grass of the Triticum family, the true origins of which have never been determined. Recent research has come closer to breeding it back to its very early forms, which will be used to strengthen or create new strains. For nearly 9 000 years man cultivated wheat in exactly the same way, introducing new varieties rarely, and usually by chance. But it was never cheap or plentiful enough to be a universal food; neither would it grow in northerly climates. Until the 19th century wheat products and wheat bread were a status symbol in Europe and America. Then the strain known as Turkey Red was introduced into North America. It began to produce such mammoth crops, so easily, that the wheat farmers of the world all wanted part of this bounty. So did the public, keen to establish their improved social position by eating only wheat bread and forgetting the barley, oat and rye breads of their forefathers. Soon Russia and Australia, too, had developed heavy-cropping wheat strains that were specially suited to breadmaking (the so-called strong wheats). In just a few years the world's wheat growers had to change every agricultural, cropping and manufacturing technique so they could cope with the size of the crop and the demand.

Cooking wheat

Perhaps because wheat is so ancient and universal it is sold in more forms than other grains. Wholewheat grains, known as wheat berries, are not often used domestically, but when soaked overnight and then cooked in water for an hour or two, make a mild and nutty contribution to bread dough, to soups and stews or to mixtures of cooked pulses or rice. If during the final minutes of cooking, you let the water almost boil away, then add milk and let that thicken up, you will have a specially chewy type of porridge that is excellent when flavoured with natural muscovado sugar. Moist, freshly harvested wheat treated like this becomes the traditional English furmenty or fruminity (or dozens of other names), once a most popular dish, which, if you believe Thomas Hardy, was often laced with rum or other liquor and then could lead to the sale of spouse and offspring. With suitable caution against such consequences, it makes a time-honoured accompaniment to venison. The jelly-like result of allowing it to sit and cool is an unusual refreshing summer treat.

Basic forms

Kibbled and cracked wheat are generally considered the same thing in the United Kingdom, but there is a difference, and the latter is also very much confused with *burgul* or *bulghur*. A kibbler is a machine that pricks the whole grains, splitting them into small pieces; cracked wheat is crushed under light pressure. In both cases the object is to split the grain to enable faster cooking, at the same time as preserving the nutritional values of the whole grain. Either can be used like whole grains and I like them soaked, cooked and then sprinkled over or incorporated into bread doughs. This makes a good basis for stuffings, too, far more interesting than pulped-up plastic breadcrumbs.
Burgul or bulghur is known commonly and incorrectly as cracked wheat but is quite different from that above. It's actually a processed food,

probably the world's oldest. Berries of the local wheat in Middle Eastern countries are cooked to a mush which is spread out to dry, sometimes having first been strained. When crisp and dry it is broken down into varied textures. To use it you simply pour twice the quantity of boiling water over it and eat it plain or flavoured when the liquid has been absorbed. It is a delicious alternative to rice, especially wonderful in stuffings, and used throughout the Middle East in highly individual and often exciting ways. Simplest is the salad made with cracked wheat and masses of very finely chopped parley and onion, known as *tabbouleh*; the most esoteric use of our taste is probably *kibbeh*, which is a wheat and raw lamb concoction of great popularity. I thoroughly recommend *A Book of Middle Eastern Food* by Claudia Roden (Penguin) which is packed with ravishing tastes and ideas of all kinds.

Wheat flakes are the result of steamed and softened berries being gently rolled under pressure. They are best used to make a delicious wheat porridge or as a major component of cold-grain breakfasts – the ubiquitous muesli. As with all flaked grains I like also to use them to change the daily flavour of mixed-grain winter porridges, for no matter how good a flavour is, I cannot abide eating or drinking the same thing day after day.

Semolina is probably one of the most widely known but least used wheat products, loved or hated depending on the standard of puddings at your school. It is often, but not always, made from durum wheat and is the boltings of flour – that is to say the hard unground pieces of wheat endosperm that do not pass through the sifter. At least that would have been the case before the roller mill. Now, semolina is simply de-husked wheat that is rollered to a state of coarseness that allows it to perform as expected. Semolina is simply a sort of coarse wheat flour.

Couscous, the national dish of much of north-west Africa is based on a fine semolina which is then rubbed patiently into a very fine flour so that every grain is coated with a film that helps keep them separate during steaming. To me the appeal of couscous lies entirely in the wonderful sauces and stews by which it is accompanied, redolent of cumin and coriander and saffron, glistening with fats and butters, burgeoning with exotic vegetables and meats. Without these it is fairly boring considering the amount of effort and care required to make it. **Wheatgerm and wheat bran** are usually used an additives to bread doughs or sprinkled over other foods. Take great care in the buying and storing of the former; indeed, only buy it if its packaging and provenance are impeccable, or it will be rancid.

Wheat flours

It is thought that there are now over 30 000 varieties of wheat, each with its own local advantages. Today's crop is estimated to be in excess of 300 million tonnes annually, broadly made up of just two types, the strong and soft wheats.

The grain of strong wheat has a relatively higher proportion (13–14 per cent) of gluten-producing protein, essential for bread dough. When water is added to wheat flour, the protein hydrates to form a continuous web of gluten throughout the mixture. The elastic gluten can be expanded by gas (yeast or chemically produced) and, being strong enough to trap that gas, thus causes the mixture to rise. The risen mixture can support both itself and the addition of whole grains, fruits and so on. The grain of strong wheat is frequently red and always long. It flourishes in hot summers and snowy winters, but cannot abide humidity.

Soft wheat grows in more temperate climates and is lower in protein (7–10 per cent) than strong wheat and thus will not give a good rise when leavened with yeast. But it is higher in starch, which contributes to the light foamy texture desirable in cake and scone making, when chemicals are used to give the rise. Soft flours also absorb less moisture, so baked goods with a low-fat content will quickly become stale. All French bread is made with French soft flour, giving the characteristic sweetness and fast staling. As this is not exported you cannot reproduce the flavour of an authentic French loaf in the United Kingdom, as enthusiasts will have discovered; but if you use soft, unbleached white flour and eat the bread almost immediately, you will get close.

Most commercial plain white flour is a mixture of soft and hard wheat blended to produce an average taste and average performance, hence the description 'all-purpose' seen on some packets. A fuller discussion of flour of all types will be found under the section on milling, pages 166–7.

There is one other major strain of wheat – the durum – which, as its name implies, is the hardest and strongest of all. Its special use is in the making of pasta of all kinds and it is suitable for semolina, too.

Wholemeal and 'wheatmeal'

The terms *wholewheat* and *wholemeal* are synonomous and indicate a flour made from the whole grain, with nothing added or taken away.

Much confusion is caused by the term *wheatmeal*, which is *not* a 100 per cent wheat grain flour, much as manufacturers would like to have you believe this. It is what is called an extraction flour and is often also sold as 'farmhouse flour'. Such a packet also tells you it is an 85 or 81 per cent flour which simply means that 15 or 19 per cent of the original grain has been sifted out, giving you a flour that is subsequently lighter in colour than wholemeal and which also gives lighter results in baking. The term wheatmeal is gradually being phased out in the UK to avoid the passing off of this for wholemeal.

Remember, if you are making bread with 100 per cent wholemeal flour the dough should *not* be kneaded, as this increases the deliterious effect of bran on the gluten.

THE DAILY GRIND

The natural result of the awakening of the public to the goodness of grains and the badness of the majority of people who process them on our behalf is an interest in home grinding. Certainly you will get maximum dietary benefit from using freshly-milled flour. And you'll need it! For even the best of the small handmills requires exertion. You must take heed of the technique instructions and set your mill to achieve a coarse grind first and then grind on with a finer setting. If you attempt to grind direct from grain to fine flour, you'll be too exhausted to cook with the result.

Food processors such as the Magimix/Cuisinart can't make flours or meals, but the big strong liquidisers such as that made by Braun are excellent. In the case of the harder wheat and rye grains, crush them lightly first in a mortar, which saves a deal of time and ear-piercing racket. Personally the effort of one method, and the noise of the other, makes me perfectly happy to belong to the 20th century, and able to purchase my needs.

Time to set matters straight, herbs are always leaves and usually green, and everything else is a spice, which includes seeds, fruits, pods, buds, bark, stalks and roots. There are many books which will give the fascinating lore about herbs but I'm sticking mainly to culinary information and include some more unusual items that may puzzle you when you come across them on your delicatessen shelf or in foreign books. Although this section does dip into the world of Islam and the Orient, it is principally concerned with European cooking.

The one golden rule for herbs and spices is to buy as little as possible and store for as short a time as possible. Although convenient, the storage of herbs and spices close to a cooker is rather silly as the heat will hasten their deterioration. Light does too, so although it is very pretty and homely, it's not a good thing to hang sprays of herbs in a warm kitchen. Find somewhere cooler and darker and they will be longer-lasting, better tasting and more rewarding.

Both herbs and spices can be used to make a remarkable number of interesting drinks, hot and cold. The rule is that leaves and flowers are usually infused in boiling water and roots, barks, stalks and so on are usually boiled for a few minutes. The former should always be brewed in a cup with a saucer over the top or in a pottery tea pot; the saucer or lid keep in the essential fumes and keep the drink hotter.

If you don't like the look of leaves in your cooking, and many people don't, then brew some strong liquor from your herbs and use that instead. Commercially, most herb flavours are obtained from essential oils. These are proclaimed as the true flavour of the herbs, pure and unadulterated. And that is the trouble. Being unadulaterated with the vegetable matter and minute trace fragrances, the oils don't reflect the essential flavour of their parent herbs. But obviously it is simpler for commercial interest to add a small amount of oil than to cope with fresh or dried herbs, and once again the customer loses out, having to make do with second best.

Herb vinegars are a wonderful way to utilise fresh bunches of summer herbs and details of how to make a variety of these useful condiments are given on **page 365**. Once you've made them you'll find them perfectly invaluable.

AGAR-AGAR	This is a seaweed, and a vegetarian substitute for animal gelatine. Instructions are usually printed on the packet, which you are most likely to find in health stores. Generally you use about a tablespoon to a ½ pt (300 ml) of boiling water. Required when making a set pudding with fresh pineapple or kiwi fruit, as they contain an enzyme which prevents gelatine setting.
ALFALFA	Very popular seeds for sprouting and with the usual raw, green flavour of sprouts. Can be brewed into a tea.
ALLSPICE Pimenta officinalis	One of my favourite devices for giving a lift to all manner of food, allspice is the dried, unripe berry of a myrtle-related tree discovered in the New World by Christopher Columbus. Its hot spicy smell and taste is similar to a mixture of the sweet spices of the Eastern world – cloves, cinnamon and nutmeg. If your mixed spice is too sweet or has lost its flavour, add some freshly pounded allspice berries. Freshly pounded or ground allspice goes very well in rice stuffings for poultry and lamb and is essential in pork or veal based pâtés, sweet root vegetables like carrots and parsnips; fruit pies and sauces, pickles and curries can also benefit. The whole berries are nice in pot pourris and ground allspice can be used for pomander-rolling mixtures. Sometimes allspice is called Jamaica pepper or the pimento or pimento pepper, but it must not be confused with pimiento, which is a vegetable.
ANGELICA Angelica officinalis	A member of the parsley family, the lovely angelica bush was once a mainstay of herb and flower gardens; its handsome foliage can grow as high as 6 ft (1.8 m) and you can make it into a perennial if you keep its flower spikes cut. Every part of the plant has been used, and the celery-flavoured leaves are still popular as the base for a tisane (herbal tea), sometimes in conjunction with a little juniper berry. The root may also be boiled for a tea, and root or seed-oil flavours both liqueurs and wines. But the best-known use for angelica is in the form of candied stalk and leaf stem for cake decoration. If you have an angelica plant or know where there is one (masses of them grow wild, usually close to rivers where there are rich, moist, shady conditions) try making your own glacé angelica.

Glacé angelica	Cut the selected stalks and stems into lengths of 4–5 in (10–12.5 cm), place them in a glass or crockery dish and pour over a boiling solution in the proportion of 1 pt (600 ml or 20 fl. oz) water to 4 oz (100 g) salt. Cover, leave for 24 hours, drain, peel and wash in cold water. Boil a syrup of 1½ pt (900 ml) water with 1½ lb (700 g) sugar for 10 minutes, add the angelica and simmer for 20 minutes, then remove and drain on a wire rack for 4 days. Reserve all syrup. After draining, reboil syrup and angelica for another 20 minutes, then allow the angelica to cool in the syrup. Drain for another 4 days, sprinkle well with caster sugar and store in airtight containers.
ANGOSTURA BITTERS	Originally a fever cure, these get their bitterness from the inclusion of quinine, but are said also to incorporate tropical spices, citrus and some rum. Of course, most of us know them only for the pink they give to pink gin, but they can be far more useful than this, if used with great discretion.
	Perhaps the most fascinating assistance they give, apart from beefing up a variety of cocktails, is to fruit salads, especially where there is a good proportion of fresh orange. Add it to the sugar syrup early on.
	Angostura bitters are quite good with creamy things and I have found them useful for finishing sauces for fish, for chicken and for pork.
ANISE SEED Pimpinella asisum	Once used to pay taxes and a supposed bringer of good luck when included in wedding cakes. The plant is an annual which grows about 2 ft (60 cm) high overall, a native of Asia Minor and probably one of the oldest known aromatic seeds. It has a sweet, liquorice-like taste with a broad spectrum of uses, from marinades to fruit salads, cakes and pickles, and is very good with cabbage dishes hot or cold, or scattered on bread dough. The tea, made by steeping the seeds in boiling water, is a good digestive after a large meal; but then so is aniseed liqueur – anisette. Anise is the flavouring of all the pastis drinks and these make a simple way to flavour fish dishes and many dried fruits. A discovery of mine is sliced kiwi fruit marinated in Pernod and served with prawns, with a lime-flavoured mayonnaise.
ANNATTO Bixa orellana	This seed gives a flavourless colour similar to that of saffron and is used for such purposes throughout

South America. Here we use it to colour our butter and such cheeses as Red Cheshire and Red Leicester.

ARROWROOT
Maranta arundinacea

The anglicized name comes from the belief that the tree's root was an antidote to the poisons on the arrowheads of the natives of the West Indies. The arrowroot we buy is the finely-ground root of a tree grown in tropical Central America. The industry was the mainstay of income for Christian missions throughout the South Pacific during the last century, and it's still not difficult to find communities who perform the tiring grinding procedure by hand.

I think it's far better as a thickener than either cornflour or flour, giving a cleaner, more translucent look to sauces and gravies without imposing a colour change. It has the additional advantages of making no alteration to taste and being particularly easy to digest. Milk puddings made with arrowroot are very good indeed for invalids and children and can be flavoured to suit the individual.

If your skin is allergic to talcum powder (which is a mineral) you can use arrowroot instead, perhaps slightly tarted-up with a little cinnamon or some other warm spice.

BASIL
Ocium basilicum

To me, the very essence of summer. Once fresh basil starts arriving in my shop, the pungent warm smell seems to attract people from miles away, and it's sold in hours. Actually a native of India and Persia, basil nowadays is specially associated with Italian cooking, but is also important in South-East Asia, Thailand in particular.

Basil's peak of culinary achevement is its simplest use – freshly-chopped on slightly chilled slices of rich, red, knobbly tomatoes; it is an insult to something so regal (to say nothing of the palate) to combine basil with those woolly orange bullets sold as tomatoes in the United Kingdom. Use basil with any tomato dish, hot or cold, including pizza and spaghetti sauces. Although some people wouldn't add herbs to ratatouille, I think a combination of basil and sweet marjoram gives a quintessential element of hot Mediterranean summers to this glorious vegetable mixture. Its peppery sting is surprisingly good with parsnips.

Pesto Genovese is a pounded sauce for pasta containing fresh basil, garlic, pine nuts and cheese but there are many variations including the French *pistou.* I've tried the small glass pots available commercially and although not quite like the freshly-made sauce, they still offer the tang of the fresh herb and I recommend them.

There is also a bush basil which has a smaller habit and leaves, and is rather more like marjoram in flavour. It seems easier to grow if the summer is not hot enough to encourage the full-sized plant. Basil grows well in a sunny window and should always be grown under cover if you only have one or two plants – once they discover basil, birds become besotted with it and can devour a large specimen in days.

BAY
Laurus nobilis

This is the leaf with which Olympic heroes and poets were crowned. I think it indispensable in any red meat dish or the sauce that goes with one; I regard it as the boards of a stage upon which every other flavour must perform. Knowing cooks use 3–4 times the number normally specified in recipes. But one shouldn't forget it has a remarkable flavour itself: try it stuffed under the crackling when you roast pork or under the breast skin of a chicken. Prunes, simmered with bay leaves, red wine, spices and a little brown sugar become the most unctuous accompaniment for game dishes; simmer until there is just enough juice left to cover the fruit, then remove the leaves and whole spices.

When you add a little wine or stock to a roasting dish, add a little bay to pull together the gravy flavours.

As the prime ingredient of a bouquet garni, bay also lends its flavour to many of the great sauces, particularly white ones, and I like to use bay when I am cooking fish; it is essential in all but the most recherché marinades. But perhaps the most interesting way to appreciate the individual perfume of the bay leaf is to use it to flavour rice; use 1 big leaf to 8 oz (225 g or 1 cup) of uncooked rice. Served with both plain or spiced food it adds a truly individual touch (but too strong a flavour can be cloying). Bay-flavoured rice is particularly good when it is to be eaten cold in salads.

Bay-leaf-flavoured custard is an old favourite and very elegant when chilled; get the depth of flavour by simmering several leaves in the milk, removing them and proceeding in the normal way.

Bay rum, beloved of 'gentlemen's hairdressers' is made of bay oil, plus essences of orange and clove,

plus black Jamaican rum.
Powdered bay is very useful in pâté mixtures and
in spaghetti sauces, but generally the leaves are more
reliable. When using them fresh, check the underside
for nasties, as my tree regularly plays host to all
manner of them.

BERGAMOT
Monarda didyma

Also known in 'olde-worlde' gardens as Bee Balm,
because its scarlet flowers are very popular with
honey bees. The crushed leaves give off a citrus-like
fragrance that has unmistakable overtones of the
exotic, and the flowers are very good to eat in salads.
The leaves can be brewed into a tea of sorts and it
was this with which American patriots comforted
themselves after the Boston Tea Party deprived them
of tea from China.
Oil of Bergamot, which flavours Earl Grey tea and
is the main ingredient in the new suntan oils that tan
you faster, has nothing to do with this plant. It
comes from a variety of eastern bitter-orange and is so
named only because its perfume is like that of true
bergamot. The Kumquat liqueur you will know from
holidays in Corfu has somewhat the same flavour,
even though it is only distantly related.

BORAGE
Borage officinalis

The cucumber-like flavour tells you what to do with
it; sprinkle it over salads, use it in sandwiches, layer
it in gelatine moulds, put a sprig in long, cold
summer drinks – especially in Pimms. A salad of
finely sliced borage leaves and fresh strawberry
halves is extraordinary and as good as it is unusual –
very. But if you do not chop or slice it very thinly,
you will be distressed by the hairiness of the leaves;
better to use only the vivid blue flowers.

CAMOMILE
Anthemis nobilis

Although not, as far as I know, used as a flavouring
herb, camomile is one of the most commonly-used
bases for a tisane. The yellow liquid obtained by
steeping or boiling the dried or fresh flowers is a
natural tranquillizer and used extensively as such in
Spain, Italy and Greece. It is also very soothing to
upset stomachs and can help relieve diarrhoea.
Blondes use it to rinse their hair, to which it adds
golden highlights.
One of its oldest uses is as a strewing or treading
herb, grown in the cracks of paving-stones to release
pleasant smells as you saunter through herb and
other gardens. It has the distinction of being a

fighter; the more you tread on it the faster it grows and it has thus become the emblem of humility. If you have space for a lawn but not for lawnmowers, plant camomile and you'll soon have a lovely and practical ground cover – which you can also drink! Vast stretches of the garden party lawns at Buckingham Palace are camomile.

CAPILLAIRE
Adiantum capillus

This rather extraordinary flavour is actually that of the maidenhair fern, and was very popular towards the end of the last century but quite unknown now.

Dorothy Hartley in *Food in England* says it was used to garnish sweet dishes in the same manner parsley is used on savoury ones. The black ribs of the fern when boiled with sugar make a thick aromatic syrup, which was usually improved with orange-flower water and saffron.

Capillaire syrup was mainly used to flavour drinks, and was thought to be a tonic – the sort of thing to take 'on rising in the morning'.

To make your own, stew 2 oz (50 g) freshly-gathered maidenhair fern in water for several hours, strain and boil the liquid with sugar in the usual proportion of 1 lb (450 g) to 1 pt (600 ml or 20 fl oz). When thick, add a good spoonful of orange-flower water and cork or bottle tightly. Miss Hartley suggests the following uses: put a dozen cherries, pounded till their kernels are cracked, into a large glass with crushed ice and a wine glass of capillaire, and top up with iced plain water (soda might be nicer). You will probably never want to make or drink capillaire, but when you come across it in a book you will now know what it is.

CARAWAY SEEDS
Carum carvi

You love or you hate these, the tiny grey sickles of sharp aniseed flavour that populate seed cakes, and some rye breads. They can be rather interesting if they are used in moderation on hot vegetable dishes and cold salads; a few sprinkled on buttery carrots are very nice and they seem to suit coleslaw and beetroot salad very well.

Caraway has a certain affinity with apples, both raw and cooked. The nicest combination for a baked apple pie is to grate half an orange over roughly sliced raw apple and then add brown sugar, butter, nutmeg and few, very few, caraway seeds. A casserole of liver and sliced apple cooked in cider is all the better for a sprinkle of caraway.

The popular Kümmel liqueur relies on these seeds for its flavour and digestive qualities. Aphrodisia, a surprisingly good herb and spice shop in New York's So-Ho district, recommends you to make your own thus: Steep 2 tablespoons caraway seeds and 8 oz (225 g) caster sugar in 16 fl oz (450 ml) of brandy for at least 1 week, shaking vigorously each day. Strain and use. I think you can make this even more interesting by using gin or vodka and by adding some thin slithers of orange peel.

CARDAMOM
Ellettaria
cardamomum

Quite one of the most aromatic spices of all, native of India and introduced to Scandinavia by the Vikings, where it remains the saviour of their otherwise bland food. Cardamom is the spice which gives that elusive extra appeal to good Danish pastries, but can also go into meat balls, marinades, curries and fruit dishes. Crushed cardomom cooked with the syrup you make for a fruit salad, and then strained out, adds a sensationally exotic lift.

Cardamom is one of the most important flavourings of Indian and Middle Eastern sweets and is also used in drinks. A tiny sprinkling over hot coffee at the end of a smart dinner party is often the cause of more comment than the most complicated and original dish.

If you like your curries fragrant rather than hot, add cardamom to your garam masala or curry mixture and go easy on the ginger and chili. Cardamom is also widely used in salamis.

The seeds usually come in their fibrous pod which should be removed; unless you crush the seeds you do not get the full benefit of their fragrance.

White cardamom

From the Middle East and sun dried, it is especially suited to hot drinks.

Green cardamom

Usually from Central America and not as aromatic as the white.

Black cardamom

The least spicy but most common.

Ground cardamom

Although available is not recommended. Cardamom is so expensive you should get every last bit of goodness by crushing your own whole seeds and anyway it loses its strength *very* quickly.

CAROB

This is a substance made from the abundant locust

bean and used as a substitute for chocolate by those who want such a flavour but little of the accompanying fat, calories or caffeine. The pod of the locust bean is cooked and then roasted and ground. The roasting caramellizes the natural sugars of the substance and gives a cocoa-like reddish brown colour. The flavour is definitely *like* chocolate, but with fudgey, caramel overtones. Mainly available in health food stores, carob can be used in cooking as though it were cocoa; to replace chocolate, use a couple of dessertspoons per chocolate square. But remember, because it is naturally sweet it can not substitute for dark or bitter chocolate.

CASSIA Cinnamomum cassia	The bark of the cassia tree is sold as 'Chinese' or 'bastard' cinnamon and it can be used as a substitute for the real thing, but it is stronger and coarser. Cassia buds are sweeter and tangier (like cinnamon and cloves combined) and especially good with cherries; you may well see them specified in recipes for Hungarian cherry soup. The use of cassia precludes that of true cinnamon, and I am indebted to the late Tom Stobart for learning that in a chemist shop cassia is another name for senna pods!
CAYENNE PEPPER Capiscum annum	Cayenne and paprika all come from the basic red pepper or capsicum but different climates produce different degrees of flavour and pungency. This is the *hot* one, sometimes sold simply as red pepper. Named after the area in South America whence it came, it is now widely grown and used in Asia. It gives colour to a garnish but adds bite rather than flavour so should be used very sparingly. Cayenne pepper proper is the ground pod *and* seed and should be a dingy red-brown; brightly-coloured cayenne has been tampered with. I don't approve of very hot food, so prefer hot paprika which is milder and more flavourful. Cayenne pepper and chilli powder are the same thing.
CELERY SEED AND SALT	The seed, when ground in a pepper grinder, can be used as a condiment and is good with fish, soups, tomato, potato salad, eggs, cheese and vegetarian nut dishes. It can add an interesting lift to a marinade if you heat the liquid slightly to stimulate the extrusion of fragrant oils from the seed. But never include the

whole seed in food: the flavour is really rather coarse and you are better off with chopped celery greens or the more subtle flavour of dill weed (even though not quite the same).

Celery salt is a mixture of salt and ground celery seed, much beloved of vegetarians and drinkers of the Bloody Mary. It is common to use too much and this is why many delicate vegetarian dishes all taste the same; but it is nonetheless a very handy helpmate when bland dishes need to be saved from death.

CHERVIL
Anthriscus
cerefolium

Really a delicate parsley, to which family it belongs. Often called French or (in America) gourmet's parsley. The subtle difference is lost on most people and in most dishes. . . . But it sounds good.

CHILLI PEPPER OR POWDER

Also called cayenne pepper and something of which I barely approve. Extremely hot, and used in Indian, Middle Eastern and Mexican cookery. If used in extreme moderation the bite can be interesting, but too much burn negates any delicacy and fragrance that may also be present.

The biggest mistake in using chilli is to imagine it gives authentic taste and tang to a chili dish. It does not. For that you need . . .

CHILI POWDER OR COMPOUND

This is a mixture of ground chilli pepper (cayenne) plus spices, the most important of which is cumin. Without cumin you cannot have real chili or chili con carne. Real chili powder is an interesting mixture which can also be used with great delicacy and to much effect in egg cookery.

When you buy chili to flavour foods check to see it is a mixture, or insist on tasting it. There are some packers who call a powder or compound by the simpler and incorrect name of just 'chili' or, worse, 'chilli'; and there are scoundrels who simply grind hot chilli and call it chili powder which it is not. You have been warned.

Correctly, chilli should mean the pepper and chili (with one 'l') means the compound.

CHIVES
Allium
schoenoprasum

Although billed as the mildest member of the onion family I still doubt the place of the raw onion flavour of any kind in serious or subtle cooking. If you disagree, you'll find yourself using it chopped over chicken soups, on sour cream garnishes, in omelettes and cheese dishes.

But 1 will concede that chives work very well as a relatively subtle onion flavour in a fish stock or cooked into a soup for a few minutes or in a poultry stuffing.

CHRYSAN-THEMUM	You'll come across these petals in a most regal Japanese soup; I recommend you try it for they give a spicy fragrant flavour. One or two flowers infused also make a delicious tea, hot or cold; they can also be added to your usual tea.

CINNAMON
Cinnamon laraceae

The spice for which the New World was discovered. Introduced to Europe in the 15th and 16th centuries from the East, mainly by returning crusaders, it soon became one of our most popular spices. Demand was so high the ruling families knew that if they could find an alternative way to the East Indies, by sailing westwards, they would be rich and secure. Hence Christopher Columbus.

Cinnamon is actually the inner bark of a fragrant type of laurel. Cinnamon sticks are rolls of this soft bark and make wonderful swizzle sticks for coffee or hot wine, for hot chocolate and, surprisingly, for hot tea, a combination which is soothing and delicious. Sticks are important ingredients in curries but should be removed before serving.

Ground cinnamon is multifarious in its usefulness. We occidentals use it specially with fruit and with cakes and pastries; try cinnamon sprinkled on thick, chilled slices of a blood or navel orange – strikingly simple and unbelievably good. The Arabs are rather more voluptuous with it. They also sprinkle it over poultry, with rose or orange-flower water. Egg dishes, sweet or savoury, also go well with this warm, comforting flavour as is seen in the American breakfast combination of cinnamon-coffee cake with eggs and bacon. Rice stuffings for lamb or whole fish benefit from the addition of cinnamon, especially if some ground almonds and a little, very little, sugar is also included.

The best cinnamon is thought to come from Ceylon, and it should be yellowish rather than reddish brown and slightly pliable. A good tree can go on producing for almost two centuries.

CLOVER
BLOSSOMS, RED
Trifolium pratense

Dried or fresh, the honey-like flavour of these flowers makes a delicious tea and can be employed to make sensational but delicate creams and ice creams.

CLOVES
Eugenia
caryophyllata

Two thousand five hundred years ago, Chinese courtiers were obliged to have cloves in their mouths when addressing their Emperor, to sweeten their breath. Our name comes from the French 'clou' meaning nail, for these unopened buds of an evergreen tree from the Moluccas look like shrivelled nails and seem as hard. They are grown commercially in the West Indies and the islands of Madagascar and Zanzibar (or the Malagasy and Mozambique Republics, as they're now mundanely called).

I regularly reach for ground or whole cloves when I'm cooking pork, rubbing some into roasts or incorporating either form in casseroles and pâtés, where I think them most important. With fruit, marinades, spiced biscuits, rich fruit cakes and mulled drinks it always works better in combination with sweeter spices such as cinnamon. I also think that orange has a special affinity with cloves, so in hot cross buns, Christmas puddings and Christmas cakes, I always add extra ground cloves to the mixed spice *and* incorporate grated fresh orange peel. The classic pomander is, of course, an orange covered entirely with cloves.

CORIANDER
SEEDS AND
LEAVES
Coriandrum sativum

The orangey bite of freshly-ground coriander seed is something I'd like to see used more in British cooking. I mix equal quantities of coriander seed, black and white peppercorns for a taste better than either one or both those peppers. In fact I now keep one grinder full of that mixture and one filled just with coriander as it makes an unobtrusive but satisfying flavour change to a huge variety of foods, sweet and savoury. It can be used in rather greater quantities than most spices. I use it with apple in pies and with anything that is remotely citrus-like; it is good on a salad dressed with lemon juice rather than vinegar. Pork goes very well indeed with ground coriander seeds, and this spice is a favourite of mine when making interesting marinades. Coriander is very nice in breads and biscuits, or in custards and is commonly used in sausages in Europe. Peas, carrots, lentils and pumpkin are other vegetables that go well with it.

Coriander is a prime requisite in curry powders and if you decide the commercial one you have bought is rather boring or just plain horrid, you can improve it by adding a generous amount of a mixture of coriander and cumin powder in the proportion of two-to-one. A sterling tip, that one; sometimes you might even reverse the proportions

The green leaves look like flat parsley but are something else entirely, with a bitter and haunting flavour which is endemic (some would say epidemic) in countries as diverse as Thailand, Mexico, Spain, Greece and Cyprus. It is used as a basic flavour or an almost inescapable garnish in the first two former countries where life can be very difficult if you don't like it. I must say I didn't mind it when balanced by, say, a lemony coconut milk which bathed a large steamed fish, but it is aggressive enough to become boring when served too often. I know one man who banned its use in his Bangkok kitchen and immediately lost his entire staff. If you want to try it, look in Greek, Turkish and Middle Eastern shops, for now we import it in vast quantities from Cyprus. Once, I'm told, it was widely used in England; our tastes have certainly become blander.

Again from New York's Aphrodisia (who claim their name is just a name and has no hidden promise), comes this recipe for a flavoured drink you can make at home. They call it Anisette, but I think it is the coriander that gives it elegance. To 16 fl. oz (450 ml) vodka add the following amounts of seeds, all crushed: 2 tablespoons (30 ml) coriander, 1 (15 ml) of fennel and 4 (60 ml) of anise. Mix with sugar to taste – about 4 oz (125 g) is right. Shake well every day for a week, longer if you can bear the tension. Strain well through several layers of muslin. It is lovely chilled as a welcomer on a cold night and an excellent comforter after a good dinner (even better after a bad one).

CREAM OF TARTAR
Tartaric acid

Made from powdered dried grapes it is a basic ingredient of baking powder. The combination of baking soda and tartaric acid together with liquid and heat is what causes the manufacture of gas and the subsequent rising of cake mixtures. If you only have baking soda, you must use something acidic in the mixture, such as sour milk or milk and lemon juice.

Cream of tartar is also used in making sweets.

CUMIN SEED
Cominum cyminu

Together with coriander, the basis of curry mixtures, and one of the most important spices throughout the tropical belt of the world, New and Old alike. Most of ours comes from Malta and Italy.

Cumin works very well with tomatoes in sauces

and goes surprisingly well with seafoods: prawns bathed in a pink sauce of tomato and cumin are wonderful. The Moroccans combine cumin, sweet paprika and tomato which is magical. It is also found on yoghurt and bean dishes. Its special tang goes very well with the bite of chickpeas, cooked whole or made into a purée.

See the coriander section for advice on how to zip up a boring curry powder mixture. Cumin and coriander make a good flavouring for rice salads, and I think that, whereas coriander and clove work extra well when orange is present, cumin reacts well with lemon – and this marriage should always be arranged when possible.

CURRY POWDER

Although really beyond the scope of this book, a few words on curry powder are probably required. The basic ingredients are cumin, coriander, cayenne and turmeric: the first two for flavour, the third for heat and the last for flavour and colour. From then on it's up to you: ginger, cinnamon, cloves, garlic and cardamom can also be included. Fenugreek adds a certain something but is over-used in many commercial mixtures, and responsible for that ghastly sour smell that hangs around cheap Indian restaurants. Green ginger root, the sharp juice obtained by soaking tamarind in hot water, coconut cream or milk, and sliced limes and lemons are also excellent ingredients. There are no rules and the mixed spice mixture which curry is, is so widespread you can have authentic African, Jamaican and Thai curries.

Curry shouldn't be thickened with flour; the use of coconut cream or a tomato and onion paste is usually enough. The latter technique is well worth noting. Fry a lot of chopped onion in oil until it becomes a mush, then stir in the curry powder and cook on until it has released all its odours. Put the meat in, seal it, then add tomato purée or canned tomatoes slowly and the mixture will gradually thicken.

You should always heat curry powder before use; it is almost pointless to add curry powder directly to a stew or casserole in the hope of beefing up a boring curry.

DILL SEED AND WEED
Anethum gravellens

The standby of Scandinavian cookery, but also found, unexpectedly, in Turkey and Greece. The seed, lightly crushed, is sharper and more pungent than dill weed, and can be used in rice dishes and breads, with fish and cucumber. It is used as a condiment in Russia.

The feathery fronds are absolutely wonderful, quite different from anything in the basic English repertoire of flavours. When dried (it is sold as dill tips) it has almost the same flavour as when fresh. It is superb with fish of all kinds, on anything to do with cucumber, yoghurt, vegetables and, surprisingly, with meat. The Turks make delicious stuffed courgettes and aubergines, filled with dill-flavoured mincemeat and cooked in a sauce of tomato and butter. Dill weed is basic to *gravad lax*, the Swedish dish of lightly pickled salmon, and the Swedes also cook their crayfish feasts with festoons of the weed. It goes well as an unexpected flavouring with spinach, particularly in a phyllo-pastry covered spinach pie.

ELDERFLOWERS
Sambicus nigra

Honey-scented elderflowers make the most sensational muscatel-like wine. It improves dramatically with keeping and then serves as both a stunning wine accompanying puddings, and an irreplacable flavouring agent. Classically, elderflower is cooked with gooseberries, but gooseberries ripen just as the flowers fade and you can miss out (Muscatel wine is a good substitute). When cooking gooseberries for a fool one or two heads of rinsed elderflower will be enough to add the required flavour. Goosberry-and-elderflower jam or jelly is particularly recommended.

Cream perfumed by soaking elderflower in it overnight is a lovely surprise with all sorts of summer fruits, strawberries and raspberries included. And by the way, although the recipes for elderflower champagne are terribly easy to make, the result is more a children's drink – very sweet, only slightly fizzy, and probably filled with clouds of dead yeast.

Elderflowers apparently pick up lead easily so should not be gathered beside busy roads. Each flat head should be smelt as it is picked for some have a distinct catty smell which, like all bad things, dominate the rest no matter how much or little you have. You can mix the florets into a cheesecake mixture or stir them into a pancake batter.

ELDERBERRIES

Like elderflowers, these usually find themselves made into wine. Provided you use a recipe that incorporates spices like nutmeg and cloves, you will, after several years of patience, be rewarded with a wine that, in my experience has all the elegance and nobility of a fine Burgundy.

I've never eaten elderberry jam, but believe it to be very good. What I have done is to combine a few elderberries with apple in a baked pie and that was very successful.

FENNEL Foeniculum vulgare	In New Zealand I was constantly chastised as a child for chewing the stalk of both fresh and dried wild fennel. No one knew in Auckland that the fabulous fresh fish hauled out of the harbour would have been even better if cooked with fennel stalks burning under it or fennel fronds in it. I had to get myself to the Mediterranean to find this out and now regard my early habits as the first sign of a natural ability to find good things to eat. Similar in taste to the liquorice-like anise and dill seeds, and somewhat interchangeable, fennel seeds are specially useful in cooking oily fish such as mackerel as they help cut the richness, and they are good in the butters which go with snails. I think the frond and the stalks should be used lavishly: red mullet and other oily fish should be stuffed full and if you have a barbecue, the dried stalks should be put on to the charcoal to smoke and smoulder just before the fish. You can put the sticks to burn under the mesh of a grill-tray, if you do not have a barbecue. Root fennel (F. *vulgare dulce*) is a different animal and quite one of the world's most delicious vegetables; its name in Italian is *finocchio*, which is also a vulgar name for flaunting homosexuals, presumably because both are highly perfumed.
FENUGREEK SEEDS Trigonella foenum graecum	Its name translates as 'greek hay' and there is a distinct hay-like quality. The bitter-sweet taste is used in the curries of southern India and over-used in many commercial powders (*see Curry Powder*). Very little, ground and sprinkled over vegetables, can be rather appealing. In Greece fenugreek seeds are eaten raw or boiled with honey. The seeds are also recommended for sprouting.
FINES HERBS	In contrast to the mixture of herbs in a *bouquet garni*, which should be robust, fines herbes should be a combination of three or more sweet delicate herbs,

such as parsley, tarragon and chervil or chives. They go very well with eggs. The mixture sold as mixed herbs, and used to excess by those who know not how to cook, is much more rugged, often contains sage and is better consigned to the back of the cupboard or, in extremis, to assist an ailing stuffing or sausage mixture.

FIVE SPICES

This is Chinese and has a very strong liquorice flavour made by combining cinnamon, fennel, anise, cloves and pepper. Pork, chicken and duck react well to it.

FOOD COLOURING

Generally, if you can do without food colouring, I think you should. The exceptions are two – children's food and absolute disaster. I suspect many people rely on colouring to cover overcooking, especially where cucumber-based food is concerned. Most colourings are very artificial and contain ingredients about which the long-term effect on the human system are totally unknown. Every year a different yellow or green, or red or blue is suspected and this is enough reason not to use colouring for children's food and drink on a *regular* basis. For fun, and from time to time, should be the rule.

In Medieval times banquets and even quite ordinary food had to be brightly coloured. Sandalwood made food red, saffron made it yellow and spinach made it green. It was gilded with egg and gold leaf, silvered with silver and most spectacular it must have been. For very special occasions I think such presentation is worthwhile and a few years ago I experimented to find out how one could recreate coloured pastry without having to find sandalwood and so on. It turned out to be frightfully easy. Once you have made your pie, you simply paint on it with undiluted food colouring of which there is now a vast range. Once it has dried, you cover it with the usual egg glaze, let that dry and bake away. Lighter colours are fugitive so if you are using light greens and yellows, only glaze for the last few minutes.

The simplest stripes look good; try diagonal stripes of bright green and saffron yellow on, say, a chicken, lettuce and cucumber pie.

Artists can really go to town. At a recent wedding I cooked a ten-course banquet for 60 people in evening dress (them, not me). The *pièces de resistances* were hot game pies, gilded and decorated and painted. One of the guests was a fairly well-known artist from Paris, so she came to the kitchen and made each pie crust into her own brand of picture. A sensation. Another time I made a fresh peach and rose geranium pie for Glyndebourne. I decorated the top (over-decorated some might say) with roses, leaves and vines of pastry and painted them carefully, leaving the crust its natural colour and only glazing the flowers and foliage. Others on the Glyndebourne lawn came to take photographs and it is still mentioned with awe. It is far more fun for a child to have their name or portrait on a pie than to be presented with blue, yellow and green striped parfaits. A damn sight less trouble, too.

One of the most commonly used colourings is caramel or gravy browning, but good cooking technique should make this unnecessary. Use minimal flour and make sure your meat is very well browned before adding liquid. Commercial gravy browning is the result of an extraordinary process that incorporates ammonia and some authorities recommend it should not be used. It is simpler to brown some sugar, dilute it with water and keep that bottled until you wish to use it.

GARLIC
Allium sativum

Garlic, like the onion, was the chief nourisher of the slaves who built the Pyramids and the common food of Roman labourer and legionary. Slowly it is becoming more acceptable in the United Kingdom and can be used with more foods than you could imagine. All meats do better with garlic and all birds should be rubbed over with a cut clove whatever else you are going to do with them: duck à l'orange is far better when the crisp skin has the tang of garlic. When frying garlic, though, beware of browning it too much for this gives a bitter flavour.

Some of the stars of the new styles of French cooking use cloves of garlic whole, still in their skins. Try this in casseroles, soups and stuffings. The flavour is mellowed somehow, and to slip the softened clove out of its skin and slowly eat it is absolute bliss.

The simplest use of garlic is to flavour butter, melted or otherwise. I also usually add lemon juice and chopped parsley and this is wonderful with hot cobs of sweet corn, as a dip for artichoke, with fresh asparagus and with broad beans. Hot vinaigrette sauce with garlic and parsley is a specially good idea with simple salads of hot or cold pulses, potatoes or mixed vegetables. If you make your garlic butter too strong, melt and cook it a little and that will reduce the harshness.

Once you get the idea there's no limit to what you can do . . . I even use garlic with fresh salmon.

If you are saddled with someone who says they loathe garlic, use it anyway and simply say it is 'a secret ingredient from Turkey (or Brazil) . . .' It's astonishing how many people do not recognize garlic when it is used with sublety.

Wild garlic, which brightens up many a corner of an English wood, is perfectly usable – the green tops sliced finely make an interesting addition to salads.

Credited with amazing medical powers, garlic seems to be accepted as good for the blood and strengthening to the throat, so is beloved by opera singers. It keeps witches and devils away, too.

The dried minced garlic and garlic powder never quite work in my opinion, usually giving an unwelcome bitterness.

Garlic salt

Is useful for final hints of flavour but you must remember it is largely salt – you'd be amazed at the number of people who don't. Make your own, if you like, by mixing three or four parts salt to one of garlic powder and use it to flavour mashed potatoes, gravies or seasoned flour.

GERANIUM LEAVES

Scented geraniums usually have rather small leaves and these have many uses in the kitchen for someone who likes exotic but traditional effects without fuss.

My favourite by a long shot is the rose geranium (*Pelargonium graveolens* and *Pelargonium capitatum*). The musky rose flavour of the leaves has dozens of uses, the oldest of which is to flavour plain or chocolate sponges. Spread the leaves over the base of the baking pan before you add the uncooked mixture. A little rose-water in the icing completes this transformation of a basic cake into something very special. Rose geranium leaves can be left in caster sugar and after a week you'll have a scented sugar that is good on soft fruit or in baking, far more interesting than vanilla sugar.

I like to chop a few rose geranium leaves into soft fruit salads just before serving, and when pressed onto the side of pats of cream cheese or unpotted

Petit Suisse and left overnight, they make a wonderful accompaniment to raspberries in particular.

Orange-, lemon-, mint-, nutmeg-, apple- and coconut-scented geranium can be used too.

GINGER *Zingiber officinale*	Grown all round the world, ginger is one of the spices that is very different dried from when it is fresh. Indeed, whereas many herbs are used dry *and* fresh, it is rare for spices to be so used. Fresh ginger is now more easily available in the United Kingdom and is well worth exploring. Peeled and sliced thinly, the combination of pungency and perfume is fabulous with stewed rhubarb, wonderful with beef, excellent with chicken and almost indispensable with fish of all kinds, particularly when poached. Always use a little more than you think for the pungency soon cooks out. I chop ginger root and squeeze it through a garlic press and often use this juice to refresh the flavour of any sauce just prior to serving. This green juice can also be put on the table for people to use as they wish. Use a garlic press to extract juice when the ginger is too fibrous to use in slices, or to chop. Ginger root keeps very well in the bottom of the refrigerator, although it might dehydrate a little. I've read you can bury it in moist earth and keep it for ages by watering occasionally. You simply dig it up when you want some, and replace the unused piece afterwards.

Dried ginger root and ground ginger have more fire but less fragrance, and I don't use dried ginger very much as it often seems to add a dimension that is medicinal rather than culinary. But of course it is *de rigueur* in cake making and then I like it enormously. Gingerbread can be many things – from a rich treacly dark cake to the thin, almost crisp, Grasmere gingerbread still only made in the village of that name in the Lake District.

Preserved ginger is dealt with in more detail elsewhere and can be used in ways that its sweetness would seem to belie. Elizabeth David recommends its use in white dough to make ginger tea breads, and it certainly goes well with ice cream of several flavours – vanilla, chocolate and coffee for example. The syrup in which it is preserved is very useful and far more elegant an accompaniment to chilled melon than the awful eye-watering dust of sugar and ground ginger usually served.

Ideally, use fresh ginger root wherever you have used dried or ground ginger before and you'll discover a world of subtlety that makes the simplest and most familiar dishes different again. It is very good with many vegetables, especially green beans. If you have made some nice stock, cook it for 5 minutes with matchsticks of ginger plus four or five other contrasted vegetables – cucumber, green pepper, celery, carrot, radish and so on and you'll have an elegant oriental soup.

To put an authentic Oriental flavour into Chinese, Thai or other dishes add chopped green ginger and garlic in equal quantities, a few minutes before serving.

Although specially associated with Eastern food, whence it originated, the best ginger comes from Jamaica.

GRAINS OF PARADISE
Ampelopsis mallaquetta

Often called for in older recipes but I've never seen it in shops. It is apparently a fairly strong sharp flavour and the best substitute is a good quantity of cardamom or black pepper or a judicious mixture of both. If you know anyone or any place associated with voodoo you might be able to put your hands on this spice, for it is integral to such charms and love potions.

GARAM MASALA
(sometimes guaram masala)

This is sweeter and more perfumed than most curry powder, usually having no turmeric and little chilli. It is bought in India as the basis for curry-spice mixtures, thus can be added to curry powders to give a more aromatic flavour without increasing bite. Mace, cinnamon and nutmeg often play a large part in its make-up. For a very gentle and elegant curry use only garam masala and slices of green ginger as the flavourings. Garam masala can also be used to finish your curries – simply sprinkle a little over the top of each serving for extra flavour and great fragrance. The difference is startlingly good.

GUM ARABIC
Acacia arabica

This natural, edible gum has virtually no scent or flavour but is used as a fixative and binding agent in scented foods and beads, as below.

If you are sybaritic enough to want scents wherever you go, you simply mix 1 part (a tablespoon, perhaps) of powdered gum arabic to 3 parts rose-water, almond oil, vanilla extract or something equally aromatic. Mix until a thick paste forms, then use your palms to roll small beads which are then left to harden overnight. They can be threaded and worn close to the skin or carried in a warm pocket from whence they will dispense their headiness. A few drops of your favourite commercial scent can also be added and you can experiment with powdered spice mixtures. To crystallize flower petals, mix 1 part gum arabic with 3 parts rose-water, brush then all over with this solution, sprinkle with caster sugar, and dry on a rack in a dry, warm place.

HIBISCUS
FLOWERS
Hibiscus
abelmoschus

Drinks are made from the red hibiscus flower throughout the Far East, in Africa, the Caribbean and Latin America. The tea, sweetened with honey, is delicious served iced. Made very strong it can be used to give food a lovely red colour and a tart, fruity taste.

HORSERADISH

This habitué of English railway cuttings is used more as a condiment than a flavouring but once you start to experiment it has many uses. Of course, when freshly grated, the root is very hot, the fumes alone making your eyes water and nose run. Thus I'm not too fond of it in its common guise – freshly grated and mixed with vinegar or a little milk to accompany roast beef – as it seems to overwhelm the meat's flavour. I recommend you look out for packets of imported horseradish from Germany or Sweden. They may be mixed with milk or cream and make a far nicer sauce. The best way to use prepared horseradish cold is to fold a little into whipped cream and then leave it for some hours for the flavours to mix. This is rather good with fish, especially smoked fish like eel or mackerel. Or, you simply buy a tube of *pepparots visp*, which is a preparation of horseradish and cream the Swedes use to smear on thin slices of reindeer meat. Next time you serve cold meats, make a very gentle horseradish and cream sauce and just see how good it is. Once you get used to using it with discretion try it in seafood sauces, hot or cold; in the former some of the heat will cook out, making it more delicate and hard to discern. I first ate horseradish with fish at the Red Fox Inn in Middlesburg Va, said to be the first 'pub' on the United States, East Coast. If not for the iced water, the huge portions and low prices, the low ceilings and panelling might have created an atmosphere just like an English Inn. But I wouldn't have been served split Pacific prawns with horseradish cream sauce in the Thames Valley, I bet.

If prepared with a very light hand, horseradish and cream sauce can be served very succesfully with grilled salmon.

HONEYSUCKLE FLOWERS Lonicera caprifolium	The woodbine's heady perfume can be captured and used to flavour creams and syrups, including ice cream (see *Flower waters*). Dried honeysuckle can usually be bought in Chinese food shops.
IRISH MOSS Chondrus crispus	Also known as carrageen, this seaweed-based product is very good for you, and is used to set liquids in the same way as *Agar-agar*.
JUNIPER BERRIES Juniperus comminis	Their ancient reputation as an appetite stimulant is probably what made the English and Dutch flavour raw spirits with the berry, thus giving us gin. The unique flavour of juniper – half bitter, half perfume – is very important in marinades, especially for game or when you want to add a gamey quality to anything. Pig's liver, usually too strong to eat by itself, becomes very good indeed if soaked overnight in milk and then marinaded in white wine with juniper berries and baked whole. The berries can help make rabbit taste like hare and lamb like mutton (although I'd rather have the flavour of those untampered with). Better to use the berry to complement the natural strong flavours of venison etc. The juniper-based flavour of gin is not used a lot in cooking, possibly because it is fairly fragile. But if it is strengthened with crushed juniper berries you get some delicious results. Gin and pineapple have an astonishing affinity, which is very appealing when hot. A layer of thinly sliced fresh pineapple doused in gin should sit for several hours, and then be cooked beneath a soufflé flavoured strongly with Galliano liqueur. To call it smashing is only to describe the effect; the flavour is *wonderful*.
LAVENDER Lavendula officinalis	I use lavender quite as much as I do rosemary. It has an extra, musky perfume that is quite addictive. The spikes and leaves can replace rosemary in almost any recipe, especially with fish and veal. Lavender and carrot soup is very special, and you can use the flowers or the spikes. Lightly, lightly is the rule and perhaps one of the best ways to use lavender is to

incorporate it in your favourite sweet herb mix; it comes as a surprise to many that it is often included in that delicious mixture Herbes de Provence.

Lavender flowers and rose-water mixed into cream cheese make a most elegant chilled cream pudding for hot summer evenings.

LEMON BALM
Melissa officionalis

Regarded as a weed by many for it is even more prolific than the proverbial pet rabbit. But that's a good thing, for then you can use it in greater quantities; it is one of the greatest bath perfumers. Strew great bunches in your bath while it is running and you'll be rewarded with a heavenly smell that would normally cost an astronomical price. It makes delicious tea, too. But otherwise, like so many herbs, its very smell and flavour dictate its use. Use it instead of, or in tandem with, lemon: in stuffings for poultry or fish, finely sliced in salads (very good) and to add a tang of taste and colour to fruit salads.

LIQUORICE ROOT
Glycrriza glabra

A natural sweetener that contains no sugar, it can be used to stir drinks or made into a sweetening brew by boiling in water. Chewing this instead of sweets is said to have helped many give up smoking, but it's also said to be an infallible aphrodisiac, specially for women.

LOCUST BEANS

see CAROB

LOVAGE
Levisticum officinalis

Looking like a huge celery and having something of the flavour, all parts of the lovage plant can be used. Mainly it is added to soups and stews. In the West Country they make a cordial with it which, mixed with brandy, is said to be the best soother of upset stomachs there is. You can make your own simply by steeping the root in brandy. It's supposed to be very good in baths, too (the leaf I presume).

MACE
Myristica fragrans

The outer covering of the nutmeg kernel and altogether more elegant. Mace is essential in fruit cookery and in pork pâtés, in chocolate dishes and with vegetables. Use it as an alternative to nutmeg, or as a way to add individuality to any spice mixtures. It is extra good in a crumble topping over rhubarb or apple. Some say it has a special affinity with the cherry, and a dusting is good with hot shellfish sauces. Mace, in whole blades or ground, should be a very pale yellow-ochre – the paler the better.

MAIDENHAIR	see CAPILLAIRE

MAHLAB

These are cherry-stone kernels and can be bitter or sweet. Available in this country in Greek stores (and probably Turkish and Middle Eastern ones, too) it gives a great density of almond/cherry flavour, and is a standby of Turkish Delight. Russians use it to make cherry *kissel* and the Greeks flavour their large Easter loaves – *Tsourekia* – with it.

MARIGOLD
Calendula officinalis

Not commonly used nowadays but the dried petals are recommended as an interesting alternative to saffron for colouring stews and casseroles, soups, breads and buns. The slight flavour can be rather exciting with poultry dishes and the fresh petals make an excellent addition to mixed salads.

Marigold flowers should be dried fast rather than slow – do it in a low to middling oven. To use them either grind the dried petals and use the powder, or brew a few petals in hot milk or water and use that.

If you are a butter or cheesemaker, marigold was the original colouring before *Annato* began to be imported. It can still add life to cream or cottage cheeses.

MARJORAM
Origanum majorana

Closely related to *Oreganum* sweet or knotted marjoram can be used in exactly the same way – with grills, tomatoes, poultry and fish. The flavour is reminiscent of thyme, but warmer, slightly spicy and definitely sweet. Although an important part of flavouring strong vegetable dishes such as ratatouille, I don't think it works with red meats like beef or game. Instead, I use it when making smoked mackerel pâté, where it seems to complement the flavours perfectly, possibly helped by the inclusion of tomato purée. It is quite fugitive and should only be added to hot dishes shortly before serving. Wild marjoram is usually the much stronger pot marjoram, and when this is grown in dry sunny places it becomes oregano. The Greek *riganis* is also wild marjoram but may be other species too.

MASTIC, GUM
Pistacia lentiscus

Another slightly liquorice-flavoured substance but with the resinous overtones you would expect from a natural gum from a tree; the precise tree is the lentisk, a type of Pistacia. The flavour is fascinating when used in moderation – it is amazing in rice pudding. And it is also used in cakes and breads.

Although related to the flavours of ouzo and retsina wine, mastic is a different substance. The Greek island of Chios makes a rather special liqueur called mastica, flavoured with the gum from their variety of lentisk, which is unique to them; the Turks use mastic to flavour their fire water – *raki*.

MINT

The large family of flavoured mints provides a simple and accessible way to start experimenting with herbs and herb teas. Any decent plant nursery will have a variety of them, most of which can be used for culinary purposes.

The two best known varieties are *spearmint (Menta spicata)* and *peppermint (Menta peperita)*. Spearmint is mellower, usually has a green stalk and is the better known form in the United Kingdom. Peppermint, thought to be a hybrid, has a definite extra fizzle on the tongue, has a reddish stalk (the darker the better) and is the proper one to use to make a good mint tea. Either can be used in basic cooking, but peppermint is less usual.

I loathe the idea of mint sauce in any form; the idea of dousing sweet lamb meat in sugar and vinegar is appalling. I even doubt its correctness with mutton. But stuff lamb with sprigs of mint, roast it on a bed of mint, and serve it with a spoonful of the juices you have pressed from that bed and you have something quite superlative. This works sensationally with chicken too, and cold minted chicken is the most marvellous picnic food.

These basic mints tend easily to overpower a salad, I find, so only add them at the very last minute and in whole leaves (cutting or chopping leads quickly to bitterness).

Other mint flavours include pineapple, lemon, orange, apple and champagne. These smaller, whole leaves are perfect for salads, for decorating or for perfuming cakes and fruit dishes (see *Geraniums*). Eau-de-cologne mint is quite pungent and needs to be used with great discretion but is wonderful in summer salads and drinks.

Dried mint works rather well in grain-based stuffings and when added to the sweeter Eastern combinations that also include currants, dried fruits and nuts, makes its own tantalizing original contribution.

Mint teas, the subsistence drink of millions of Arabs in tea shops, are also beloved of the French, the Italians, the Greeks, the Austrians – they must be the most popular of all tisanes – and can be made in many ways. The Moroccans make it by plunging stalks of peppermint into a pot of brewed gunpowder green tea, and very nice it is, too; in Egypt they simply brew up with fresh bunches of leaves. But in all cases they sweeten it rather too dramatically for my taste. Like them, you can use whole bunches, leaves or chopped leaves on their own, or you can combine mint with any other black or green tea. You can use them fresh or dried. It is always refreshing and enormously soothing.

Mint is used in cold drinks, too – in the famed mint julep of the southern United States, or in a wonderful Pimms, which is doubly good and dangerous if made with champagne rather than lemonade.

Pennyroyal, a member of the mint family, has extra dimensions of flavour that I recommend. It also grows wild, even more of a recommendation.

MIXED SPICE

Although generally a mixture of cinnamon, nutmeg and cloves or allspice, a really decent mixed spice can include far more than that, so don't be afraid of experimenting to get a really good spicy taste rather than just a sweet and aromatic note. Dill and fennel seeds give a liquorice flavour, which is good in conjunction with clove overtones. Coriander and cumin both give warmth and can be added together or individually. Ginger adds bite as well as flavour. Cassia serves to heighten the cinnamon taste. Fenugreek can also be used, and Elizabeth David adds pepper to her spice mixture (and if she says it's all right it must be). Finally, mace adds elegance, and cardamom an unmistakeable touch of the exotic (but can easily overpower, so be careful).

MONOSODIUM GLUTAMATE

Perhaps the most reviled flavouring additive of all. But it does have an important role to play if used with responsibility. Both salt and monosodium glutamate work in the same way to stimulate our taste buds – neither 'brings out the flavour of the food', they stimulate *us* to taste more of what is there. Because we are all different, we all need different quantities of salt or MSG to get broadly the same results in our mouths. The problem is that salt has a flavour of its own and the more you use, the more it begins to dominate; it can also be addictive and when taken in large quantities is thought to contribute to some heart diseases.

MSG is virtually tasteless and you can use masses of it without it being intrusive. This is why it is so widely used commercially, for massive injections of MSG can give apparent flavour to the weakest mixtures – the huge quantities of MSG stimulate our tastebuds into a veritable spasm of sensitivity. It can thus reduce the cost of food by making the flavouring ingredients go far further; unfortunately it is often the manufacturers who go too far.

The use of comparatively huge amounts of MSG to super-excite our taste buds when there is little intrinsic flavour in food is what gives rise to the so-called Chinese restaurant syndrome. Diners at Chinese restaurants often start with a delicate soup – in fact this is thin rather than delicate and any apparent flavour is achieved by lots of MSG – which, going straight into an empty stomach, can cause giddiness and other side-effects. The cure is simple: don't eat soup in a Chinese restaurant if your stomach is totally empty. MSG is in no way the bogey-man fanatics make it out to be and, like everything else, has its place when used properly.

MUSTARD

There are three types of mustard seed – white, brown and black and all three are from plants of the cabbage family. Combinations of ground seeds (flours) or mixtures of the coarsely-crushed seeds together with a variety of liquids are what give the broad palette of mustard flavours.

Although introduced to us by the Romans 2,000 years ago and thought of as basic to English cookery we actually use it for very little other than on our plates and for 'devilling'. And I think the introduction of the rather sweeter American mustard, that coincided with the invasion of the hamburger, has done more to create interest in the United Kingdom than the tiers of gaudily packaged prepared mustards that come from everywhere and contain everything.

Mustard flavour only develops when the crushed or ground seed is in contact with water; both salt and vinegar inhibit the development of flavour, as will very hot water. Mustard powder, even when used to flavour, say, a cheese sauce, should first be mixed with water and left for 10 minutes.

It is also important to remember that the hotness

and flavour of mustard disappears with time and cooking; thus you should add mustard to any sauce or casserole only five minutes before serving. The seeds, or lightly crushed seeds, keep their virtue relatively longer than does the powder.

Having a germicidal action, mustard is used as a preservative, which explains its use in piccalilli.

As well as the types of mustard listed below, there is a mustard oil, more easily available in Indian shops. Very hot, it is a good way to get a controllable heat plus interesting base flavour into curries if you use it instead of a blander oil.

English mustard

Sold as a powder or ready-prepared and usually made of brown and white mustard seeds, with the addition of wheat flour if it is for the UK market. English mustard sold in the US is pure ground mustard seed. Mix with cold water and leave to stand between 5 and 10 minutes, which allows the pungency to develop. Personally I think this is quite horrid and the use disguises any flavour the accompanying food may have. But if you then mix it with milk, cream or a mixture the flavour is mellower and more of a complement. Those who insist on ruining their food *and* their palate might mix mustard with malt or wine vinegar and even add horseradish, which is what they do to Tewkesbury mustard.

Prepared English mustard is not quite as strong as the freshly-made kind.

French mustard

A broad term this, covering many mustards which in general are far less strong than the English type, mainly through being mixed with other aromatics, thus lessening the proportion of heat to flavour. Dijon mustards are mixed with grape juice only, whereas the Bordeaux usually have herbs added. Either are excellent for spreading on steaks or other meats before grilling or roasting, and give a touch of interest when mixed into a good mayonnaise. Currently popular to the point of swamping the market are French mustards made with whole or crushed grains, the red-wax-topped Moutarde de Meaux being first and best known. Although I've seen some peopie in print say they are not much use for cooking I think they are *most* useful for they add visual interest as well as flavour. Use them liberally in stuffings (the heat cooks out, remember) or in vegetable purées.

German mustard	This is usually mild and sweet, often with an important herb content. Austrian mustard is often tarragon flavoured (at least the one I buy is).
American mustard	Sweetened with sugar and made only with the milder white mustard seed, this is made into a creamier consistency than we are used to. Thus it can be spread with a nonchalance that would strip your mouth if it were the English type. It's the only mustard to eat with hamburgers or frankfurters, and an interesting base for sauces. It can contain a lot more additives than other mustards, which are largely unnecessary in view of mustard's own preservative abilities.

Making your own mustard is easy with a pestle and mortar: try and get a variety of mustard seeds and grind some into powder, some into pieces. Honey goes very well in mustard mixtures, but isn't a good idea if you are going to coat meat or fish for grilling, as it will caramelize and burn.

NUTMEG Myristica fragrans	Nutmeg must be used sparingly and should always be grated from a whole nutmeg for it loses its flavour and develops a soapy, thin flavour when ground and left. It is extraordinarily flexible, equally at home in sweet and savoury dishes. There are very few cheese dishes, for instance, that do not benefit from the addition of nutmeg (although perhaps those which include tomato, like pizza, are better without it). But fondues, soufflés, sauces, rarebits, cheesecakes, salads and sandwiches all benefit. Nutmeg is a prime ingredient of mixed spice and thus important to cake and biscuit cooking, particularly in association with apples. Hot green vegetables are good with nutmeg, specially green beans and spinach. It is very good with many meats and excellent in pâté; fine-textured sausages like frankfurters and bologna invariably include some.

You can buy nutmeg graters, but it's just as simple to run a kernel up and down the finer side of a grater or to scrape with a knife. Once upon a time the gentry used to carry their own nutmeg and pocket-sized silver grater partly to flavour hot chocolate and partly for swank. Because they were so common they were little valued and few were preserved: now they are among the rarest small pieces of silver. I've seen only one in 20 years of looking, but I presume there are more.

The large evergreen nutmeg tree looks like the pear and is distinctly sexed; only the female produces the fruit, which looks like a small yellow plum. Inside lies the nutmeg in a case, which dries and becomes mace.

ORANGE-
FLOWER WATER

A standby of my kitchen, as it was in every English kitchen until well into this century. For some inexplicable reason (perhaps the increasing victory of mediocrity?) both this and rose-water suddenly fell from favour after a reign that lasted from the days of the crusaders, who first brought them to Europe.

Distilled from orange flowers, the liquid has a sort of brilliantine scent which can be offputting. But once it is sprinkled over food this softens and becomes as fragrant as moonlit nights in orange groves (yes, it *is* romantic). The Arabs still use it lavishly on every conceivable type of meat dish, in breads, pastries, cakes – and you. In Morocco, for instance, it is frightfully good form for a host to have his guests sprinkled with orange-flower water by servants after dinner. If it happens to you and you're also drinking good wine, I suggest you quickly clap one hand over your glass.

With peaches or strawberries orange-flower water is extraordinarily wonderful. Even simply mixed into cream and used to top almost any dessert it will be a wow. It will be more difficult to convert you to sprinkling it over lamb stews, over chickens and over roast kid, but once you've tried it . . .

The variety we buy here is often called citrus-flower water and comes from Greece where I suspect that lemon blossoms are also used, giving the brilliantine effect. In Egypt or Morocco there is a water that is softer and richer and I recommend travellers to get some, or you can lean on adventurous friends to bring some back for you.

Orange-flower water combined with almonds, pistachios, rose-water and honey is what gives such flavour to the range of Arabic pastries now available in London.

PAPRIKA

There is more ignorance or confusion about this spice than any other. Although there are dozens of flavours of paprika they all come from two basic plants, which you would recognize as capsicums or red pepper. One is a native of the western hemisphere and one a native of the east, and their product equally can be simplified into two categories, the hot and the sweet. A recipe that includes paprika as an ingredient but that does not say whether it should be hot or sweet is no recipe at all, in fact in most countries where it is indigenous to the cooking there is usually not a choice as most houses actually mix the two to get a taste to their own liking. The combination I most like is three parts of sweet paprika to two parts of hot.

In Hungary or Spain you can buy both hot and sweet paprika but here, where even some of the spice distributors seem not to know there are two types, you will generally find that so-called Spanish paprika is only marginally sweeter than so-called Hungarian paprika, which might be slightly hot. The difference in flavour can be obtained several ways. Usually paprika is the dried and ground flesh of red peppers, which avoids the bite of including the seeds. Hotness can be obtained by the inclusion of a proportion of the seeds and sweetness is often added with sugar, which is why the Spanish or sweet paprikas tend to caremelize easily.

If you wish to add a little heat to paprika at home, judiciously mix in some cayenne pepper, which is also sold as chilli powder (don't buy chili powder or compound for this as they are different things).

Don't be alarmed at the amount of paprika called for in some recipes, you *do* use a lot – 3–4 teaspoons (20–30 ml) for 1½–2 pints (900–1200 ml) of liquid is nothing. I usually only put in half the specified amount when starting to cook and add the rest ten minutes before serving.

Paprika of both types is excellent with tomato-based sauces and in Morocco is used in conjunction with cumin powder, an unexpected but excellent combination.

Just to show how easy it is to be wrong about the cuisine of other countries, here is an official Hungarian definition of the basic types of food flavoured with paprikas. Note that the beef goulash in a rich tomato sauce, flavoured with sour cream, that we all know and love doesn't exist. (What's more, paprika only became popular in Hungary a century ago.)

Goulash or Gulyás: more a soup than a stew, made with onion and chunks of potato as well as small pieces of pasta (*Note* – no sour cream).

Pörkölt: a stew with masses of finely chopped

onions, braised rather than boiled, and with a thick sauce.

Tokány: less onions and little paprika, finished with mushrooms and sour cream.

Paprikás: *all* the dishes made with paprika and finished with sour cream or sweet cream. Always made with white meats – fish, fowl, veal and lamb (red meats and fatty birds like duck and goose are never used for these dishes).

PARSLEY
Petroselinum
crispum

The only things you may not already know about parsley are:

1. The best flavour is in the stalk so use that for flavouring stocks, soups and so on.

2. Chewing parsley does neutralize the odour of onion or garlic on the breath.

3. Don't use dried parsley; it nearly always has a hay-like quality that is the antithesis of its appeal when fresh.

4. Flat-leafed parsley, also known as French parsley or petroushka tastes the same as curly parsley; but green coriander leaf looks similar, so beware as both are more readily available than previously.

PEPPERCORNS
Piper negrum

Possibly the most important spice in the world – certainly the most widespread in use. Native to India and the Far East they were the basis of the earliest trade between East and West, and at one time all manner of public debts, dowries and rents could be paid in them – hence the origin of the peppercorn rent.

All colours of peppercorns, black, white, and green, come from the same climbing vine, and the variations are due to the manner and timing of harvesting.

Black peppercorns

Aromatic and sharp tasting, and beloved of food writers who demand freshly-ground black pepper with everything. These are the whole peppercorns picked when slightly under-ripe and dried and sold in their entirety. Black pepper is indeed very good but it is dangerous in the hands of those frightful people who *will* screw it all over everything before so much as even asking if the food in front of them is seasoned. When used in cooking it is better not to add it too early for it tends to go rather bitter; whole or coarsely ground pepper put into a casserole about 10 minutes before serving is *much* better than the same added at the start of cooking. Try it and see. Of all the uses for black peppercorns, I like them ground onto thick slices of slightly chilled red Moroccan or beefsteak tomatoes. Ground black pepper is also very good on strawberries; it takes some nerve to try this one but I do recommend it.

White peppercorns These are the whole peppercorns left to ripen fully on the vine and then soaked to remove the outer husk. The creamy corns underneath are hotter than black pepper but do not have its extra perfume and full flavour. The main use for white peppercorns is in fine stocks (but black ones taste better I think) and for flavouring sauces that would look nasty with black pepper pieces floating about. Thus you would use white peppercorns in béchamel sauce, in scrambled eggs, cream soups, quiche mixtures and so on (you can always put some black pepper on afterwards). A combination of white and black peppercorns is rather interesting to have in a peppermill, and sometimes I add coriander seeds to this mixture. In France small allspice berries are often added to white and black pepper, and that is very good indeed.

For some reason white pepper has always been more popular than black on the English table and it's only since long frocks, sandals and scrubbed pine have come back from continental holidays that the latter has become popular. I can only imagine that we've preferred the simpler, hotter flavour because it *was* less perfumed and 'foreign' tasting.

Green peppercorns These have made a strong impact on the fine food market over the last 10 years. Mainly from Madagascar, they are exactly what they say they are – underripe peppercorns, and really most delicious. Being quite soft they crush into butters or marinades; the colour is useful and the flavour has heat and a truly wonderful aroma that is quite unique. Be very careful only to buy green peppercorns which are packed in brine; those packed in vinegar lack elegance and usefulness.

The brine from green peppercorns is actually a useful flavouring agent itself, just right for adding a dash to a stock or sauce, particularly for fish. To keep green peppercorns once you have used some turn the remainder out of the tin into a screw-top jar and just cover them with extra medium strength brine solution. They'll last for months in the refrigerator and that brine will soon take on their flavour. It may go black, but the peppercorns will be fine once rinsed; make more brine and recover them.

Steak au Poivre made with green rather than black peppercorns is delightful: I'm tempted to think this is the proper way to do this overdone and often palate-searing dish. Green peppercorns go very well with fatty meats and thus complement well a duck or goose.

Dried green peppercorns need to be ground or crushed and don't have the subtle overtones or flavour of the tinned ones.

Red or pink peppercorns

Let the colour warn you – these can be dangerous.

Pink peppercorns, which quickly became the *ne plus ultra* of nouvelle cuisine in the United States, never caught on in the United Kingdom, and just as well. Still, when I tried them, I found the flavour perfectly wonderful, something truly new, and my excited broadcast had hundreds of people scouring the shops, in vain. Although suspicious of why I could not determine their exact provenance I decided to use them in a tight-security dinner for five very highly placed politicians. Just two days later I discovered the ghastly truth: pink peppercorns are not peppercorns at all but the processed berries of a pesky plant known as Florida Holly, a relation of poison ivy. They can cause nausea, giddiness and fainting, and can stimulate the eruption of excrutiatingly large and painful haemorrhoids!

It will be many years before I dare ask for, or tell, the secrets – political, medical and physical – of that dinner party! Why, I may have wiped out a whole generation of our future leaders, so to speak.

The United States Food and Drug Administration have now suspended imports.

PICKLING SPICE

This mixture of spices, with a few herbs like bay thrown in, has more uses than for pickling onions. I use it to flavour vinegar for my red cabbage, use it to flavour wine or cider when sousing mackerel, sprats or sardines. There is no agreed recipe for pickling spice, but a quality blend would have mustard seed as its main component and fragrance and interest can be added with most of the following: coriander seeds, peppercorns, ginger root, allspice, dill seed, chillies, fenugreek, whole cloves, mace and cut bay leaves.

Sousing is such a good way to 'do' fish, especially the bony sardine; long slow cooking lets the vinegar dissolve the bones which in turn act with the liquid to form a jelly.

POPPY SEEDS *Papaver rhoeas*	You'll have to take my word for it, unless you are quite mad, and have unlimited time – there are 900,000 tiny blue-black poppy seeds to the pound. The mild, nutty flavour is very rich when mixed with such other ingredients as egg, almonds and sugar as a filling for middle European or Russian cakes and breads. I find the seeds often have a strange, bitter taste that stays on the tongue for ages, but am told this never happens if you first roast poppy seeds by baking them in a moderate oven for 5–8 minutes until a light golden brown. Roasted poppy seeds are quite nice when incorporated in salad dressings or in dips. They can be added to rice or included in cream sauces for noodles or other pastas.

Commonly they are sprinkled, unroasted, over unbaked bread, bread rolls and savoury biscuits, in which case they are usually first mixed with salt or sprinkled with strong brine to add extra flavour. There is a white poppy seed which is used in Indian cooking.

Originally from Asia, poppy seeds, *Papaver rhoeas* are now widely grown in Europe, especially Holland. Those who are weak of will should not worry about possible addiction; opium and morphine come from the different *Papaver somniterum*.

QUATRE ÉPICES	A great standby of the French and available commercially there. I'm told that it is made up from equal amounts of ground white pepper, cloves, nutmeg and ginger. But, like our sweet mixed spice, there is room for considerable variation of proportion, usually to do with the amount of cloves. It is used on sweet vegetables like corn and squash, with bacon, beans, dried peas and mushrooms. It can also be used over grilling meat and should then be mixed with a little salt as this will help spread the flavours more evenly.

Quatre Épices, like all ground spices, should only be made in small quantities, kept dry, cool and airtight and used quickly.

RAS EL HANOUT	You won't come across this spice unless you go to Morocco, one of my favourite countries from a food

standpoint, but you could make it. *Ras el hanout* is
the ultimate mixed spice, a culinary guide to the
countries conquered, visited or lusted after by the
Muslim nomad, soldier and proselytizer. Its name
means 'top of the shop' for that is where the spice
merchant will keep it, far from robbing hands. Many
of the contents are strange to us and its claim to be
aphrodisiac as well as fragrant is based on the
inclusion of something I thought was apocryphal –
the Spanish fly or cantharides. You can buy *ras el
hanout* ready ground but then you might not get the
best quality and certainly won't have the best fun.
This comes only with watching an expert put
together the unground ingredients, weighing this,
counting that, wrapping each one separately. A good
ras el hanout customer is honoured and treasured.

There are five different peppers included –
Guineau pepper, long Indian pepper (*Piper longum*),
black pepper, grey cubeb pepper and monks' pepper,
which comes from Morocco. Fragrance is given by
cardamom, mace, galingale, nutmeg, allspice,
cinnamon, turmeric, cloves, ginger, lavender
flowers, rosebuds, cassia and fennel. Orris root,
cyparacee, ash berries, bella donna and quite a few
untranslatable things will also be included. Then to
top it all the metallic glint of whole cantharides,
counted more carefully and tellingly. When you get
them home, grind and mix them; the perfume is
quite intoxicating, and although meant to be used in
winter dishes to heat the blood, hands, feet and other
extremities, I find it does very nicely all through the
year. So far the expected libidinous effects of Spanish
fly – although carefully monitored – have remained
undetectable. Either that, or my guests aren't letting
on.

ROSEMARY
Rosmarinus
officinalis

The thin spiky leaves of an attractive bush, rosemary
has a camphorous, piney, smoky flavour, specially
liked in Italy but often hated elsewhere. Lots of food
writers don't like rosemary and some cooks worry
about the spikes 'getting' everywhere; I can't
understand either point of view. The warm, smoky
flavour of rosemary is quite unlike anything else and
when used discreetly makes an incomparable
contribution to good eating. If you are worried about
the spiky leaves, then grind them. Or, like me stick a
whole branch of the fresh stuff into a sauce for 10–15
minutes; this is more than enough for its perfume to

be transferred, then I yank the branch out leaving only a few potentially offensive bits.

Rosemary twigs are also extraordinarily good for perfuming barbecued or spit-roasted food; this was dramatically demonstrated to me when I arrived in a thunderstorm at a converted medieval nunnery in the South of France to ask if I could stay for an unspecified time with two people I had never met. One was a morose Swedish writer, the other a Frenchman, and both were caretaking the magnificent house during the winter. They were as pleased to see me as I them, for life was lonely, and they decided on an indoor barbecue and that night I dined on spit-roasted breast of lamb cooked over masses of rosemary. Conversation was tricky as none of us spoke each other's language to a noticeable extent, and there was the complication of a large and incontinent pet ape of some sort who shared the banquet.

The most common uses for rosemary are with all cuts of lamb, with chicken, shrimp and prawns, in bread, in sauces that contain tomato, and in conjunction with lemon or orange to finish simple butter or grilling sauces. Some dried rosemary or a small sprig of fresh is excellent when brewed with Indian tea – very good for relieving tension headaches.

Rosemary is for remembrance and where it grows it is said to show that the woman rules the house. I think it should be grown far more, especially as hedges, when it makes something dense, aromatic and useful. Many holy places in the Moslem world are surrounded by such protection for there rosemary is credited with powers of purification.

ROSES

Rose buds and rose petals dried or fresh, are the bases of all manner of wonderful things, but not, it seems, in Britain. You need to go to India or to Turkey to get the best jams and preserves made from red rose petals and I think those of the latter by far the best. Roses make an extraordinarily good wine, and petals can be used to perfume sugar in the same way as vanilla beans or geranium leaves. Crushed rose petals ground into a fine powder are a delightful flavouring for fresh fruit and are incorporated in a lot of Arabic mixed spices. Crystallized rose petals are nice cake decorations or garnishes for special puddings or soft fruit dishes.

Whenever using roses for culinary purposes it is advisable to cut off the white part of the petal. Red damask roses are traditionally best but there are now so many strong-scented varieties that rules are pointless. If it smells, eat it. A few rose petals in a salad look and taste good, rose jam is great with a traditional cream tea, and pink petals are wonderful on Summer Pudding.

Rose-water (eau de rose) is *really* the way to use the glory of the rose. Distilled from red roses, it was hardly possible to cook unless you used this, throughout the Moslem world and Europe right up to the death of Queen Victoria. Now almost forgotten here it is still vital in the Moslem world, sprinkled into everything and over you.

Do, I beg you, go out and get a bottle and start experimenting. It is wonderful with milk-poached pudding grains, especially barley and rice, goes surprisingly well with poultry, and is really best with things chocolate and fruity. If you bake a chocolate cake with several rose geranium leaves underneath it, mix a chocolate icing with plenty of rose-water for something out of this world. Or flavour a particularly rich chocolate soufflé with rose-water, serve it while very runny in the middle, after only 20 minutes baking, and serve it with a little hot soft fruit purée (loganberries would be very good).

Soak dried fruit overnight and then serve them with chopped pistachios and lavish sprinklings of rose-water and orange-flower water – people will think you have done something expensive and difficult.

Rose-water goes very well with cream cheese or cream and, as with orange-flower water, you can make much of ordinary puddings by using it. I once made a banquet pudding out of profiteroles stuffed alternately with orange- and rose-flavoured creams, and held together with the lightest caramel. Pouring cream was chilled and also flavoured with rose-water and the whole concoction was finished with a scattering of rose petals. The scents were bewitching and the flavours tantalizingly difficult to identify. Rose-water-flavoured cream or syrup goes specially well with raspberries and fresh peaches.

Florentine curd pudding is an old English curd cheese, egg and spinach custard tart with the addition of currants, spice and rose-water and a 'talking point' end to a meal – well, when did *you*

ever have rose-flavoured spinach for pudding?
Rose-flavoured vinegar is excellent too.

After all that I suppose I should tell you what the
stuff tastes like. It tastes like it smells, very rose-y
but surprisingly spicy and slightly smoky. There is
no rule about how much you use, sometimes I like to
use very little and other times find I can get away
with making the flavour very strong indeed – for
instance to flavour a syrup for sliced oranges or with
raspberries. I repeat, get out and buy some, and give
yourself the pleasure not only of recreating the food
of our forefathers, but also of inventing new ideas
with the broader range of ingredients at our disposal
today. Make sure it is triple-distilled or it will be
useless.

RUE Ruta graveolens	This bitter aromatic herb is not very fashionable in the kitchen nowadays, but if you come across some it should be used with great moderation with the lighter-flavoured red meats and poultry and perhaps with potatoes. The only time I've actually enjoyed it is in combination with *grappa*, the fiery Italian equivalent of *marc*, which in turn is a fairly rough spirit distilled from what's left after wine has been pressed – skins, pips and pulp. The Sardinians put a long stem of rue into each bottle of their grappa, for rue has an ancient tradition of being a digestive aid. *Grappa con rutta* turns a pale green and has a most appealing extra perfume and flavour. A man, whom I was assured was a *bandito*, walked into a bar in Alghero and ordered a 'dynamite' (with Italian vowels of course) and was poured a huge glass of grappa con rutta. After I had expressed a liking for this drink, the same man agreed to send me some made illicitly by him in the mountains. Its arrival was accompanied by checking of windows and doors, two cars full of very big men, and a number of hissed sentences which I presumed promised death either through drinking too much at one time, or revealing my source. Apparently the punishments for bootlegging are as severe as for kidnapping, which was their other interest in life. You have to be careful to whom you talk in Sardinia.
SAFFLOWER Carthamum tinctorius	This flower can give the same colour as saffron and thus is substituted for it but it doesn't have the same subtle flavour. It was used by American Indians to colour breads and porridges, by Japanese courtiers to

dye their lips, and is used in Mexican food. It is also
known as American, Mexican or Fake saffron.
Safflower is more important as a source of a low
cholesterol cooking oil.

SAFFRON
Crocus sativus

Delicate and very expensive, for saffron comes only
from the stigma of a certain crocus. They can only be
picked by hand and it can take almost a
quarter-of-a-million stigmas to make just one pound.
It has been used since time immemorial and the
Phonecians used it to colour the crescent-shaped
cakes that were eaten for Ashtoreth, goddess of
fertility; her rites and name have become our Easter
and our hot cross buns are directly traceable to these
earlier Phoenician offerings. Saffron goes particularly
well in doughs, and saffron cakes and scones and
breads are specialities as far apart as Sweden and the
West Country, Russia and Spain, Italy and Armenia.
With fish it is superlative; both bouillabaisse and the
Spanish rice dish paella are impossible without it.
The Italians use it a lot with rice in their lovely moist
risottos.

Saffron is available powdered and in stigmas. Some
say the powder is often made of ingredients other
than true saffron. If so I don't think it matters for
I've not been able to tell the difference and I think
the desecration to be imagined. When you use
stigmas, dry them gently in a warm oven, crumble
them and then pour over a little boiling water to
draw the colour and flavour. It doesn't look good to
include the whole threads in a dish.

Next time you make a white wine and cream sauce
for seafood stir in one or two sachets of powdered
saffron. The warm, slightly sweet, slightly bitter
flavour and the wonderful colour transforms
something quite ordinary into a treat. You need so
little to make such a large difference I really can't
think of it as expensive. If you think your sauces
wouldn't stand saffron – for instance because it
would change the colour incorrectly – there are other
ways to use it. I often mix it into an egg yolk and use
this as the glaze on pastry coffins or vol au vents in
which seafood is going to be served. You get a
glorious golden glaze and a tantalizing flavour.
Saffron also gives an intriguing lift to rich
tomato-based sauces – try it with tomato-casseroled
lamb, perhaps also adding a mixture of hot and sweet
paprikas.

SAGE Salvia officinalis	The time-honoured flavouring in the true blue British sausage, but you'd be hard put to find many that do actually contain it. Pork and veal together with goose, tomatoes and cheese, are the best foods with which to combine sage. Fresh sage tucked under the crackling of roasting pork works very well and the classic veal dish is *saltimbocca*, in which thin slices of veal are wrapped around ham and fresh sage.

Sage and onion stuffing is traditional for poultry but I can't think why the commercial variety is so popular – possibly because so few people have tasted the fresh leaves? Most dried sage tastes distinctly like a musty damp room smells, and that is not what the fresh herb does. The worst perfidy thrust upon sage is the use of its name in association with Derby Sage cheese, that stuff with the green marbling. They use sage oil and colouring and you can read what herb oils are all about in the introduction to this section. I can't think why people bother to eat it. Especially now there is a Sage Lancashire and Sage Cheshire on the market in which rolled sage leaves are incorporated. No colour, no oil and perfectly delicious; a good way to convert someone to the pleasures of sage, as I had to be.

The affinity of sage with tomatoes is why some people suggest you crumble a sage-flavoured cheese over a tomato salad.

SARSPARILLA Smilax officinalis	The root of a plant indigenous to tropical America from Mexico to Peru, sarsparilla is used to flavour a drink with so-called tonic properties. Certainly sarsparilla tastes as though it should be good for you, rather like combined wintergreen and chewing gum if early teenage memories serve me well. Then it enjoyed a brief vogue as a soft drink flavouring, but the emergence of Elvis Presley shortly afterwards quickly returned us to coca-cola, which is flavoured by berries from the cola plant and once also included extracts from the coca plant, source of cocaine; *its* instant success was hardly surprising. If you want to try sarsparilla, look in Jamaican communities; the best root comes from there and they still drink it as though it were life's blood.

SALT	Salt is the simple name for sodium chloride, an essential part of our body chemistry but, like so many things we take for granted, its role can be misunderstood, and it may be used to our detriment.

237

The problem is that salt can be addictive, or at least the flavour can be, and too high an intake is thought to be dangerous to the heart. To begin with, do you know how it works? Salt does not alter or improve the flavour of food one iota, other than to add its own, or in the case of salt-preserving to hinder or help the development of flavour-giving bacteria.

What salt does is to stimulate the taste buds of the tongue to discern what flavour is inherently present, and the more salt present, the greater the stimulus and the greater the flavour reward. But – the more salt you use, the more you taste the flavour of the salt rather than of the food.

It does not necessarily follow that someone who uses more salt than you has a saltier flavour in his mouth; his tastebuds might need a higher degree of stimulation to experience the *same* taste as you. But the risk of a high salt intake is that eventually the salt taste becomes paramount, and that is bad for you and boring for the cook. Like sugar, salt is present naturally in a great deal of the food we eat, especially that which is processed, and it is worth taking a really hard look at the amount added and the amount really needed. Are you *really* tasting the food? or are you tasting salt?

Types of salt

There is a difference between the salts you can buy, a matter of how they are made, whence they come, and with what traces of other chemicals each is mixed.
Rock salt: this is mined in ready-formed crystals, and is the deposit of a long-gone dried sea or other waterway. It is invariably mixed with a great number of other tastes, some of which you may not like, so it is an idea to taste rock salt before you buy. It can be even better than the more common –
Sea salt: evaporated from the sea and thus bound to include a number of other trace elements and chemicals. Yet it is perfectly safe and free from anything nasty.

The broad spectrum of ingredients which complement the sodium chloride is what recommends sea salt to the health experts. I simply prefer its flavour.
Bay salt: is a cruder form of sea salt, often rather greyish as it is less likely to have been purified in any way. It will be flavourful and is commonly the salt used for preserving and brining.

Common or kitchen salt: this is made by extracting salt from the earth by dissolving it in water, pumping this brine out, and evaporating off the liquid.

There are various forms, and this is what used to be made into the solid blocks. Vacuum salt, that is salt that has been extracted and purified in vacuum, is 99.9 per cent sodium chloride, but this is usually then turned into

Table salt: the purity is interfered with by the addition of starch or other chemicals to promote free running. The combination of such essential purity and additives makes it pretty boring of flavour and perhaps this is why so much is used.

Iodised salt: salt to which iodine salts have been added as a necessary dietary supplement in some countries as defence against goitre. It has a definite taste of its own, but is vital where needed.

Flavoured salts: sometimes called seasoned salts, these are traditional for flavouring meats but were usually made at home with preferred mixtures of cloves and nutmeg, peppers, and some of the sharper, sweeter herbs. Garlic salt is increasingly popular but beware when you buy it – check the label and you might find it also contains monosodium glutamate.

Celery salt is beloved of vegetarians and can be very delicious if used with infinite restraint. Quite simply, it is salt pounded with celery seed.

Hickory-flavoured salt is a favourite in the United States and a company in Norfolk is experimenting with the production of herb-smoked salts, to which I look forward.

You can try pounding any fresh or dried herb with salt, and they keep for a long time.

If you wish to dry-salt fish or meat, salt with large crystals gives better results.

Although a fine preservative, salt behaves rather strangely when deep-frozen. Whereas salted butter keeps far longer than unsalted butter in a refrigerator, salted butter should only be frozen for a month. Unsalted butter can be stored three times as long. The salt content is why dishes containing bacon cannot be frozen for very long periods. Strange isn't it?

SASSAFRAS
Laurus sasafras

One of the very first exports from the United States to Europe, the root and bark of the aromatic sassafras tree can be made into a warming drink and it is the root from which American root beer is made.

In Creole cooking the leaves are ground and made into *filé*, a strange green powder that has a thickening effect on hot liquids, but which must be used with great care or the results can be most unpleasant and stringy. It is the most important ingredient in some gumbos, the important rice dish of Creole food. If you don't have *filé*, you can replace it with a little cornflour, which will do the thickening but won't add the strange flavour which I would describe as a cross between eucalyptus and marijuana.

Sassafras isn't very expensive and it is worth asking someone travelling to America to bring you back some.

SAVORY
Satureia hortensis

Often confused with thyme. Summer savory has a slightly more peppery taste and the leaves are longer. It is particularly good with beans and often grown between rows of broad beans for it repels the black fly which normally attacks the latter. What grows together gets eaten together and the French are very fond of savory with broad beans; I think you should try it too, otherwise use it where you would thyme. It is generally used much more on the Continent than in England and there is a good but expensive 'mi-chèvre' (half-cow, half-goat milk cheese) coated with savory, which is called *sarriette* in French. There is a winter savory but it is inferior.

SESAME

Extremely versatile and used in the Near, Middle and Far East for aeons, the sesame seed has only recently become popular in the West, mainly due to increased travel and the growing influence of Eastern diets.

Raw, the seeds have high nutritional value and a sweet nutty flavour and can be made into a milk, but are generally used as a sprinkler over breads, in casseroles, sauces, pie crusts, puddings, and so on. When browned lightly in butter they are excellent on almost every type of vegetable or on plain noodles. Sesame seed bars make terrific snacks as long as you have good teeth.

We are probably more familiar with sesame in halvah and as tahini. Halvah is a Turkish/Greek/Israeli confection made of ground sesame seeds, honey and flavouring. It can have all manner of other ingredients including dry milk powder and dried fruit. The Poles make excellent halvah, for some reason, and their chocolate-flavoured one is particularly good.

Tahini is sesame butter, ground sesame seed with nothing added or subtracted; it can be used just as you would peanut butter and is also used to flavour salad dressings when thinned with a little oil and lime or lemon juice, or to flavour dishes like hummous, a paste of chick-peas. Vegetarians use it as a substitute for butter in pastries and bread, for it makes one of the best oils of all for cooking. Marco Polo was one of the first to extol its virtues in the West, but he probably didn't know it was so good for those on low-cholesterol diets.

If you wish to cut down your salt intake, *gomasio* may be the answer. It is Japanese, but not so strange it can't appear on your, more ordinary, table. Toast sesame seeds, mix with salt in the proportion of five-to-one, crush or grind and keep in an airtight container. I like it sprinkled over food rather than in it.

If you are offered a tahini that is rather darker than you expect this may be because it has a lower oil content; some Greek storekeepers say that a proportion of commercial tahini is made from what's left over after the seeds have been lightly toasted and crushed to extract the oil. I can only surmise there are several ways to make it, and you buy and use the type you like best.

SORREL AND
WILD SORREL
Rumex acetosa

If you were a horse and called a sorrel, you would be a bright reddish chestnut colour. If you were a plant you would be green, and bear acidic leaves which can be steps to rare gastronomic heights. You would also be as rare as hen's teeth in stores throughout the British Isles even though you grow wild. Sorrel looks a little like dock or anaemic spinach; the cultivated leaves grow quite big but the wild is sometimes not much bigger than a man's thumb. Some shops (ours) sell it fresh but I earnestly recommend you grow it; in California it is sold in supermarkets. Although used raw in salads for contrast, it is mainly a superb flavouring for sauces; I personally don't like the sorrel soup which is every other book's basic sorrel recipe.

To make a sorrel sauce you first melt the de-stalked leaves over gentle heat in lots of butter. They shrink prodigiously, a couple of handfuls of small leaves end up as a puddle on the bottom of a saucepan. Try not to brown them. Now sprinkle over a little flour and some more butter and cook gently for a few minutes, which gives you a strongly flavoured roux. Add liquid that suits your dish to make the sauce. You can use white wine or milk or cream, but be careful about curdling. Stock is good, especially vegetable water, for although the sorrel is strong it can end up just being acidic and having its flavour overshadowed by strong sauce ingredients.

Now, how do you use your sorrel sauce? Well, it's outstanding with fish, especially eel, salmon and sea trout. It is excellent with sweetbreads, giving a wonderful contrast of sweet and sour and is very good with eggs and with young green vegetables. I like to make this sauce and then put it into the choke-free centre of baby or teenage artichokes, so you dip into it with the cooked leaves. Provided it is not too strong, sorrel sauce also makes a nice change on asparagus spears, too.

One point: it isn't worth simply chopping sorrel and putting that into a white sauce or hollandaise; unless it is reduced the flavour isn't strong enough.

TABASCO	Very hot, but with the redeeming quality of having flavour as well. Tabasco is the trade name for a chilli-based sauce that was originally from Louisiana but which is now made in the UK under licence. It should be used in amounts so small you will scarce believe it, particularly when employed for such drinks as a Bloody Mary. Although recommended by the manufacturer for almost every type of dish, it is far better with creamy fish or pasta dishes. Smoked mackerel pâté is changed remarkably by a few drops, and if you can only buy sweet paprika for a dish where you want a mixture of sweet and hot, then a drop or two of Tabasco will be a reasonable substitute. But note: use it miniscule drop by miniscule drop.
TAMARIND	I mention this because, although from the Eastern kitchen, it does have relevance to ours; you buy the fruit of this tropical tree dried. When you soak it you get a sour juice which can be used instead of lemon juice. It's a very up-market substitute to be sure, but dried tamarind keeps an extremely long time and will save many a dish that needs some bite.
TARRAGON	A necessity in every herb garden and kitchen, basic

to French cooking, and to anyone who cares about fine flavours. It is warm and aromatic but must have both bite and an air of liquorice. There are two sorts – the Russian and the French – but I recommend you only use the French for the Russian will add a flavour not much more useful than fresh lawn clippings.

Tarragon's great affinity is with all dairy products and with eggs, hence its appearance in classic sauces, and I always try to get some into savoury soufflés. It is extraordinarily good with melted butter over virtually every vegetable but does have a special relationship with courgettes. This also applies to chicken, and chicken roasted only with butter, a little lemon and fresh or dried tarragon is really hard to beat. When you cook chicken, courgettes and tarragon in the same dish the result is . . . well, try it for yourself. A lesser known affinity is that of tarragon with lamb, another recommendation; so is lobster baked with tarragon.

Tarragon is essential to sweet, mixed herbs and wonderful in a herb mayonnaise for serving with cold fish, specially salmon, when the bite of the tarragon is a good foil for the smoothness of the flesh. Tarragon vinegar is one of the finest of all the flavoured vinegars and adds instant elegance to almost anything. Vinegar is often overlooked as a finisher for casseroles and sauces, but shouldn't be.

Tarragon is better for being grown with lots of sun, but its flavour is very changeable, being affected by the slightest variation in soil and climate. No two plants taste exactly the same so always test the strength on your tongue when using tarragon.

THYME
LEMON THYME
WILD THYME
Thymus vulgaris;
Thymus citriodorus;
Thymus serphyllum

A favourite herb of such long standing that the ancient Greeks used it as an incense to purify their temples and Greek thyme honey from Mount Hymettus is regarded as the best in the world. Certainly thyme is one of the all-time favourites of bees.

There are many different types of thyme, most of which are useful in cooking. Basic and wild thyme are related in flavour, with the wilder being the headier. Lemon thyme is more citrus than thyme but has a lovely flavour and gives a clue to one of thyme's greatest affinities – lemon. Other rarer thymes have the flavour of caraway and should only be used with great discretion.

Thyme loves tomatoes and tomato sauces, goes well in savoury sausages and stuffings and indeed is fairly basic in my opinion. Dried thyme imported from the Med may be very much stronger than the fresh but weaker stuff from a damp English garden. You have to be careful. White flesh, rabbit, veal and poultry go well with the slightly sweet-sharp flavour and is good with garlic. Nearly all vegetables like thyme but carrots are its best and prettiest companion.

TURMERIC
Curcurma longa

The brilliant yellow colour and pungent flavour of turmeric is basic to picallili and curry but well worth exploring in its own right. Related to the ginger, it is the plant's ginger-like root that is used. The flavour is mellow, perhaps peppery; used as a saffron substitute there is no similarity in flavour and the practice can have unfortunate culinary consequences. Use it on rice dishes, in stews, fish dishes and in kedgeree; mixed with a little butter and garlic it can make an interesting enlivener of vegetables.

VANILLA BEAN
Vanilla aromatica

This is the fruit of a climbing orchid native to Mexico but now grown throughout tropical areas. If stored in a closed (*not* airtight) jar, it improves with keeping. So widely used it is barely regarded as a flavour at all – how often do people refer to vanilla custard or ice cream as 'plain'. You shouldn't use the bean itself to eat, and I don't agree with some suggestions that you grind it to mix with sugar.

Its basic uses are to flavour milk or sugar syrups in fruit or pudding dishes; the classic ploy is to store the bean, in closed jar with caster sugar and to use the flavoured sugar (also good in coffee or tea drinks). If you use a piece to make a syrup, don't throw it away, rinse and dry it and it will be good for a dozen or more times.

Don't worry if you see what looks like long fine white hairs on a vanilla pod; this is a sign of high quality.

There are many substitutes for vanilla so when you buy liquid vanilla flavouring, ensure it says vanilla essence or pure vanilla essence.

Vanillin is a white powder used to give vanilla flavour and although it has the same chemical formula of the ingredient that makes vanilla beans smell it is, only half the story. If it means anything to you it is $C_8H_8O_3$.

ICE CREAM

In the days when Saturday matinée movies were preceded by a stirring serial and Walt Disney cartoons, it used to cost 6d to sit downstairs and 9d to lord it in the superiority of the balcony. I used to be given 9d, which meant an invidious choice. Did I sit upstairs and command considerable social envy? or did I sit downstairs, enjoying the status of a 2d ice cream, save 1d, and have two ice creams next week? The ice cream plan usually won. If I'd studied social history in my first 10 years I could have saved myself the trouble of choosing, for ices have always had a greater social cachet than mere position. The Romans and almost every other ruling power spent fortunes having snow and ice rushed over great distances so they could freeze food and so astound *hoi polloi*. In England and America, lesser fortunes relied on the building of underground ice houses in which to store winter's ice, so providing them with the means to make cooling ices and sorbets, a special need in the humid summers of the southern states of North America.

It was the society-levelling Americans who popularized ice cream and it's very much part of everyday life for millions and millions of children and adults. Huge containers of ice cream are stored in the family freezer, to be scooped into as a snack from breakfast to bedtime. But, like so many convenience foods now in the public domain, much of it has very little in common with the real thing, other than temperature. In fact, true dairy-based ice cream simply doesn't exist as far as most major producers are concerned: their product contains no cream and any milk is probably added in the form of powder. The fat, so essential to the texture and enjoyment of real ice cream, is nearly always from the oil palm, at least it is in the United Kingdom. Thus, if the EEC continues on its, legislative way, it will soon prohibit such products being called ice cream, which would be a good thing. This isn't necessary in Australasia and in some of the stronger dairying states of the United States, where the real thing is protected as a birth right.

Ice cream in its simplest form was once just flavoured and frozen cream and even this probably didn't appear until the 18th century. Ices had been closer to what we would call sorbets; it's thought the Chinese invented these concoctions of fruit; that the Italians took up the idea and then introduced it to the rest of Europe. Charles I it was who first fell for them in this country, protecting the recipe with a sentence of death for anyone who divulged it. The classic form nowadays is a flavoured egg custard made with milk or cream. The best I ever ate was made in an old-fashioned ice cream churn or dasher, in which the mixture is turned over and over again surrounded by salted ice. It takes a long time and a lot of patience but gives such a wonderful silken result. Other recipes give smooth results too and you can also buy small electrically-operated machines which will churn ice cream in the freezer or the ice-box of your refrigerator. But, although rather satisfying to do, it may not be necessary. In the last several years there has been a distinct move back towards the commercial making of true ice cream, in the United Kingdom at least. In London there are three independent brands and one of the big manufacturers of vegetable-oil ice cream has also brought out a 'real' range. They are all perfectly delicious and sport original flavours that immediately make bought ice cream a possibility (as it once was) for even the grandest dinner party instead of it being the 'easy' answer to the end of meals, particularly at sordid 'banquets', wedding 'breakfasts' and Rotary dinners. With hazelnut or kirsch dairy ice cream I serve hot cherries jubilee. With chocolate goes some home-made crème de ménthe sorbet, vanilla accompanies sweetened chestnut puree and rum. . . . and so on, the possibilities are infinite.

If you can buy only vanilla and you want something more interesting, or if you can buy only a non-dairy ice cream it is very easy to reflavour these. Softened, not melted, ice cream is easily flavoured with fruit, alcohol or some mixture of both. Try chocolate or vanilla ice cream with crushed peppermint candy, strawberry or raspberry with swirls of liqueurs, mocha combined with sliced marron glacés, strawberry folded with purée of peach or mango, fudge with orange juice and passion fruit pulp . . .

You need to leave the ice cream to soften in your refrigerator for an hour or so. Then chop it into a bowl, beat it quickly, add the chilled flavouring and serve straight away. If you've kept the ice cream cold enough you can refreeze it to serve as 'your own' flavour ice cream a few hours later or simply to store until you want it.

MARGARINE

The most amazing thing I learned about margarine lately is that most people pronounce it incorrectly; it really *should* have a hard 'g'. Other than that, the great misapprehension is that it contains no butter or milk. Quite wrong, for apart from kosher products, all margarines rely on milk or butter for a great deal of their flavour or texture.

Margarine (sometimes oleo margarine) is essentially a fatty food made from oils and fats to resemble butter. It was invented in the 19th century by Mege Mouries, a Frenchman, and was patented in 1869, as a cheaper and less perishable source (than butter) of fat for the diet of the poor and of the armed forces.

The United States is today's largest producer and the popularity margarine lost in the United Kingdom after the war due to its rationing-related stigma has been regained because of advertising-related concern over cholesterol levels and because it is undeniably easier to use than butter straight from a refrigerator, makes good-looking cakes and lasts extremely well.

There are many types of margarine, the variety made possible by varying the type and proportion of oils and fats used. Generally vegetable oils are the base but fish oils are often included, too. Statutory regulations vary from country to country, and in the United Kingdom the moisture content must not exceed 16 per cent and there must be no more than 10 per cent butterfat. Although there may be no preservatives, emulsifiers and antioxidants are allowed and all margarines must have added vitamin A and D.

The method of manufacture has changed little since its invention. A suitable oil is purified and, possibly, bleached and emulsified – this is then blended with an aqueous milk preparation and then chilled. Thus as well as the flavour variety inherent in the blend of oils used the milk can also be treated to affect flavour in the same way as it is ripened with or without a bacterial culture to influence the flavour of butter. When the milk and oil emulsions are mixed, other flavourings, salt and colouring are also included and then the mass is kneaded to achieve homogeneity.

That doesn't sound too bad, does it? And generally it isn't if used cold. It is when it is heated that margarine displays its bastard heritage for none tastes like butter when hot or after heating. This is why I said it only made good-*looking* cakes; the difference in flavour is noticeable. If it is marginal, this is because the margarine has a very high butterfat or other milk constituent. Yet even this is not enough, in most cases, to disguise the often unpleasant flavour changes of heated margarine. Apparently the chemistry of what happens to butter when it is heated is only little understood; thus the delicious aroma of melted butter cannot be copied in the laboratory. Instead, the food scientists put ever more milk products into margarine and hope this will suffice.

Presently, advertising is informing us that butter and margarine have the same calorie content, which is generally true. Some margarines also have very high cholesterol content. Even those that do not, have other additives which cause concern in some circles.

It seems that most butter substitutes are made more to satisfy a need for economy in the kitchen rather than responsibility to solve any major health threat.

So, on balance, I find the blessings of margarine very limited, and almost non-existent once it comes to cooking. It would be far simpler, and almost certainly healthier, simply to continue eating butter, but to eat less of it. Or to switch to olive oil, which has no ill effects on anything.

MILK

Milk must be the world's most important food, even though it is still largely ignored in China and miscellaneous easterly places. It is fashionably railed against as being the source of much cholesterol-related disease but I think the benefits it can bestow generally outweigh the disadvantages.

The modern reliance on products made from milk, or containing milk derivatives, is extraordinary and makes it difficult to imagine that the entire American continent and all the great South Pacific had no knowledge of milk as a human food before the arrival of the European. It is even more astonishing to remember that for all its health-giving potential milk was until a century ago one of the most dangerous of all foods, contaminated with tuberculosis, adulterated with water and worse, dirty through lack of hygiene and a dearth of sealed containers – and usually sour. And that was just the stuff in the country. The few people trying to improve soured milk and rancid cheese used such things as borax and formaldehyde. The herds and their maids were respectively dirty and slatternly, equally contributing to one another's painful demise. Yet it is these same milkmaids that are so romantically sung and portrayed. The reason is quite simply a continuous publicity stunt of the first degree. The job *had* to be made to appear to be romantic, for no girl in her right senses would otherwise choose such back-breaking work at such unsociable hours. When Marie-Antoinette toiled for minutes at a time in the rustic dairy farm (le Hameau) she had built in the purlieus of Versailles, she was as much employed publicity *pour encourager les autres* as Margaret Thatcher visiting mines under an illuminated helmet. The French queen had real dairymaids to do the real work. Perhaps it was the dairymaid's requisite brawniness that gained them such universal admiration; but the flush on their cheeks was more likely to be tubercular than virginal. Milkmaids needed to be as strong as a bull (the more personal domestic duties of which she might also have had to supervise) and needed a stomach quite as strong as the forearms which heaved pails of milk and wheels of cheese.

I've never been able to drink fresh cow's milk and at times in my life have been forbidden all kinds of products even remotely associated with it, including tranquillisers, which like most drugs are sweetened with milk sugar, lactose. I often found it simpler to stick to a Jewish Pareve (milk-free) diet and wish I had had the nerve to present my charge card at Selfridges Kosher Counter. Yet I look with pride at today's huge milk-fed children (have you been to Japan recently?) for it was an ancestor that prodded the whole operation into being, by first applying scientific methods to raise cattle exclusively for dairying.

John Christian of Cumberland was first cousin to Fletcher Christian of the 'Bounty' and head of the family. After his first wife died he married Isabella Curwen, last representative of one of England's ten oldest families. By combining the names, estates and fortunes of the Christians and Curwens with his extraordinary gift for advanced agricultural thinking John Christian Curwen made himself into a one-man vanguard of experiment both on the farm and in mines. His achievements are many and include organizing the first agricultural shows. Early in the 19th century he noted that the Cumberland town of Kendal had more milk carts and fewer child deaths than other parts of England. Deciding this was evidence that milk was vital for health and growth, he consulted the few other people who had come to the same conclusions (notably in Scotland) and then set about to do something about it. By 1813 he had eschewed the traditional longhorn for shorthorn cattle and was getting an average daily milking yield of 10 quarts per animal.

He achieved these unheard of results by unheard of methods: he actually planted grasses and clovers in his fields instead of letting nature take its course; he stall-fed the animals and made much use of oil cake, and thus established the country's first true dairying herd. And what did he do with these vast quantities of milk? He distributed them free to the poor of Workington, much to the amusement and derision of other landowners; it was the world's first organized free-milk service and later John Christian Curwen introduced legislation into Westminster that is now acknowledged to be the first step anywhere in the world towards the Welfare State. This remarkable man is almost unknown, perhaps because he refused a peerage twice.

It wasn't until the 1860s and 1870s that anyone else began seriously to establish specialized milking herds. Not only did they get on to a profitable band waggon, they also utilized the waggons of the new railway system, which allowed transportation of country milk to the towns for the first time. By 1900 the Great Western Railway alone carried 25 million gallons in one year, the produce of 50,000 cows. Remember, the unpasteurized, unchilled milk of the time would have soured and curdled terribly quickly as it was carted over the rutted roads of the time. Indeed, rail-transported milk still did as often as not, so country milk was not much better than that from the horrible town herds, which were tethered or wandered wherever there was room, and milked and fed and calved there, too. In 1865 and '66 there were widespread epidemics of cattle plague which decimated the town herds to a state from which they never recovered.

Cooling and refrigeration were gradually introduced through the 1880s and 1890s. About the same time the first milk purity laws were passed and by 1900, with the invention of milking machines and the establishment of wholesale dairies, there was a distinct improvement in hygiene and a decline in milk-linked disease. But milk was still transported and sold in bulk, often by horse-drawn cart and didn't begin to be pre-packed until the 1920s. Even at the end of the 1940s I remember running barefoot in the morning down the garden to collect the billycan from under the letterbox after it had been filled by our milkman – this was in Auckland.

In 1923, Britain officially recognized the benefit of pasteurization – the process in which milk is heated to 71°C for 15 seconds and then cooled quickly. Since then the strictest safeguards have been rigidly enforced to protect us from contaminated milk or diseased animals and our average consumption of 242 pints per annum is 4 times what it was a century ago.

Sweet and soured milks for drinking

I once went to a lecture on food hygiene in a catering establishment and the bacteriologist speaking said that with all his knowledge of the horrors of food poisoning there was only one thing he would categorically not do, and that was to drink unpasteurized milk. He said that many disease-free attested herds in this country still manage to include animals with notifiable disease, including, in his opinion, tuberculosis. If you are in the position of only having raw milk to drink, you should boil it, or failing that, leave it to ripen until it has a definite sourness; the gradual increase of lactic acid in souring milk acts as a germicide of sorts and makes it marginally safer. If undisturbed the acid-producing ripening process continues until the lactic acid level solidifies the milk protein, making sour curds. Although goats and sheep are tuberculosis-free, they can have other nasty diseases, but less commonly, so their unpasteurized milk is generally safer.

The fact that a high-acid content makes milk safer is behind the popularity of so-called fermented milk drinks which are also easier to digest. Interestingly, they are found in both cold and hot countries – whereas I though only the latter had need of preservative methods. Fermented milk drinks are made with the addition of a specialised culture of lactic-acid-producing bacillus; they have the specialised ability to give the milk a pleasant tang and thicken it slightly but do not let the process continue to form a curd unless left a very long time. In general these products are less sour than yoghurt and although usually used as a drink, have their uses as bases for summer soups and in cooking. In Sweden you can buy all types of fermented milk and throughout the Middle East, including Israel, they are very popular, as they are in Middle Europe and the Balkans – indeed the only such product available in this country is Smatana, which is of Balkan origin. You can get something similar by adding water and sugar to plain yoghurt, another common Eastern practice. Other fermented milk drinks include leben and kumiss.

Buttermilk is possibly the best milk-derived but non-fermented drink and is what's left after you churn cream (milk fat) to make butter. If made from unripened cream it is quite sweet; ripened cream gives buttermilk with a slight sourness.

Cultured buttermilk has a bacterial culture added to it, a culture of bacteria similar to those that naturally curdle milk to make cheese but which are killed by pasteurization. Thus, cultured buttermilk ripens and thickens slightly, becoming slightly acidic as the lactose (milk sugar) is turned into lactic acid. If you want to use buttermilk in a cooking recipe it must either be cultured or made from unpasteurized ripened cream or it will not have the acidity necessary to interact with baking soda and so form a leavening gas. If you use sweet buttermilk in cooking you have to exchange the baking soda for twice as much baking powder or add a squirt of lemon juice.

Most buttermilk here and in the United States is made from skimmed milk, so isn't buttermilk but fermented skimmed milk; the real stuff is often sold as 'churned' buttermilk.

Soured pasteurized milk is not safer from germs than soured raw milk. Quite the reverse. All manner of bacteria can make milk sour and thicken and most of those that settle and grow in pasteurized milk are downright dangerous. You should dissuade friends and children from drinking soured pasteurized milk.

Milk and your health

The vitamins and minerals and proteins and so on of milk, and its abilities as a cure-all, are far too complicated for this book. In any case the structure changes according to the animal and its food, as well as the time of the year. It's more important to know how and when to use milk. For instance, hot boiled milk takes far longer to digest than cold milk, as all milk clots very quickly when it hits the stomach and hot milk clots even faster into an even harder curd and this can put a strain on a delicate stomach. Hot milk should be drunk as slowly as possible to allow the stomach to cope with it properly. Whole milk and skimmed milk take exactly the same time to digest and the soured or fermented milks including yoghurt take least time of all.

There is direct medical evidence to support the belief that warm milk helps you sleep. Apparently milk's calcium has a slight hypnotic effect on nerves, genuinely aiding a temporary relaxation of the body; anything else containing available calcium would be as effective. A word of advice to the elderly: a diet heavily balanced in favour of milk, acceptable to infants, who are thoughtfully born with a special store of iron, can lead to anaemia or at least an iron deficiency in the adult. The accompanying lists show the various ways in which you can buy milk in this country, and in a few others as a matter of interest.

Goat's milk is rather more easily available nowadays, both fresh and, rarely, dried. This is partly because it is more widely recognized that many children and some adults simply cannot digest cow's milk and when given it have constantly upset digestive systems. The exchange of cow's milk for goat's milk apparently can cause a miraculous improvement in health. For information about raising goats or obtaining goats' milk or goats' milk products (you can buy ice cream made from it at Harrods) you should write to the *British Goat Society, Rougham, Bury St. Edmunds, Suffolk.* They have excellent literature, especially *Dairy Work for Goatkeepers,* which includes advice on how to make cream, cheese and yoghurt from your goat's milk.

There are very few milking sheep kept in this country, although from time to time a customer at my Portobello Road shop has brought in some home-made cheese. But more dairying herds are being established and the resultant yoghurts and soft cheese, sometimes flavoured with herbs, are a great success in London at the moment. These are the first mass-produced sheep's milk cheese produced in the United Kingdom for many centuries, and really rather a good addition to the market, as fresh sheep's milk cheese is often called for if you are entertaining visitors from Uzbekistan, Azerbaijan or Armenia. Well, you never know . . .

Types of cows' milk sold in the United Kingdom

Unless it has a green foil top or a foil top striped with green, all milk sold in the United Kingdom is heat-treated in one way or another.

Pasteurized milk: the basic silver-top milk. Made with milk other than that of Jersey, Guernsey or South Devon cows, so is white rather than creamy, and has only thin cream on top.

Channel Islands and South Devon milk: the gold-top milk, made only from Jersey, Guernsey and South Devon cows (who may of course live anywhere in the British Isles). It is a richer colour because of a higher carotene content and has more, thicker cream on top.

Untreated milk: this raw milk is hard to find but will have a green foil top if from most cows or a striped green and gold top if it is unpasteurized gold-top milk.

Homogenized milk: this is red-top milk. By forcing full milk through a tiny valve under pressure the fat (cream) globules are reduced in size and then do not separate from the milk and rise to the top. This results in a milk with a richer creamier texture and taste, which is also more easily digested as it forms a much softer curd during digestion. Homogenized milk is not often suitable for making cheese.

Sterilized milk: usually sold in what look like French

wine bottles and capped like beer. This was the first type of preserved milk marketed, about the turn of the century, and tasted pretty rotten I understand. Homogenization changed that. Sterilization destroys bacteria and other micro-organisms more completely than pasteurization. Generally the milk is heated, homogenized, bottled and hermetically sealed. Then they are heated to about 110°C for 30–40 minutes. This high temperature causes slight caramelization of the milk sugar giving a definite 'cooked' flavour. It will last for two or three months without refrigeration as long as the container is unopened. Personally I wouldn't bother, now that we have:

UHT or Long-Life milk: this milk is heated to 132°C for 1 second then packed under sterile conditions into aluminium foil lined containers. It lasts unopened for months (it's usually date-stamped) but is just like ordinary milk once opened. The advantage is that its flavour is exactly the same as pasteurized homogenized milk; those who say they don't like it are usually comparing it to ordinary silver-top milk, from which it is certainly different. It is apparently quite the best of all for making yoghurt.

. . . and in other countries

In America plain milk is as difficult to find as sweet cream is in France. There is enormous emphasis on low-fat (partly-skimmed) milk and milks which are also fortified in some way, and although good to drink can do strange things to cooking. Flavoured milks are very popular and easy to buy, and fermented kefir comes in an extraordinary range of natural flavours.

In Australasia, where milk drinking is as much a religion as Marmite and rugby, you usually get only one type of milk, and that's the equivalent of our gold-top. But you also get rather good flavoured milks, especially the chocolate one. Milk bars, which are sort of like dairies here, but more like echoes of the soda shops of the US in the 30s, 40s and 50s, still make fabulous milk shakes containing real ice cream – the flavour range is exceptional – and often uses real fruit bases. The well-known Sanitarium shops, which are terribly old and well established health food shops, also sell lots of healthy drinks and have a special meal-in-a-glass which includes milk, ice cream, wheat germ, lecithin and other goodies. Ice cream sundaes are still made and in many dairies you can have a take-away fruit salad of tropical fruits put into a carton and topped with cream and ice cream –

a fabulous lunch to enjoy in Sydney's Hyde Park on a hot day; there's more than enough flesh about, both rare and roasted, to balance its fruitarianism!

Storing milk

Heat and light are the two worst enemies of milk, both of which destroy or affect flavour and vitamin content. So you must take it inside as early as you can and keep it cool and dark. If you don't have a refrigerator, keep it in a draught – the floor is always cooler than a table top. Cupboards should only be used if they are well ventilated.

The old-fashioned method of keeping milk cool works very well: you put the bottle or jug in a basin half filled with cold water and cover it with butter muslin saturated in cold water. You can also leave milk wrapped in a wet towel in a relatively warm place and it will become quite chilled – an interesting point to remember when on picnics.

Everything that comes into contact with milk should always be rinsed in cold water *before* going into hot; this avoids the formation of a film which is almost impossible to remove.

Pasteurized milk should keep in a refrigerator an average of six days.

Commercially-frozen milk is pasteurized and homogenized and frozen extremely quickly by using a special brine solution. Domestically frozen milk can be problematical – it is better to freeze only cartons of homogenized milk.

Condensed and evaporated milk

Invented for the easy transportation and storage of milk's goodness, all of these products have inbuilt problems of nutrition. But today's better methods of milk preservation have led to less dependence on condensed milks, especially in the poorer countries and they cause very few dietary problems now. **Condensed milk** diluted according to directions is easier to digest than ordinary milk but basic imbalance in favour of sugar and against fat is inherently bad and it should never be used in the diet for extensive periods. Nevertheless, a couple of generations of inhabitants of hot countries are hooked, and every beverage, including tea, is served with condensed milk, a habit I recently noticed sweet-toothed Englishmen quickly adopting in Bangkok. Usually the milk has been reduced by two thirds.

Evaporated milk is a term usually used for *unsweetened* condensed full milk whereas condensed milk usually indicates sweetened full milk or sweetened skimmed milk.

Milk powders

Milk powder is quite simply milk with most of its water content evaporated to produce solids with a moisture content of 5 per cent or less. It is made in quite a lot of different degrees of fat content, from full milk down to skimmed milk; all except the latter are homogenized before treatment.

There are two main ways of preparing this invaluable powder. The first spreads milk thinly on hot revolving rollers. The water evaporates leaving a film of solids which is then scraped off. This gives a powder which does not reconstitute readily and usually gives very lumpy results when mixed with water. The alternative method pumps milk as a fine spray into a chamber of hot air. As the water quickly evaporates the powder falls to the floor. This reconstitutes very easily.

Whole-milk powder contains all the nutrients of milk except vitamin C, thiamin and B12, which are affected by the heat of the process. Skimmed milk powder contains almost no fat and the other varieties of powder vary according to their original constituents. Provided the storage temperature is moderate-to-cool, milk powders keep a very long time. Those containing fat are liable to rancidity on exposure to air.

There is also available a range of dried milk powders that include non-dairy or vegetable fats, the advantage of which as far as I can tell is purely that of price. This mixture or total use of non-dairy fat is what gives us the 'whitener', a milk or cream substitute sprinkled on to hot drinks in place of the real thing. Palm oil is the usual source of such fat, although manufacturers are not required to state the exact fat used.

Mushrooms, dried

Those fine, wild and wonderful mushrooms from the French forests are best known in this country in dried form. *morels* are wrinkly and pocketed, like a prune or brain. *Ceps* are large and brown on top but honeycombed underneath. *Chanterelles* and *girolles* are elegant, golden and spindly.

Usually you are instructed to soak these dried mushrooms in water before use, but I'm sure much of the flavour gets thrown away if you throw this away, too, I tend always to use the water, stock or wine in which they have been soaked, or I put the dried mushrooms into a prepared sauce and let them hydrate in that, so that there is a full mixing of flavours.

All these mushrooms go well with other earthy foods, especially wild rice or with barley, and this is particularly when you should use the soaking water, to cook the grain.

Morels are exceptionally good as a garnish when stuffed with seafood or a purée of some sort and will make a contribution to special poultry stuffings.

Italian dried mushrooms are usually ceps and the Polish variety is either sliced field mushrooms (cultivated I suspect) or a stronger flavoured type usually found whole and strung into garlands. Although expensive they are cheaper than the French ones and can be used more lavishly; if you put them into, say, a pâté that is going to cook for a long time, they will swell with the meat juices and add their flavour too without going soggy and shrinking as would fresh ones.

The simplest use of cheaper dried mushrooms is to cook them gently from dry in cream and to use this as a sauce for pasta, fish or grilled meat; it should take about 20 minutes. If you do not have a lot of cream, then do the rehydrating in white wine or vermouth and when the mushrooms are soft and the liquor has reduced, add cream then.

NUTS

Nuts are fruits with a hard or leathery casing around an edible kernel. But not everything commonly referred to as a nut is one: for instance, peanuts are technically legumes, brazil and cashew nuts are seeds, and tiger nuts are tubers. 'Nuts to all that' you might say, but you'd be overlooking a very important source of protein, fats, minerals and vitamins, which is why vegetarians are so keen on them.

In Europe the fruit of the oak, the acorn, was part of earliest man's diet, Pliny calling the oak 'the tree which first produced food for mortal man'. Remains of acorns have been found around the Upper Great Lakes in settlements dating from at least 2000 BC and the early Yosemite Indians made a porridge out of them. Almonds and pistachioes are referred to in the Bible and right up until the end of the 18th century, almonds and walnuts were blanched, pulverized and soaked in water to provide a staple milk.

As well as being edible in their own right, nuts are very important commercially in a variety of ways. The main such usage is in nut oils: the oil from the hazelnut is widely used in cosmetics and soap making, almond oil is used for moisturizing creams, and a rather nasty component of the whole cashew nut is actually employed in making plastics.

There's hardly a country in the world that does not have an indigenous edible nut, but here in the West we seem to have settled for rather a short list.

ALMONDS

Probably the world's most popular nut, Britain imports about 15,000 tonnes annually, mainly from Spain. Other important producers are Italy, France, Portugal, Morocco and the Canary Islands. The United States is now largely supplied by the fast-expanding Californian industry.

The pretty almond tree, with its ornamental blossom, needs soil that is rich to a depth of 12 feet (3.6 m) and that has very good drainage. It starts to bear useful fruit in its third or fourth year and increases its yield annually for 12–20 years. Harvesting must start as soon as the outer hulls are fully split open; if they are left too long the nuts stick tightly to the shell and are known as 'sticktights', a dreaded situation if you are in to almond growing. Usually the nuts are dislodged from the trees with long thin poles but in California the pole has a padded mallet-like head and this collection method is called 'chubbing'. Immediately after hulling the nuts are put in the sun to dry – if this is delayed the shells darken in colour. They're left to dry for 2 days to 3 weeks depending on the weather.

This is one nut where you need to know something about types:

Bitter

Although very important in many dishes where just one or two round-out an almond flavour, these are very harmful if eaten in quantity. They actually contain the deadly-poisonous prussic acid, 'given away' in detective stories by its lingering smell of bitter almonds. Very hard to come by I find, but an excellent adjunct if you use almonds a lot in cooking; they work like lemons, orange on other fruit, bringing out all the essential flavour of the sweet almond without intruding itself. You can get something of the same flavour, without the intensity, by using cherry or apricot kernels.

Californian

A new type grown only in California with advanced techniques and irrigated orchards. Used mainly by confectioners.

Californian Nonpareil

The principal variety grown in California, it is of medium width but quite flat.

Jordan

Mainly grown in Malaga and Alicante and sometimes called the 'finger' almond as their long, slender shape resembles the little finger. Jordan almonds are the sweet dessert kind and extensively used in cooking. Graded according to size, large Jordans are sold retail, and the small ones go to confectioners who need a long variety for making sugared almonds. These are the ones with which the eyes of oriental beauties are compared.

Valencia

Grown in Spain and Portugal, these are the flatter, heart-shaped nuts, with a rougher, tougher skin and less sweet flavour. Sold mainly for cooking, they're usually blanched and skinned and used widely for cake decoration, specially for Dundee cakes.

The various forms of almonds

Whole blanched or unblanched halves: used mainly for cake decorating when they are all the better for being lightly toasted or roasted all through, and in some Chinese dishes, notably with deep-fried seaweed. If you are going to use them *in* cakes they really should be roasted first, or otherwise they will soften during cooking. If you want to finish a sauce with whole or halved blanched almonds then they should be added only a few minutes before serving, again to conserve crispness.

Flaked almonds: one of the most useful of all ingredients in a kitchen. They are expensive but you need very few to add flavour and interest to an extraordinary variety of food. They should usually be toasted but for use in cream sauces can be left their natural colour.

Toasted or fried in a little oil or dry-fried in a non-stick pan – they finish off salads superbly and are excellent in sauces with rich fish and seafood, as their crispness complements the solidity of such flesh. Wonderful with potatoes, peas, beans and squashes. Creamy tomato sauces, white wine sauces and richer pasta sauces containing cream are all much the better for the addition of a few flaked almonds.

Toasted flaked almonds convert ice cream into something far more interesting and make a simple two- or three-fruit salad into a speciality of the house. An easy way to smarten up a simple cold pie or mousse is to whip cream, flavour it with orange-flower water and then fold in toasted almond flakes. Almost good enough to serve by itself – or perhaps with a mountain of baby meringues. My newest use for them is incorporated into meringues; add some untoasted flakes to the mixture and cook a little longer than usual. The almond will toast and flavour the meringues, which are all the better for being flavoured with such liqueurs as Mandarine Napoléon or Crème de Cacao.

Slithered and nibbed: these fancier shapes, one long and thin, the other short and sort of fat, are mainly recommended for special decoration or where you want to add some texture – in a nut stuffing, for instance. In most cases flaked almonds would be as good, and probably cheaper.

Ground almonds: another invaluable standby and I'm sorry that soaring prices don't let me use them as lavishly as once was possible. They add wonderful richness and moistness to fruit cakes, make superb custards and tarts, transport stuffings into heaven, enrich sauces, and generally lift the ordinary into the extraordinary. I prefer to grind my own, for ground almonds can be very soapy and it's hard to know whether this is because of intrinsically low quality or staleness; it's not worth the risk. When seedless white grapes are in season spread some on a good short pastry shell and cover with a mixture of 4 oz (125 g) of ground almonds, 2 eggs, some cream, and some sugar to taste. Bake in a gentle oven until set and serve warm. Truly wonderful.

BRAZIL NUTS

It may come as no revelation to you to be told that the brazil comes from Brazil but you might not know that it isn't a nut but a seed. It's actually one of the 8 to 24 seeds arranged like segments of an orange inside a globular fruit 2–4 in (5–10 cm) in diameter.

Other names by which it is known include butternut, creamnut, castanea, paranut and niggertoe. The nut's rich flavour indicates a very high fat content and it also contains protein, iron and thaimine, one of the vitamins necessary to prevent *you* going nutty.

Harvested between January and June from trees which grow as high as 115 feet (34.5 m), brazil nuts are not much used in cooking, but there is no reason – other than expense – why they shouldn't be. They're very good with chocolate.

CASHEWS

Native to Central and South America, the cashew was taken to East Africa and India in the 15th century and now grows abundantly along their coastlines. Related to the American poison ivy and the poison sumac, the tree and its fruit must be treated with great care. The nut – which isn't a nut but a seed – looks very odd on the tree, rather disturbingly like a worm eating its way into or out of a soft, fleshy apple. The cashew apple which surrounds the seed/nut in its shell is used to make jams and jellies and drinks.

The seed is enclosed in two shells between which there is a brown oil that blisters human skin; this oil can be collected and used as a lubricant, an insecticide, and in the production of plastics. After the whole nuts are detached from the apples they are left to dry in the sun.

The traditional method of extraction begins with the burning of the nuts amongst logs. This causes the tough outer shell to crack but the burning of the oil releases intensely injurious fumes. Modern methods get over this by roasting in enclosed cylinders. Either way, the inner shells still have to be broken open, usually by hand, and the kernels heated again to remove the remaining skin. I wonder who first bothered to cope with all this fuss and danger – they must have been *very* hungry.

The Chinese use toasted cashew nuts in combination with chicken and pork, at least those living in London do. I use them in stuffings for pork and chicken and they are my favourite snack. Otherwise I don't know of much specialized use for them in food.

CHESTNUTS

Chestnuts roasting on an open fire are an essential component of any vision of old England – and Tin Pan Alley. What the songs don't tell you is that pieces of red-hot, burst chestnut shell fly in all directions, burning you and your carpet. If you wish to sin with Elinor Glyn – or some other kind of her – there are ways to protect yourself *and* eat your chestnuts. You can buy a small enclosed pan with holes in it with which to roast chestnuts, thus ensuring the safe pursuit of other traditional fireside activities. The combination of fireside and chestnuts has also been used to tell amatory fortunes. Dorothy Hartley tells us in her seminal *Food in England*: 'It was a fortune-telling trick to name the row of chestnuts set along the top bar of the hot grate, and the first 'name' to pop was to be the first lover to pop the question. If he jumped into your lap, you had him; if he popped into the fire and was burnt up . . . well, you didn't!' (She doesn't elaborate on what 'had' means.)

Chestnuts are different, and interesting, for a large number of reasons. They are the only nut we treat as a vegetable and, as they contain the least amount of oil and most starch of any nut, are the most digestible and the only ones that can be turned into a useful flour. Personally I find the shelling and peeling of fresh chestnuts a bore and for most recipes the tinned or dried kind are perfectly adequate; and I wouldn't begin to try to make the wonderful commercial, vanilla-flavoured purée, the discovery of which converts any cook into a better cook as far as puddings are concerned.

If you do want to prepare your own chestnuts, the simplest way is to pierce the flat ends, put them into boiling water for 5 minutes or so and when cool enough to handle you can remove the shell and skin very easily. Every one has their favourite method and if yours isn't the same as mine I don't know enough about it to argue. The important thing to remember is that chestnuts generally don't, in their natural state, have a great deal of flavour, and that without care even this can be diluted.

There are several varieties of chestnuts, which mainly differ by having one or more nut inside the shell. Only when there is a single floury nut in the shell can it be called a marron; and the best of these are held to come from the Ardèche, a beautiful French region of lakes, rivers, pine and chestnut-tree clad hills. It was once a centre of the French silk trade, but when there was a slump in 1882, a certain Clement Faugier set up a chestnut-processing plant in a town called Privas. Faugier is now the most famous marron-producing firm of all, and still run by descendants of its founder.

Chestnuts can be bought in a wide variety of states, all of them worth your investigation.

Chestnut flour

Mainly found in Italian stores and almost exclusively used in Italian kitchens. When mixed with water it makes a non-elastic dough (there being no gluten content) and this is made into fritters, porridges of various kinds mixed with cream, milk, water or oil and an extraodinary yeast-leavened cake flavoured with aniseed. It is also used for a chestnut-type polenta.

Dried (dehydrated) chestnuts

Expensive but an excellent standby in the larder of any imaginative cook, so buy plenty when they are in the shops at Christmas. Provided they are stored in a cool place, dried chestnuts keep for at least 18 months. All you have to do is soak them in warm water until they can be bitten through or cut with a knife; but you can be more inventive than that.

I simmer the dried chestnuts gently in red or white wine spiced with cinnamon, nutmeg, a little orange peel and bay leaf. Or I'll cook them with red wine, a little garlic and some small pieces of fatty bacon, for chestnuts take to fat and smoky flavours like anything. Either way, reduce the liquid until it just covers the chestnuts. These reconstituted and reflavoured chestnuts are then ready for roughly chopping into stuffings and sauces, to add to brussel sprouts (a classic combination), or to serve by themselves with roasted meats and poultry. Another wonderful idea is to drain them after reconstituting then turn them in a hot caramel of butter and lightly-browned sugar; very gala, very simple.

You can also reconstitute them plainly to mash with sugar and spices and vanilla as the basis for sweets and puddings. If you want to use whole chestnuts or chestnut halves in any dish I think the reconstituted dried ones have more flavour than those in tins (in fact I'm sure of it). As dried chestnuts are invariably from Italy it may have something to do with the variety used.

Chestnuts make excellent additions and stretchers to casseroles. In this case I often don't reconstitute them first but put them into the cooking liquid in the dried state. This way they make their contribution to the overall flavour and benefit in turn from all the flavoured fats and liquor; if you used ready constituted chestnut they would be more likely to give their flavour out and take nothing back. Chestnuts are specially good foils to the richer winter stews that include pieces of fat bacon, and are wonderful with pigeons and pork dishes of all kinds.

Purée (plain)

Not something you might use a lot of, but its concentrated flavour and delicious rich colour is useful. Mixed with breadcrumbs, chopped celery green, some brandy and a little onion or garlic it makes a simple moist stuffing for veal or poultry. Or it can be added to a pancake mixture to make fritters that will go with all manner of meat dishes. It's quite common to accompany duck with chestnut purée in some form; you might simply mix in some cream, salt and pepper, beat in one egg to each 5 fl. oz (150 ml) of purée, and gently bake this beneath the roast for 40 minutes or until it has a crisp brown crust. This would then be a superior chestnut polenta. You might also consider mixing in some whole, uncooked cranberries before baking.

Purée (vanilla)

Perhaps one of the most delicious things you can buy in a can. No, not perhaps – *definitely!* Too rich and sweet for most people to eat as it is, so what you do is this: fold it gently into equal quantities of whipped cream, then add a tot of brandy or sherry for good measure. Simplicity itself, it is truly heavenly.

Here are just a few of the ways I have used this mixture. It can be crammed into freshly-made profiteroles, perhaps with a black cherry in each that has been soaked in black rum for a while; stick the profiteroles together in a pyramid shape with light caramel. For a wedding at which 60 guests in formal dress sat down in candlelight to a ten-course dinner, I had to make a pudding which would also serve as the wedding cake. So I sandwiched one chocolate and one vanilla meringue together with this chestnut cream mixture, thus achieving a very pretty three-tone colour graduation. These were then built into a mountain some 3 feet (90 cm) high and, having alternated the way they were presented, the mountain appeared to be made in stripes of white and brown. It created a sensation when brought in -- but nothing compared to that caused when served up, for each plate was sauced with a mix of puréed black cherries and black rum slightly thickened and glossed with arrowroot. The bride said it was worth getting married for.

Chocolate goes well with chestnuts and with the chestnut and cream mixture; next time you want to make a spectacular cake, bake a couple of chocolate sandwiches (use Betty Crocker mixes for something really rich and fail-safe), join them with ½ inch (1.25 cm) of the mixture then mix icing sugar with more of it. You might sprinkle orange or coffee liqueur onto a layer of the cake; you could also add a layer of fresh mandarin sections, or more black cherries, a combination which is also foolproof. If you make the mixture taste more of cream than chestnuts, you can serve it with almost any fruit, but it's fantastic with strawberries and raspberries.

I'm not going to give you *all* my best ideas but here's a last one worth remembering; make some millefeuille squares from puff pastry, split and rebake to crisp right through. When cool, spread thickly with the chestnut and cream mixture then arrange unsweetened strawberry halves which you have soaked in orange juice or liqueur (the juice is better) and then drained. Cover these with the top layer of the millefeuille, then if you have the time and inclination, glaze each with some lightly-coloured caramel which you should allow to run willy-nilly over the edges.

Marrons glacés   Made only with the marron chestnut, which is preserved by repeated boiling and soaking in syrup. But are they *really* worth the huge prices? No unless you add brandy (even *more* expense) to the syrup.

COCONUT

The coconut has been admired for countless generations, and relied upon for far more than food and romantic backdrops. Our earliest civilizations, in the Indus Valley, certainly ate them and the Chinese have included them in their diet for almost as long and are thought to have been the first to use coconut meat and milk in confectionery. The tree is probably native to India, the coasts of south-east Asia, South America and the Caribbean and could have got to the South Seas in several ways. In the first place the coconut is an extraordinarily hardy traveller and can survive in salt water for a long time then happily take root on hitting land. Alternatively, the Polynesians may simply have taken some along when they settled on the islands from various parts of south-east Asia; or later invaders from South America could have carried them as suggested by the great Kon-Tiki expedition. Those in the Bahamas were planted in the famous pink sands after Columbus had found them further south.

Every part of the coconut palm is useful and the Sanskrit word for it means 'tree which furnishes all the necessities of life'. The leaves are used for walls, thatching and packaging; the trunk is used for building; the hair covering the mature nut makes coir matting; the oil from the meat appears in cosmetics, soap and suntan oils; the meat itself is food, either fresh or dried (copra); the milk is used for cooking or for making wine; the shell is an eating or drinking bowl, or, for centuries, the top-people's travel souvenir. In 14th-century Venice, if you wanted to keep up with the Marco Polos, you would have to have had a silver-mounted *noce di coco* in your palazzo. As late as the last century polished coconut shells were still being mounted in silver and sent home by the adventuring scions of European families.

But there's always something new, even with such an ancient food. Clever – or lazy – men in Thailand now have trained monkeys to shin up the palms and carefully choose nuts of the preferred degree of ripeness and pick them, which saves their owners either (a) doing it themselves or (b) paying someone else. The state of ripeness of the nut is rather important, for although it will drop to the ground all by itself when nice and ripe, the milk contained in the younger, green coconuts is more plentiful and more delicious. When I stayed in a beach hut on an otherwise deserted 20-mile strip of burning white sand on the Gulf of Siam, I was impressed to find that our host had thoughtfully imported lads to shin up the trees to gather fresh coconuts each morning, so we could drink that cool and refreshing liquid. What he had overlooked was to tell us that it has a decided laxative effect – something we found ourselves learning *a posteriori*.

The name coconut is based on old Portuguese and Spanish words which mean 'grinning face', a reminder of the appearance of one end of the nuts, on which there are three darker spots looking like eyes and a mouth. Dr Johnson referred to it as the 'cocoanut', which was an accident, but it took a long time for the spelling to revert to its original.

The coco-de-mer is a double coconut of enormous size found only on two islands of the Seychelles; polished specimens have become the new tourist status symbol and their undoubted resemblance to oiled and sun-tanned buttocks or voluptuous female thighs ensure they are noticed by the neighbours.

If you don't fancy coping with whole coconuts, the meat and milk can be bought in two basic forms.

Desiccated or flaked coconut

Particularly popular in Australasia, where desiccated coconut is put into or onto more sweet and savoury dishes than Dame Edna Everage could ever poke fun at. Lamington cakes are squares of sponge coated with chocolate syrup and coconut and are as essential at a Down-Under christening as the vicar. Coconut bumblebees, coconut ice and coconut-sprinkled fruit salads and curries will be as life blood to the newly named child. Actually, it is very good in all these foods, specially in curries, with which it can also be seved as a condiment.

Coconut cream and coconut milk can be made from desiccated coconut by covering, say, 6–8 oz (150–200 g) with boiling water and leaving it to cool. Then put the coconut into a sieve or some muslin, and mash or squeeze it to extract the creamy-white liquid. If you leave it thick is is 'cream', or you can dilute this with water to make 'milk'. The liquid inside a coconut is not that used in cooking.

Cream of coconut

Although you can sometimes buy *coconut milk* canned it has usually been adulterated and sweetened. Better to buy a solid block of cream of coconut which lasts for ages, is pure, and can simply be reconstituted by dissolving an amount in hot or boiling water. The thicker it is the richer, obviously, and as both thick cream or thin milk it can be used like the dairy product; thick coconut cream curdles if heated to boiling point. This is done deliberately in West Indian and Malaysian cooking. Thick coconut cream spread on top of a grilled pork chop or roasted chicken gives an interesting and instant lift to otherwise ordinary food. Even such basics as vanilla ice cream, sliced oranges or grilled bananas are magically transformed; and used with care in association with finer fruits like strawberries or the wonderful mango, thick, chilled coconut cream makes child's play of creating new desserts during hot summer months. I always keep coconut cream in the refrigerator.

You don't always have to *eat* it; coconut milk is terrific in long summery drinks with rum and fruit juices. A hot evening, a barbecue, some friends, some coconut cream, assorted fruits and alcohols and you'll have a memorable party – or, if you are lucky, a party that no-one remembers!

I like to finish a spicy, gingery curry sauce by leaving the solid coconut cream to melt in the liquid, and it can add new dimensions of flavour to the most unexpected vegetables – I think you'll like sliced aubergine baked gently in coconut milk spiked with a few rings of green chilli peppers.

Whole coconuts

If you do find yourself the owner of whole coconuts in this country this is what you do. First shake it close to your ear to ensure it has plenty of liquid inside; if it does not, throw it away. Then, with something long and sharp, pierce two or three of the soft 'eyes' at the base so that the milk can be poured out. Now you can split the nut, either by a sharp blow on its equator, or with a fine-toothed hacksaw.

In the Pacific Islands you would then coarsely grate the flesh using one of the most obscene-looking techniques ever devised. You use a vertical wooden shaft mounted at knee level, the end of which is a sharp, curved metal blade. Women straddle the shaft so that only the up-curved blade shows and then screw the coconuts on the blade to loosen the flesh, and this is how copra is made.

You would find it as easy to break the half shells into smaller pieces and lever the flesh off. You can leave the thin inner skin on or off as you like. Cut into small pieces and chilled slightly, coconut then makes an excellent snack or accompaniment to cold meats and poultry for a barbecue or picnic. You can grate it roughly, skin and all, to incorporate into sauces or scatter over fruit, or follow an 18th-century English recipe by boiling the lot with a pint of milk until this is highly flavoured and use the milk to make coconut bread, which you do by replacing your usual milk or water in any favourite dough or scone recipe.

HAZELNUTS

Hazelnuts are cobnuts are Kent cobs are filberts; the only difference is technical and determined by the relative length of the nut to the husk, cobs usually being rounder and filberts somewhat longer. In the United States all type are called filberts, a name originally given because they usually ripen on or about St Philbert's Day, August 22nd. In Europe, filbert usually denotes a hazelnut that has been cultivated. The 15 species of shrub and tree from which this small and important nut come range in height from 9–120 feet (2.7–36 m) and belong to the birch family. They need deep well-drained soil with plenty of sun, and thus Turkey, Italy and Spain are the chief producers. The finest nuts are said to come from trees best described as Eurasian – the European and the giant hazelnut. Hybrids of these with the American and Beaked Filbert are also excellent producers. Constantinople nuts is a trade name for Turkish hazelnuts, and for those from Spain are known as Barcelona nuts. In New Zealand we call them monkey nuts . . .

From a culinary point of view hazelnuts are essential to a great part of the finest traditions of European cake-making and confectionery, when they are usually used in ground form. Although there is some argument as to whether one should use hazelnuts, almonds or both to make praliné I think the purely hazelnut variety infinitely better (not that it probably matters one jot).

Like almonds, hazelnuts taste much better when lightly toasted, or, if you have the patience, slowly roasted until golden all the way through. Lightly crushed they are good to sprinkle over fruit dishes, in cereals, muesli, yoghurt, cream and with green vegetables. They are specially good with the aristocratic mangetout, or with broccoli, particularly if bathed with some garlic-ridden butter.

Toasted hazelnuts, whole or chopped, crushed or ground are quite one of the best additions to stuffing and make a fascinating addition to meat gravies and game sauces. I recently stuffed boned trout with a mixture of grated celeriac, chopped hazelnuts and garlic, baked them in a hot oven and served them with a dollop of chilled sour cream – perfectly simple and quite memorable. So too are strawberries served with whipped cream stiffened with ground or chopped hazelnuts.

Finely-ground hazelnuts are the basis of many regal Middle-European cakes, and for the increasingly ubiquitous hazelnut meringue 'gâteau'. Hazelnut oil is one of the newest ingredients of nouvelle cuisine; it is worth saving for use on special salads – but only to be given to those who appreciate things heavenly. As they used to say on Marmite jars, Too Much Spoils The Flavour.

MACADAMIA NUTS

A relatively new arrival on the international scene and virtually unknown in Europe, macadamia nuts are something of a cult food in America, particularly in Hawaii where Macadamia shops are as shiny and well-staffed as service stations used to be. There they've done more things with macadamia nuts than you can – or would want to – imagine. Every kind of chocolate shape, every kind of jam, jelly and marmalade, every kind of cake biscuit, cookie and character includes the macadamia. Mark my words, a macadamia Muppet is only *just* around the corner.

The most extraordinary thing about this nut is that the tree upon which it grows is Australian, a native of Queensland and New South Wales. It looks something like a pale, fat hazelnut and has a slightly strange, fatty, waxy texture and a taste that can only be described as 'nutty', perhaps slightly buttery. The ones I've been sold as cocktail snacks were all helped with a little coconut oil, so perhaps there's not all that much unaided flavour. So why the fuss? Well, good marketing strategy excepted, they have a most valid claim to the world's very serious attention for they have an exceptionally high protein content and are being studied as a new and simple alternative protein source in remote tropical areas. If you manage to get some you will probably find them so expensive you won't dare use them. Best plan is to pop into a Macadamia shop on Waikiki Beach and taste one or two of their confections for free.

And the name? Yes it is associated with the man who pioneered the use of a tar mixture on our roads; the nut was one of Mr Macadam's later interests.

PEANUTS

Peanuts, which are not nuts at all but legumes, are also called groundnuts, earth nuts, monkey nuts . . . and goolers. Yes, that's right, monkey nuts *and* goolers. Perhaps because of such names, peanuts hide underground, the dying flower actually managing to burrow in such a way as to protect her offspring. At harvest time the entire plants, except for the deepest roots, are pulled up and left to wither in the sun for a day. Then they are built into large stacks around a stake with the pods towards the centre to protect them from the weather. In 4–6 weeks they are ready to be used to make all manner of goodies – peanut oil, peanut butter, salted peanuts, spiced or dry-roasted peanuts, or the peanut sauces that make Indonesian foods so original and full of flavour.

Traces of peanuts have been found in ancient Peruvian mummy graves and from its native South America it has now spread to India, Indonesia, China, West Africa and the United States.

Peanuts are very much more good for you than their usage as monkey food would suggest. Pound for pound, they have more protein, minerals and vitamins than beef liver, more food energy (calories) than sugar and more fat than double cream.

PECAN

Native to North America where it was widely used by the Indians who called it 'pecan' (a word describing all nuts that have shells so hard they need to be cracked with a stone). As well as eating its meat, the Indians ground it into a milky liquid for use in gruels and maize cakes, a combination which would be very good. It is now grown in a belt stretching from New Mexico to the Carolinas, and as far north as Illinois; South Africa and Australia also cultivate some.

The pecan is claimed to have the highest fat content of any vegetable food, with a calorific content similar to that of butter. The trees grow anything up to 160 ft (48 m) high with a span of up to 70 ft (21 m) and so harvesting is mainly by variations of beating branches or shaking the trees. Shelling is difficult, and a labyrinth of conveyors, blowers, reels, fans, graders, pickers, dyers and packers can take up to three days ultimately to separate the kernel from the shell and sort it into uniform grades; this complicated processing is the reason for its relative expense. Although most pecan trees are wild and grow on the banks of rivers and creeks, there is also a cultivated variety made possible by the experiments with grafting successfully carried out by a Louisiana slave in 1850. The cultivated tree produces a nut with a thinner shell and thus gives a better yield.

Whole pecans are sometimes available in markets in this country and recognizable by their red-grey-brown shiny appearance, something like an acorn without its cap. They can be infuriatingly difficult to crack – using a hammer often disintegrates the shell *and* the nut, or forces splinters of one inextricably into the other. The best way is to hold two nuts on one palm and squeeze; one of them should crack right round the middle and the two halves can be extricated. Well, that's what *should* happen . . .

Pecan halves and pieces are increasingly available in the United Kingdom in specialty stores, and worth every penny. Good in sweet pies, vegetable purées or dessert pastries that include spices, they are often said to be interchangeable with walnuts, but in my opinion the substitution could only be made for reasons of economy. The pecan has a far richer and more elegant flavour, without the acidic bite of the walnut. If you ever want to bribe me, give me pecan pie: I'll do anything – before, during *and* after.

PINE NUTS OR PINE KERNELS

These delicious morsels really are from pine trees, usually the stone pine, but other pines may be the source. Pine nuts are an essential for Middle Eastern food and are also widely used in Italy and Greece. Those seen in the United Kingdom usually come from China.

The small, moon coloured nuts are rich and oily and taste of the merest whisper of pine resin, but are perfectly addictive once you begin to eat them.

They are an important ingredient in the famed *pesto* of Genoa, pounded with fresh basil, garlic, oil and parmesan into a pasta sauce. But generally they are browned lightly before being used, either in a little oil or in a dry non-stick pan, which is easier.

To convert any rice dish, even plain rice into something Levantine, browned pine nuts with or without chopped pistachios is all you need. Added to a saffron or turmeric scented pilaff they are even better.

Once sweetened, I find they make a delicious and unexpected garnish for simple puddings like ice creams and lemon mousses; they go very well with fresh, lightly-flavoured cream cheese, too. The most spectacular way to sweeten them is first to brown a little butter (carefully) then to add some sugar and let that caramellize before you add the nuts. The sugar and butter will coat the nuts with a crunchy toffee; I first did this to top poached whole satsumas, served in their syrup with rose-water flavoured cream cheese.

PISTACHIOS

This is the most maddening nut of all – once you eat one you have to eat another, then just one more . . . until your fingernails ache and bleed from opening the shells; you cry out for liquid because of the salt, and your surroundings are littered with raped shells. But what bliss!

I've not been able to discover why pistachios are nearly always sold still in their shells, slightly cracked open and salted. Perhaps they keep better that way (as good a reason as any). They can also be bought shelled and unsalted, which is what you use for cooking.

This green nut, rich and decorative with its wine-red skin, is grown from Afghanistan to the Mediterranean and in the United States where it is specially popular as a flavouring. It is expensive and has always been so, for there are records of complaints about its prohibitive cost from Ancient Rome. Of the more accessible places, Aegina in Greece's Saronic Gulf produces the most wonderful, and no visit to this island can be considered unless you are prepared to gorge yourself. Strangely it is the only place in Greece they grow.

They are invaluable for decorating, chopped finely over sweet or savoury food, hot or cold. Pistachios are essential, chopped roughly, in good Middle Eastern pilaffs which also include saffron and toasted pinenuts. Finely chopped pistachios are part of the fillings for Greek, Turkish and Arabic pastries and are also excellent in poultry stuffings. But Europe has never really taken this nut to its heart – or stomach – and it appears only rarely as the flavouring in specialized cakes or ice creams, usually in association with a muddy green colouring which has nothing to do with its natural state of affairs. In fact most pistachio flavouring is achieved by artificial means and tastes more like almonds, which is a terrible let-down. I always send pistachio ice cream back if it tastes of almonds – especially if it is expensive and served in a restaurant with airs.

To get the really bright green colour which looks so good, boil the nuts for 30 seconds in water and then peel away the skin; if the nuts do not brighten they are not of the best quality.

TIGER NUTS

These are the least nut-like nut of all, for they are actually tubers. Looking like a cross between shrivelled peanut and extruded, dried dog food they are perhaps better known under their Spanish name – *chufas* or *alchufas*.

Mainly eaten as a snack they have an extraordinary chewy texture and flavour, not unlike coconut crossed with brazil nut. Apparently they were very popular before the last war but disappeared with the corner shops. Harmony Foods of London, who are responsible for putting them back on the market, say they have had letters from old people telling them how much they appreciate seeing them again.

In southern Spain you drink them rather than eat them, in a very popular beverage called *horchata*. This is made by soaking the nuts overnight (start with hot water) then putting them all into the liquidizer with the water. Drain well then put the residue back into the liquidizer again with a little more water. Drain again then put the residue into muslin, tighten that and squeeze the remaining milk. It is a really refreshing drink served chilled and if you've ever wondered what people do in a Spanish *horchateria*, now you know. Horchata can also be heated very slowly indeed in a double boiler and it will eventually thicken to make a custard.

Tiger nuts are rarely used in cooking, but when soaked, apparently go well in apple pie.

WALNUTS

Walnuts have been with us a long time and used just as long. The Greeks used them lavishly and still use them as prodigiously in sweetmeats and pastries. The Romans spread walnut trees wherever they marched and may have introduced them to the British Isles; some can be seen preserved in the volcanic ash at the Temple of Isis in Pompeii.

There are several types of walnut. The black and the butternut grow in the eastern states of North America; the English or Persian walnut is common throughout Europe, the Middle East, China and has been introduced to the United States. The nut of the English variety is usually picked green and dried or ripened off the tree.

It's a particularly versatile nut, found successfully in sweet and savoury dishes throughout the world. It has a rather astonishing affinity with tomatoes and the Caucasian combination of tomato and walnut sauce is sensational. Perhaps the simplest 'gourmet' dish of all is a bowl of sliced tomatoes (but rich, red ones, needless to say), just slightly chilled and soaked in walnut oil. I also like them crushed together in butter with green peppercorns, to make a savoury topping for such tasty flesh as pheasant.

Walnuts were once crushed and soaked to make milk but the almond variety is the only flavouring of this kind now made. Vegetarians like walnuts and use them extensively, usually eating them in combination with cracked cereals to form their vegetarian steaks.

Pickled walnuts are increasingly hard to buy, and like so many traditional English foods they seem to be disappearing because commercial manufacture is *un*-commercial. Some are made, but it is usually easier to buy them bottled from America; however, these are sweet pickled which is not to many people's taste.

The grading of walnuts calls for a mind besotted by minutiae and such a predeliction would be of some help in buying them too. The best advice when buying walnut halves is to remember that light is right – the lighter the colour the higher the grade. If you are being asked to pay exceptionally high prices, the half nuts should not only be pale, there should be no surface chipping and no smaller or broken pieces present, both of which are signs of a lesser grade.

Remember when you are making cakes or pies with walnuts, that if they brown they often become very bitter.

OILS

Put simply, an oil is a fat which is liquid at normal temperatures. Although earliest man in northern Europe relied on animals for fat, the rest of the world looked to vegetable oils. The type varied according to locality. In Mesopotamia sesame seed oil was used and records survive of the 'best quality' being bought for Nebuchadnezzar's palace. In Anatolia it was almond oil; in the Americas oil from the peanut, maize and sunflower; in China and south-east Asia they used soya and coconuts. Before the introduction of the olive, you would have used radish seed oil in Egypt, walnut and poppy-seed oil in Greece. Poppies of a different type were used in northern Europe, as well as oil from flax and the cameline.

Not all these oils were used exclusively for cooking, nor are they now. Pliny gives an explanatory quote which I vote the most tantalizing of any. He said: 'There are two liquids especially agreeable to the human body, wine inside and oil outside,' And I shouldn't think he was speaking of salads al fresco . . .

The Egyptians used olive oil (and buttermilk incidentally) as a lubricant for moving heavy building materials. Homer mentions it as an aid to weaving and it has been used to make soap since the days of ancient Rome, where it also powered lamps. In Minoan Crete oil was considered part of the king's treasure and an important commodity for earning foreign exchange.

Oils were also used as protective agents on ships' hulls and in painting.

Modern emulsion paints, which are now water soluble, are descendants of tempera, an emulsion in water of oil and pigments stabilized with vegetable gums or egg yolks.

Oil's uses pharmacologically are manifold, and far more sophisticated than the purgative spoonful of castor oil. This perhaps is the time to simplify the vexed question of saturated and unsaturated fats and all that.

Animal fats have a high level of so-called saturated fats. These are solid at normal temperature and are believed to increase blood cholesterol, leading to hardening of the arteries and heart problems. Vegetable oils mainly contain poly-unsaturated fats, which are always liquid unless specially treated. They in turn contain something called linoleic acid which when eaten with food helps actually lower the cholesterol level and aids the burning up of carbohydrate, preventing its conversion into fat. This is not to say you must throw your butter out the window, but rather, as in most dietary matters, try to strike a balance of what you like, what makes you fat, and what might help prolong your life. Butter is not an assassin, nor is safflower oil an elixir of everlasting life.

The accompanying list will graphically illustrate the relationship between the major sources of fats in our diets.

The major uses of vegetable oils are for cooking, and as the basis of margarine; they also go into cooking fats, salad dressings and ice cream.

THE MAJOR TYPES OF CULINARY OIL

Cottonseed

Widely used in vegetable oil mixtures and in oleo margarines, especially in the USA. In these products it has usually been bleached but when used to pack seafood (especially from Japan) it has slight colour and, to me, a rather unpleasant taste and texture, some of which I think remains in the butter substitutes. It is the second most important seed oil, produced mainly in Russia, the United States and China.

Olive oil

Indubitably the king of oils, though many English people cannot get used to the idea of oil being enjoyed for itself. But it is important to remember that olive oil is a most important flavouring agent, and now the good stuff is so expensive this is its major function in my kitchen and I use blander oils for most frying. Although it's a shame to do so, richer olive oils can be diluted with fine flavourless oils, giving economy and a less obtrusive flavour for salads and general purposes.

Every country makes oil of different basic flavours and many grades, and only experiment will tell you which suits your palate better. Generally the further south and the hotter you go the stronger the flavour of the oil. Which should mean that French oil is less strong in flavour than that of, say, southern Italy or Greece. Experiment with small bottles and then lash out to buy a 1 gallon (5 litre) can, for you will save huge amounts. Olive oil is mainly monosaturated oil and thus neither a threat nor a help to one's cholesterol problem. It also lasts a very long time without being affected by air, though it should be kept in the dark.

The best grade of olive oil is made simply by crushing the fresh, cold olives, with no heating or other processing. This is the virgin oil and may then be pasteurized. It should be very green and have the rich throaty flavour that instantly conjures up thoughts of sun. Marchese Emilio Pucci, the aristocratic Italian designer of playwear for playgirls, has had olive groves and vineyards in his family since the 12th century. He markets unpasteurized virgin olive oil from Tuscany, which costs a great deal of money but is delicious enough to drink by the spoonful (which I understand can do wonderful things for your skin).

All the other grades of olive oil are expressed by pressure under heat and many have an undoubted bitterness. Some are white and all rancidify fairly quickly. The lowest grade oil is made from windfall, preserved or fermented olives, and needs chemical treatment to make it colourless. Mainly designed for industrial use, it is often found adulterating higher quality oils in the interest of economy and profit but such mixed oils are very interesting, nonetheless. If you like just a little of the olive oil taste and have a limited budget, I suggest you look at some of the Italian oils, often called 'Green oil' (Lupa brand) or Olivette. You get colour and flavour from the percentage of olive oil contained and you get economy from the other vegetable oils. As far as I know it is all good pure oil and it is very popular with our customers, who know a good thing when they taste it.

Next time you are at a loss as to how to make simple vegetables taste interesting, add a little warmed olive oil and some lemon juice. In stews or casseroles, too, just a few spoonfuls really will make a remarkable difference. And when you start to cook like they do in Provence and Italy it is ridiculous to consider your food authentic unless it has masses of olive oil. Ratatouille without a lot of olive oil is just not on. Although I know this will sound terrible to many, even fried eggs taste extraordinarily good and different when done in olive oil or oil and butter. And where ever there is garlic, there olive oil must be, too.

Palm and Palm kernel oil

The oil palm is native to West Africa and although its existence is barely even suspected by most Europeans it is a most important part of our diet . . . especially if you like ice cream products.

The brilliant red fruit of the oil palm grows in bunches averaging 26–32 lb (13–18 kg) in weight and if properly cultivated the tree produces a higher yield than any other oil-producing plant per acre. Each palm fruit is built up like a miniature coconut with a thick fibrous pulp on the outside and a hard kernel inside. Palm oil is obtained from its outer layer and this red substance is an essential ingredient to the food of Brazil and Nigeria. But it adds a flavour not readily appreciated by others ie non-natives. More refined palm oils are staples in India and Asia and some edible fats include refined palm oil.

Kernel oil is an altogether harder oil, rather like that of the coconut, and it has two uses that some would say are indistinguishable, and others would argue are poles apart. One use is in soap, as Hollywood stars constantly remind us in return for huge fees. If the name is honest, there is olive oil in this soap, too. The other use, as *no-one* reminds you, is as a major substitute for milk, butter and cream in 'non-dairy fat' foods. Palm kernel oil, after suitable treatment can be whipped and frozen into believing it is cream and subsequently ice cream It is the major fat used in ice creams in this country and the basis for the kosher *pareve* whips, creams and ice creams.

Peanut oil

This is specially important in the catering trade for, as well as having no taste, it can be used to fry at an extremely high temperature without unpleasant smoking or other side effects. The combination of high temperature and lack of taste means you get crisper food faster and that the fat has had no opportunity to penetrate. The nut has an oil content of 45–50 per cent, which is used in fats, ice cream and margarine.

Poppyseed oil

Another oil popular simply for its lack of taste, an asset in some sorts of cooking. It is sold as *huile blanche* (white oil) in northern France and Paris, where it enjoys greatest popularity.

Safflower oil

Comparatively new on the market but all set to become market leaders. Safflower, seeds of which have been found in Egyptian tombs of 2000 BC, was originally grown for the colour of its florets, which give a cheap imitation of saffron. When synthetic dyes began to displace safflower it seemed doomed, but then it was discovered that the oil obtained from the same florets and their seeds has the highest percentage of poly-unsaturated oil known – 78 per cent. The major producers are now Mexico and the United States who between them produce over half a million tons of seeds each year. If you really are worried about your cholesterol level, this is the one for you (but sneak some olive oil too, from time to time, just for pleasure).

Sesame seed oil

A very ancient oil, used as much for flavouring as anything else. It can be clear or a nice reddish brown depending on whether the seeds have been toasted or not. Marco Polo was impressed enough to write about it and it is still widely used in India and the Orient, specially in confectionery and bakery.

Soya bean oil

Although used in China for the past 4,000 years, the first shipment did not arrive in the United Kingdom until 1908. It is one of the top four in the poly-unsaturated league and is an extremely good keeper. Soya bean oil also has quite a high smoking point, which means it will fry or deep fry at a temperature high enough to ensure it will not pass what little flavour it has on to the food. It is now the leading type of vegetable oil in sheer quantity. As well as margarines and cooking fats the oil is used in paint, printing ink, soap, cosmetics, varnishes and insecticides.

Sunflower oil

The very high percentage of polyunsaturated oils in this oil make it very important indeed, and it is widely used both as an oil for salads, cooking, fats and margarine. It is very good for frying also but perhaps a little expensive for this use on a regular basis. The sunflower is a native of Mexico but grown in many parts of the world, particularly south Russia. China, Hungary and South Africa also grow enough to be useful but Great Britain, although it has an eminently suitable climate, produces a very small crop indeed.

New varieties developed in the Soviet Union have increased the oil content of seed from 20 to 40 per cent.

See also

walnuts (p.275) and **hazelnuts** (p.270).

Pasta and Noodles

Even though an Italian word, pasta is about as exclusive to Italy as palaces and royal families are to Great Britain. Marco Polo did *not* bring it to Europe from China – that is a 19th-century American fabrication. And firm, *al dente* pasta is better for you than well-cooked pasta. Now, having shattered the basic misconceptions, here are some facts.

All pasta is based on a kneaded paste of strong (usually durum) wheat flour and water to which eggs are sometimes added. Its origins are the same as those of cheese – no-one knows when, where or by whom. Ancient Etruscans, Greeks and Romans enjoyed it – indeed the *noodles, nouilles* and *nudeln* of modern Europe are clearly rooted in the Roman *nodellus*, a word which means little knots and describes what happens to long strands of pasta when on your plate. Even the Arabs have their own noodles, the *trii*, which they introduced to Sicily long ago, in sumptuous recipes. More surprising than pasta's long history is that it was only rarely eaten in post-Roman Italy until the middle of the 19th century, and even then those who ate it all lived in the south. The people of the north used rice as their staple starch product.

Pasta products seemed spontaneously to have become popular again with pockets of populace of southern Italy around the 13th century; they had been known there since the Greeks colonized this part of the Mediterranean. This was all well before the appearance of the tomato, so pasta was served with sharp fish or vinegar-pointed sauces or with the voluptuous flower-scented creams and cheeses that dominated European cooking after the return of the crusaders. When the tomato arrived it was found to flourish most fulsomely near Naples, and soon the inventive proprietors of the rumbustious Neapolitan inns and *vermicelli* stalls were offering a rich reduced tomato sauce as an optional extra dressing for their pasta products. In 1860, when bearded Garibaldi led the One Thousand into southern Italy from the rice-eating north, this army learned to like the combination and when they returned home they took their new tastes with them, permanently altering the style and flavour of northern Italian cooking. At about the same time, new strains of wheat made wheat flour more readily available and both north *and* south Italy ate more pasta than ever before. Now the north claims as its own several of the most popular pasta sauces – *pesto* and *salsa Bolognese* in particular.

Many European countries have used long thin noodles in one way or another for centuries, often with or instead of vegetables. The smaller, cut shapes, called macaroni generically, were more often made into sweet puddings. But almost always the pasta was cooked for hours, reducing it to a muciferous mush. This would be horrifying to the Neapolitans who like their pasta not *al dente* but *verdi verdi*, which to us would seem barely warmed through, let alone cooked. But you are wrong if you think this would be dangerously indigestible. Quite the reverse. Firm pasta encourages you to chew more, breaking it into small pieces and mixing them with the important digestive enzymes of the saliva. The well-cooked stuff slips down the gullet in great dollops, landing heavily in the stomach with no such enzymic help to assimilation. Thus the digestive trouble begins. But if your trouble is other than of the stomach, you may care to know that a decent meal of spaghetti and tomato sauce is said to supply significant amounts of vitamin E, which is of specific benefit to the reproductive organs (trust the Italians and French to know this). Still, they *have* given us a clue. Both know the tomato as the 'love apple': *pomo d'amore* and *pomme d'amour* respectively.

In other parts of the world, broadly similar food has been known for aeons. Think of the orientals with their noodles, steamed or fried, and the tiny steamed parcels of dough, the *wonton*. The Russians' *vareniki* are like ravioli, little pillows of pasta, stuffed with cheese, with cabbage, with fish or strawberries or poppyseeds or almost anything. And in Thailand they make all manner of white or transparent noodles in a fascinating manner which I saw in a jungle village in the infamous Golden Triangle. They don't make a dough which is rolled out and cut. They make a thick sludge of mixed rice and soya flour, which is ladled into what look like huge icing bags with a many-pierced nozzle. From some height and with considerable dexterity, thin strands are extruded directly into a vat of water aboil over open charcoal fires, in which they congeal immediately. In seconds they are looped out and hung to drip-dry under teak-leaf-thatched roofs in great opalescent skeins. They don't last long in the humidity so the agile villagers had their work and their fortune cut out for them to supply, as they did, nearly all the local district. But the concomitant pigs, scabrous dogs and mucous-choked children cut them right out of my diet.

There seems to be no end to ingenuity when it comes to making noodles. In Vietnam a particular type of cellophane noodle, thin and transparent, is made with a flour of dried mung bean and in other parts of South East Asia, gram flour, made from a type of pea is used. The Chinese make a batter of whatever flour they can get, spread this on an oiled platter and steam until transparent; it is rolled and eaten with chopped green onion and revived dried shrimp. In Japan the great pasta speciality is *soba*, a spaghetti-type product made with a proportion of buckwheat; you can buy this in the United Kingdom.

Hungarian egg drops – *tarhonya* – are well worth finding. These small pellets of egg pasta are fried a golden brown before being covered with water to cook. The nuttiness is delicious and once you have eaten them with a paprika-rich goulash, mashed or boiled potatoes will never do again.

Then there's America. It is the United States that has led the march of pasta so steadily to the top of the post-war popularity poll. It was they who popularized the idea of eating Italian pasta as a main course, which it never was: Italian purists would also say it should only be eaten as a first course at lunchtime and never in the evenings. It was almost certainly someone in the United States who invented *canneloni*, *tagliatelli* with cream, ham and peas, *carbonara* sauce, and the notion of cold pasta salads. But the chances are that these innovators were also of Italian extraction, and not *all* progress is a bad thing. When thousands of Italians emigrated to the United States it was pasta they wanted more than anything, and it had to be Neapolitan. It was this export demand that allowed the great pasta families to mechanize and then sell their products all around the world. Not long ago, just one of these companies was selling 2,000 tons of pasta products a *day!*

As you might expect, mechanization has had some effect on commercial Italian pasta. Eighty years ago you could find 250–300 different shapes, but now the number is probably closer to only 50 or 60 – and that includes new monstrosities like spacemen and flying saucers.

To those who have not been brought up with pasta it can be an extraordinary experience to discover the amazing range of flavour pasta can have, all obtained by varying the thickness and shape of the same combination of wheatflour, water and, possibly, egg. Spinach juice or tomato purée can be added to make green (verde) and red (rosso) pasta. Pasta is very simple to make and doubly delicious when fresh rather than dried. The fun of making it can be as addictive as the pleasure of eating it. But before you dash into the kitchen, here's an attempt to guide you through the maze of the most common categories and shapes of Italian Pasta.

KINDS OF PASTA
Pasta lunga
(long pasta)

From the tiniest *cappelli d'angelo* (angel's hair) to **thick and broad** *lasagne*, with every type of *spaghetti, vermicelli, linguine, ziti, fettucine* and *tagliarelli* or *tagliatelli* in between. With or without holes. Once nearly all the thinner *pasta lunga* was made up to 5 feet (1½ metres) in length and looped to dry like wool. Now it's usually cut into 8–12 in (20–32 cm) lengths.

Pasta corta
(short or cut pasta)

The best known in these categories are the rounded, hollow pastas, usually cut on the bias and which may be smooth or grooved. These include *macaroni, rigatoni, penne* and the newcomer, *cannelloni*. This category also includes the shapes and shell types, so wonderful for holding sauce-juicy chunks of meat or seafood. *Lumache* (snails), *conchiglie* (shells), *gnocchi* and the elbow-shapes also come into this category.

Pasta ripieni
(stuffed pasta).

Ravioli in all different sizes is the best known, I suppose, but *tortellini* which look like belly-buttons are much more delicious, I think, and *cappelleti* which look like head scaves tied on the chin. There are varieties of stuffed dumplings, called *angolotti*, but these are rarely seen commercially.

Pastina

These tiny pieces of dried dough are specially made for serving in soup and are most usually seen as egg drops, squares or bow ties (*farfalli*); then you must also include novelties such as alphabet pasta, tiny animals and the aforementioned visitors from outer space.

Pasta all'uovo
(pasta with egg).

Here the flour is mixed with a proportion of egg that varies but should never be less than 1 per lb (500 g) of flour. It is nearly always made into *pasta lunga* products but every type of pasta may be made with egggs. Much of the very good pasta that comes from Israel is made with eggs.

TYPES OF PASTA

There is no recognized rule for any shape or type of pasta. Spaghetti is generally known as being round and thin but without a hole; the diameter (and subsequent flavour) varies enormously without any change of name. So the following can only be arbitrary; and is based more on what you might buy easily rather than what is being made in the village kitchens of Italy.

Bucatini: a thick, hollow version of spaghetti.

Capellini: very thin, flat or round noodles (*capelli d'angelo* being the thinnest of all).

Cappelletti: 'little hats'. This is a stuffed pasta, like a small peaked and tied headscarf.

Conchiglie: seashells. Available large or small, smooth or ridged. Excellent for trapping the tastiest bits of seafood or meat sauces and attractive in cold pasta salads.

Farfalli – farfallini etc. A bow-tie shape often with crinkled or diamond-cut edges. Made by pinching the middle of a square of pasta.

Fettuccine: a blood brother of *tagliatelle, fettuccine* originates from Rome, is usually made with egg, and is narrower and thicker than its relation.

Fusilli: a spiral-shaped pasta.

Gnocchi: this should be made with starch or purée of something other than wheat flour. Dry mashed potato or pumpkin are the most common but flour is also included. The proper shape is a small oval that is slightly folded and serrated.

Lasagne: the broadest pasta noodle, smooth or ridged. *Lasagne verdi*, like all green pasta, is coloured with spinach. Lasagne is one of the few pastas not dressed with sauce at the table. Instead it is layered with *béchamel* and *ragú* sauces and returned to the oven to be baked (*Lasagne al Forno*).

Linguine: another flat, thin noodle.

Macaroni: a generic term for all commercially-made dried pasta. But in general use is often used to mean only the well-known cut, tubular pasta. There are many lengths and sizes of such *macaroni*.

Orecchiette: these 'little ears' are shaped just like that, and suit salads and chunky sauces.

Pansotti, panzerotti: a triangular, stuffed pasta.

Penne: specially used to indicate a hollow short pasta cut at an acute diagonal angle – up to 1 in (2½ cm) long. The shape is reminiscent of the end of a sharpened quill, hence the name.

Quadrucci: these little squares of noodle are used in soup and in today's prosaic times are liable simply to be labelled 'egg squares'.

Ravioli: best known of the stuffed pasta, they are square-shaped and can sometimes be found quite big.

Rigatoni: ridged and tubular, sometimes curved, but without the pointed ends of *penne*.

Spaghetti: thin strings of pasta, without holes. Called *vermicelli* (little worms) in southern Italy. There are thinner varieties called *spaghettini* and *vermicellini*.

Tagliatelle: a long, thin egg noodle, the speciality of Bologna, one of Italy's greatest food centres. There is also a green one – *tagliatelle verdi*.

Tortellini (and **Tortelli:**) a stuffed pasta, more or less of a twisted ring shape which look like perfect belly-buttons. Can be bought fresh or dried in many English cities; in London they are available deep-frozen, having been imported from Italy. They are a good ingredient for a timbale – the great rich pie of pastry and pasta.

Wholewheat: don't be duped by the breathless wonder with which assistants in smart shops point out wholewheat pasta. Well over a century ago, and for ages before that, all pasta was probably like this. But by the time it became internationally popular white flour was easily available. The Veneto, the area about Venice, still makes *bigoli*, a thick type of spaghetti, from wholewheat flour. Wholewheat pasta is perfectly delicious and, dare I say it, pretty, too.

COOKING PASTA

The manufacturers don't necessarily know best and often tell you to cook your pasta longer than is necessary. The Italians say that 'pasta likes friends' meaning you need to keep an eye on it when it cooks. The slightest variation in thickness, humidity or amount of water will affect the time it takes for your pasta to be to your taste. There is a tradition that says some Italians reckoned theirs was ready when a handful flung onto the wall stuck there; I've never been able to find necessary details of type of wall, distance thrown or style of delivery and so have gone for the more mundane tooth test. Boring but effective.

You must use as much water as possible so that

each pasta piece can swell unhindered. I always put some oil in the cooking water as this stops the pasta sticking together when drained. Classicists say you should never pour pasta into a colander but take it out of the water with a large fork or spoon. Do what you will, but don't rinse it in cold water and then expect to reheat it without it going sticky (the only exception to this rule is lasagne). When the lasagne is cooked, run cold water into the cooking pot and gently move the lasagne sheets until separate and cool in the running water. Then take them out and lay them on a tea towel to drain and dry.

Generally, it is regarded as bad practice to toss your cooked pasta in its chosen sauce. Rather you should put the hot pasta into a dish, let it sit for a few minutes, when it will almost miraculously absorb the moisture on its surface then pour the sauce over. The mixing is then done at the same time as the serving which looks better and protects the pasta's texture and shape.

French pasta cooks in just a few minutes. Complicated shapes, like shells, *should* be drained in a colander, and gently turned so the water caught in the interior drains away.

SERVING PASTA

Because it is a simple food, pasta specially suits simple accompaniments. But which sauce goes with what pasta? Every sauce goes with every pasta. But some are better than others. For example it can be pointless to serve a *pasta lunga* with a very thin sauce or with a sauce filled with large chunks of meat or seafood; in both cases the sauce will slide from the pasta and need to be eaten separately. Such sauces are enjoyed more when served with the complicated shapes of *pasta corta*, which can catch the sauce in pools or trap the morsels of flesh. But even this rule can be ignored if you have the wrong type of pasta in the cupboard.

Here are a few tips on basic pasta sauces.
Butter sauces: melted butter flavoured with chopped garlic, herbs and a dash of olive oil makes one of the best and clingiest dressings for pasta lunga. If you want to ignore the above advice, some seafood, snippets of cheese, cubes of ham or salami, croûtons or lardons, black olives or cornichons might also be added. It is correct to serve some ravioli and gnocchi with melted butter; often the former is served with butter that has been allowed to brown slightly.

Cream sauces: the simplest cream sauce is simply a reduction of double cream. For two, reduce ½ pint (300 ml) double cream to half its volume and then flavour according to your store cupboard. An excellent way to proceed now is to add some of the juice from a tin of baby clams or Danish mussels which have been preserved in brine or their natural juices. Add also some tomato purée, until there is a rosiness rather than ruddiness. Continue reducing until a coating consistency and only then add salt and, if you have some, a teaspoon or two of brandy.

When your pasta shells or *lumachine* or *penne* are cooked and well drained, serve on to hot plates, then quickly toss the clams or mussels in the sauce before serving. A little oregano is good with this. So is a sprinkle of mixed hot and sweet paprika.

Should you want a creamy sauce for noodles, then reduced and flavoured cream is really the best way. This is also true when preparing a creamy sauce for *tortellini* or *cappelletti*.

Meat sauces: the basic tomato/beef sauce or *ragú* does not need complication or expense to be good. First you must brown the minced meat with onions and a little celery. Then cover the meat with plum tomatoes that have been tinned in tomato juice including all this juice. Add some bay leaves and then let this simmer gently for several hours – the larger the quantity the longer the time. No garlic, no herbs, no red wine and definitely no expensive cuts of meat.

At the end of the long cooking the meat will almost have dissolved into the reduced sauce, the flavours will have combined and the colour will be wonderful. Finish with some black pepper and salt if you think it is necessary. Should you wish a higher colour or even stronger tomato flavour then use as your cooking liquid, tomato purée, diluted only slightly, or add some, in the way outlined under my piece on that subject, towards the end of the cooking. This is the sauce which is also the basis of lasagne making. But for that layered and baked dish, the *ragú* is mixed, swirled rather, with equal quantities of a thick, but simply flavoured béchamel sauce. Do not accept as lasagne layers of pasta and undercooked or watery mince; without the texture and contrast of the béchamel sauce it is horrid and dry or greasy.

Tomato sauces: the simpler the better. If you have tomatoes in your garden which are rugged and red and sun ripened then simply chop them up and cook them gently with some olive oil, strain them or liquidize and strain, then reduce further. But don't bother to attempt this with the orange bullets you buy in the guise of tomatoes. If you don't have the goodies in the garden and you can't buy the wonderful marmonde tomatoes now being imported, then open a couple of cans of plum tomatoes and reduce them into a sauce as above. Onions and bay leaf are the only additions to consider.

But you have to be quite patient about reducing the liquid enough, and also take care that it does not burn or caramellize. Then a few minutes before serving, add some sprigs of fresh herbs, like basil, thyme or mint, let the flavour draw, drain and serve. Dried herbs work as well, but I recommend you strain them out, too.

Cheese: Yes, Parmesan and other cheese do go nicely with pasta dishes. But please don't add it regardless. Such piquant cheese is to be considered an alternative to salt and pepper, and so on some dishes, especially the creamy seafood sauces, the additional flavour of cheese is quite wrong.

The use of grated Cheddar cheese, spongy and stringy, adds little but bother, unless it is dissolved into a sauce completely. Even so it is pointless using something mild as you spend more trying to get flavour than if you simply bought less of a biting parmesan, for all its expense. I blame the Italian restaurants themselves for the propagation of 'Parmesan with everything'; at least eating chips with everything does not mask flavours which some chef has, or should have, been creating for hours.

ODD WAYS
WITH PASTA
LEFTOVERS

I often find myself with some leftover pasta, cooked or uncooked. The latter is often hard to find a use for, though as it keeps so well perhaps this is only a problem of space rather than economy. Here are some ideas for using small amounts of cooked pasta and appearing to be creative at the same time.
With vegetables. Almost any hot vegetable dish that includes a sauce or is in itself rather wet can be extended with pasta shapes. Ratatouille becomes even more filling and nourishing. Cauliflower cheese, brussel sprouts or leeks in a cheese sauce plus pasta make a snack a meal; it looks good if you've used wholemeal pasta.
With casseroles. Cooking dried pasta or reheating

cooked pasta in the juice of braises, stews and casseroles gives you a meal in one container. And you retain all the vitamins of the dried pasta instead of throwing some away in the cooking water. Liver and bacon is good with pasta in it; so is goulash, with added paprika and sour cream. Braised steak that is too wet and sloppy can be saved by cooking noodles in the liquid.

With fish. Leftover fish incorporated into a rich white sauce with a sharpening of green pepper, cheese and Tabasco is a nice combination with small macaroni shapes. Bake a crisp golden brown in the oven. Smoked fish would probably be better.

With salads. Although a recent innovation cold pasta in salads is becoming very popular. It can either be the basis or an ingredient. As the former, consider adding a few highly-flavoured ingredients to pasta tossed in good olive oil and lemon juice whilst still warm – some smoked sausages or frankfurters, some rollmops and sour cream with onion, salami and gherkins, for example.

As an ingredient pasta can go into almost any salad. It's specially good in the classic *Salade Niçoise*.

When incorporating pasta with a poultry salad, use the Polynesian idea of including fruit, too. Mix pasta with chicken, avocado and pineapple, or with turkey, apple, nuts and celery plus some orange segments.

With fruit. Provided they are not oily, cooked pasta shapes make interesting additions to cooked fruit. Toss the cooked shapes in a little sugar and cinnamon or in some syrup. They are particularly good with puddings made with dried fruit and with apple – you'd be surprised how good is a layer of small, buttered macaroni at the bottom of, say, an apple crumble. I'd be inclined to pour a little cream or milk over the pasta, so it could be absorbed with the dripping juices of the apple whilst in the oven.

Fried. It is not only noodles that can be fried. Simply ensure that your leftover pasta has been well and truly dried and dump it into deep, hot oil or fat, cook until brown, drain and serve. It is specially good mixed up with masses of fried onion or crisp-fried onion rings.

PÂTÉS, TERRINES AND GALANTINES

Well done you, if it's ever occurred to you that many pâtés were simply sausages without skins; you are right. Pâtés and terrines are based on chopped or minced pork in combination with liver and, sometimes, salt pork or bacon. They were originally a method of preserving miscellaneous parts of the pig by first sterilizing (baking) and then sealing (with fat).

The difference between pâtés and terrines is now largely eroded and either name is applied arbitrarily by those who manufacture them. Originally pâtés were the ones that might be turned from the containers in which they were baked and terrines stayed in their earthenware bowls.

Almost any type of meat could be minced also into the basic pork mixture. Often the additions were layered, a favourite way to present a pâté featuring more unusual flesh, pheasant or wild boar for instance, but unless the technique was superb the flavour of that flesh was absorbed by the more ordinary surroundings. It is usually better to distribute specialty flesh, plus stock made from its bones, throughout the mixture, in my experience.

Today, we tend to make terrines and pâtés with a low fat content, and this has changed flavours and storage techniques; a properly made traditional pâté keeps uncut for months under its layer of fat in a cool cellar, whereas many modern products become uneasy after much shorter storage. On the other hand most commercial pâtés are so preserved as to be almost indestructible, far more likely to damage you than themselves. In fact most of the huge range that has flooded the market over the last decade is everything *but* what it claims to be – traditional. Most are liquidized then stabilized with thickening agents, extended with cellulose or soya, coloured by the roseate action of nitrites, flavoured with herb oils rather than the real thing, enriched with soya flour or milk powder and overloaded with mono-sodium glutamate to overstimulate your tastebuds into recognizing what little meat is contained. The effect is such that they can be transported over hundreds of miles, stored for weeks and still look fresh ages after they have finally been broken from their vacuum wrappings. Wonders of modern science or the home economist they might be – wholesome, honest and simple they are not.

Of course, these are the products which have been

the vanguard of the growth of delicatessen in this land and anything is good that starts people on the road to eating more adventurously. For some years my London delicatessens manufactured pâtés the traditional way. They had a naturally long life and a big following, even being flown privately to New York for dinner parties. We no longer make them, but it is gratifying to see a number of small companies copying them, even down to using the same type of bowl and simple decorations. I feel I once made a real contribution to the food of the metropolis, but wish I knew what went in to those copies.

If you have a food processor, pâtés and terrines are exceptionally simple to make and very satisfying. The ingredients are cheap and easy to obtain. Ignore absolutely those recipes with zillions of ingredients or amazing ideas. (I even know someone who wanted to put choux pastry into chicken liver pâté, saying this is what he was taught at a well-known catering college).

Galantines are those multi-coloured, large sausages with strips and stripes of brightly-coloured meats and vegetables in a finely textured pâté, held together by a wrapping of fat. Originally the container was the whole skin of a fowl or it was the boned carcass of this or some other bird. Some are available commercially, but I implore you to taste them first for the ones which looked best to me turned out to have least flavour. It seems the flavour of too many commercial pâtés, terrines and galantines is contributed by the additives rather than the animal upon which the product is based.

STORING PÂTÉS, TERRINES AND GALANTINES

It is better to treat all charcuterie products as if they were fresh produce; keep them well-wrapped and well-chilled. Those including a lot of onion are more likely to go sour.

PEAS, BEANS AND LENTILS

The British call these pulses when they are dried, but that term is little understood elsewhere. These most ancient of foods, cheap and nourishing, are looked upon in this country with much disdain, largely for reasons which are difficult to argue against.

Perhaps the most common complaint about dried peas, beans and lentils is that they are boring and associated with sandals, long hair and beards (and that is just the women). There is much basis for this prejudice and the serious perpetrators of characterless lentil rissoles have only themselves to blame for the failure of their regimen to grip our imaginations. If only they knew they could be as original with these foods as they are with their clothes . . .

The other oft-heard complaint is wind. This is a very real and sometimes painful problem for many people, but a little sound knowledge and advice will sort this out in most cases. First concentrate on the thinner skinned varieties, which cook faster, as they seem responsible for fewer side effects. Then, always soak *and* rinse *and* parboil them before cooking.

Our digestive systems will adapt to new diets in an extrardinary way if we give them the chance. If you think you would like to introduce more peas, beans and lentils into your diet – and there is every culinary and health reason so to do – start by regularly including some in moderate amounts in other foods. In just a few weeks you will be able to enjoy red kidney beans, or a chick pea salad with rarely a grumble.

All the pulses are excellent sources of protein and carbohydrate but are slightly unbalanced in protein content and for balance need always to be eaten in conjunction with other types of protein, cereal, seed and nut, or dairy. This is generally done without thought, as eating baked beans on toast, or scooping hummous with pitta bread.

Pulses have no fat content but it is difficult to find many enjoyable recipes that do not add this in some form or another. They have the advantage of containing a high degree of dietary fibre, and this is most important, especially as we get older, when the general trend towards eating softer food means food might take many days to pass through the alimentary canal, and this unquestionably exacerbates any illness and contributes to general ill-health. Even small amounts of pulses (or whole grain cereals) in the diet can make a major difference to health in the elderly, and is good practice for all others.

BUYING AND STORING PEAS, BEANS AND LENTILS

Although good keepers, all peas, beans and lentils will toughen with age and many reach a stage where even the most determined soaking and cooking will never soften them. It is better to buy them in smallish quantities from shops that you expect sell enough to have a regular turnover of stock. Do check, if they are in bulk, for excess dirt or insect contamination, but expect some. And don't bother with stock that is broken.

Store them cool and dark.

In canned form they are more expensive, but a few tins of cooked beans are a godsend standby. Heated and drained and dressed with oil and garlic as a salad basis, puréed, or drained and reheated with a herb-rich garlic-laden tomato sauce they make a fast vegetable stew appear to have taken you days to make. Of course, they instantly bulk out a soup, casserole or ready made salad, too, if someone should come knocking upon your door whom you do not wish to send away. I think beans are good hot or cold but never at room temperature.

GENERAL COOKING ADVICE

Cooking times are given under individual entries. These are just a few words about methods of cooking.

There is continuing discussion about whether all these products need to be soaked, and certainly if the soaking is not done properly fermentation can begin which gives an unpleasant flavour. My experience is that soaking in cold water can enhance the flavour by starting the germination process (the same as the malting of grains) and it certainly cuts down on cooking time, a saving of expensive energy. Generally speaking, overnight, or from morning to afternoon, is enough – allow plenty of room for expansion, especially for chickpeas, and keep fairly cool.

If you have forgotten to soak your pulses in cold water it is possible to plump them faster, by bringing them up to the boil in water, simmering for 5 minutes then turning off the heat and leaving until cold – for at least 2 hours.

Soaking water should not be used for cooking any pulse if you are afeared of wind problems. Either drain it off and put the pulses into fresh cold water, or rinse them very thoroughly under running water.

If you have persistently bad digestive problems you might try the equivalent of blanching at this stage, bringing the soaked pulses to the boil in fresh water, simmering for 5 minutes, draining and rinsing before cooking in more fresh water.

It is essential that salt should never be added to the cooking water until the beans are thoroughly cooked or they will be tough.

Acid in the water can also toughen beans and thus it is not a good idea to cook them in a tomato purée, for instance. Better to cook them first then add them to a rich stock or vegetable-based liquid that has been prepared separately. Cook on to let the flavours mingle.

Onions are also acidic and thus better added towards the end of cooking, after the beans have softened.

There are many famous bean, pea and lentil dishes to be found in the cookbooks of the world but I have to say that I always end up cooking beans the same way – with tomato, lots of garlic, fresh herbs in a bundle and lots of fat – bacon, goose or butter. Often the fat, bacon and garlic will come largely from chunks of Polish boiling sausage. But be brave with peas, beans and lentils. With chickpeas, use cumin and coriander and tomato paste and olive oil when they are warm – just enough tomato to bind them together, and serve sprinkled with chopped chives as a salad. Mix red, black and black-eye beans together in a salad.

Serve cold tuna fish with cannellini in vinaigrette as a starter. Mix leftover butter beans with chilled orange slices, black olives and segmented tomato.

To make a succulent sauce for any hot beans, take up to a quarter of cooked ones from the saucepan, add water, stock or tomato purée to them and cook to a mush (you might even purée them then). Return to the drained beans and cook on. A real chili should have a sauce of softened purée-like beans like this. Beans in their own sauce are excellent hot or cold, and reheat well, too – witness the famous *refritos* of Mexican and Tex-Mex cooking.

Whenever a bean recipe fails to excite you finally, and you have added enough salt and extra fat and more garlic, then add red wine vinegar teaspoon by teaspoon. The difference will be wondrous, and fast.

Neither should you overlook the flavouring

possibilities of oil. Olive oil is almost *de riguer* unless you have very fatty bacon or a tin of goose fat. But beans cooked simply with tomatoes and then finished with a spash of walnut oil make a superb accompaniment to poultry and, after setting in a refrigerator overnight, the most memorable cold salad. Better with garlic, it goes without saying.

Lamb, especially the cheaper fattier cuts, go well with beans. I like to cook neck of lamb in tomato with garlic sausage and some fresh thyme then to add in cooked haricot or butter beans and cook on for enough time to allow the beans to melt into the sauce and absorb the fat. Just put the pot on the table and let them help themselves.

As far as lentils go, I adore lentil soup with a pool of butter, some sliced sausage and chopped pickled cucumber on top. Brown/green lentils haven't figured so much in my diet, but I do remember being served pigs' trotters that had been simmered in them and that was a good winter dish.

Be bold. But take care in the beginning, don't cook with salt in the water . . . and make sure your red kidney beans really *are* boiled hard for at least 15 minutes.

Pressure cooking

This really is the way to get your beans tender or cooked in short time. My advice, gleaned from Rose Elliott's *The Bean Book*, is that you should use 15 lb (8 kg) pressure, cook for a third of the usual time and always include a few spoonsful of oil as this prevents foaming up, which might clog the valve.

ADZUKI OR ADUKI BEANS

Small, ochrous-red and sort of pillow-shaped, these are an oriental bean and have long been regarded as the best of them all in Japan, China and Thailand. Unknown to the West until George Ohshawa introduced the macrobiotic diet earlier this century, they are now much favoured here because they are the most 'yang' of beans, and because they have an appealing, strong, nut-like flavour.

I've always preferred them eaten as sweets covered with sugar or made into a paste for those luminous and often glutinous sweetmeats of the East. But they are also served savoury; the most famed version is Serkhan or Festival Rice from Japan. Rice is tinted with the pink cooking water of adzuki beans, then the two are mixed together.

The bean is the seed of a bushy plant which grows

up to about 30 in (75 cm) high. Juice made from adzuki beans is still prescribed by oriental herbalists to help kidney problems.

Cooking adzuki beans

Cook at least 30 minutes, perhaps longer. When mixing with cooked rice, begin with a proportion of about 1 part adzuki to 8 of rice. This mixture is similar, by the way, to the rice and peas of Jamaican cooking. In macrobiotic cookbooks you will find suggestions for soups and desserts; I like the sound of one that cooks together adzuki and dried chestnuts, makes a purée of the mixture flavoured with cinnamon, and bakes that in a pie crust. The pie is served with cream and almonds.

BLACK-EYE BEANS

These beans are actually peas, a variety of cow pea and this is why they are also called black-eye peas in the United States. To add to the confusion, they are the seeds you find in the yard-long bean. I find I like the rather savoury flavour and interesting appearance of these more than the plain haricots. They cook comparatively faster too and I believe many people find them lighter on the stomach, too. Essential to Creole cooking and the related soul food.

Cooking

Soaked beans take 30-45 minutes to cook.

BROAD BEANS

Not very common in their dried form, and unrecognised by most because they are brown rather than the expected green. But I like them for their bigger size and flouriness. Although it is nice to have a bit of a chew sometimes, the skins of these take expectations of mastication too far. You either have to skin them after cooking, or buy the more expensive ready-skinned variety.

Cooking

These should have a good long soak and will then need about 1½ hours cooking – but less, of course, if you are using those wihout skins.

BUTTER BEANS OR LIMA BEANS

Many books divide butter beans from Lima beans but I'm sure they are the same thing. If they aren't, it doesn't matter for they are both large, white, flat and aristocratic of flavour. They should not be cooked until pulpy, but must be very well cooked and pre-soaked for they have some rather unpleasant constituents.

Baby lima beans are pale green and usually sold

fresh or frozen. Opinions vary but I think baby fresh limas are quite the best for mixing with sweet corn to make succotash, even though I have seen recipes which required cooked, dried ones.

Cooking Smaller ones will take 45-60 minutes; bigger ones will take 15-25 minutes longer.

CHICKPEAS OR GARBANZOS
With their spicy, peppery flavour, appealing golden colour and hazel-nut shape, these are amongst the most attractive of all dried pulses from any point of view.

They are the main ingredient in hummous, that standby of Middle Eastern, Greek and Cypriot restaurants, but one also found in Spanish and Latin American cooking and make excellent additions to soups as well as fascinating salads. They mix well with other vegetables, too, and I always like to have some on hand.

Cooking This can vary enormously. Older types may take up to 3 hours or more but newer types, the ones most likely to be bought here, should be cooked in something over an hour. They rarely go out of shape and are much nicer, I think, when rather floury, for then they absorb somewhat more easily the oils, spices and flavours with which they can be mingled.

FUL MEDAMES
Fundamental to Egypt for countless centuries, these are round and brown. Like broad beans, they have a tough outer skin and a rough but enjoyable flavour that welcomes the vigour of garlic, oil and onion.

KIDNEY BEANS
This is the biggest group of beans and the one which causes much confusion. Simply, all beans which are kidney shaped without being flat, are kidney beans. There is a variety of colour and flavour – but they *are* all kidney beans. Here is a guide to the most common ones.
Black beans: very popular in the Caribbean and in the southern United States, these shiny, very black beans are the most similar of all kidneys to the better-known red kidney beans. They cook to a firm satisfying texture and have a meaty, full flavour. Used by themselves or with other beans they make an attractive change to the look of your cooking.
Borlotti: (also rose cocoa beans) streaked with rose or crimson, and all the better for being pale of colour

these are specially popular in Italy and excellent tinned examples are available. They seem usually to require little soaking when dried, and they have a rather sweet, soft texture.

Cannellini: a small white kidney bean that is absolutely interchangeable with haricots. In Italy cannellini might mean other white beans, too. These are almost always the right bean to use with rugged Italian sausages and with lots of garlic and tomato of some sort make excellent cold salads dressed with good olive oil.

Flageolet: these are very young haricots removed from the pod before they are ripe. Thus they are a delicate green, sweet and tender. By far the most expensive and a very special accompaniment to fatty birds, to young lamb or to hot ham.

Haricot: these creamy kidney beans are perhaps the best known of all, for they are *the* beans for baked beans. In this country in 1979, 850 million cans were consumed. Extraordinarily adaptable, they are the basis for the varying versions of cassoulets in France, cooked with bacon or goose fat. Some say they are called haricot because the French included them in their stews called haricots, but the late Tom Stobart says 'haricot' is really a corruption of the Aztec word *ayecotl*, which I am inclined to believe.

In America they are known as navy beans; and just to add to the confusion they are often shaped more like a cushion than a kidney.

Pinto: a shorter, fatter, patern, squarer version of the borlotti, speckled and savoury of flavour.

Red kidney beans: because delicatessen counters discovered they were nice to eat cold as a salad, and because chili con carne has proliferated, these are as well known as white haricots now. Their rich colour and texture and full flavour make them worth the popularity, but recently it has been discovered that they can kill. Red kidney beans must be very well soaked and very well cooked until really soft; during cooking they should actually boil for 15 minutes.

Their uses abound throughout Central and South America and the Caribbean; they are the basic chili bean and, like their black brothers, add considerable spice when mixed with whites or other beans.

Cooking

The average time for cooking these beans is 1 hour, but haricots can be stubborn and need longer so be prepared to exercise patience.

LENTILS	One of the first-ever crops in the East, lentils are richer in protein than other pulses, except for soya. They have a very high calorie content too, so even though lacking some of the essential amino acids they make an important food staple, especially in Third World countries.

There are two basic types but both have many names:

The red lentil: also known as Egyptian or Indian lentils.

These look reddish but are the ones that cook into a yellow-gold mush. They are vital to all sorts of winter soups and go extra well with contrasted sharper vegetables like garlic, onion and green peppers.

Green or brown lentils: also called continental lentils. It is generally these lentils that are mentioned in European cookbooks, old or new. They keep their shape when cooked and have a stronger, earthier taste than the red ones, which blends very well with smoked meats, fatty pork, herbs and onions.

Cooking

Unsoaked red lentils take 20-30 minutes to cook, and soaked ones will cook in about 15 minutes. Green lentils take much longer; soaked ones 30-45 minutes, unsoaked 1-1¼ hours.

MUNG BEANS

An entrancing dark, frosted-olive green, mung beans are one of the basics for making into bean sprouts but can be cooked as any ordinary pulse. Like the red adzuki they are quite soft and sweet when cooked.

Cooking

Cook between 25 and 40 minutes.

PEAS

Provided you can suspend both belief and memories of what other people may have done to them, dried peas can be an excellent, honest and sustaining food. They are available whole or skinned and split, green or yellow; the green seem harder to find but I prefer them. Peas rarely hold their shape which is why they are put into soups or made into soups. It is always a surprise to taste how sweet they are, which is why they are a natural accompaniment to salted meats.

Cooking

Cook for about 45 minutes. If you want to keep some semblance of shape, use a minimal amount of water and watch carefully.

PICKLES, PRESERVES AND OLIVES

For some reason, pickled cucumbers cause much confusion to new delicatessen customers, perhaps because we have little real equivalent in our own cuisine. What is a 'new' green? or a dill pickle? and are gherkins really cucumbers, too? A few words about the processes involved in pickling cucumbers, olives and other vegetables will put most things in order for you.

A pickle can mean any food preserved in acid (vinegar) or salt.

It is well known that salt in solution with water is a preservative, because in a strong brine bacteria cannot multiply and cause putrefication. But too much salt in food can mean an unacceptably hardy flavour to many. Luckily, a process called lactic fermentation can be employed to preserve vegetables with rather less than a saturated brine.

All fresh vegetables contain sugars and have a skin covering of micro-organisms which can be controlled to our advantage. If you quickly put freshly-gathered vegetables into a brine that contains only 8-11 per cent salt, the purrefactive bacteria will be inhibited but those which act to ferment sugars and make lactic acid proceed – it is the same process that sours milk naturally, of course.

Lactic acid is a preservative, too, but does not have a marked flavour; yet it is not powerful enough to be a sole preservative. So once lactic fermentation is complete, the lactic-brine is replaced by a brine of 15 per cent salt and about 1 per cent lactic acid, then neither fermentation or putrefication is possible. Lactic acid is often combined with acetic acid, the acid of vinegar, to dilute the latter's sharpness, especially in pasteurized packs.

If vegetables are placed directly into a 15 per cent brine solution or into a mixture of brine and vinegar, this is called non-fermentation brining.

The degree of lactic fermentation, presence of herbs and flavourings, temperature of brining and quality of the initial produce, will all flavour these products. The presence of air causes the growth of bacterial moulds on the top of lactic-brines, but are harmless and can easily be scraped away. The produce, though, should always be kept below the surface of the liquid and should be kept away from light as much as possible.

Products which are pasteurized in liquid are likely to have a lower lactic or salt content, because of the

302

additional sterilizing action of heat treatment.

Preserving in vinegar or acetic acid alone works because it short cuts lactic fermentation by providing from the start a high enough acid level to kill or inhibit all bacterial action. Some items require a mixture of salt and vinegar to control their unique infestation. Onions are pickled by being cooked in vinegar; and when this process also includes fruits, spices and herbs you get spreadable pickles and, by including sugar, chutneys. Make the same products smooth and you have sauces, and ketchups.

Beetroot

Bottles or tins of small pickled beetroots, usually from Scandinavia or Germany, are very useful indeed, cold as a garnish or hot as a vegetable. Drained of their preservative liquid (those from Scandinavia are less sharp) and heated in some orange juice and butter, with a little lemon for accent they become quite special. Excellent heated in sour cream which is spiked with horseradish, with garlic, with parsley or with paprika – or any combination. Didn't know they could be such fun, did you?

Brown fruit sauce

The HP sauce and relations. Good for flavouring mayonnaise into which you wish to incorporate poultry or vegetables. Date syrup is the base for many, especially HP sauce, but vinegar, onions and fruit of other kinds are also essential. It is easy – and right – to make fun of those who use these and other sauces with no thought for the cook, but like every product that has survived on the market, fruit sauces have their place and time. Give me a good game pie or pork pie and I'd much rather have such a sauce than a mustard; I like them slightly cooled, too, which removes any unnecessary sweetness.

Chutneys

As this book is trying not to get involved in the cuisines of the East, better simply to say that Indians would not recognize our chutneys, even though the word came from there. Chutneys are hot and spicy, based on fruits, always contain both vinegar and sugar and should be quite coarse in texture; often the major fruit has been brined separately, and is added to the cooked base sauce at the end of the cooking process. Mango chutney is the best known, but peach is very good, too. Chutneys mix well with mayonnaise and can also make quick interesting hot sauces for cold meats; for instance, heat a few spoonsful of mango chutney, splash in a little citrus juice and the merest touch of brandy.

Cucumbers

Cucumber products are generally lactic fermented.

Salt cucumbers are treated the most simply of all and after fermentation are put into a plain brine. No other flavouring is incorporated.

Sweet and sour cucumbers: have extra flavour added to them by mixing vinegar or acetic acid into the second brine. A variety of other herbs and spices might also be used. But these are more usual in:

Dill cucumbers: these rely heavily for flavour on the fresh fronds of dill but the brines can also contain peppercorns, red peppers, garlic, grape, black currant, oak and cherry leaves, bay, parsley and horseradish.

New green cucumbers: are simply lightly salted and ready to eat in a few days, whereas dill pickles can take up to three months to taste right.

The secret of retaining crispness and developing flavour in pickled cucumbers is to allow fermentation to progress at a low temperature. New green cucumbers are usually cured in a warm spot and must then be eaten quickly whilst being stored in a cool place or they will soften and lose flavour, colour and texture.

The techniques and ingredients are accessible to anyone, so when the markets are flooded with ridge cucumbers, have a go at making some of your own pickles. Traditionally, pickled cucumbers are sliced lengthwise or diagonally and eaten as a relish. Very good with salt beef, hot or cold, and I also like dill cucumbers with smoked fish, especially salmon. Any hot or cold smoked meat or sausage is transported into a different part of heaven by the addition of some slices of a crisp cucumber pickle.

Gherkins: what the French call cornichons. These are usually baby or dwarf cucumbers, and they make nice decorations when cut almost through their length several times and then fanned out. I find their flavour too determined even when they are *real* gherkins. Which are not baby cucumbers at all but a relation and native to the Caribbean.

Capers

Tom Stobart described these as tasting 'goaty' – they are certainly unusual and can be unusually awful if not used with the greatest discretion. They are the unopened flowers of a Mediterranean plant that grows like a creeper. Good ones are expensive because the gathering cannot be mechanized – I believe that the life of the flowers is so short you must gather each morning or miss out altogether. They are not lactic fermented, but put into jars of a vinegar-brine, which preserves by the joint action of acetic acid and salt.

Use? On the few occasions I have enjoyed eating them they were always first soaked (in water or milk) and used with great restraint – cooked gently in a sauce as a flavouring rather than served as something to be eaten in its own right. Mr Stobart, who was enthusiastic, says he always combined them with grated lemon rind and garlic and I can imagine how good that would be with fish. Perhaps I'll give them another try, when I've saved some money. Two things I'm certain about – you should never buy cheap capers, and they must always be covered with liquid, or they develop a taste that makes goats seem positively fragrant.

Preserved ginger

This is one of the great mysteries of Christmas. Everyone seems to be given it, but almost no-one knows what to do with it, other than to slice it onto some ice cream. In fact there are many uses, and here are just a few.

Preserved ginger in slices, or chopped, together with a little of the syrup, is delicious on melon and far better than the silly idea of using powdered dry ginger. It is equally good with fresh or poached pears and can be used for baking in a host of ways, with apple, with peaches, with soft fruits in pies, sponges or crumbles. It is also very good with chocolate sponges; in fact if you put pears and ginger at the bottom of a chocolate sponge mixture you will turn out a memorable pear, chocolate and ginger upside down pudding . . . it looks better when baked in a ring mould.

Fine slices are a nice addition to any fruit salad, and can be added to home-made ice cream, especially when also flavoured with honey.

Preserved ginger, also called stem ginger, can rarely be used in savoury cooking, but might be included where there is already a mixture of sweet and sour in the sauce, or where the meat is very fatty, say with duck. But fresh green ginger would probably be better.

Mushroom ketchup   Few people make this or any other type of ketchup at home now, but a well stocked larder once always contained a selection of sauces made from ingredients as diverse as cucumbers, oysters, fruit and vegetables. Mushroom ketchup is one of the few that survived and when you can find it (made commercially) buy it more as a flavouring than a sauce to lay on the side of your plate. It is made by an interesting process using salt, which when sprinkled on mushrooms will extract the liquid from them. This is heated and flavoured and bottled. Commercial mushroom ketchup often contains soya sauce nowadays, which makes the apparent salt content even higher; it is so high that mushroom ketchup becomes interchangeable with anchovy essence, but that is no bad thing. Use mushroom ketchup only at the end of cooking to strengthen or add interest, in the same way that celery salt, soya sauce, anchovy essence or garlic and ginger juice might do.

Mustard Pickle   What the Americans call piccallili, a word that almost no-one can spell anyway.

Olives   An extremely ancient cultivated crop, the olive and its oil have been one of the three staples of Mediterranean trade since time immemorial. Together with wine and wheat, Rome or any other Mediterranean power with expansionist objectives used the strange fruit to bargain, seduce and support. In Crete, where olive oil was part of the royal treasury, olives were being cultivated over 5,000 years ago. Mediterranean countries are still the major producers, with Spain and Italy providing over 50 per cent of the crop. Greece and France make an important contribution and trees imported into California and Mexico created the basis for large localized industries.

Like apples or pears, olives come in all shapes, sizes and flavours. There are two major types: those that you eat and those from which you extract oil. The soil, climate and type of tree will all affect the type and flavour, thus there is no easy guide.

Green olives are just that, picked in September or October before they are ripe. They are uncommonly bitter and to remove this unpleasantness are put into concrete vats containing a soda solution which generates heat and cooks the olives, softening and sweetening them. After washing they are put into casks of brine and left to ferment in the sun, which can take up to three months according to the weather. The fermentation further softens the flesh and gives the characteristic greenish-yellow colour.

Black olives are left on the tree until December until fully ripe. They are slightly less bitter and do not need to go into a soda solution. Instead they are put into boiling brine or sterilized some other way before being preserved in the manner favoured by the area.

In Morocco you can get a beautiful violet/mauve olive, which has been picked when half-ripe and split before curing; a much darker violet colour is typical of some of the highest grade Greek olives, the Kalamata and Amphissa.

In most Mediterranean countries the only things allowed near olives are the soda solution, brine, vinegar and oil. In California they have developed a new process in which by bubbling oxygen through the brine green olives are oxidized into black olives.

Spain prefers to grow, eat and export the green olive and of these the best are the queen and manzanilla, a speciality of Andalucia whence both sherry and flamenco. The queen is large, deep-green, fleshy and plump; the manzanilla a light-green, finer-textured and with a silky thin skin. They use them in cooking, too.

France grows and enjoys both colours and once they have been processed she then further flavours them with a bewildering variety of herbs and spices. Outside the crenellated walls of Aigues-les-Mortes in the Camargue I counted 25 different types on one stall, some in brine, some in oil, some in oil and vinegar. Some were in marinades of onion or of garlic, others were perfumed with sun-strong herbs from the hills of Provence – thyme, rosemary, lavender and bay. Still others were soaking in rich liquids textured with chilli peppers, black peppercorns or lightly crushed coriander seeds, one of my favourite flavourings.

In Greece, where 90 per cent of their production is black olives, they even grow types which are sweet enough to eat straight from the trees; the island of Mitilini is reputed to have the best of these. Different soil types and different tastes give a choice of very interesting olives. The northern part of the country prefers smooth, shiny black olives (*gialeres*) whereas the southern part is partial to wrinkly-skinned ones (*thrúmpa*).

Once treated, olives can be stored in brine, or oil, or oil and vinegar. The more expensive the olive the higher the quality and quantity of oil used to preserve and flavour it.

In my experience very little oil is used in storing the majority of olives imported into this country, the highest percentage undoubtedly being that in the olives from Kalamata. But don't be afraid to alter the balance yourself, especially for black olives.

First, rinse off the brine and then make a light oil and vinegar mixture with the emphasis definitely on the oil, which must be olive. Then add some slices of lemon and some oregano, and let this get to know itself for a while. Sometimes I also add a couple of crushed cloves of garlic, some crushed coriander seeds or bay; use all or some in any balance you like.

I have to say that green olives in cooking are not my favourite thing; used with infinite discretion in cold food, especially in the lighter new pâtés and mousses, they can be delicious and pretty. But in hot sauces and hot dishes they are most intrusive and, although happy to be disabused of my opinion, I can't remember ever enjoying such a dish.

Black olives are far more acceptable – slices of shiny black olives make excellent decorations that just *might* be truffle.

Buying and storing olives: the most important point about buying olives loose is the chance to choose; there are so many types that it is silly to buy on looks alone. In any case the prepacked ones are really very expensive.

If you live in a small community where bulk olives are unobtainable, don't hesitate to buy in quantity elsewhere when you can. Keep them dark and cool and add oil to help extend their life. Refrigeration is not necessary but they are all the better for being kept dark. To prevent mould forming on brine, add a slice of lemon to a jar once you have opened it.

Pitted and stuffed olives are a great favourite, if not to eat then for decorative purposes. The most popular are those stuffed with red pepper but there are others. I specially like those stuffed with an almond and specially dislike those stuffed with onion or anchovy. Orange and lemon peel are sometimes found in eviscerated olives and both are marvellous but more likely to be encountered at a *tapas* bar in

Spain than in Ilkley. The stones that have been extracted, mainly by machine nowadays, are often used for low grade olive oil and the resultant pulp is an animal feed. Now, you didn't know that before did you?

If you like an olive in your martini, it is essential that it is a pitted manzanilla; refuse any that is either stuffed *or* intact.

Onions

Almost everyone knows more about onions than me, because I dislike them very much. Onions seem to me to represent all the worst of British cooking, onions with everything and vinegar on your chips. I simply do not believe that *every* sauce or stew or soup needs onion as a basis and I know that Cheddar cheese, caviare and tomatoes, among other things, are far nicer if they are not massacred by the acidic sharpness of raw onion which then stays on the palate to disfigure your wine taste or pudding. Pickled onions are worse. Eat them if you like, but keep your distance.

Piccallili

This is a law unto itself. First the vegetable content should be crisp, and so it is lactic fermented or brined rather than being boiled in a sauce like other pickles. The sauce itself is thickened with cornflour and made from onions, garlic, spices, vinegar and, of course mustard, according to each manufacturer's specific recipe. The usual vegetable content is silverskin onions, gherkins and cauliflower florets. The yellow colour is turmeric, or should be. Some commercial manufacturers use colouring instead, because turmeric fades in sunlight.

Pickles

This is really quite a broad term when you think that olives, onion, piccallili, beetroot and cucumber can be called pickle. Other mixed pickles vary from the delicious Italian examples of crisp mixed vegetables in a light, vinegary brine, which are excellent as hors d'oeuvres, to the Oriental bottles of lime pickle, mango pickle, and so on. As pickles last so well buy one or two really excellent examples to use from time to time they give a welcome lift to ordinary food. For all that I love pickled walnuts I can't think of a commercially available English mixed pickle that is better than those made by such Indian companies as Ferns; but English pickled peaches, oranges or pears, occasionally available, are very good.

Red Cabbage

With or without apple, this is a very cheap tinned vegetable that goes a magically long way. Always cured on the day it is gathered, red cabbage can stand a lot of cooking – allowing you to improve it at home so that it tastes home-made. Sliced or chopped apple, bacon and spiced vinegar make the usual combination – make the vinegar by simmering a few spoonsful of good wine vinegar with a dessertspoonful of pickling spice, drain and add. Garlic and orange juice with hot and sweet paprika is another wonderful combination; so is garlic and juniper berries and gin. A touch of molasses give colour and body. Red cabbage is first choice with any hearty meal, especially game dishes or fatty continental sausages.

Sauerkraut

The truth about sauerkrat is no less astonishing than that about soft roe or salami. It is made the same way a farmer makes silage for his cattle, indeed the smell can be distressingly similar. Sauerkraut is white cabbage that has been subjected to lactic fermentation but it is rarely drained and re-brined. The sauerkraut you can buy in tins is very good but has been cooked, of course. If you are lucky enough to buy it uncooked (we manage to get a few barrels from Holland each year) you can eat it like this but it is more usual to drain and rinse it and then to flavour it with bacon, onion, garlic, apple, carraway, wine – even champagne. You cook it for up to an hour; it should not be mushy but have absored the cooking water or liquid you have used, which should have equalled half the original volume of the sauerkraut. Cooked together or separately sauerkraut and rugged pork sausages, bacon or starchy vegetables all belong to one another. The *choucroutes* which are served in varying ways throughout France are nearly all more filling and rich than expected; and a version into which champagne is poured really does exist. I ate it in Cognac, where they know a thing or two about food – it was delicious but I don't think I'll do it again; I had a conscience about doing *that* to champagne.

Walnuts

Green walnuts which are not too young are pickled regularly in England, where the weather would not guarantee they would ripen anyway. They are brined but not lactic fermented, then dried at which stage they turn black. Storage and final flavouring is done in a vinegar, flavoured according to taste with spices, garlic and so on. Americans tend to make the vinegar mixture sweeter than we do. Very hard to find nowadays and generally too highly flavoured for most people; but it's worth trying the American sweet pickled walnuts, which are less strong. Use them as you would any other pickle, but especially with cheese or cold meats or raised-crust pies.

Worcestershire sauce

This is one of the few good things to come out of the Indian Empire, and is also an echo of everyday life in the Roman Empire. The Romans would have been lost without their *garum*, a sauce made by fermenting and maturing the liquid that small fish give off when silted and left in the sun in barrels. It sounds awful, but after much maturation it ends up being only slightly salty and barely fishy; nothing similar remains in the West, but in the East similar fish sauces are used as freely as we use salt.

When such sauces are mixed and matured with extra ingredients – vinegar, molasses, garlic, the bitterness of tamarind and much more that is secret – you get something like Worcestershire sauce. There used to be many of these spicy, hot, salty sauces, made from recipes brought back by gourmand colonels from the India of Queen Victoria. Some were manufactured for distribution and some were kept as private stocks. Lea & Perrins Worcestershire sauce was first made as a private stock but forgotten about by the owner. Eventually the barrel was about to be thrown away by the custodians, some pharmacists, who bravely decided to check on the contents. They discovered that the long sojourn in their cellar had transformed a sharp and unpleasant liquid into something with possibilities, and started to make it commercially. Thank goodness.

In Thailand I noticed it used with great abandon by much of the populace, and in Australasia it is used as often as dessicated coconut, which is saying something. But it *is* extraordinarily good for pepping up boring food and for adding unrecognized piquancy and interest to mayonnaise, soups, aspics, sauces for fish, herb butters and mince dishes, especially hamburgers. I like to use very little on a lamp chop, rubbed in both sides and left to sit an hour or so before cooking. You know, of course, that a Bloody Mary is bloody awful without Worcestershire sauce.

For thousands of years the pig furnished virtually all of the meat of the European peasant and was prized both for its ability to prosper where other animals starved and for being almost totally edible.

For city dwellers, too, the pig was a mainstay. The urban poor scavenged the pigs who scavenged the litter of the filthy streets. Street pigs, which were usually ownerless, were common in New York well into the 19th century and in Naples until even more recently – they were the only street cleaning service this notoriously grubby city could maintain.

It's just as well the pig is the most prolific animal after the rabbit (one sow is supposed to be able to accumulate almost 6.5 million descendants in a mere 12 years). For it is still *the* meat of much of the world, especially about the Pacific and South East Asia.

China is the leading pork producing and eating country, and the CIA doubtless had nefarious reasons for attempting to estimate the number of pigs raised there. At the beginning of 1978 they reckoned the world's most populous nation cared for over 280 million of the creatures, almost three-quarters of the world population of 400 million. Hungary is second to China for the inventiveness and number of ways it uses its pigs, and Denmark raises enough pigs per year to equal two-and-a-half-times its population of 5 million.

In Europe, Austrians head the pork eaters table with an annual consumption of 84 lb (38 kg) per head.

Americans eat an average of 70 lb (31 kg) per year of pork products but the West Germans beat that with a consumption of 74 lb (33 kg) per head. Britons manage only 25 lb (11 kg) of pork products per person each year.

Almost every fact about the pig is superlative. For every 100 lb (45 kg) of feed, a pig will produce 20 lb (10 kg) of flesh whereas cattle would struggle to covert the same amount to 7 lb (3 kg). Pigs are also the animal world's most efficient converters of carbohydrates into protein and fat.

Neither is any animal easier to preserve. Once the pigs had been fattened on the last of the summer's fruits and vegetables each cottager would in turn hire the slaughterman, and neighbours would come to help quickly preserve the pigs' flesh. The fine rear legs were made into hams, salted then smoked or air dried. Other joints were put into brine cures until needed – salt pork. Some bits and pieces were minced and flavoured and cooked and put under protective coatings of the pig's fat – the pâtés and terrines. The same minced flesh and back fat might also have been forced into cleansed intestines to make the sausages, saucissons and salami to be slung from rafters. The belly and loin were salted, dried and smoked to make bacon and if your pig was the type that had a long jaw, its cheeks were similarly treated (these would be called chaps). The head was made into brawn. The small intestines were chopped and used as stuffing for sausages, chitterlings or andouilletes, or they were dried for later use as sausage casings. Even the blood was made into black puddings, thickened with barley or oatmeal and textured with glistening blobs of back fat. Only a few choice pieces, like the liver and the trotters, were enjoyed fresh with the neighbourly helpers – if there was a real abundance. For the liver could also be used in faggots and pâtés, and the trotters could be boiled and stuffed and kept for ages in their own jelly or under fat.

Even then the dead pig kept working for you for its dung is one of the best manures of all and throughout winter the rain would wash the nutriments back into the soil, there to feed new growth in spring. When Mao decreed he wanted there to be one pig per person throughout China, he was more practical than the king who merely wished there to be a chicken in the pot of each peasant.

Modern husbandry, refrigeration and transport give us fresh pig meat and offal throughout the year, and thus many cured pork products are increasingly difficult to obtain. Those that are marketed often cut corners and are certainly far less salty or smoked than the originals, for once given the chance, modern palates decided to avoid the flavour of well-preserved meats. Indeed, today's processing methods have so changed the flavour of today's pig and its products that the general public are tending neither to recognize nor like, say, a genuine ham, which is relatively dry and dense. Instead they prefer the moistness and bright colour of products which have artificially high water contents, and have been battered and re-shapen into a false and often slimy tenderness. Sad.

Still, if you shop and eat with care the pig offers

pleasure still. And if you like to cook this can be multiplied, for many of the traditionally preserved dishes can be made with butcher's meat and still represent economical and satisfying cuisine. Pâtés and brawn are the easiest example, but I've cured a ham in central London with little problem.

Even to the uninitiated it must be obvious that the avalanche of pork products that tumble through our shops and supermarkets are largely variations on a very few themes. As with cheese, it is more important to be able to recognize the basic groups, to understand the manufacturing process and the ultimate aims. After that it is really up to you to get out and taste, and decide what you like.

In France you would go only to a *charcuterie*, for they specialize in pork produce. Charcuterie is also the word widely used to describe the products that follow.

UNCOOKED, AIR-DRIED MEATS

The best-known products in this category are the salamis of Italy, the *saucissons secs* of France and the 'raw' hams such as the Parma, Bayonne and Westphalian. Most are meant to be eaten raw, but English air-dried hams are usually cooked.

Salami and saucissons

It is a dreadful shock for many to learn that a salame is actually raw pig meat; even more are mortified to the point of nausea to learn the origin of some salami casings. And almost no-one believes that the white powder on these skins is not flour or 'preservative' but an artifically encouraged bacterial mould.

Salami and saucisson secs are the same thing, so for simplicity I will use mainly the former name.

Salami are made from raw pork minced with back fat and, sometimes, beef. In France a variety of spices and herbs plus salt and pepper will be added. Italians use fewer spices and herbs but are more likely than the French to incorporate beef. An Italian salami made only of pork will bear a metal tag stamped with an 'S', if beef is included it says 'SB'. It is a commonly held fallacy that most Italian salami include garlic. Some do, but it is rare, for it is likely to go rancid. There are salami with a garlic-like flavour, but this is rarely induced by garlic itself.

Both Hungary and Switzerland make a salame flavoured with paprika, well worth seeking out, but some are really very hot.

The flavour of salami is first determined by the

proportion of meat to fat and then by the texture to which each ingredient is minced. In my experience the larger the pieces of meat and the lower the proportion of fat, the sweeter the salami; look for the plump Jesus de Lyon if you like this style. If you like strongly flavoured salami, go for those with a fine texture and/or high fat content, both of which can be judged by sight of the cut edge; the Italian Milano or the Hungarian are popular examples.

Further effects on eventual flavour can be expected from the casing into which the basic preparation is forced. Ideally they should be the cleansed intestine of the pig. As each part of an intestine harbours or attracts different types of bacteria and accompanying enzymes, so will each part donate a different flavour to a salami. A long thin salame will dry at a different speed from a thicker or shorter one and this will affect the outcome, too. Some of the casings are quite extraordinary; in the instance of the large saucisson called Rose de Lyon, the last few feet of the pig's large intestine is used, including the sphincter. Thus the saucisson's name has nothing whatsoever to do with its rosy colour.

Once the prepared mixture is encased it might then be tied overall with string in a traditional manner or simply tied both ends so it may be suspended. With minimum attention in a constant temperature, the salame should lose about 35 per cent of its weight through evaporation of its water content. The time taken may vary from a few weeks to many months depending on the size and the degree of dryness required. Some Italian salami are cured not in air but by being pressed between boards. The boards, which absorb the liquid expressed, are changed at regular intervals and these products, immediately recognizable by their flatness, thus cure faster than those left to evaporate in the air.

During the air-curing process some salami will regularly be wiped free of exudate, some will not; some may be dusted with talcum to seal any holes in the casings, others will be dipped into herbs or black pepper. In Hungary and Italy a fine white ambient white bacteria is encouraged to grow on the skins, because the enzymic action of its by-products further tenderizes and flavours the meat.

Of course modern techniques have been applied to salami, too. Many have artificial casings and may even contain preservatives. The startling pink of

Danish salami is due to the meat being pre-salted, a process which incorporates saltpetre, and that gives rise to the hue. I understand that the meat is sometimes slightly cooked, too.

The theory behind the preservation and long life of all air-dried products is that all bacteria dangerous to humans require water to flourish. Salami's combination of high fat content and low water level means a properly-made and stored salame is impervious to the attention of putrefactive influences. But manufacturing techniques which do not allow proper drying can make a salame very dangerous indeed to eat. When the French government tested salami samples from throughout the country they found that only the largest and oldest manufacturers could be relied upon consistently to be absolutely safe. I will never eat a salame that is soft or spongy in the centre or that smells sharply; it may simply be too young but it could also have unpleasant digestive effects. I think one of my life's most memorable mornings was spent in the search of salami facts, when I visited the Caby factory, outside Lille in the north of France.

Uniformed staff greeted me under a pristine Union Jack. I was issued with wellingtons, a hat and coat, all too big. My visit unexpectedly coincided with the arrival of a consignment of pigs and I quickly plunged into a far fuller picture of the manufacture of French salami than anticipated. From the slaughter and disembowelling of the animals (which meant ducking streams of steaming blood), and right through every part of the butchering, the cleansing of the intestines, the mincing, chopping, seasoning, packing and drying, the whole astonishing experience was viewed by me with a frozen smile and the smell of hot blood in my nostrils.

At the end of the long tour I was grateful for the offer of a drink and some lunch on the premises. Too late I realised I would be offered platefuls of assorted pork products – salami, pâtés, sausages, indeed everything that could be made from what I had seen squealing on trotters all too recently. Every bit of politesse was needed to strike the necessary balance between enjoying my hosts' proudly presented products and my revolving stomach. Now I eat salami more than ever. But that lunch *was* difficult.

Hams   Such sweet, air-dried hams as Parma, thin slices of which are constantly assassinated by luke-warm hunks of dreadful melon, differ from salami in two ways: (a) they are always brined before drying and (b) they are left whole. True hams are made only from the detached rear legs of the pig; if perchance the leg is cured still attached to the side of the animal it should actually be called a gammon, but this is how Wiltshire hams are cured.

The traditional way to get fine flavour and texture from an air-dried, uncooked ham is to begin with dry-salting. The raw meat is rubbed with dry salt at regular intervals. This slowly draws the fluids from the flesh, which in turn dissolve the salt which is absorbed back into the skin. The high salt content preserves the flesh, as bacteria cannot flourish in such conditions. There is always the risk that the brine will not penetrate right to the bone and the unsalted meat there will go off, causing a very nasty taste and potential danger known as bone taint.

It is by the addition of sugar and spices to the salt that different styles of cure and flavours are encouraged; and naturally the food given to the pig will also have some influence. The famous Virginia hams should be made from pigs fed on peanuts and peaches; the Smithfield (which is in Virginia not London) pig should dine on acorns and other wild nuts before being fattened on corn and peanuts. I suspect few of the animals responsible for furnishing the 'Virginia' Hams sold in the United Kingdom have ever seen a peanut, let alone a peach.

A faster method of salting is simply to soak the meat in a brine bath, but this always leads to a tougher end product. The newest technology of all automatically weighs each raw ham and then injects it with a predetermined proportion of brine, using a major artery as the point of entry. By using the animal's natural channels of communication the brine travels quickly and evenly throughout the flesh. Results seem better than the brine bath, but experts say they can easily detect a certain toughness.

Once salting is completed the ham must be dried. This can be done green (unsmoked) or after being smoked and once again the time and type of wood used will influence the flavour. In Ireland peat smoke is used, in Virginia apple and hickory wood are popular and here oak is common.

Smoking and drying, which allow the final development of flavour, can take as much as 24 months and this is why real hams are so expensive; the cooked pressed hams, hams for slicing and those sold sliced will have been salt cured but not dried – indeed they have extra water added to them. Sometimes air-dried hams are boned before curing, some are boned after curing. Beware of boned hams that have too obviously been pressed into an even shape. This is often done after curing but before drying and so some of the liquor is expressed which is not conducive to great development of flavour. Given the choice, it is better to choose a ham which has been cured whole then de-boned.

It would be pointless even to attempt to estimate the different types of air-dried hams produced, even in this country. For those who make them on a farm will do it differently each time, and even the well-known ones will vary a little. But if you have the inclination, luck (and money) here is the guide to what you may find in stores.

Bradenham: smaller than most hams, the Bradenham cure includes molasses, thus making it also one of the most expensive hams. It has a very black skin and a highly individual flavour, drawn both from the molasses and spices such as juniper. It has been made in Chippenham for just over two centuries and needs to be soaked for a good 72 hours before being baked.

Suffolk: this is also quite sweet and is smoked before being allowed to develop its 'blue bloom'. I rather like this one for it is a rich colour and has a good full flavour.

York: well-known even in Europe where anonymous ham will also be sold as Jambon d'York. A real York should be mild and pink and might have been smoked to varying degrees. A dry salt cure is used, so any sweetness is due to careful tending during the maturation, which takes 3–4 months and should be accompanied by the growth of a green mould. A York needs only to be soaked 12–24 hours before cooking.

In France, Jambon de Bayonne is the best known. This is eaten raw and differs from the hams of Spain and Italy by being lightly smoked. Otherwise look in local charcuteries for Jambons de Campagnes, which are simply local variations and depending on their excellence will be recommended for use as they are or for cooking.

One of my favourite hams of all is the

Westphalian, from Germany. It is a darker colour than many and quite smoky. I know some experts, such as the lat Tom Stobart OBE, believe its smoky taste is better without accompaniments but I think the more assertive flavour is a fine complement to a really succulent pear or syrupy fig, which sometimes overwhelm the delicate Bayonne or Parma.

Prosciutto is simply Italian for ham; if you want Parma or one of the other excellent air-dried hams you must ask for *Prosciutto crudo*. Sea salt is used for genuine Parma ham cures and the drying may take as long as two years; it is never less than 8 months. Hence the expense. It is easy and common to call any air-dried Italian ham by the name Parma; it is always worth checking the skin, for genuine Parma hams have a distinctive brand burned into them.

Once you start looking, you will find that most European countries have air-dried hams that are worth exploring. The Dutch have the smoked Guelder ham and the Coburger, which is only the top part of the ham. The Swiss make an excellent *Röhschinken*. The Spanish *jamon serrano*, can be excellent but is often chewy; the Belgians are justly proud of their *jambon d'Ardennes* and the Prague ham, which should be from Czechoslovakia, of course, is considered the best ham of all to be served hot (I'm still waiting for my first sample). Of all the rare and wonderful treats I have enjoyed I specially remember home-made hams on the Isle of Elba, encrusted with peppers and herbs in a way I've seen no-where else. Almost mahogany in colour, the flesh resisted the teeth but then released a flavour that hung on the tongue for hours. With a glass of chilled Elban wine and a sun-warmed peach direct from the bough, I had lunched enough, and hardly ever better.

OTHER AIR-DRIED MEATS

Although some countries go to great lengths to dry mutton and lamb these end up being rather too special in flavour for any but the initiated or the starving. But there are several beef products that are worth exploring. They are *Bresaola* from northern Italy and *Bundnerfleish* from the Grisons in Switzerland. Fatless and very hard, they were originally fillet or some other lean cut and are never chopped or minced. To serve, they must be sliced very thinly indeed, and although I was constantly served these translucent, scarlet slithers with smart aprés-ski drinks in Gstaad I always thought they tasted of soap. Even when served on a plate, and moistened with excellent olive oil and a little lemon juice, I find air-dried beef overrated. I far prefer *coppa cruda*, from Italy. This is a piece of air-dried pork, from the neck I believe, pressed into a skin. It has often some quite noticeable runs of fat throughout; *coppa cruda* is essential in antipasto, sweet and satisfying and acceptable to those who do not usually like salami. Swiss *Rospeck* is air-dried belly of pork or streaky bacon.

Laxschinken, too, is a great but rarer treat. This is the lightly-salted, slightly dried, lightly-smoked loin of pork, wrapped in fine fat. It is soft, meltingly so, and its name means salmon ham and should be served just below room temperature in quite thin but not too thin slices, and never cooked.

I suppose *biltong* from South Africa should be included here too. It can be almost any kind of meat but the source makes little difference – it is all pretty filthy except for ostrich biltong. That is absolutely filthy. *Pemmican*, by the way, was air-dried buffalo meat, somehow combined with cranberries. As well as being a staple of the American Indian, it was popular with early Arctic explorers. The modern equivalent in the United States is something called *jerked beef* or *jerky*; it is strips of sun-dried beef, and last time I was in Los Angeles *everyone* carried some around as a calorie-low way to assuage hunger. Now I understand they eat nothing but strawberries, unless it is Wednesday when they eat nothing but pineapple, and jerky is only available where people hunt and shoot and fish.

Serving

Salami and saucissons are made to be eaten simply, with bread, and perhaps some cheese and a few unobtrusive pickles. The Scandinavians and Dutch and Germans tend to serve them for breakfast.

In general I don't think salamis should be cooked, but a leftover end piece of salami might be cut into chunks to finish a spaghetti sauce or for inclusion in a salad. Or you can roll slices around a flavoured cream cheese as a snack. Oh, it should *always* be skinned, unless it has been coated with herbs or peppers. If you have a piece which you are to slice yourself, peel it first.

You are unlikely to have a whole Parma or a Bayonne to yourself, but if you do, take extreme care when removing the tough skin prior to slicing. For maximum enhancement of the sweetness of raw hams served just a little below room temperature; too warm and they will start to sweat, too cold and the flavour will be hidden.

I grant that melon is a good accompaniment if it is a fine specimen but fresh figs or a juicy pear, again not too cold, are infinitely better. It is also good to serve such a ham sliced onto a plate and scattered with an excellent dressing made with olive oil and lemon juice or a mildly flavoured wine vinegar. As a wrapping of flavour and excellence for special vegetables, whole truffles – even fillets of fish – translucent slices of uncooked ham cannot be bettered. But the more robust flavour of the smoked Westphalian ham is usually more appreciated than the rather fragile unsmoked or lightly smoked varieties.

The end of knuckle pieces are delicious when diced and thrown into a sauce, or a pasta dish, or when finely minced as the basis of a stuffing; but do check for rancidity.

The raw beef products are eaten sliced extremely thinly, sometimes also sitting in a little first-class olive oil mixed with a little lemon juice, or less wine vinegar.

Storing air-dried products

Whilst they are still whole, air-dried products are better kept out of the refrigerator and simply hung in a cool, well ventilated place. But once they have been cut they must be treated with care. They may not go mouldy, but will easily go rancid, particularly if they are already sliced. Even the flavours of the more robust salamis are actually rather delicate and likely to be swamped by something powerful in a refrigerator, so always wrap these products well in cling film, but let them warm a little before eating them, otherwise the essential sweetness will be lost to your palate.

SAUSAGES IN SKINS

Fresh sausages: these are the sausages made for immediate use and thus are as often made from fresh meat as from slightly salt-cured meat, which gives a little more flavour and colour because of the use of saltpetre. This type is known as Röhwurst in Germany.

This section specifically deals with sausages that have not been treated after they have been put into their skins and which must be cooked before eating.

In England the fresh sausage is the famed 'banger'. Although we seem always to have included bread or cereal in many of our sausages it is thought to have been the Industrial Revolution that increased the content to its now high but accepted level. The need for cheap, filling food for the thousands of labourers who had left the country for the city meant that traditional sausages were extended with a variety of cereals or farinacea. Don't be persuaded by phrases such as 'all-pure pork' or even 'beef' sausages. The rules about naming sausages refer to that proportion that may not be other than meat, i.e. if a certain type of sausage is allowed to have 30 per cent filling and the *rest* is all pork it will be sold as all-pork.

Beef sausages have become slightly easier to buy, because they are popular with the many new Muslim inhabitants of the country, who can't eat the pig. Yet again, don't be misled. Most 'beef' sausages also contain a proportion of pork. Look carefully at the label if you want to avoid a Holy War.

There are few truly fresh sausages sold; most having been treated in some way or another.

Sausages with casings

American breakfast sausages are generally smaller and slimmer than British sausages. There is considerably less cereal and they are also more coarsely cut and generally rather peppery or with a distinct herb flavour. Some are smoked and these are my favourite, especially with buckwheat cakes and maple syrup. These are always a pleasant surprise, and infinitely more interesting than the English kind.
Bratwurst: this famous German sausage is more and more available in the UK. It can look like a rather longer, straighter, thicker frankfurter or a thicker, uncooked English sausage. Either way the filling will be chunky and there will be nothing but pork, fat and flavouring inside the skin. Bratwurst are used in many ways: they can just be boiled in water and served with sauerkraut or, more simply, with masses of hot buttered green cabbage and mashed potatoes. I think they are better if, having been boiled for about 5 minutes until cooked through, they are then gently browned in butter. They are sometimes sold 'scalded' in commercial packs, meaning they have been slightly cooked to give them a longer life. Either way they make a welcoming and satisfying winter dish.
Chipolata: essentially a smaller English sausage, very popular with children and those with barbecues.

The name is derived from *cibolla*, Italian for chives, for they should contain some of this member of the onion family. I'd be surprised if you ever found one that did. Cook as you would the English banger.

Contechino: this might well be described as the Italian bratwurst, but it is considerably bigger, usually weighing about 1 lb (½ kg). It should be pricked slightly and then cooked in simmering water for several hours. Again, I also like to finish it off by browning it in a little butter or fat.

Cumberland: one of the few traditional British sausages that remains and that tastes something like it should. Essentially a pork sausage with a minimum of bread or cereal, coarsely cut and peppery . . . You can buy it readily in Cumberland, and each good butcher has his own recipe. It comes in coils and should be baked slowly in the oven until golden brown and swimming in its own fat. Its pepperiness and the fat combine marvellously with excellently mashed potatoes and a simple green vegetable like cabbage, which has an affinity with virtually every hot sausage of merit.

English beef: generally a paste of beef *and* pork with permitted fillers and perhaps a little herby and peppery. Not very common other than in the north of England and in Marks and Spencers (but most of theirs have pork as well).

English pork: there are as many of these as there are manufacturers. Generally made from a paste of pork and other ingredients to enhance flavour, extend and preserve life.

Here and there you do find a butcher who will go to some trouble to achieve a degree of authenticity, i.e. to include detectable amounts of sage and a few pieces of meat to chew upon, even if they are gristly. For one there is a butcher in London's North End Road market who makes wonderful herby sausages.

I'm afraid we put up with bland sausages simply because we put up with them and that's that. The cost of increasing the texture and enhancing the flavour by including some decent herbs would seem to be negligible. Up north tomato-flavoured sausages are made, and they can be quite good, especially in Carlisle's market.

Undoubtedly there is only one way to cook sausages if you have the time and that is slowly, unpricked in a very low oven. It may take 45 minutes, but the skin turns a wonderful colour, the flavour is nutty and the smell they make whilst they are gently roasting makes even the least good one taste better on the plate, expectation being the greatest stimulus to enjoyment.

Salsiccia: this is the generic Italian term for all sausages, fresh and cured. Few are available here, and those that are are usually like bratwurst, which is a suitable substitute.

Saucisses: French sausages: saucissons are air-dried salamis.

Toulouse: this is the most famous French fresh sausage and available in fairly good versions in ths country at specialist butchers – certainly in Soho. It has a high meat content and is further flavoured with quatre-épices. The French have a variety of fresh sausages, none of which contains anything but pork and flavouring. They are usually thinner and longer than ours. The best I ever tasted were offered to me by a four-year-old French girl on a beach by the walled city of Aigue-les-Mortes in the Camargue. They were crammed with chunks of chewy pork, with tiny slices of garlic, leaves of fresh thyme and coarsely ground pepper. The meat had obviously been lightly cured for it was bright red. The sausages had been cooked by the little girl's family over an open fire and they were quite simply superb. When I asked what name they had, the answer was, 'Oh, no special name – they're just the saucisses that our local charcutier makes.

Zampone: this Italian sausage is stuffed into the skin of a pig's trotter and is probably rather rare in its uncooked state in this country; if you find it at all it has probably been scalded to lengthen its life.

Cook in the same way as Cotechino, perhaps slightly longer, to ensure the skin is deliciously gelatinous. It is specially good with hot pulses and potatoes.

| SAUSAGES WITHOUT CASINGS | Some sausage mixtures are sold without the usual skins. In England this is simply called sausage meat and is much used, although I wish it were not, as the base for stuffings. If you buy some, mix it with fresh herbs, breadcrumbs, grated lemon rind some mace, nutmeg and black pepper, perhaps a little wine or vermouth, and then bake it in pastry. It makes delicious picnic fare. The French *crepinettes* are usually made from minced pork, but sometimes other meats, seasoned and spiced and wrapped in a |

piece of caul fat; thus they are similar to our faggots which usually include some degree of offal as well.

Perhaps the best known of other uncased sausages are the Greek *keftethes* which are really meat patties, I suppose. Beef or veal are the usual bases and there is always a proportion of breadcrumbs, onion and the obligatory oregano and mint. They are not the same if they are not cooked in very hot olive oil.

SMOKED DRIED SAUSAGES

Cervelat: this finely-minced salme-like sausage, usually a mixture of beef and pork, is packed into a long gut and smoked a golden brown. The texture and mild flavour are popular with those who are not normally keen on charcuterie.

Landjaeger: a popular snack with skiers, these robustly-flavoured small sausages usually have a flattened look as they are pressed between boards for smoking. They should be quite hard and dry and consist mainly of spiced beef. Red wine is incorporated into the mixture, too. Excellent with hot wine or cold beer.

Katenrauch (wurst): a coarse, heavily smoked sausage usually cut on the diagonal to give oval slices.

Mett (wurst): this can be many things and each area will have its own, i.e. Braunschweiger Mettwurst, Berliner Mettwurst, etc. Made from pork and beef, it is air-dried then cold-smoked. It has a very smoky flavour and this one can be heated to eat with, say, cabbage. Sometimes made as a spread, too.

Tee(wurst): spicy and salmon pink and smooth but available in many variations. Ruegenwalder Teewurst is considered the best and is made only of pork and spare rib bacon. Usually sold in small sizes and is also available as a spread.

Shinken(wurst) (or ham sausage): a Westphalian speciality of coarsely chopped or flaked ham, mild and tender. Schinkenplockwurst has large pieces of fat but is easy to cut. If the colour is dark this indicates a high beef content, otherwise the meat used for this one is pickled pork.

SCALDED SAUSAGES, SMOKED AND UNSMOKED

These are what the Germans would call *Brühwurst*. They are usually rather finely minced and sometimes smoked, but always lightly cooked to prolong their life and preserve their texture. This is by far the largest group of sausages, and many are for slicing.

Bierwurst: a large, German slicing sausage which does not contain beer, but which is excellent with it.

It is always eaten cold and has a peppery flavour. *Bierschinkenwurst* is the same thing with small chunks of ham included.

Chorizo: although Spanish by name, this paprika-flavoured sausage is made by a number of countries and is not always scalded, e.g. the Hungarian paprika-flavoured salami. There are hot and sweet versions made in France and in Spain. They may be cooked whole or in slices and make an excellent addition either way to dishes of beans, cassoulets and that sort of thing. Genuine Hungarian paprika sausages are much harder to find nowadays but worth the money; they are called *Gyulai* – similar products are now being made in London.

Bockwurst: this is really a subsection all of its own and the name is used generically for most sausages that are extremely finely ground, like frankfurters and wieners and knackwurst.

Boiling ring: this Polish sausage, which is usually tied into a horseshoe shape and weighs about 1 lb (½ kg) is chunky, garlicky pork lightly smoked. Basically cooked like the frankfurter, it is invaluable for adding to things in slices, especially cassoulet, bean casseroles, and rugged poultry dishes. Also eaten cold.

Bologna: many things to many people. Known in America as baloney, and in Australasia as luncheon sausage. It is finely-minced pork with a peppery taste, sometimes smoked and usually made in a fattish shape. Quite good sliced and fried but usually eaten in bread rolls or as part of a mixed hors d'oeuvres

Cervelas: not to be confused with cervelat which is German and a type of salami, this French *saucisse* is not unlike a shorter, thicker frankfurter, but might contain garlic and is often slightly dried. Cooked like the frankfurter and its family. In Switzerland it is also called a *Chlöpfer* and served grilled.

Cheerios: always referred to as 'little boys' by my mother. These are 'cocktail-length' saveloys or frankfurters, useful for parties. Usually red-skinned, they are often also called 'weenies', which takes us back to mother, I suppose.

Fleischwurst: sometimes called *Extrawurst*. This is a slicing sausage, one of the nicest of the finely ground types. It is pale, firm but moist, and variations contain garlic, pistachio nuts or pieces of red pepper. Their decorative appearance makes them perfect for *aufschnitz*, which means a selection of sliced meats –

what the Americans call cold cuts. I know the Swiss make excellent sausages of this type.

Frankfurters: these should be made from a paste of fine pork and salted bacon fat and be cold-smoked, which gives a yellowish colour to the skin. Often they are made with whatever is to hand I think and even in Germany such sausages can have lots of fat or none at all. Frankfurter is now a name for any long thin sausages and in the United States you can buy chicken, turkey, ham or beef frankfurters. Once they get around to making one with fish, that really *will* be a fish finger. To heat these and other similar sausages, put into cold water and bring slowly to the boil – they will burst if you plunge them into hot water. Sliced frankfurter is delicious in hot or cold potato salad or a salad of cold french beans. A frankfurter is what you usually find in a hot dog – except when you find a *wiener*.

Garlic sausage: one of the best-known slicing sausages and made by most European countries. The French ones are usually fairly fat and in an artificial casing; sometimes they include chunks of ham and thus are simply a ham sausage containing garlic. There are some thinner Polish types which have a wrinkly brown skin and are only a few inches in diameter. I think they are better than most; ask for *krakowska*.

Ham sausage: together with garlic sausages, the big two of the slicing sausage trade. Chunks of ham in a paste of ground up ham, stablizers etc. Again the Polish variety is usually a better choice.

Jagerwurst: finely-minced veal and pork with a very peppery taste, sometimes with green peppercorns.

Kabanos/kabanossi: piquant, highly-smoked chewy pork sausages that are very thin and long. There are two types, the soft and the dried – one is simply older than the other. The soft one makes an excellent snack or, cut into thick slices, a good addition to salads. The hard one is popular for chewing but better sliced and cooked, especially in a dish that has lots of either garlic, tomato or beans, or all three.

Knackwurst: short fat frankfurters, really, usually tied together in strings.

Mazurska: not a dance but music to anyone who is a Polish sausage lover. Like a slightly larger 'banger' in size but filled with chewy pork, garlic and pepper, and smoked. Simply heat in water and serve with buttered cabbage or spiced red cabbage and some good relishes. Perfectly indispensable for cooking in winter dishes but equally wonderful sliced and served cold in summer. One per person is usually more than enough.

Merguez: thin, very spicy sausages brought to us from Algeria via France. Nice barbecued or cut up into casseroles.

Mortadella: the big fat one for slicing. There are many, many, many types and some horrid stories – this is the one that really was once made with donkey meat, I think. The best types should include green pistachioes but all have cubes of fat, thus it can be disagreeable if warm. Chilled enough to keep the fat solid it is nice on fresh crusty bread or in mixed platters, but not memorable.

Mysliewska: a dry short sausage of pork that is heated in water like a frankfurter. Coarse and chewy and quite peppery, but I prefer the mazurska.

Saucisson: confusingly, the Swiss name for a delicious smoked sausage containing ham, brandy, leeks and paprika. Served hot.

Saveloys: a corruption of the French cervelas as far as etymology goes, and a corruption of most other things as far as the product generally goes. It should be made from finely minced pork and, like a fat frankfurter, should also be smoked. But they often have a scarlet coating, perhaps with some artificial smoke flavour added, and this colour should be a warning if you are looking for something of quality.

Schüblig: a lightly-smoked, fine Swiss sausage with a thick skin. Served hot.

Tuchowska: another slender Polish sausage of pork, coarse but solid and smoked, excellent cold but can be sliced into casseroles; slightly wetter and fatter than *wieska*.

Weisswurst: varying in size but always very white and firm. Strangely, I have seen them sold as white bratwurst. They should be made of veal, perhaps with some chicken, and often include parsley. Like bratwurst they are specially good if they are first heated in water and then browned in fat or butter. A little mustard is all they need as an accompaniment.

Weinerwurst: first cousin, if not brother, to the frankfurter, but often shorter in length; the *real* 'little boys' (see 'cheerios').

Wieska: one of the basic Polish sausages, long but tied into a horseshoe shape. A pork sausage, relatively dry and lean. Eat cold or heated.

COOKED OR BOILED SAUSAGES

Nearly always based on offal or blood or some such combination, these products (the German *Kochwurst*) are steam-cooked in their casings.

Black pudding: (*Blutwurst/boudin noir*) based on blood thickened with cereals like barley or oatmeal and often with cubes of back fat and onion flavouring. This is made in many qualities and sizes and is usually sliced and fried to serve hot, especially for breakfast. Some skin it first, some don't (I don't). The French *boudins* are often more delicate, containing cream and spices. The Polish *Kashanka*, available in this country is rather firm, and is usually made in a natural casing. *Rotwurst* is a variation, spicier and coarser.

Brawn: made properly, with lots of pepper and *big* pieces of meat, brawn can be the most delicious of charcuterie treats. It should be made from the many contrasting meats of a well boiled head set in an aspic from its own cooking. The English brawn stops there but continental ones often put the whole lot into gut, or even a stomach (the Poles do). This is much better if served slightly chilled with a sharpish accompaniment, like a vinaigrette sauce, pickled cucumber, gherkins and olives. If you make your own, defy tradition and add herbs and spices. Orange and lemon peel, finely chopped garlic, horseradish, chives, mint, thyme, and mace, whole peppers – white, black or green – make the normally bland dish into something quite marvellous. It is doubly good, if you have well flavoured the cooking stock, with vermouth, bay and citrus in particular. Germans call this *Sulzwurst* and the French *fromage de tête*, which is why Americans call it head cheese.

Haslet: this is specially English, a sort of meat loaf made only from offal and which should be cooked in a lace of caul fat . . . not often available and not often worth eating. But it could be. Eaten cold or hot in slices.

Leberkäs: a speciality of Bavaria, but not often special, for it is a baked meat loaf with a high liver content – and meat loaf is nearly always awful unless you make it yourself. Thinly sliced and grilled or fried it can be fine in Bavaria, but those we find here are usually too crammed with filler and preservative. The Swiss *fleischkaise* is also a meat loaf, but contains little liver. It is served sliced, hot or cold.

Liver sausage (*leberwurst*): The price and quality depends both on the amount of liver actually included and the type of liver used. Generally such sausages are made with pork liver and pork meat. Some are firm enough to slice and wrapped in fine fat, others are meant to be spread and these are often richer in flavour. There are variations also in the texture of the mixture and the inclusion of spices, onion and so on. The most expensive are made only from calves' liver (*Kalbsleberwurst*) or from goose liver. None is usually heated before use, but if they are rich and full-flavoured some of the slicing liver sausages could be fried or grilled or heated on toast, perhaps as an accompaniment to game. Mix some good sausage with a little brandy and crushed green peppercorns to make good stuffings for *petites bouchées* or to slide under the skin of a roasting fowl.

Tongue sausage: one of the best-looking sausages for making arrangements of *aufschnitz* or cold cuts, the German tongue sausage (*zungenwurst*) is usually a superior blood sausage in which whole pieces of tongue are suspended. Generally it looks better than it tastes.

COOKED HAMS

Cooked hams, boneless and meant for slicing, are the charcuterie counter's equivalent of sliced white bread.

Now there are some exceptions, usually from the Continent, but this is generally what happens, and it is important that you begin this voyage of discovery at the end rather than the beginning. First, most ham is not ham, (that is from the rear leg of the animal), not even that in a ham shape, and what you are buying is as much water as anything else.

Pork for such products can come from all parts of the animal, and is always cured in a salt brine; those sold as Virginia hams probably have some sweeteners added to the cure. Once this is completed the meat is shredded and tumbled to make it even in texture. Then it is pressed into moulds, either square, 'd' or ham shaped and steamed to prevent weight or moisture loss. Oh yes, and the animal has been treated in such a manner that the flesh retains far more moisture than normal.

All this is done to bring a cheaper product to the market, you understand, and there must be some merit in that. But how sad to see people preferring this literal dilution of one of our oldest foods, thinking real ham too dry or too strongly flavoured. You do get what you pay for with ham, and the bottom end of the scale in cooked hams is tasteless, and barely worth eating nutritionally.

OTHER PRODUCTS

Bacon products are not usually thought of as being from a delicatessen, although sometimes these are the only shops where good quality bacon can be bought. The most useful I know is the *spek*, which is simply the very best back fat, salted. Some is plain, some is smoked and some smoked with paprika.
Thinly-sliced or cubed, all can be used to add richness to cooking, for rendering or to make crisp *lardons*. The paprika spek is eaten as is, very thinly sliced, an interesting experience.
Bozcek is Polish and is lean belly of pork, salted, smoked or unsmoked, cooked or uncooked. The cooked smoked *bozcek* is delicious sliced and eaten with mustard and can also be fried or grilled. The raw *bozceks* are the best way I know to get a smoky bacon flavour into any dish, from pâté to casserole.

In Switzerland pork chops are smoked and make a smart but expensive picnic dish. These are called *Rippli*. It might be cheaper perhaps to go for *kassler*, which is made by various countries, this is the eye of the loin, salted and smoked. Cut thin or thick it is succulent and delicious in sandwiches, salads or *aufschnitz*. It makes the most superior and attractive looking ham for ham and eggs.
Laxschinken is harder to find than ever, but is perhaps the finest pork treat. It is the fillet of pork very lightly salted and smoked then wrapped in fine bacon fat. It is soft and pale and always eaten raw. The name means salmon ham for there is a simlarity in texture to the raw or the smoked fish, but there must be none of its flavour.

If you can find smoked spare ribs, the rib cage that is, not the boneless cuts sold as spare ribs in the United Kingdom' these are wonderful cooked slowly in the oven or stuck into tomatoey stews to add flavour and vigour.
Pastrami: Common enough in the United States but only now beginning to appear in the United Kingdom. Pastrami is, or should be, salted and spiced brisket of beef. Firm of texture and covered with black pepper and other spices, it should be sliced extremely thinly and served cold or hot, specially in sandwiches – who hasn't heard of pastrami on rye?

When you are planning a cold buffet, the bite of pastrami can be a welcome relief amidst the sweetness of ham, chicken and turkey.

SALADS

As we see delicatessen counters and individual delicatessen shops increase, even more people will eat the salads they sell, usually made in bulk commercially. Most good independent shops also make a variety of their own salads or try to look as though they do by buying from the more inventive small suppliers. These usually include a salad made of red kidney beans with green pepper and or onion rings, sweetcorn and red pepper, cucumber in yoghurt, celery apple and raisin, carrot and raisin, and sometimes a salad based on cold pasta. All can be good and useful; but ensure they have been kept cold and also fresh. Personally I would buy no commercially made salad containing onion unless it was made the same day as nothing sours faster than chopped onion. Salads made with lettuce and tomato are rarely seen as they tend to go soft quickly, but I've always found that when we made tomato and leek salad we sold as much as we could make every day. The secret is not to dress it until it is sold, or to sell dressing separately.

The most usual salads you will come across are:

Coleslaw

Based on raw, shredded or thinly sliced cabbage, usually with some carrot and in a creamy mayonnaise-type dressing. Some do contain onion but it isn't really right to do so; it's better if you add your own if you must have it. Grated apple, orange rind, some bacon bits, sultanas, drained crushed pineapple, hot and sweet paprika, garlic, black pepper, mustards, lemon juice or parsley can all be added. Olive oil makes a smooth difference, and don't be afraid to add extra mayonnaise, or to add some cream, soured cream or yoghurt.

As well as being served as a side salad, coleslaw is delicious in great thick sandwiches, especially with sliced roast beef.

Potato

Generally sold rather bland, which is just as well because, you can do things to it and call it your own. As usual, I warn against those that contain onion, as this is pervasive and sours readily.

Soured cream rather than mayonnaise is the best addition to bought potato salads, together with green herbs, garlic and horseradish, or strips of tinned red peppers. Otherwise add strips of cooked sausage, sliced frankfurters, bacon pieces, small cubes of cheese and gherkin, salt, dill or fresh cucumber and prawns, mussels, anchovy fillets – or any combination; for instance, to make something Scandinavian, use soured creams and lots of dill. Mix tomato sauce or purée, black olives, garlic, parsley and Mozzarella cheese to make pizza-potato salad, and top with oregano and anchovy fillets.

Prawn

This is essentially a coleslaw in a mayonnaise-type dressing with tomato purée and paprika which also includes prawns. Naturally there is a high amount of preservative of one kind or another to keep this wholesome. It makes a good filling for a roll or sandwich as well as an accompaniment to cold, hard-boiled eggs. Of course, a touch of garlic juice, some ready-mixed mustard or chopped parsley, added at the same time as cream or soured cream to give more body, are all worthwhile considerations.

Russian or vegetable

It is so simple to make a basic Russian salad nowadays with the advent of frozen mixed vegetables, but you should always follow the system recommended for making good potato salad which is to douse the warm vegetables with a vinaigrette dressing or they will never have enogh flavour when cold. A lemon-flavoured mayonnaise completes the dish when the vegetables are cold.

Bought Russian and vegetable salads tend to be a little lifeless, but this is understandable, for they have a long way to travel and a long time to last. Nevertheless if they are helped along they might be the basis of something more exciting. Usually you must compensate for an excess of vinegar in the dressing in which it comes, essential to help give them a longer life. As usual a good mayonnaise, soured cream or whipped cream will sort that out. Then you can add other vegetables you may have. A true Russian salad was a wonderful confection, always containing meat, fish and poultry. You could do the same.

As with all vegetable dishes, garlic would help and so would Worcestershire sauce, Tabasco, chilli sauce, the freshness of parsley and the sharpness of orange or lemon. If it can stand the extra sharpness, tarragon vinegar can make a world of difference to Russian salad. If you have some fresh tarragon chop this into or over the salad; mint can help too.

Always serve such salads rather cold; this is why the flavours must be strong.

SNAILS

Snails, usually from France, are available two ways, in tins or frozen. The tinned ones sometimes come also with empty shells.

If you think carefully, it is not the snails you enjoy but the butter, usually redolent of garlic, so the bother of stuffing snails back into their shells, then pulling them out again with special and expensive instruments seems a bit silly. Snails are even nicer (or the butter is) on little beds of pastry or in tiny vol-au-vents.

Other places serve them other ways and the most interesting alternative is a red wine sauce flavoured with anise – either the seed or some suitable alcohol; fennel seed can also be used, and I believe these ideas come from Sicily.

Snails are now being bred for the table in England once more, in the Mendips, as they were by the Romans, but they seem rather small.

SOUPS

I'm not much of a soup person and rarely buy it in tins, mainly because I so loathe the school of cooking that invariably begins recipes with a tin of tomato or mushroom soup. Yet I know that many disagree with me and so I have made the effort.

I have yet to taste a seafood soup that tasted of seafood rather than cereal and I think the English ones are worst of all. There is an excellent range of Norwegian fish soups that are sold dried in foil packs and these can be made up with cream and milk and a touch of brandy into extraordinarily good seafood sauces as well as passable soups. No one knows they are from a packet.

The most useful tinned soups are the beef and chicken consommés. They are currently fashionable, at dinner parties, when whipped up with sour cream or cream cheese, curry or danish 'caviare' but I hope that like all fashion this will cease. A more sensible use is to serve consommé hot with a selection of very finely sliced vegetables including garlic and green ginger which habe been poached in the soup for a minute or so to crispen and brighten them.

SUGARS, SYRUPS AND HONEY

Pure sugar is sucrose, a white carbohydrate ($C_{12}H_{22}O_{11}$) with a sweet flavour, obtained mainly from sugar cane and the sugar beet; but some countries obtain sugars from palm trees, maple trees and from sorghum, a type of millet. Before such sugar was discovered by the western world, honey, fruit and such vegetables as the parsnip and carrot were the major sources of sweetness.

From a dietary point of view extra sugar (including honey) is unnecessary in an otherwise balanced diet. Enough 'energy fuel' can be obtained from the starch of cereals or from the galactose and fructose of vegetables and fruits respectively, and the advantage of using such sources of sugar is that it is ingested with other vitamins and minerals. But don't be fooled by honey. Its sweetness is sucrose broken down into invert or simpler sugars; the minimal amount of other good things honey contains in no way compensates for the damage done to teeth and health by eating more sugar than you really *need*. Honey is not a substitute for sugar – it is an alternative source of something you shouldn't need. But, having said that, I also know few people – myself included – can live without either the flavour or the silken texture sugar adds to food. So I'd better stop lecturing and start explaining.

CANE SUGAR

Once the white gold of merchants, for whom one cargoload of just 100 tonnes would be worth £1 million, sugar is now simply the world's most common sweetener.

Whence the cane from which it is extracted came, no-one is quite certain, but it is likely that it was the Solomon Islands in the South Pacific. Different cultures produce different sugar-related mythologies, the most titillating of which hails from India. It is said a King Subandu found a sugar cane growing in his bedroom, from which issued a prince Ilshvaku, reputedly a direct ancestor of the Buddha. I've heard some fine excuses for being found with a sweet young thing in your bedroom, but *really* . . .

As they seem to have been refining sugar since as long ago as 3000BC, Indian communities also seem to have been the first to have cultivated it on any scale. The knowledge spread slowly east to Indo-China and later ebbed west into Arabia and Europe. By the 5th century BC the Persians could both refine sugar and form it into loaves but were jealous of their techniques. Alexander the Great's general Nearchus commented in the 4th century BC on a reed that produced honey without bees and the Arab Conquests carried sugar further westwards so that by the 8th century AD it was being grown and processed in Spain and southern France. But it was not officially mentioned in England until the 12th century, when it is referred to in the court rolls. By 1544 there were two refineries in London.

Early sugars had charming names; one was *Zucchero Mucchero*, flavoured with musk. This sugar was the highest Egyptian quality and generally available only in the Middle East. *Candi* was, as you might guess, like rock candy – clear chunks made by boiling sugar syrup; five types might be found in the apothecary's shop: simple (unflavoured), rose, violet, lemon and red gooseberry. Montreal Mill came not from Canada but from a Syrian town to the south of the Dead Sea. Caffetin came from Caffa in the Crimea and was wrapped in palm leaves, which explains its 17th-century name, palm sugar (this term is now used for something else, see page 342).

During much of its history, sugar was used as a medicine, for it was far too expensive to use as a food or sweetener. As late as 1736 it was listed alongside the precious gems among the wedding gifts of Maria-Teresa, later queen of Austria and Hungary.

For a long time Venice controlled the sugar trade, but the discovery of the New World radically altered this. In the days of Christopher Columbus, sugar cost at least £20 a pound weight in modern terms, so on his second voyage west Columbus experimented with growing the cane on Santo Domingo in the Caribbean and found it grew faster and better there than anywhere else. The European crowns fought long, hard and expensively for the new sugar-producing areas. At the end of the Seven Year's War in 1763, England had a difficult choice over which French colonies to keep as indemnity, the tiny sugar islands of Martinique and Guadaloupe – or unmeasured Canada. She plumped for the latter only because certain she already had the better sugar islands.

In England, rapidly becoming the new hub of the sugar trade, technical developments in refining pre-dated the Industrial Revolution. By 1750 there were more than 150 factories producing over 30,000 tons of white sugar a year, which at an average of something over ½ oz (15 g) per cup would sweeten 63,000,000 servings of tea.

By the 18th century you usually bought loaf sugar which was refined sugar pressed with syrup into a very hard lump and then shaped into a loaf or cone. It was used with great care, for it was both expensive and highly-taxed. In the kitchen books of Mary Senhouse, my grandmother of nine generations ago, you did careful annotations of when a loaf was bought, how much was used and when. Sugar didn't come into general use until 1874, when Gladstone removed the tax, a blessing about which dentists have had mixed feelings ever since.

Processing sugar cane

The 10–24 ft (3–8 metres) high sugar canes are harvested in tropical sun in ghastly conditions, as any reader of the Australian novel *The Thornbirds* will know; but now this is increasingly done by machine.

The root of each cane is left in the ground to sprout again, a technique known as 'ratooning' and which can be repeated for up to six years. The freshly picked cane deteriorates rapidly, so is processed as quickly as possible.

First the sugar cane factory will clean it and shred it to expose the inner core. This is then crushed and sprayed with hot water to form a juice to whch linestone is added. Filtration under vacuum leaves a clarified liquid which is then concentrated. This thickened juice is boiled in steam-heated pans – still under vacuum – until something called 'massecuite' is obtained, a mixture of sugar crystals and 'mother syrup'. Centrifugal machines spin the mix separating it into crystals (raw cane sugar) and cane molasses. The raw cane sugar which is 96 per cent sucrose plus impurities and a coating of molasses then goes to the refinery. After softening by warmth, more centrifugal force is applied to separate the liquid sucrose from the molasses and impurities until one is presented with a clear amber syrup that is pure sucrose. This is decolourized before being turned into crystals by low boiling under vacuum. Different sizes of sugar crystal are made by variations in the final boiling.

BEET SUGAR

The other source of refined white sugar is the sugar beet, and from the outset you can be assured that the sugar from both is exactly the same thing – pure sucrose. Any differences in taste are the result of the processing technique used – or of imagination. Used as animal fodder and a table vegetable as far back as Roman times, the sugar beet didn't begin to be taken seriously as a sweetening source until the 18th century. In 1575 Olivier de Serres had ascertained beet sugar to be 'like a sugar syrup and is very beautiful to see because of its vermilion colour', but he did nothing other than look at it. In 1747 the German Andreas Marggraf extracted sugar from beet and made it solid for the first time and then in 1802 one of his pupils, Achard, set up a sugar factory in Silesia with the help of the King of Prussia; but the quality was low and the price high.

It was Napoleon who finally put beet sugar on the table. Suffering from the British blockade he enlisted the aid of the French Academy of Sciences, and the chemist Delassert finally made sugar from beet into a viable commercial proposition. Nowadays sugar beet is Europe's principal source of sugar. Much of England's comes from Norfolk and thereabouts, and experiments continue to produce better strains that can be grown in more parts of the world more easily. Hilleshog is a Swedish company which has a beet breeding station just outside Norwich. Their chief scientist is Kjell Ohlund and his work is making a major contribution to improving the English beet crop.

Processing sugar beet

The sugar beet arrive at a factory to be washed and cut into 'V' shapes, 'cosettes'. Together with hot water the cosettes are fed into a tower or slowly rotating drum so that the sugar can dissolve into the water. Then in other tanks this syrup has lime added to it and then carbon dioxide is bubbled through which forms a precipitate to carry out the impurities. More careful filtration follows, then a sulphur dioxide treatment and then concentration until you have the final syrup which can be crystallized from cane in the same way as sucrose.

CANE AND SUGAR BEET PRODUCTS

Note: None of the *natural* brown sugars can be obtained from beets.

Molasses sugar
Black Barbados or Demerara molasses

This is fairly difficult to find outside sugar cane processing areas. It is a very strong tasting sugar with a high molasses content and a rich, almost black colour. The sticky texture and taste are similar to good treacle toffee.

Muscovado sugar
sometimes called
Barbados

The most common naturally-dark sugar, this is extracted after the mother liquor has made three trips through the centrifuge. It is the last time the producer can extract sugar from the almost exhausted source. Thus the crystals are very small and one-seventh of their weight is molasses, which forms a coating on each crystal.

Light Muscovado is a creamier-coloured muscovado with a lower molasses content than true muscovado. It is ideal for cakes and puddings where you want extra flavour; the darker sugars aren't generally recommended for cake making.

Demerara sugar

This highly important and delicious natural brown sugar is crystallized from syrup that has been only partly discolourized and filtered during boiling. The large sparkling, yellow crystals are about 98 per cent pure sucrose and 2 per cent molasses and thus quite refined, but at least give you some of those vital minerals. It takes its name from the county in Guyana where it was first produced. But now there are other types of Dem., as it is affectionately know, and it can be made by adding cane molasses to refined white sugar, which could thus be beet sugar. It will have exactly the same qualities and you will always know if it has been made for its name must be qualified. Demerara on a packet means it was made from cane sugar in the country in which the cane was grown. Other types, such as 'London Demerara' indicate that it has been artificially made and the qualifying adjective usually indicates this was done in a refinery close to the point of consumption.

There is almost no nutritional difference between Muscovado and Demera sugar.

Demerara is excellent for flavouring cooked or new fruits, and for cereals. It is traditionally used to sprinkle on fruitcakes and biscuits before baking, to give a crunchy topping. It can replace white sugar in virtually every recipe where you do not mind the addition of a little colour.

Molasses
Blackstrap molasses

This is the rich concentrated syrup remaining after cane sugar syrup has been through the several boiling and separating processes necessary to extract almost all the pure sucrose. It contains some sucrose and other tyes of sugar as well as everything that refined white sugar is missing; in fact 8 to 10 per cent of molasses is vital minerals including iron, copper, calcium, magnesium, chromium, phosphorous, potassium and zinc.

There are various colours and grades, depending on how much sugar is left in the liquid. The darker the molasses the less sugar it contains. All types can also contain sulphur, which is used in some refineries – unsulphured molasses is usually light coloured and better flavoured. Some cane growing areas will simply reduce cane syrup over heat and call this sweet golden liquid molasses; but this is never sold commercially that I know of. Molasses is mainly used these days to flavour baking, in Creole cooking and to add flavour to the water when boiling hams.

Treacle

This is much sweeter than molasses for it is actually the full syrup that has only had a proportion of the sucrose removed from it, and again can only be made from cane sugar although golden syrup might also be added to it – the label will tell you. Used mainly for puddings.

Other than those natural brown sugars from the cane, it's all sweetness and white, for further refining produces a crystal that is practically 100 per cent pure sucrose, and it is this white granulated sugar which is usually demanded and to which the refineries and factories are basically geared. There is no proof that refined white sugar is in itself more fattening than the natural brown sugars; but the latter are nutritionally more valuable and balanced, *relatively*.

GOLDEN SYRUP

Terribly popular but, like 'brown sugars', a little dishonest. It is a syrup of refined sugar plus something called invert sugar plus colouring from the original sugar syrup. Invert sugar is sucrose (a complicated sugar) broken down into it components, the two simple sugars called dextrose and laevulose. If you must have a syrup, treacle is probably a marginally better choice; but I wouldn't put anybody off a golden-syrup flavoured steamed pudding!

If you are American you cannot buy golden syrup so you must use corn syrup and, if you like, colour it with some brown sugar of one kind or another.

TYPES OF
WHITE,
REFINED SUGAR

These are classified according to grain size.

Rock or candy sugar	Huge sugar crystals, often strung together. It is used for sweet making as it does not burn easily.
Granulated sugar	Although varying from country to country each grain is usually about 1 mm.
Caster sugar	Useful for cake making, drinks and decorating where the smaller grain either dissolves faster or looks prettier. Usually under .25 mm in this country. In the USA the grain is even smaller and called superfine or Baker's Special; one can be substituted for the other.
Icing sugar	Called confectioner's sugar in the United States of America, this is made by grinding small crystals, and cornflour is usually added to prevent caking.
Cube sugar	This is produced by moulding and pressing selected granulated sugar with sugar syrup which cements the crystal. On drying it is very hard and this is presumably based on the process which formed loaf sugar.
Preserving sugar	Specially suited to such work as its large crystals dissolve slowly and do not settle in a dense layer on the bottom of the pan – therefore there is less stirring and less chance of your jam buring.
LIGHT AND DARK SOFT BROWN SUGARS	These are a swizz, being fully refined white sucrose crystals to which flavouring and colouring syrup have been added. They might give you colour and flavour but will not include the minerals of the real thing.
COFFEE CRYSTALS	These stupid, over-expensive, maddening things, thought to be the height of sophistication in far too many restaurants and houses, seem carefully planned to ensure you either enjoy the complete cup of coffe in all its bitterness before the crystals begin to melt, or that you drink it stone-cold, by which time some of the crystals might have melted. I can't think why anybody buys them.
SUGAR IN COOKING	The most important contributions to cooking made by sugar are its preserving qualities and its lightening of cake mixtures. Sugar's preservative qualities give us jams, jellies and preserves, for a high sugar level prevents the growth of bacteria or the action of enzymes. It is

important that sugar is used when freezing fresh fruits and some vegetables, as the temperatures of a freezer are not low enough to kill or dissuade the attentions of enzymic actions which putrefy such goods. In addition the presence of sugar or sugar syrup in frozen soft fruits or berries prevents the formation of ice particles which break up the structure of the fruit and cause them to disintegrate when defrosted. Cream, butter and egg yolks all freeze better if sugar is added and cakes and biscuits will freeze well if they have a high sugar content.

Sugar in a cake mixture helps keep the gluten of the flour soft and pliable, allowing it to expand thereby giving volume and lightness.

I know it is popular but I cannot bring myself to use sugar when cooking peas or tomatoes. If you need sugar either you have been soaking the peas, which removes their own sugar, or are using unripe or English salad tomatoes, for which there is no cure – or perhaps you have used too much salt . . .

OTHER SWEETENERS

The usual substitute for sugar is honey another natural sweetener which was replaced by refined sugar when it became generally available.

In the United States there is much use of corn syrup, made by hydrolysis of the corn starch, that is, a chemical splitting into component sugars together with the addition of water. If you find a recipe that calls for corn syrup, you can replace it with golden syrup, but remember that it will give added colour, for corn syrup is colourless.

Less common nowadays is sorghum, a relatively natural product made by concentrating the stalk juice of sorghum, which is a type of millet.

Maple syrup is the reduced, sweet sap of the North American sugar maple (*Acer saccharum*) and varies in sweetness, colour and flavour depending on how much it is boiled down. Used hot specially on pancakes and waffles or with bacon; otherwise as a flavouring for ices, sweet sauces, icings and baking. Sometimes crystallized to make maple sugar.

Palm sugar: this is made from the sap of a variety of palm trees. Moist and tawny gold, it has an appealing caramel or fudge flavour and is less sweet than cane sugar. To approximate palm sugar (for Thai cooking for instance) mix equal quantities of Muscavado sugar and molasses.

ARTIFICIAL
SWEETENERS

Also known as non-nutritive sweeteners, these were originally developed to assist diabetics and others who needed to cut down their sugar intake for health reasons. But now they are very widely used in food manufacturing, particularly in carbonated and still drinks.

Saccharin was discovered at the Johns Hopkins University, Baltimore and had its centenary in 1979. First marketed in New York in 1884, it has exactly 100 times the sweetening power of sugar. It gives me kidney pains.

Sodium cyclamate was discovered at the University of Illiois in the late 1930s and became very popular in drinks and other manufactured goods from 1950 to the early 70s. It is now prohibited in many countries as evidence shows a possible link with cancer.

The other such product is or was Dulcin or Sucrol, no longer used because it turned out to be toxic.

HONEY

From the dawn of civilization honey and such vegetables as the now lowly parsnip were the only form of sweeteners known to Europe until the introduction of cane sugar; but this was so expensive and rare until the late 19th century that honey must be regarded as having been one of the world's most important foods.

Like sugar syrup today, honey was used also as a preservative, for its low moisture content and high sugar content combine to prevent the growth of bacteria and moulds. Honey, recognizable by appearance and taste, has been found in Egyptian pyramid burials at least 5,000 years old. Yet it is *not* truly sterile. It often contains spores of various kinds, including the fatally dangerous botulism. The precise type of botulism spore is weak enought to be dealt with internally by children and adults but babies under a year old should not be fed honey that has not been pasteurized.

Is honey one of the elixirs of life? No. Like yoghurt, it is credited with content and power based on wishful thinking. A typical breakdown of commercially available honey would show it to be almost 75 per cent levulose and dextrose, together known as invert sugar, plus a tiny amount of the more complicated sucrose and other, lesser sugars. As invert sugars are what our digestive system makes of sucrose, or refined white sugar, you see that honey is largely a predigested way to increase our intake of a substance we do not really need. The rest of honey is mainly water.

Now, when honey is eaten straight from the comb it also contains pollen, wax debris and colloids (apparently dissolved substances) and these certainly add extra vitamins and minerals. But these must all be extracted from honey that is to be bottled or stored or they will stimulate the formation of crystals. I'm afraid that unless she eats only unrefined honey this substance is not the secret of Miss Cartland's complexion or of her energy.

The story of the manufacture of honey is as astonishing as every other fact about the bee. Quite simply, honey is a processed concentrate of the sugary nectar that collects in the base of flowers. The effort required is phenomonal for although in some places a bee might obtain a full load of nectar from just one blossom (the Australian eucalytpus for instance) in others it may have to visit up to 1,500 flowers for the same harvest. So well designed is the honey bee that it can carry almost its own weight of nectar whereas the most efficient aircraft only carries a payload of 25 per cent its weight.

It takes 300 bees about three weeks to make 1 lb (½ kg) of honey and an average hive has 10–15,000 flying honey bees. Australia holds the record for production, as its hardwood trees have huge reservoirs of nectar in their flowers. One keeper there harvested an average of 786 lb (356 kg) honey from each of 400 hives in a year. It has been estimated that this represents the collection of over 1 ton of unconcentrated nectar every day – even amidst eucalyptus trees the number of bee journeys is almost beyond comprehension.

The freshly collected nectar is stored in a special honey stomach from which the bee can siphon off enough to keep going, and here's another silly estimate .... it is thought a bee could fly four million miles at a steady 7 mph on one gallon of unconcentrated nectar.

Back at the hive the nectar is transferred to an indoor worker and the pollen in the bee's leg sacs is collected by others. The nectar is handed from mouth to mouth, worker bee to worker bee, and this is what digests the original complicated sugars and reduces the moisture content from 70 per cent to between 15 and 20 per cent, thus making what we call honey. As the hive's interior is a constant 32°C, further natural evaporatio is subsequent to this process.

The point of all this work is to give the bees a store of food during winter. It is sometimes thought that much of the world's cheaper honey is made by feeding bees sugar syrup but this is incorrect. Because their natural food has been taken from them for our tables, the bee keepers are forced to feed bees on sugar syrups or lesser honeys throughout winter simply to keep them alive; none is converted and stored as honey.

You doubtless know that honey is stored in the hives in honey combs, made from wax that is itself perfectly amazing. But beekeepers want bees to make honey not wax and so commercial hives are supplied with combs of other, reusable substances. Once it is time to collect honey the combs are removed from the hives and de-capped, that is the wax plugs from each cell are removed, usually by some heat process. The honey is extracted by centrifugal force or by pressing and if you were going to eat it quickly there's nothing more to do but to clean the combs and replace them in the hives. Otherwise the solid particles of pollen and wax must be removed or crystallization will begin. Sometimes new honeys are stored unstrained or only partly refined and later heated to 52°C for several days to liquidize them before further treatment. Once bottled, honey is usually heated again, to about 62°C, which helps give a shelf life of 6–9 months.

Even the strained and pasteurized sugar syrup called honey nevertheless contains enough oils and essences from its origins to present an enormous range of flavours and styles. Most commercially available honeys are blended for uniformity of appearance, flavour or price and an inexpensive honey may well be a mixture from the products of America, China, Russia, Australia and Africa – some giving colour, some texture, some flavour and some economy.

The rarer the flower from which the honey has been extracted, the more expensive will be any unblended, single-flower honey, like clover, orange blossom, linden, yucca and so on. My absolute favourites are the fragrant orange blossom and linden or lime blossom honeys; believe it or not, honey making is quite common in central London and those who live close to the great lime trees of Hyde Park make honey with a perfume that is quite intoxicating.

If you like a medium richness and fullness of flavour, clover honey is a medium sort of choice. The big flavours come from the hotter countries like Mexico or Australia, even if from mixed blossoms. Although it is rather dark, New Zealand manuka (or ti-tree) honey has a full sharpish flavour which makes a nice change. Otherwise the queen of honeys is said to be the Greek Hymettus, flavoured with the wild thyme that grows on the mountain of that name although others think acacia honey from middle Europe is better. It is worth looking for more unusual single-flower types when you are on holiday especially in the Balkans or about the Mediterranean. I understand there are rose and raspberry blossom honeys made there; in France there is lavender honey and rosemary honey. Other than commercial types there are said to be over 300 single-flower honeys in the United States alone.

And English honey? Well, it is delicious but why is it so very much more expensive? Presumably because dismal summers encourage less nectar and therefore less honey . . .

Honey styles

Honey in its natural wax combs is very difficult to find and expensive whey you do, due to the popularity of reusable, artificial combs. If you can bear to chew the wax it is the most nutritious honey of all and may have some claims to providing you with the life-enhancing goodies missed from refined sucrose or refined honey. But don't make the usual mistake and store it lying down. Bees don't. Close examination will show that each cell slopes back from its cap of wax, precisely so it can stand upright without leakages. This is how you should keep it too. **Clear honey:** even refined and pasteurized clear honey is likely to crystallize eventually and if so all you need do is to stand the sealed container in cold water and slowly bring it up to a temperature into which you can just put your fingertips. Keep the water at this temperature or remove the honey and let the process continue, slowly, under stored heat. The container must be sealed and it is also an advantage if it stands on a trivet or saucer in the saucepan.

It is untrue and silly to say that granulated honey is in any way 'off' – if you see it being sold off cheaply, buy it and treat it carefully and it will be as good as new.

Set honey: the opaque honeys are really crystallized or granulated honey and this effect is obtained by stirring or whipping. But if you give such honeys the above heat treatment they will revert to clear liquids.

Storage and cooking

Like most natural products honey is adversely affected by light and heat. It can stand warm places but prefers there not to be too great a fluctuation of temperature. Honey also frosts in very cold conditions, caused by bubbles or air being forced out as the honey shrinks. When it expands again, on reheating, these bubbles remain and are most difficult to remove.

As the individual oils and perfumes of a honey disappear with heat it is pointless to use very fine, rare or expensive honey in cooking. It does have flavour contributions to make to cooked fruits and exotic pastries and sweetmeats but should always be added after cooking, so it simply melts into or over the food.

Should you wish to use honey in cooking then use something quite ordinary, especially in baking. To convert recipes which use sugar, calculate that honey and sugar have the same sweetening capacity weight for weight; by volume it is almost twice as sweet, that is one dessertspoonful of honey is equal to almost two dessertspoons of refined white sugar. Naturally the water content of honey means you must adjust other liquids to compensate. Honey is seen suggested as an ingredient of mustards, salad dressings, ice creams, icings, face packs and hair rinses and it can be very good in all of them. Sometimes it can be ravishing. If you were to purée about 1 lb (½ kg) of avocado flesh with 4 dessertspoonsful of clear honey and about ¼ pint (150 ml) of citrus juice, say orange or lime, and then freeze, whip and re-freeze this in the usual way you will have sorbet with a fascination that no sugar, real or other, could have given. Sometimes you might add a generous teaspoon of grated orange rind, as well, for extra sharpness. If you can get them, squeeze the pulp from some ripe passion fruit and place that as a topping.

TEA

If you are sincerely interested in fine flavour, and will take some time to experiment, you will eventually agree with me that tea is an infinitely more interesting and satisfying drink than coffee. Yet, for reasons I have been unable to discern, the English, second only to Eire as tea drinkers, generally drink the most bitter, undistinguished and harsh teas in the world.

Tea's great advantage over coffee is that it is difficult to spoil its flavour, for the liquor is never boiled, at least in this country, and thus the extraordinary differences between hundreds of distinctive varieties of tea can easily be discerned, and you can match your tea to your mood or your meal.

Tea is a liquor made by steeping in boiling water the dried, top leaf-shoots of a type of camellia. The habit of drinking it began in China, where tea was certainly used as a beverage by the sixth century. By the eighth century it was popular enough to have been taxed; about the same time the Japanese adopted it and began their amazing ritualizing of tea making and drinking.

It was not until the mid-17th century that tea began to be seen in England, first imported via Holland. There wasn't much of it, even though Charles II's Portuguese queen, Catherine, had popularized it in court and aristocratic circles. But by 1689 the East India Company had begun direct importation and in 1721 was given a monopoly in the trade by Parliament. By the mid-18th century tea was so popular it was the principle drink of all classes. It was perhaps the first hot drink the poor had ever had and, as with white bread they were determined to keep up with the nobs, even though 1 lb (½ kg) of the very cheapest tea probably cost a third of a working man's weekly wage. There was plenty of it, however, because England had the ships to bring it from China. Russia became a tea drinking nation early in the 17th century because their tea could go overland by caravan, which was considered a better way to transport tea than by exposing it to salt air.

The taxes on tea imported into this country were exorbitant and led first to an enormous trade in smuggled tea. Anxious for the lost revenue, Prime Minister Pitt compelled the East India Company to import enough tea to supply all needs without raising prices and smuggling ceased. Some would say that the drinking of tea is also what finally ended London's gin era when there were twice as many burials as baptisms.

The suspiciously close liaison between Parliament and the East India Company was an important contributor to the loss of the American Empire. In 1765 Parliament decided to tax the colonies and their imports. When they refused to pay the tax on tea, the colonists quickly generated a smuggling trade from Holland. The East India Company forced Parliament, who acted like a subsidiary company, to give them absolute rights to the tea trade with the American colonies – they were to take tea direct, cutting out the European exporters and the American importers. Resentment and self-interest erupted and the colonists decided to forgo tea. In December 1773 the first East India Company ships arrived in Boston. On the night of the 16th a group of colonists dressed as Red Indians threw the tea into the water. Tea parties at other ports were quickly organised. Parliament closed Boston's port . . . and it was war.

Fifty years later the great Indian tea plantations were established, but the huge growing market of America was not interested.

GROWING AND PROCESSING

The tea bush (*camellia sinensis*) is native to a fan-shaped area that starts in Vietnam and expands westwards to Assam and eastwards into China. The plant is remarkably free with its affections and, like humans, almost every new bush can be quite different. As the flavour of tea is also affected by soil, temperature and weather, like grapes, some way had to be found to control consistency, at least within small areas. Today cloning of specially suitable plants seems to have curbed tea's propensity to individuality.

Only the top, two, very new leaves and the emerging leaf bud between them are plucked to make tea, something that has never been successfully mechanized. In some areas the gathering can continue year round, in others there are dormant periods. But there are always better and worse times for picking. The best are called the flushes; the first flush is early in Spring, the second a little later, and the third flush, after summer, gives the autumnal teas. In between is when the standard teas are collected.

There are four types of curing process, each of

which gives a distinctive and easily recognizable type of tea leaf and flavour.

Green tea: the original tea, most teas that first came to this country would have been this style. Once the leaves are gathered they are withered and dried immediately. This preserves colour and means the tea will have a definite taste of vegetation. They are light and refreshing.

Oolong tea: after the initial withering, leaves for oolong tea are slightly crushed which begins oxidation (or fermentation) of the leaf, accompanied by a change of colour from green to brown. Oolong teas are only half-fermented before being dried and they have a beguiling sweetness, often reminiscent of peaches. They are the most expensive but most rewarding teas. Often there are special vintages and they are wonderful after-dinner drinks in summer.

Black tea: the tea with which we are most familiar. The withered leaf is crushed and then fermented fully, until it is a rich brown. Then it is dried.

Smoked: a few teas are dried over smoke, which gives a distinctive tarry flavour.

The processed leaves are now sorted according to size, first into large leaf and small leaf or broken leaves. There is much confusion about the grades of tea and I do not intend to add to that by giving you lists that are relevant only to tea blenders. Suffice to say that terms like Orange Pekoe and Broken Orange Pekoe are neither indicative of quality nor of style, nor of flavour; they simply tell you what size of leaf has been employed. And dust? So many people say they *know* tea dust is swept from the floor and used in tea bags, and . . . well you've heard them. In fact Dust is the proper name for the smallest pieces of tea leaf and can be of all qualities; perhaps the confusion would go if the term was changed but I fear it is too late for that.

Once, all tea was large-leafed, or orthodox; quality, unblended or green teas will still be like this. Now we also have something called CTC tea. This is a process invented in 1928 which cuts, tears and curls the leaf into smaller pieces, which gives a faster, stronger brew in the cup.

As well, we have tea bags, invented earlier this century by an American who started taking his samples about in silk envelopes. It is theoretically possible to get respectable tea from the modern bags, or would be if there was not such insistence upon speed. Read on and you will find out why.

STYLES AND FLAVOURS

If you start in Sri Lanka and work upwards through India you can generally guess at the style of tea which comes from each growing area, they get stronger as you go north. Sri Lankan teas, still sold as Ceylon teas, are fragrant and refreshing, making a slightly sweet, red-gold liquor with very little acidity. Most tea drunk in New Zealand and Australia, and many of the American blends are Ceylon rather than Indian teas and even when made strong remain clear. They are amongst my favourite teas.

In the south-west of India you find the Nilgiris teas, sometimes available unblended. A little more assertive than Ceylonese teas, and picked all year round.

Up north you have Darjeeling and Assam teas. Darjeeling teas are described as the champagnes of tea. Really they are the muscatel of teas for this is the flavour you have from a fine, orthodox leaf Darjeeling. The plantations are high above sea level, which is apparently an advantage, but there is an acidity, or briskness, that can overpower what subtlety there might be in some of the lesser produce.

Assam tea is the most powerful of all, usually strong, dark and very pungent. I have drunk an Assam made with tea that literally glowed with golden tips, a sign of quality not of twigs as so many think; made with only half a teaspoon of tea per person and brewed for the right amount of time it was very delicious indeed, but had been imported privately. Most Assams are blended, and need to be.

China teas, whether green, oolong or black can be strong of colour and flavour but never have the acidity of Indian and Ceylon teas. Although not traditionally drunk with milk in China, some are quite robust enough to be so treated, if they are all- or partly-black teas.

Just a word about blending, which is another subject for experts. Teas are blended after they have been dried and, like coffee, they are usually blended within each of the many grades. It can be fascinating to make your own blends of tea, but if you have respect for food, blend only similar qualities. For instance, many people like to blend the scented Earl Grey mixture, or smokey Lapsang Souchong with a plain black tea, and they can be good. But it is better to do this with an identifiable Ceylon or Darjeeling than with an anonymous mixture of tea from all round the world, just as you would not mix highly roasted coffee beans with light roasted ones.

Here is a necessarily brief list of some of the teas you might buy or read about:

African: usually from Uganda or Kenya and used for blending: some Kenyan teas are thought of very highly.

Assam: the richest and most acidic tea, with many golden tips in the higher grades.

Brick tea: finely ground tea compressed into a block. Grate some into a cup or teapot. Green or black but not up to much; it's what Tibetans carry in their pockets.

Caravan: usually indicates a blend of black, large leaf China teas, imitating the flavour of teas that went by camel to Russia.

Ceylon: always black tea, tips noticeable in better grades. If you find labels stating 'high-grown' or distinct names, they should be very good quality. Perfectly delicious and fragrant and strong without being pungent.

Ching Wo: a basic black China tea with good round flavour. Might be drunk with milk.

Darjeeling: often sold as a 'self-drinker', that is, unblended. It is high-grown and smells like rich wine but has a fair tang on the tongue.

Earl Grey: a black tea, sometimes just of China teas, sometimes of blends. Flavoured with oil of bergamot, a type of citrus. Each company's idea of what it should taste like is different.

English Breakfast: there are two types. The original was a blend of China teas, and so was fragrant. Some remain of this type but most are now stronger, perhaps a mix of Ceylon and Assam.

Formosa Oolong: this is the only oolong tea usually seen in the West. Spectacularly good if you find a vintage or silver-tipped Formosa Oolong, and can afford it (as much as £2 for 4 ozs(125 g)) you really will have drunk the champagne of teas.

Gunpowder: the name is given because this very high quality green tea has a metallic grey sheen to it. It is the best of the green teas and usually the one used in Morocco for making their mint tea.

Hyson: was the old name for green tea.

Irish Breakfast: blended Assam teas and thus

fiercely strong, perhaps to cope with hangovers.
Jasmine: this can be green tea or black tea or a
mixture. It includes jasmine flowers which give the
elegant perfume and flavour, but goes rather bitter.
It is the basic Chinese restaurant tea.
Keemun: perhaps the best black China tea that is
easily available. There is a sweet, slightly nutty
flavour that is strong enough to take milk. Good to
mix with a touch of Lapsang or to go with an Earl
Grey blend that has some finesse.
Lapsang Souchong: the only smoked tea I know that
is available. It is a large leaf China tea and the flavour
it gives is decidedly tarry rather than smokey. Can be
very refreshing but must not be made strong or it can
be nauseating.
Lemon tea: usually a black tea including bits of peel
and some lemon oils. Better achieved with tea and
fresh lemon.
Nilgiris: black tea from south west India, rather like
Ceylons, but not so refined.
Russian: Russian tea, grown in Georgia and fairly
ordinary.
Seychelles: hard to find, and unexceptional without
being awful. But they do blend one tea with vanilla
and that is surprisingly good.

MAKING TEA

You draw it, mash it, stand it or brew it. In
Australasia you might boil it in a billy can over an
open fire, and you certainly boil it in Turkey and
such places. But, apart from *not* boiling it, European
tea making is simple:
1. Boil water taken from the cold tap; water from the
hot tap may have been kept in the tank a while and
have lost much flavour. The flavour of your water
will affect your tea, but there is little that can be
done about that – you just have to get used to it.
2. Shortly before the water boils, pour some into a
tea pot, let it warm thoroughly, pour it out.
3. Add the tea, using rather less than 1 teaspoon per
person – see 5. below – and forget the one for the
pot, a marketing ploy if ever I heard one.
4. Take the pot to the kettle – never the other way
around – and pour the boiling water into the pot.
5. Let the tea infuse. Most people do not leave tea
long enough, confusing colour with strength.
Orthodox leaves require 5–7 minutes to develop
flavour and colour, and the CTC blends need at least
2 or 3. Naturally this gives stronger colour and

flavour than when you only brew for 1 minute, so you need less tea and get a finer flavour. That is real economy and true value for money.

If you *must* use the tea bags and are quite convinced you cannot taste the bag or the string, or do not care, you must let them brew, too. The colour that comes quickly from most modern teas, and specially from tea bags, is from teas called Bright Colouring Africans, included simply because they colour water so quickly. To dip tea bags in and out of hot water a few times is to retrieve only a small percentage of the flavour and colour that is inside. 1 tea bag will make 2 or 3 delicious flavourful cups of tea if allowed to brew for 2 or 3 minutes – either do it in a tea pot, or brew in 1 cup or mug, divide the brew between others then top up with more water. When I gave this advice on BBC TV's Pebble Mill at One, a woman wrote to say I had all but saved her marriage as until she allowed tea bags to brew, she was constantly insulted by her husband about her tea.

I can't stand milk in tea, but I know it can divide man from man. The Royal Geographical Society abounds with tales of expeditions which found itself noting who was MBT and who TBM – milk before tea or tea before milk – and socializing accordingly. Scientifically, tea added to milk distributes the fat globules of the milk more efficiently, giving a richer, milkier flavour. Sugar is unnecessary with fine teas but essential with most of the wicked blends sold in this country. Russians drink tea with strawberry or raspberry jam, Tibetans mix theirs with rancid yaks' butter, and the men who work in Indian plantations mix their tea with sweetened condensed milk; the latter have an excuse, for much tea grown in India is far too assertive to be drunk unless blended, and these men are probably drinking unblended tea. Lemon may be used in strong Indian or Ceylon teas, but it is thoughtless to use it in China or scented teas, as they should be enjoyed for what they are.

FLAVOURING
YOUR TEA

One distributor in Canterbury makes tea with almost any flavour you can imagine, including peach, pineapple, cherry and orange. The peach is actually rather good. He also makes spiced tea, which I recommend thoroughly; there is an American spiced tea called 'Constant Comment' which includes orange peel as well as spices and it is quite the most calming and rewarding drink I know on a cold day or when you are not feeling well. For simple spiced tea add 1 or 2 in of cinnamon stick to each 2 teaspoons of high quality black tea and brew the usual time. Vanilla, clove, allspice and citrus juice or peel are all possibilities too, but use great caution for many spices give a bitter flavour if you are too generous.

Herb-flavoured teas are quite common. Whereas an Egyptian will make mint tea just by infusing mint leaves, the Moroccans plunge mint into China tea, usually a gunpowder green. Mint can also flavour black Ceylon or Indian teas, but you are more likely to want some sugar. Anyway it is very settling to the stomach. When you are tense and headachey you may find that rosemary tea works to give you some relief. Simply put a good sprig or two of fresh rosemary into the pot with a black tea, or sprinkle in a little dried rosemary and let it brew a little longer. Many green herbs from which you would make tisanes are more palatable when mixed with a tea to which you are more used.

For a hot tea punch, boil 6 cups of water from cold with 6 whole cloves and half a cinnamon stick; simmer a few minutes to extract flavours. Pour on 1 tablespoon (15 ml) good black tea in a warmed teapot. Brew for 5 minutes then stir in the strained juice of 1 orange and ½ lemon. It may be sweetened.

Iced tea

Not very popular in this country but a way of life in the United States. The great secrets are that the tea must be pretty strong, must not be made with hot water, and should be served with lots of ice.

You begin by putting cold water on to tea or tea bags and leaving that overnight. You get lots of good flavour with no bitterness. This should then be well chilled, either by itself or with fruit juices and spices. The best combinations I know are tea and pineapple juice with slices of orange and some cinnamon sticks. Apple juice also goes well with these cold tea punches.

Cooking with tea

If you really want to get some tea flavour into fruit loaves, you must make a very strong brew in the proportion of 1 oz (15 g) of dried tea leaves to 1 pint (600 ml) boiling water or other liquid. Only then will it be worthwhile. Tea makes delicious sorbets and ice cream, but for those recipes, you'll have to wait for the book that follows this one.

TRUFFLES

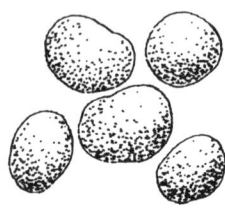

When an author as august as Colette describes a fungus as the 'most capricious and most revered of black princesses' you can be certain it is rather more than a mushroom. The truffle, black diamond of cookery, is one of the rarest of all the world's exotic treats; in Perigord in France, regarded as the epicentre of truffledom, they cost 1600 francs per kilo in 1982 when still uncleaned and straight out of the soil. That's about £5 an ounce and on top of that we have to pay for processing, transport and for the profits of those who sell such delights.

Truffles have been popular and acknowledged as special for thousands of years and like all rare things have been credited with aphrodisiac powers, particularly by Francis I of France, but I suspect this was rather a matter of expecting more for your money than passing gastronomic gratification.

The flavour of black truffles is found in nothing else – indeed it isn't found in truffles most of the time. The delicacy is fugitive, easily overpowered and expected to perform tasks of which it is incapable. It is more a perfumer or catalyst than a flavouring and the true flavour is only passed on to other foods by standing together or cooking together very gently for a longish time. Truffle is best with other fragile flavours, such as exalted foie gras or creamy scrambled eggs. Although a standby of buffets, banquets and ballrooms, the practice of decorating with slithers of cold truffle is nonsensical and wasteful in the extreme – the truffle has not been brought to full flavour and the food will not be perfumed by it. Far better to use slices of black olive which have been blanched to desalt them. An extraordinary number of people will believe it is truffle if you tell them so; everyone will if you don't.

The 19th century was blessed by a boom in the truffle harvest, as is manifest in cookery books of the time which use truffles like we use tomatoes. It was nothing to be served a whole one as a starter, baked in an oven with a little madeira and seasoning, and served on a crisp, white linen napkin. Now the harvest is around 100 tonnes a year when conditions are right. You need warm rainy summers to follow a spring in which the right types of breeze have encouraged the spores to travel, settle and germinate. Dry summer weather can reduce the harvest by at least 25 per cent.

Truffles are gathered between the end of

November and mid-March or so. They're probably at their best in January. Usually they are found under oak trees in 'burnt' areas, so-called because no other vegetation can or will grow there. They can only be found by being sniffed out by trained dogs or pigs, all of which contributes to the high cost. But if they grow under oak trees, are there no English truffles? Well, there *is* an English truffle, the Bath or Red truffle, but it has largely been lost to us by the creeping of our towns and cities into our fields and by a dearth of those who have the knowledge to train animals to find them. However, I once had a Lithuanian working for me who said regularly, 'Oh I know where to find truffles all over England'. Initial excitement gave way to inertia on my part, a dampening of disbelief. Imagine my face when he returned months later with a small paper bag full! There were black ones and white ones – and one extraordinary fragrant one the like of which I've never come across before or since. I knew rather less about truffles than I do now and probably ruined some of them in my experiments – but . . . truffles to *experiment* with. My friend told me he knew where to go because he had actually sown the spores all over England, having brought them from Europe after the war. I've not seen him for years now, but somewhere in England there are treasures as valuable as any Graeco-Roman silver hoards.

There are two major types of truffle, the black and the white. The black truffle – *tuber malanosporum* or *tuber brumale* – is best known as the Perigord truffle. Its dark flesh becomes jet black when fully ripened. Found only in France in Perigord-Quercy, Provence, the Comtat Venaissin and the southern slopes of the Cévennes.

Tuber Magnatum is the white Piedmontese truffle which has a white flesh and smooth yellow skin. Less expensive than the black, it is slightly more pronounced in flavour and usually eaten raw, grated finely over pasta or on a hot brioche, a specialty of sidewalk cafés in Florence. Neither type has yielded to being cultivated with any success in France or Italy.

Although supples are hard to come by, some of the Arabic countries are growing and harvesting a type of white truffle commercially. They grow in sand, especially in North Africa. In few, very few shops in London you can buy a tin holding well over 1 lb

(½ kg) in weight for something in the region of
£8-£10 (Christmas 1981).

Their flavour is very light but the excitement they
give is enormous. With a huge hot cheese and
cucumber soufflé I served a great bowl of sliced
white Egyptian truffles, gently poached for a few
seconds in a reduction of dry madeira. The
astonishment was so extraordinary I'll never do it
again. The soufflé got cold as the table stared at the
truffles – and everyone thought I was so rich they
stopped bringing bottles of wine when they came to
dinner. If you do find these, buy them and use them
extravagantly, to layer pâtés, smother scrambled
eggs, stuff rolls of smoked salmon, float in
consommé, flavour seafood sauces for pasta. Brush
them well first to remove the sand and soak in some
reduced sherry or madeira with a touch of salt and
pepper first.

Black truffles are sold fresh, tinned or bottled.
After the laborious brushing and peeling and sorting,
which can only be done by hand, truffles stay fresh
for just three to four days and will be sold in the
chilly winter markets of French villages whole or in
pieces. Otherwise the truffles are preserved in one of
two ways; they are either cooked before canning or
bottling which gives some control over weight loss,
or they are slightly salted and sterilized after packing
which keeps all the flavour and bulk but converts 25
per cent of the weight into liquid. If you have a fresh
truffle and wish to keep it, poach it in madeira and
leave it in this liquid, itself a wondrous addition to
sauces. The chart on p.372 gives the official French
gradings for canned or bottled truffles.

Frankly, though, I am disillusioned. I've never
been knocked out by the flavour of a black truffle,
even when it has been left for days to perfume a
sirloin of beef. In fact the flavour that seems best is
that of the madeira in which a truffle has been
poached. Even the whole, baked truffle I enjoyed at
the Ménage à Trois restaurant in London's
Beauchamp Place wasn't such a thrill as, say a slice of
foie gras or a few spoonsful of caviare. I'll walk a
long way to eat freshly grated white truffle, but the
black ones? I don't understand the fuss.

VEGETABLES

Artichokes

Tinned vegetables have largely had their day, well and truly replaced for flavour and colour by the frozen varieties. But there are some that are distinctly better, more convenient, or solely available when so processed.

Artichoke hearts are an excellent addition to any cold hors d'oeuvres, and I like to slice them in half. They should be served with a good vinaigrette, in which they have soaked for some time.

Artichoke bottoms, *fonds d'artichauts*, the little cap of solid, nutty tasting artichoke with no attached leaves, tastes just as good from a tin as fresh – well, almost. They make good additions to mixed buffets, or sliced into salads. They may be sliced and dressed as a rather high-class salad themselves, perhaps with a few cold peas, orange segments, some olives and a few anchovy fillets. They are best served at grander dinners when warmed and filled with a vegetable purée. Green pea is most traditional but anything with the bite of lemon or garlic will work . . . celeriac, brussel sprouts with nutmeg, carrot with allspice or thyme, and so on.

Celery hearts

These, too are not so different from braised fresh celery. Sprinkled with lemon juice, a little chicken or beef stock and some butter they reheat wonderfully. They are also good braised in a little walnut oil and garlic and served with chopped walnuts.

Hearts of palm

Only available here in tins. The shoots of a palm tree, and the best are usually from Brazil. Serve chilled with vinaigrette or mayonnaise, as though asparagus. Better if you give a little tropicality, so flavour either type of dressing with lime.

Sometimes the pieces can be woody and rather unpleasant, so if you are serving them for a special dinner it is wise to check each piece individually, and to have a spare tin on hand.

As a substitute for asparagus they always work, so serve with smoked salmon, with gulls' or quails' eggs, with smoked fish or with a barely-warm *sauce maltese*.

One of the few times I have used toasted cashew nuts is to chop them over hearts of palm.

Mushrooms

Don't bother, whatever the ubiquitous home economists say.

Peas	Apart from mushy, or processed, peas which are a world unto themselves, tinned peas have been cancelled out by the frozen variety. Petits pois à la française, which are cooked with baby onions and some lettuce, or should be, also retain a devoted following. I suspect this is based on nostalgia rather than inherent quality.
Potatoes	Because they are generally small and waxy, tinned potatoes are very good for making salads that do not fall to pieces. But heat them slightly before dousing with a vinaigrette and garlic or cloves, even if you are later to mix with their mayonnaise. To ring the changes, mix only with soured cream and dill, or with a mixture of half yoghurt and half mayonnaise. Colour slightly with tomato purée, add horseradish sauce, some poached cucumber and a few prawns – that really is something very special, created for the magazine improbably titled *Titbits*.
Pulses	All the kidney beans, chickpeas, borlottti and cannellini type of bean are excellent from cans, but see the section on these for suggestions as to use.
Red peppers	Red peppers in small tins, which have the advantage of being peeled, are sweet and colourful and delicious. Cut into strips they finish a salad far better than the raw ones, can be added to scrambled eggs, puréed for stuffings, added to pasta and fish sauces . . . they are one of the best things of all to have in your larder. And the opened ones last ages in a refrigerator. If you really like peppers, simply drain well, dress with garlic and good olive oil plus a splash of lemon juice of vinegar for a simple but robust accompaniment to plain grilled lamb chops, chicken or pork dishes. Good mixed with slices of artichoke bottoms, too.
Sweet corn	Whole kernel or cream-style these taste just about as good as you would make: see Grains for uses.
Tomatoes	Food is not possible without tins of plum tomatoes processed in their own juice; so called breakfast tomatoes in brine are harder and boring and meant to be grilled in the morning, but not in my house. Tinned tomatoes make the perfect medium in which to cook other strongly-flavoured vegetables, like

okra, or to make sauces for almost everything, cabbage, cauliflower, beans and peas especially. But they are better when reduced thoroughly over heat, first squashing the whole tomatoes. When quite reduced, liquidize, and strain out the pips and return to heat for final reduction. Only then throw in some herbs, fresh or dried, and when the flavour is strong enough strain them out too. Finish with a few drips of olive or walnut oil, a few drops of red wine vinegar, salt or celery salt (but be very restrained with them all). Black pepper should only be added at the last minute.

For a memorable and easy sauce for grills or well-flavoured fish, make a plain tomato sauce as above then add some very fine chopped garlic or some garlic juice. Let this mellow a few minutes then toss in a great deal of coarsely chopped parsley. Let heat through and reach a brilliant green then serve immediately.

You could also reduce the tomatoes without straining and with little stirring, so that texture remains. This is excellent with some precooked bacon pieces added as well as garlic, parsley and pepper and used to top such soups as artichoke, carrot or parsnip. Add double cream or soured cream as well.

A reduced tomato sauce flavoured with fresh mint is far better with lamb than mint sauce, and an interesting pasta sauce. Tomato and orange with a dash of Tabasco or chili seasoning is good for fish.

Tomato and basil, well chilled is a welcome change with cold poached salmon. Rich with paprika, cumin and butter, tinned tomatoes are wonderful for casseroling chicken; with bay, thyme, parsley and onion they give pulses more appeal and oxtails cooked with tomatoes, Guinness and celery is so good no one has had less than two helpings. I may use tinned tomatoes too much, but so far no one has complained: they're also cheap.

VINEGAR

The basis of vinegar is acetic acid, and thus a vinegar-like flavour can be obtained by diluting man-made acetic acid with water. But it would be of little culinary use, for real vinegars can be as complicated of flavour as the finest wines or ales, from which they should be made.

The souring of wine or ale is a natural process and is the result of the oxidizing of alcohol to form natural acetic acid, which will happen to any alcoholic liquid with less than 18 per cent alcohol when exposed to air. But it is not enough simply to open a bottle of wine or ale and wait for vinegar. The process must be controlled of speed and temperature, or the original liquid will go off in its own direction, losing flavour or picking up others before the acetic acid level is high enough to inhibit any further bacterial action of flavour change.

The three most common types of commercially available vinegar are malt, wine and cider.

Malt vinegar

This is made from soured ale, that is an unhopped beer. Brown malt vinegar is coloured, usually with caramel. It is actually less sharp than wine vinegars but does not carry with it the advantages of other aromas and flavours. It is usually distilled to increase its strength. Spirit vinegar and distilled vinegar are almost always made from malt vinegar and are the same thing. White malt vinegar, distilled or otherise, has simply been decolourized by a charcoal process.

Wine vinegar

Do not take it for granted that all wine vinegar will reward you with a kaleidoscope of wondrous flavour. It will only be as good as the wine from which it was made, and only if it was also made by the slow, expensive Orléans process, which protects all the natural aromas of the wine. Most wine vinegar is *not* made this way, as, like most ingredients of excellence, Orléans-style vinegar costs more. It really is worth buying Orléans wine vinegar if you care about your food, and want a wine vinegar.

Cider vinegar

People are drinking it, prescribing it – almost worshipping it. If you would believe only half of what people – especially Americans – say, it is the elixir of life. Well . . . some people don't even like the flavour and generally I find it a little intrusive, appley and honey-like, which is not unexpected I suppose. But it does come into its own when you are pickling fruit – peaches, pears, plums and so on. Then it is wonderful. It is made, of course, from soured cider.

Specialty vinegars

A sherry vinegar will be expensive but a revelation. The 'brown' flavour – there is no other word for it – is mellow and exciting. A great treat well worth looking for. Otherwise we are most likely to buy red or white wine vinegar that has been flavoured after manufacture with a variety of herbs, petals, or fruit. Best known, and most useful, is tarragon vinegar, but you can easily buy dill, shallot, chilli and garlic varieties. Less known are basil and lemon vinegars.

All these varieties are made easily at home by infusing any of the above ingredients in a bottle of vinegar in a warm place for several days.

Vinegars-flavoured with raspberries, strawberries, blackcurrants or blackberries were once the basis of sweetened summer drinks, when diluted with iced soda water, and very good they were too. But now unsweetened fruit vinegars are back on the market and making a mark in some of the more advanced restaurants. Raspberry vinegar is a sensation on beans, cauliflower or raw spinach and blackcurrant vinegar is excellent with liver.

All these can be made, if you have the fruit, by soaking say 1 lb (½ kg) of raspberries in 1 pint (600 ml) vinegar for 5 days on a warm window ledge, removing the fruit and replacing with another 1 lb (½ kg) and leaving another week. Strain and store in a cool place. You could add more raspberries and you may also sweeten it somewhat. I used this vinegar, together with some of the pickled raspberries and some fresh, to make duck with sweet and sour raspberry sauce for His Excellency the Chinese Ambassador when he visited a house at which I was cooking in Scotland, during the summer of 1981. He asked if I had learned to cook in Peking, his home town, which I thought a compliment. It did look – and taste – exceptional.

Cooking with vinegar

Vinegar is basically used to help preserve, as in pickles and chutneys, or in dressings on a salad. But judicious use of vinegar as a flavouring agent is a secret you will be pleased you know. The merest whisper of vinegar can miraculously transform the flavour of a lifeless casserole, especially if it is a rather fatty one.

A touch of vinegar enlivens dishes and sauces based on tomato; and you should remember the affinity wine vinegar has with soft fruits. The slightest hint of red wine vinegar can really make a raspberry or strawberry dish, hot or cold. To be really arcane, you might make yourself some rose-petal vinegar in the way you would raspberry vinegar, but frankly if I had *that* many fragrant rose petals I'd macerate them in vodka or gin with a few rose-geranium leaves for good measure. It makes an after dinner drink or flavouring agent of considerable astonishment.

Very reduced vinegars, especially the flavoured ones, are the key to many *nouvelle cuisine* sauces, added, say, to the cooking juices of some quickly fried liver or fish, and sweet and sour sauces are nothing without vinegar; but they are improved if you use a good quality one. The use of vinegar in bread dough is a cheat's way to emulate the flavour of real sour-dough. You only need a scant fluid ounce (25 ml) of cider vinegar for every pound (½ kg) of flour. But can anyone explain to me why the English put vinegar, *malt* vinegar, on fish and chips?

These are a distinct trap for the unwary and the easily swayed. Most waters thought of as mineral waters are no such thing, but bottled *pure* waters. You choose to drink these pure waters because they taste better than water from the tap or because their blandness will not affect other fine flavours, such as a single malt whisky. If they are gassed, you might choose them for their refreshing fizzle, always improved by a squirt of lemon juice and a slice of the same. Perrier, Malvern and San Pellegrino, as well as some of the Scandinavian waters, are all pure waters and their mineral or health value is relatively low, unless you count the good effect drinking any water has.

True mineral waters have a recognisably 'different' taste, claim to help kidneys, digestion and so on, and compete with one another by these and the claims of their advertising agencies. Truly medicinal waters, like those of Bath, taste so awful you have to be very sick, very silly or very fashionable to gag them down.

When abroad, you are certainly sensible to use bottled waters for drinking, tooth cleaning and ice making . . . but stick to well-known brands from reputable sources, even if they cost more. An Italian survey showed, some years ago, that most bottled waters were more contaminated than the tap waters they replaced! The best time for drinking water for flushing the system and good health is half an hour before you eat or drink anything else in the morning. Drinking large amounts of iced water when you are very hot will chill your stomach, the effects of which are worse than food poisoning, for which they are usually mistaken.

Some chefs cook with mineral or pure waters, saying that Vichy water, for instance is essential to cook real *carrots Vichy* – this is unlikely, for the special effect of the Vichy water is undoubtedly due to the common salt that is added to it. Contrexéville water contains magnesium sulphate, better known as Epsom salts, which is one way of losing weight if you drink enough; it would be no good at calming a troubled traveller's digestion, and this is an example of the care that should be taken when choosing mineral waters. Most are alkaline, though, and can help soothe acidity to some extent.

The rule in the United Kingdom is to choose pure waters if you do not want to interfere with other flavours; drink mineral waters because you like them and can afford them. Abroad, drink and use either for the sake of good sense, but read the labels or mineral water bottles in case it is doing the reverse of what you expect.

Sparkling waters like Perrier make excellent mixers, especially half-and-half with white wine in emulation of hock and seltzer, or with medium sherry, an excellent mid-morning drink. Mixed with orange juice, sparkling waters make a Buck's Fizz without kick or sugar; slightly sweetened fruit vinegars may be diluted with sparkling water for original and refreshing summer long drinks, or if you simply wish to look as though you can drink more gin and tonics than *anyone*, drink a sparkling water straight with a slice of lemon and cucumber. Have you ever tried cucumber in gin and tonic? it makes a miraculous change of flavour that is perfectly addictive, and it does somewhat the same for Perrier, too. Once you know how, even water can be fun . . .

YOGHURT

Although rather 'foreign' and 'funny' to a lot of Europeans, yoghurt is another of the world's oldest processed foods, together with bulghur wheat. Pharaohs and Israelites enjoyed it in Egypt, Greeks and Romans employed it medically and the Arab world has long respected it, a Damascene extolling its virtues in a book written in 633. Even these are *un peu arriviste* as it is thousands of years older than that. Some go as far as saying it could have been accidentally discovered at the dawn of the Neolithic age, some 10,000 years BC; this is unlikely as domestication of animals didn't start until 4,000 years later.

Yoghurt differs from soured milks in that it cannot form naturally other than by an unlikely accident. It is formed by the addition of two specific bacilli (lactobacillus bulgaricus and *streptococcus thermophilis*) either in culture or in a portion of previously made yoghurt. Accidental contamination by something containing these lactobacilli is how the whole thing would have started. The process which evolved eventually gave surefire way of enjoying safe milk which could also be stored, invaluable in hot climates and for travellers. The people who made yoghurt weren't aware that by first heating the milk and then introducing bacilli that can defeat the attacks of the most dangerous invading germs they were utilizing two of man's surest safeguards against infection, heat and acid. All they knew was it tasted good, seemed easy to digest and was a reliable source of energy and sustenance. Persian invaders took it to India, where bare yogis mixed it with honey as part of their strict diets 2,000 years ago. When the nomadic Bulgars of Asia settled in the Balkans in the 7th century they too brought yoghurt and, like the Mongol hords of Ghengis Khan, had used it as absolutely basic subsistence for they made it from the milk of the mares upon which they rode.

Yoghurt was probably first seen in Europe some time in the 16th century, but apart from pockets of fanaticism and monastries it remained virtually unknown until the early part of this century. Metchnikoff, leading light of the Pasteur Institute noted that the Bulgarian people had a life expectancy almost twice that of the richer and, it was thought, better-fed Americans. Much research lead him to the belief that the large amounts of yoghurt ingested by these people was the answer and he subsequently succeeded in isolating the two bacilli responsible for turning milk into yoghurt. Now it was possible to make yoghurt commercially and save Western man, or so it seemed. It wasn't until 1925, nine years after Metchnikoff's death, that a Spaniard called Carasso opened the first yoghurt factory, in Barcelona. This was the Danone company, still a major producer. It was many years before propaganda, sweetening and flavouring made yoghurt into the widely available and generally abused food it has become.

Yoghurt took such a long time to reach universal acceptance simply *because* it was supposed to be so good for you. The benefits were trumpeted far and wide by leathery spinsters and bearded doctors with accents, both quite certain to deter the British from embracing anything. The basis for confusing yoghurt with the long-awaited elixir of life was a misunderstanding of internal bacteriology. It was argued that because the bacterias in yoghurt were both alive and similar to those in our intestinal systems, and were demonstrably able to overcome all manner of dangerous other bacilli, they would fight and eliminate the dangerous putrefactive bacilli in our bowels. Even the distasteful process of digestion would thus be made sweet and healthy and then, harbouring no nastiness, our bodies would survive decades longer. Today there is a stong echo of this teaching in the belief that yoghurt restores the intestinal flora damaged or massacred by antibiotics. All this wishful thinking, even accepting that different scientists get different results from their tests. It is probable that the only lactobacilli that can live and work in man are those that come *from* man; the strains to make yoghurt are not of this provenance and doomed to death inside us. Which is not to say there are no advantages to yoghurt at all.

The major advantage offered by yoghurt, other than its purity, is that its predigestion of protein by the bacilli make its components – especially the sugars – more quickly available to us, up to three times faster than would be the case with milk. As part of any diet with a balance of good food, exercise and rest, yoghurt is invaluable. But no more invaluable than milk. In dieting to lose weight it can be advantageous if used in an unflavoured, unsweetened state and if made from skim or part skim milk. Flavouring doubles the calories but even so still has less than say ice cream or a sweet pudding. The fact that it is substantial and satisfying is more important than its calorie count; by eating yoghurt you don't eat something worse. If weight really worries you then the substitution of low-fat yoghurt wherever you would normally have cream can be very useful and delicious – in baking soups, stews, sauces and fruits.

The only specific medical advantage that is claimed for yoghurt nowadays is the possibility that it actually inhibits cholesterol production and might even actively lower it. Of course experts disagree, but this is one that is well worth following up. And now the burning question – is your yoghurt live or not? The answer is invariably yes, whatever the package says or does not say. But some are less live than others, the addition of growth inhibitors to lengthen shelf life make them distinctly enfeebled, fighting for their own existence rather than winning bacterial battles on your behalf.

In the interest of high sales, long life and profit, this cheaper yoghurt is first 'extended' by dilution with some liquid then emulsified and restored to something like its original viscosity with a chemical stabiliser, which works like gelatin. A natural yoghurt has a certain graininess but altered types are detectable by being jelly-like, and smooth on the tongue. This treatment combined with low-temperature storage means the further growth of the bacilli is inhibited, extending the yoghurt's life and emasculating the preservative quality of its acidic content. But even these yoghurts will eventually bubble and fizz and go 'over the top' if left long enough. Higher quality yoghurts which have not been extended or stabilized artificially are likely to produce a thicker texture and a whey-like liquid, which can be stirred back gently. Vigorous stirring or beating causes yoghurt to thin considerably and in this state it is often used as a refreshing drink throughout the Middle East; in Turkey it is mixed with soda water, which is even nicer. If you want a really thick yoghurt, like that used in India, the simplest way is to hang yoghurt in muslin as though it were cheese curd and let this drain.

Cooking with yoghurt is varied and exciting, and some very good books have recently been published. My favourite is *The Book of Yoghurt* by Sonia Uvezian (Pitman); recipes for pancakes, sauces, cakes, puddings and more are included as well as many hints and tips about substituting yoghurt for cream, milk and mayonnaise. As far as making yoghurt at home is concerned it seems quite simple once you know how, but I've never made it so can only repeat two bits of advice (1) do as Sonia Uvezian does, or (2) buy a yoghurt maker.

Everyone I know that does make yoghurt swears that UHT/long life milk gives the best and creamiest result, possibly because it is homogenized. But you can use any milk, including that made from powder. Evaporated milk can be used and every kind of milk discussed in the opening of this dairying section can be or has been used.

Bulgarian yoghurt was traditionally made with goat's milk which gave rise to the widely held belief that only this is proper yoghurt. Although that is untrue, it is true that goats' milk yoghurt is specially delicious and is slowly becoming more widely available. Just recently a small firm in the UK has started marketing sheep's milk yoghurt, which I think is better than the goat's milk type. I earnestly recommend you to try it if you see it.

An Israeli scientist has perfected a way to make a dried yoghurt. When the powder is reconstituted with water, it is ready to eat in 1 hour without special care. If and when this is marketed it will be invaluable for store cupboards, travellers and outdoor activities.

There is a third bacillus sometimes included in yoghurt cultures, lactobacillus acidophilus. I've only seen this sold commercially in health-conscious California and it seemed that such yoghurt was smoother in texture and flavour; but this may have been simply because it was sweetened with honey.

COOKING WITH YOGHURT

Unlike cream, yoghurt will infallibly curdle if added to hot liquid which is subsequently boiled. You should let the yoghurt come to room temperature then whisk it in the hot liquid just before serving. Otherwise you can stabilize plain yoghurt by heating gently and thickening with cornflour.

PERMITTED FLOUR ADDITIVES

Flour additives Additives permitted in all flours, except wholemeal, in the United Kingdom (see p. 12)

(see p. 12)

Additive	Function	Comment
ammonium persulphate	strengthens gluten	minimal usage, mainly Scotland and N. England
ascorbic acid (Vitamin C)	strengthens gluten	widely used in the new 'fast-dough' techniques
azodicarbon-amide	strengthens gluten	newly permitted; mainly in new techniques
benzoyl peroxide	bleach	widely used, destroys vitamin E
chlorine	bleach; strengthens gluten	used only in commercial cake flour
chlorine dioxide	bleach; strengthens gluten	widely used, often combined with benzoyl dioxide; destroys vitamin E
L cysteine hydrochloride	weakens gluten	combined with ascorbic acid in new techniques
potassium bromate	strengthens gluten	widely used with the two main bleaches
sulphur dioxide	weakens gluten;	used only in biscuit-making

Note It should be remembered that these additives are in no way connected with the synthetic vitamins and minerals which are also found in white flours.

TYPES OF TRUFFLE

Official French gradings for canned or bottled truffles

Description	Raw material	Appearance
'Finest Quality'* truffles, peeled or cleaned	Ripe truffles with firm flesh, black in colour	Whole, of equal size and colour, approximately round
'Extra' truffles, peeled or cleaned	Ripe truffles with firm flesh, blackish in colour	Whole, slightly irregular
'High-grade' truffles, peeled or cleaned	Truffles with fairly firm flesh, which may be relatively light in colour. Grey truffles are acceptable.	Whole, non-uniform, slightly damaged
Truffle pieces	Pieces of truffle which may be darkish in colour	Minimum thickness 0.5 cm.
Truffle peelings	Narrow strips of truffle peelings which may be dissimilar in colour	Maximum breaks 30 per cent

*The description 'Finest Quality Cleaned' may be followed by the phrase 'by napkin'.

INDEX

A

Aduki, Adzuki beans 297
Afghanistan: Bread 9
African tea 352
Agar-Agar 197
Alfalfa 197
Allspice 197
Almonds 259
    types 260
    forms 261
Ambassadeur 93
American breakfast sausage 322
Anchovy 127
Angelica 197
    Glacé Angelica 198
Angostura bitters 198
Anise seed 198
Annatto 198
Apples, dried 120
    tinned 159
Apricots, dried 120
    tinned 159
Arborio 183
Armadine 120
Armenia: Bread 9
Arrowroot 199
Artichokes 359
Artificial sweeteners 343
Assam tea 352

B

Babke 15
Bagel 15
Bananas, dried 120
Banon Laitier 72
Barley 169–71
    types 169
    flour 170
    meal 170
    sugar 170
    water 170

Basil 199
Basmatti 183
Bath buns 15
Bay 200
Bayonne Ham 318
Bay Rum 200
Beans, dried 294–301
Beaufort cheese 72
Beef products (with Pork products) 312–31
Beetroot 302
Bel Paese 84
Bergamot 201
Bierwurst 325
Bilberries 159
Biltong 320
Bismarck herring 139
Black beans 299
Blackeye beans/peas 298
Black pudding 329
Black tea 350
Bleu d'Auvergne 72
Bleu de Bresse 72
Bleu des Causses 73
Bloaters 137
Bloomers 15
Blue Vinny 64
Bockwurst 326
Boiling ring 329
Bokking 139
Bologna Sausage 326
Bondel 73
Bondon 73
Borage 201
Borlotti beans 299
Boursault 73
Boursin 73
Bouquet Garni 211
Bozcek 330
Bradenham Ham 318
Bratwurst 322
Brawn 329
Brazil nuts 262
Bread and Baked Goods 9–27

Bread
  sliced loaf 10
  in diet 11
  brown 11, 16
  wholemeal 11, 25
  storing 26
  freezing 26
  refrigerating 26
  thawing 27
Bresaola 319
Brick cheese 97
Brick tea 352
Brie Fermier 73
  Laitier 73
  eating 53
  Californian 97
Brioches 15
Broad beans 298
Brown fruit sauce 303
Buckling 138
Buckwheat 171–3
  forms 172
  cooking 173
Bunderfleish 319
Burrino 96
Butter
  General 28
    using 29
    clarified (ghee) 31, 33
    cooking with 32
    storing 32
  Types
    Farmhouse,
    slightly salted,
    unsalted 31
Butter Beans 298
Buttermilks 252

C

Caboc cheese 619
Caciocavallo 84

Caerphilly Cheese 66
Cambazola 89
Cambridge Cheese 66
Camembert, Fermier 74
  Laitier 74
  eating 53
  Californian 97
Camomile 201
Cannellini beans 300
Cantal 74
Capers 304
Capillaire 202
Caprice des Dieux 74
Caprino 83, 96
Caravan Tea 352
Caraway seeds 202
Cardamom 203
  types 203
  in mixed spice 222
Carlsbad Plums 122
Carob 203
Carré de l'Est 74
Cashew nuts 262
Castello 93
Caviare 129
  presentation 131
  mock 132
  storing 132
Cassia 204
  in mixed spice 221
Cayenne pepper 204
Celery hearts
Celery seed and salt 204
Ceps 258
Cervelas 326
Cervelat 325
Ceylon tea 352
Chabichou 75
Chapati 9, 16, 25
Chaps 313
Chanterelles 258
Cheddar Farmhouse Cheese 66
  uses 21
Cheerios 326

Cheese[1] **33–97**
   principles 33
   history 35–39
   manufacturing companies 39–97
   buying 41
   serving 43
   with wine 45
   cooking with 47, 50, 97 (*see also*
   individual entries)
   storing 50
   freezing 51
Cheese[2]
   types (by manufacture) 52–5, 58
   vegetarian 57
   types of milk 58
   fat content 58
   ripening 59
   seasons 60
Cheese[3]
   British 61–69
   Scotland & Islands 65, 69
   Northern Ireland & Eire 66
   French 69–80
   Greek 80–82
   Italian 82–86
   German, Dutch & Swiss 87–92
   Scandinavian 92–95
Chelsea Buns 18
Cheesecakes 16
Cherries
   Black 159
   Red (morello) 161, 202, 204
   kernels 220
Chervil 205
Cheshire Cheese
   Red, White, Blue 67
Chestnuts 263
   forms 264
   purées 265
   marrons glacés 163, 266
Chêvre 75
Chickpeas 299
Chili
   powder, pepper or compound 205

Ching Wo 352
Chipolata 322
Chives 205
Chocolat, petit painsau 21
Chocolate 98–101
   types 101
   cooking with 101
   substitute 204
Chollah 18
Chorizo 326
Chrysanthemum 206
Chufas 275
Chutneys 303
Cinnamon 206
   in mixed spice 222
Clams 134
   juice 135
Clover blossoms, red 206
Cloves 207
Cob/coburg 18
Cocoa 98–101
   substitute 204
Coconuts 267
   forms 268
Coffee 102–113
   basic types 104
   processing beans 104
   choosing 105
   blending 106
   styles (countries) 107–9
   decaffeinated 109
   Instant 110
   additives/storing 111
   making 112
   cooking with 113
Coleslaw 332
Colouring, food 212
   caramel 213
Comté 75
Coppa 320
Coriander seeds and leaves 207
Corn 173
   types and forms 174
   flour and meal 175

Cornichons 304
Cotechino 323
Cotswold Cheese 67
Cottage Cheese 53, 118
Cottage loaf 18
Cottonseed oil 278
Coulommiers 75
Crab 135
Cranberries 159
Cream 114–8
  types 114
  abroad 116
  cooking with 117
  nouvelle cuisine 117
  storing 118
  soured 116 (uses 227)
Cream Cheese 52
Cream of Tartar 208
Crema Bel Paese 84
Crème Fraiche 116
Crème Fleurette 116
Crispbread 18
Cristallo 183
Croissants 18
Crown loaf 19
CTC tea 350
Cucumbers 304
Cumberland Sausages 323
Cumin seed 208, 227
Currants 123
Curd Cheese 52, 118
Curry powder 209

Derby Cheese 67
Diet breads 19
Dill seed and weed 209
Dolcelatte 84
Double Gloucester Cheese 67
Doughnuts
  ponshki, loukoumades,
    olliebollen 19
Dried Fruits 120–23
Dunlop Cheese 69

E

Earl Grey tea 201, 352
Edam 90
Eel 133
Eggs 124–6
  hen's eggs 124
  other types 124
  cooking 126
  storing 126
Elbo 94
Elderberries 210
Elderflowers 210
Elvas Plums 123
Emmental 90
English beef sausages 323
English Breakfast tea 352
English pork sausages 323
Enriched breads 20
Esrom 94

D

Dairy Product Substitutes 119
Danablu 93
Dambo 95
Danish loaf, pastries 19
Darjeeling tea 352
Dates 121
Demerara 339

F

Farmhouse loaf 20
Fennel 211
Fenugreek seed 211
Fermented milks 252
Figs, dried 122
Fines Herbs 211
Fiore Sardo 84

Fish 127–56
Five Spices 212
Flageolet beans 300
Fleischwurst 326
Flour
 extraction 11, 195
 additives 12, 371
 milling 166
 stone-grinding 167
 roller mills 168
 wholemeal v wheatmeal 195
 farmhouse 195
Foie Gras 157
 types packaged 158
Fonds d'artichaut 359
Fondu au Raisin 75
Fontainebleau 75
Fontal 84
Fontina 84
Food colouring 212
Formosa Oolong tea 352
Fougéru 76
Fourme d'Ambert 76
France, good breads 10
Frankfurters 327
French bread 20
 baguettes, ficelles, longuets, pain
 de campagne, de menage
French toast 26
Fromage Blanc 76, 117
Fromage de Monsieur 77
Fruit, tinned and bottled 159–62
Fruits Glacé 163
Ful medames 299

Garlic 213
 powder 214
 salt 214
 wild 214
 sausage 327
Garum 311
Geranium leaves 214
Gherkins 304
Ginger fresh, dried 215
 preserved 305
 in mixed spice 221
Gingerbread 215
Girolles 258
Gjetost 94
Golden Syrup 340
Gooseberries, tinned 160
Gorgonzola 84
Gouda 90
Grain 165–95
 composition 166
 milling 166
 sprouting 190
Grains of Paradise 216
Grana 85
Granary loaf 20
Grappa 235
Greengages, tinned 160
Green tea 350
Grissini 20
Grits 176
Gruyère 90
Gum Arabic 216
Gugelhopf (Kugelhopf) 20
Gunpowder tea 352

G

Galantines 292
Galotiri 55
Gammelost 96
Gaperon 76
Garam Masala 216
Garbanzos 299

H

Halvah 240
Hams 316–19
 types, uncooked 318
 cooked 330
Ham sausage 327
Haricot beans 300

Haslet 329
Havarti 94
Hazelnuts 270
  oil 270
Hearts of Palm 359
Herbs 196–224
  drinks 196
Herrings 137–41
  red 139
  fillets 139
  salt 140
  Baltic 140
Hibiscus flowers 217
Hominy 176
Honey 343–7
Honeysuckle flowers 218
Horseradish 217
Horchata, horchateria 275
H.P. Sauce 303
Hyson tea 352

I

Ice cream 245–6
  oils in 280
  substitutes 119
Ilchester Cheese 67
Irish Breakfast tea 352
Irish moss 218

J

Jagerwurst 327
Jarlsberg 94
Jasmine tea 353
Jerked beef, jerky 320
Jesus de Lyon 315
Juniper berries 218

K

Kabanos, kabanossi 327
Kalbsleberwurst 330
Kasha 171
Kassler 331
Katenrauch 325
Keemun tea 353
Kefir 252, 255
Kidney beans 299–301
  red 301
Kippers 138
Kissel 220
Knackwurst 327
Kumiss 252
Kummel 203
Kumquats 160, 210

L

Lancashire Cheese 67
Landjaeger 325
Lapsang Souchong tea 353
Lardy Cake 21
Lavender 218
Laxschinken 320, 331
Leavening 12
Leben 252
Leberkas 329
Leicester Cheese
Leiden
Lemon Balm 219
Lemon tea 353
Lentils 294, 301
Lieder kranz 97
Lima beans 298
Limburger 91
Liquorice root 219
Livarot 76
Liver sausage 329

Locust beans 219
Lovage 219
Lychees 160

M

Macadamia nuts 271
Mace 219
Mackerel 141–3
Mahlabi 220
Maidenhair 220
Mainzerkase 91
Maize grain, meal 175
Mango 161
Maple Syrup 342
   with buckwheat 173
Margarine 119, 247–8
Marigold 220
Marjoram 220
Maroilles 77
Marrons glacés 163, 266
Mascarpone 83, 96
Mastic Gum 220
Matjesfillets 140
Matjesherring 139
Matzoh 25
Mazurska 327
Mealie-mealie 175
Melba toast 26
Merguez 328
Mettwurst 325
Milk 249–57
   ripening 34
   pasturized, dangerous curdled 34
   soured 251
   fermented 252
   goats' 253
   types in UK 254
   storing 256
   condensed 256
   evaporated 257
   powders 257

Milk loaf 21
Millet 177–8
Mint
   fresh and dried 221
   sauce 221
   teas 221
   julep 222
Mitzithra 81
Mixed spice 221
Molasses 339
   sugar 338
Monosodium Glutamate 221
Monsieur, Fromage de 77
Monterey Jack 97
Morels (morilles) 258
Mortadella 328
Mozzarella 85
   uses 21
MSG: *see* Monosodium Glutamate
Mung beans 301
Muesli 181
Mungster Latier 77
Münster 91
Muscovado sugar 338
Mushrooms, dried 258
Mushroom Ketchup 305
Mussels 143
Mustard 223
Mustard Pickle 306, 309
Mycella 94
Mysliewska 328
Mysost 94

N

Nagelkaas 96
Navy beans 300
Neufchatel 77
Nilgiris tea 353
Nutmeg 225
Nuts 259–276

O

Oats
Oils 277–81
   saturated and unsaturated 277
   major types 278
Olive oil 278
Olives 306–9
Onions, pickled 309
Oolong tea 350
Orange-flower water 226
   uses 123, 202, 206
Orkney and Islay Cheese 69
Oysters, smoked 144

P

Palm kernel oil 279
Palm oil 279
Palm sugar 342
Paprika
   Sweet (Spanish) 226
   Hot (Hungarian) 226
   in Hungarian dishes 227
Pannetone 21
Pareve (milk free)
   products 119
Parmesan 85
   Argentinian 97
Parsley 228
Pasta 282–91
   kinds 285
   Types 286
   cooking 287
   serving and sauces 288
   leftover recipes 290
   Pasta Filata (plastic curd cheese)
   55, 83
Pastrami 330
Pastry, colouring 212

Pâtés 292
Paw Paw 161
Peaches, dried white 162
Peanuts 272
Peanut oil 280
Peas, dried 294–301
   tinned 360
Pecans 272
Pecorino 85
Pemmican 320
Pennyroyal 221
Pepparots visp 217
Peppercorns 228
   four colours 228, 230
   in mixed spice 222
   warning 230
Pesto 199, 273
Petit Suisse 78, 273
Piccallili 309
Pickles 302–311
Pickled Walnuts 276
Pickling spice 230
Pimento, pimento pepper 197
Pineapple 161
Pine nuts, kernels 273
Pinto beans 300
Pissaladière 22
Pistachios 274
Pistou 200
Pitta 9, 21
Pizza 21
Plums 162
   in Chocolate 122
Poivre d'Auvergne 78
Polenta 175
Pont l'Evegne 78
Popcorn 176–7
Poppy seeds 231
Poppyseed oil 280
Pork products 312–31
Port du Salut 78
Potatoes 360
   salad 332
Prawns 146

Prawns – *continued*
    pate 148
    salad 333
Preserves 302–11
Prosciutto 319
Provolone 86
Prunes 122, 200
Pulses 294–301
Pumpernickel 22, 25

Q

Quatre Epices 231
Quiche

R

Raclette 96
Ragusano 86
Raisins 123
Ras El Hanout 231
Reblochon 79
Red cabbage, pickled 309
Red herrings 139
Red Kidney beans 300
Red peppers 360
Rice 182–7
    forms 182
    wild 184
    coconut 186
    fried 187
    savoury 187
    with bay 200
    stuffings 206
Ricotta 86
Roe 145
    caviare 129
Rollmops 141

Roses, buds and petals 233
Rose Cocoa beans 299
Rose de Lyon 315
Rose-water 223
    uses 101, 123, 206, 217, 218
Roquefort 79
Rosemary 232
Royalp 91
Rue 235
Rum babas 23
Russian or vegetable salad 333
Russian tea 353
Rye 87
Rye bread 24

S

Saccharin 343
Safflower 235
Safflower oil 200
Saffron 236
    uses 16
Sage 237
Saint Nectaire 79
Saint-Paulin 79
Saint Marcellin 79
Salads 332–3
Salami 314–16
Sally Lunn 24
Salmon 149–54
    smoked 150
    to slice 151
    storage 153
    tinned 153
Salsiccia 324
Salt 237
    types 238
    garlic 214
    cutting down 241
Salt Cod 148
Sandwich loaf 24

Samso 95
Sarsparilla 237
Sassafras 239
Saucisses 324
Saucisson (also see Salami) 328
Sauerkraut 310
Sausages 321–31
    fresh 320
    with casings 322
    without 324
    smoked, dried 325
    scalded 325
    cooked 329
Saveloys 328
Savory 240
Sbrinz 92
Schabzieger 55
Schinkenwurst 325
Shropshire Blue Cheese 68
Schubling 328
Sesame 240
Sesame seed oil 281
Seychelles tea 353
Shellfish 127–56
Shrimps 146
    potted 147
Sliced bread 10
Slimming breads 24
Smatana 252
Smoked Salmon 150
    uses 15
Smoked tea 350
Snails 334
Soba 284
Soda breads 24
Soft fruits, tinned 162
    with vinegar 363
Sorrel and wild sorrel 241
Soups 334
Sour-dough bread 24
Soured cream 116
    uses 227
Soya bean oil 281
Spek 330

Spices 196–224
    drinks 196
Split-tin loaf 25
Sprouting grains 190
Sticky rice 183
Stilton Cheese 68
Stromming 140
Sturgeon 154
Suffolk ham 318
Sugar 335–42
    Beet 337
    Cane 335
    type and products 338
    alternatives 342
Sultanas 123
Sunflower oil 281
Surstromming 140
Sweetcorn, tinned 360

T

Tabasco 242
Tacos 25
Taleggio 86
Tamarind 242
Tahini 240
Taramasalata 145
Tarhonya 284
Tarragon 242
Tea 348–55
    Styles and flavours 351
    making 353
    flavouring 354
    iced 355
    cooking with 355
Tellemey 97
Terrines 292
Teewurst 325
Thyme, Lemon thyme, wild thyme 243
Tiger nuts 275

Tilsit 92
Tin loaf 25
Tomatoes, tinned 260–61
Tomme 79
Tortilla 25
Toulouse Sausages 324
Tongue Sausage 330
Treacle 340
Triticale 191
Trout 155
   smoked 155
Truffles 356–8, 372
Tsourekia 16
Tuchowska 328
Turmeric 244
Tybo 95

U

Unleavened bread 25

V

Vanilla bean 244
Vegetarian cheese 57
Vienna loaf 25
Vinegar 362
   types 362
   herb vinegar 196
   tarragon vinegar 243
Vinny, Blue 64
Voll korn Brot 23, 25

W

Walnuts 275
   pickled 276
   oil 275

Walton, Cheese 68
Waters, bottled 365
Whitebait
   European 133
   in New Zealand 133
Whiteners 119
Weinerwurst 328
Weisswurst 328
Wensleydale Cheese 68
Wheat 191–195
   forms 192
   flours 194
   soft and strong 194
Wheatmeal 195
Wholemeal 195
Wholewheat 195
Wieska 328
Wild rice 184
Windsor Red Cheese 69
Worcestershire Sauce 311

Y

Yeast 12
   types 13
   equivalents 13
   use 14
   dies 14
   refrigerating 14
   freezing 15
Yoghurt 367–70
York Ham 318

Z

Zampone 324
Zungenwurst 330
Zwieback 26